The THREE AGES of ATLANTIS

"Diego Marin is a physicist who has spent many years in his quest for 'Atlantis.' His book is a well-researched and stimulating piece of detective work as well as a great read for all the devotees of this intriguing topic."

ROBERT BAUVAL, AUTHOR OF *THE ORION MYSTERY*, *BLACK GENESIS*, AND *BREAKING THE MIRROR OF HEAVEN*

The
THREE AGES
of
ATLANTIS

The Great Floods
That Destroyed Civilization

DIEGO MARIN, PH.D., IVAN MINELLA,
AND ERIK SCHIEVENIN

Bear & Company
Rochester, Vermont • Toronto, Canada

Bear & Company
One Park Street
Rochester, Vermont 05767
www.BearandCompanyBooks.com

Bear & Company is a division of Inner Traditions International

Copyright © 2010, 2013 by Diego Marin, Ivan Minella, and Erik Schievenin

Originally published in Italian under the title *Atlantidi: I Tre Diluvi che Hanno
Cancellato la Civiltà* by Eremon Edizioni
First U.S. edition published in 2013 by Bear & Company

Library of Congress Cataloging-in-Publication Data
Marin, Diego, 1983–
 [Atlantidi. English]
 The three ages of Atlantis : the great floods that destroyed civilization / Diego
Marin, Ph.D., Ivan Minella, and Erik Schievenin ; translated by Valentina
Buccella. — First U.S. edition.
     pages cm
 Originally published in Italian under the title Atlantidi: i tre diluvi che hanno
cancellato la civiltà by Eremon Edizioni in 2010.
 Includes bibliographical references and index.
 Summary: "Scientific and anthropological evidence for multiple Atlantean
empires and the global catastrophes that destroyed them" — Provided by
publisher.
 ISBN 978-1-59143-179-4 (pbk.) — ISBN 978-1-59143-757-4 (e-book)
 1. Atlantis (Legendary place) 2. Civilization, Ancient. 3. Lost continents. I.
Minella, Ivan, 1989– II. Schievenin, Erik, 1989– III. Title.
 GN751.M32513 2013
 001.94—dc23
                                                                    2013016367

Printed and bound in the United States by P. A. Hutchison

10   9   8   7   6   5   4   3   2   1

Text design by Brian Boynton and layout by Virginia Scott Bowman
This book was typeset in Garamond Premier Pro with Galliard used as the display
typeface

To send correspondence to the author of this book, mail a first-class letter to the
author c/o Inner Traditions • Bear & Company, One Park Street, Rochester, VT
05767, and we will forward the communication, or contact the authors directly at
www.gruppopangea.com or **dmarin.math@gmail.com**.

To Pietro Marin, the strong man.

Note to the Reader

This work contains references to numerous people, places, and structures, some of which are referred to by multiple names depending on the tradition they come from. In order to help you keep these straight, a list of these terms and their meanings and synonyms is provided in the glossary at the back of the book along with two time lines of the travels of the Pelasgian peoples and how they were known in each region for your ready reference. The authors have also provided a map outlining the three routes of the Atlanteans and important locations discussed throughout the book (plate 1) and a map representing the territories of the Sea Peoples along the Mediterranean Sea (plate 2). These can be found at the beginning of the color insert.

Now at last I have Plato's Lost Dialogue translated entirely.

The Greek original is lost, so I've used the Arabic text I found in
an Italian monastery years ago and always thought was a hoax.

Now I wonder . . . could this remarkable book hold the secret to
long-lost Atlantis?

Probably not. No one will publish it, that's certain. The fear of
ridicule is too great.

To be safe, I've sent a copy to Pearce.

CHARLES STERNHART ON *HERMOCRATES,*
THE LOST DIALOGUE OF PLATO
LONDON, 1922

■ ■ ■

ET IN ARCADIA EGO

CONTENTS

ACKNOWLEDGMENTS

We would like to acknowledge and thank all the people whose help and support have overwhelmed us from the first moment we decided to write this book. First and foremost, we wish to express our gratitude to Mr. Mario Pincherle and his life companion Giuliana Cristianini Volpi for their warm and friendly hospitality in allowing us to consult their great collection of books, many of which are now unavailable.

Special thanks to Leonardo Melis, who generously provided information and photos of the Shardana people. His help was essential, and offered at no cost. Also thanks to him and his friend Rossellini for the photo of the Kadesh battle engraved in the temple of Abu Simbel (including the graphic that highlights the four Shardana warriors). Thanks to Sandro Mainardi for his graphic of the V division of the Duat.

We would also like to give thanks to Roberto Giacobbo, author and host of the Italian TV program *Voyager,* for attending our meetings in Bassano del Grappa and welcoming our proposed projects with interest, and for the foreword to the Italian edition. We are deeply grateful for his guidance and encouragement, as well as for the ongoing collaboration between the Geographical Research Association (originally PANGEA) and the *Voyager* team.

We wish to thank Dr. Gisela Lochmüller, Italian representative of the Association for Research and Enlightenment, which through its work allowed us to overcome national and continental boundaries. Thanks for the precious information on the ARE's excavations in Egypt.

We cannot be grateful enough to the *Hera* magazine staff, particularly Franco Cappiello (publisher), Gianfranco Pecoraro (director), and Massimo Bonasorte (editor in chief), for believing in us from the start, when the book was nothing but a dream. Thanks also to Adriano Forgione for publishing our inquiries each month in the *Fenix* magazine.

Thanks to Syusy Blady and Patrizio Roversi for taking us with them on the trip retracing the route of "the people of the sea."

We also give thanks to architect Daniel Baldassarre and professor and artist Vincenzo Bianchi for the guided tours of the Sabine strongholds and the extensive discussions on the matter. We wish to thank Marco Zagni and the Akakor Geographical Exploring group for the new contacts provided and for future explorations.

Thanks to Michele Rossi for discussions on the *Voyager* forum.

Special thanks to Elena Lancetti for encouragement, for her translations from hieroglyphic, and for getting us involved in the conferences held in Brescia.

Also thanks to Lilly Astore, host of *Dimension X,* for inviting us on her TV program and for continuously urging us to not give up. Thanks to the "Terra Incognita" group for promoting our book on the web and to Mirko Dal Pastro for promoting it in our area. Thanks to Cristian Bertollo, Matteo Sonda, and Enrico Golin for logistical support.

We warmly thank Dr. Stefania Marin for proofreading this book in its early stages. We would also like to convey thanks to the department of archaeology at the University of Padua.

We are thankful to Jon Graham for considering our work with patience and without prejudice.

Thanks to Giada Rossi for more than we requested: keeping the contacts for us with the publishing company from the United States, getting herself involved in our project, and deepening our research. Thanks also for the English translation of the conclusion and for the errors brought to our attention.

Many thanks to Michael Bolognini's group, the Geographical Research Association, for its organizational effectiveness, the instrumentation devices and tool supply, and all the projects we carry out together.

We would like to acknowledge the importance of all the authors and researchers whose works have opened our minds—among them, Graham Hancock and Robert Bauval have inspired us the most. We can't give enough thanks to Mr. Bauval for putting us in touch with the Inner Traditions publishing company and for having always deemed us worthy to pursue this research.

Finally, heartfelt thanks go to our parents—Diego's dad Maurizio (who always says "never give up") and mom Ornella; Ivan's dad Dino and mom Mara; Erik's dad Pieretto and mom Lilia—for their unending love and support.

To all the above individuals, and the friends whose names we cannot list and who have assisted us in one way or another, we feel very much indebted.

BEYOND THE MIRROR

Our world is gone now, smashed by the wars.
Now I am the keeper of his body, embalmed here in the Egyptian
ways.
I followed him as Pharaoh, and have now ruled forty years.
I am the victor.
But what does it all mean when there is not one left to remember
the great cavalry charge at Gaugamela, or the mountains of the
Hindu Kush when we crossed a 100,000-man army into India?
He was a god, Cadmos. Or as close as anything I've ever seen. [. . .]
He changed the world [. . .], [building] a great empire, not of land
and gold but of the mind, the great Hellenic civilization spread
across the world.
But how can I say? How can I tell you what it was like to be young
and have big dreams and to believe, when Alexander looked you
in the eyes, you could do anything?
In his presence, by the light of Apollo, we were better than ourselves.
I've known many great men in my life, but only one
colossus . . .

PTOLEMY I SOTER,
DIODORUS OF ALEXANDER THE GREAT
(367 TO 283 BC)

■ ■ ■

Atlantis, the island of the blessed, the home of the gods; there it was, where the oceans flow together, beyond the muddy shallows where the keels stopped and the cargo ships unloaded. There it was, in the middle of an island, on a mountaintop, designed in concentric circles reproducing the celestial spheres, where it would sink its roots underground in deep tunnels extending underneath the sea.

Three times the raging waters broke against its walls covered with gold, silver, and obsidian, extracts of its natural mines. Three times it was destroyed and rebuilt elsewhere, in different places on Earth. Three times, three floods, beginning 15,000 years ago, when the end of the last ice age wiped out 60 percent of the habitable land.

A meteorite or perhaps a patchy accumulation of ice at the poles was sufficient to destabilize our planet, a little rolling ball lost in space. The entire Earth's crust shifted over the mantle of the planet, dragging along all the continents without altering their positions in relation to one another.

The old polar caps approached the equator and melted; the North Pole moved from Hudson Bay (Canada) and reached its current position, while the Antarctic, once a green paradise watered by rivers, became a cold desert of ice.

Its inhabitants, the Cro-Magnon (called "early modern humans" in current scientific literature), had to hastily gather supplies and escape while huge waves of melted ice, six hundred meters high, hurled against the continents, extending for hundreds of miles over the land. Entire regions became arid due to the disappearance of seasonal monsoons, while in the New World seventy species of mammals became extinct. The water shifted its weight from the glaciers to the oceans, triggering terrible earthquakes with magnitudes of 8 to 9 on the Richter scale, causing the eruption of all previously extinct volcanoes, whose ashes obscured the sky for decades. The human species was reduced to less than a hundred thousand individuals.

If it happens again, or better, when it happens again, our technology and progress will be of little use: skyscrapers will fall, roads will crack, and power stations will switch off forever. Slowly, the forest will overcome the city, and the few survivors will not be able to explain to their children what a television or a computer was, and above all, they will not be able to assemble them. All the more so if you consider that today even the most titled and intelligent of us are skilled only in extremely specific sectors. Nowadays, no one follows the whole production process—from the procurement of raw materials to the final output. In less than ten thousand years all our plastic, metal, and silicon goods would be consumed and forgotten; only the carved stone may remain intact during such a long period, a silent witness of our distant past.

This text aspires to piece together the story of the first civilization that human memory recalls. Although enriched throughout centuries with fantastic and esoteric elements, this story has preserved intact the body of real events and reveals what happened on Earth in the years following the last ice age when civilizations were extinguished and humankind was brought back to the state of hunter-gatherer. Many think it is just a fairy tale, but it only requires a re-reading of history without prejudice to unveil the solid reality hidden in the myth.

Stories from the oldest civilizations tell that survivors of an earlier era arrived in their territories in order to teach arts and sciences and were soon worshipped as gods. Exiles who had escaped on ships from the catastrophe gripping Antarctica, they had many names, and in this work we quote fourteen: Pelasgians, Danaes, Oceanides, Cainites, Vampires, Titans, Giants, Tyrrhenians, Cyclops, Shekelesh, Atlanteans, Italanteans, Arii, and Viracochas.

We find records of these civilizers in all the oldest writings of Greece, Egypt, Phoenicia, Assyria, Persia, Samothrace, and Phrygia. Homer believed they were all Oceanites, generated from Oceanus (*Iliad,* book 14), while Herodotus considered them Pelasgians. Strabo interpreted this name as "divine," like Homer with the Phaeacians of Malta, to highlight their closeness to the gods. In Orpheus's hymns they were specifically mentioned as Titans but sometimes were also called Uranides, Atalants, or Pelasgians.

Similarly, Hesiod used one or the other name. In his hymns, Orpheus uses the term "Titans" in reference to the Sun, Saturn, Hercules, Apollo, Diana, and Mercury. Iapetus, that is Janus, or Saturn, belonging to the same oceanic lineage as the other gods, is called Uranides by Homer and placed in exile in Tartarus (where he, Iapetus, led Ulysses) on the west coast of Italy. Mercury is called Atlantean by Homer because he was the grandson of Atlas. Hesiod defines Atlas and Circe as Oceanites (Hesiod, *Theogony*). Homer gives Circe the same appellation (*Odyssey*, book 5), whereas Calypso is referred to as Atlantean—even though they belonged to the same lineage: "The Atlantean smiled, and stroked him with her hand, and spoke, and addressed him." Hesiod gives the appellative of Oceanite to Electra, Circe's sister who brought the Cabiric cult to Samothrace and, according to Herodotus, was Pelasgian. Virgil, referring to Electra's son Dardanus, defines him as Tuscan. Homer calls Persephone, kidnapped from Sicily, Oceanite, and calls Tyre, daughter-in-law of Aeolus, lord of the Italian islands bearing his name, Uranide because she was the daughter of the struck Titan Salmoneus.

All the writers mentioned propose that the Sicilian Cyclops descended from Titanic lineage and were indeed a remnant of this people. The Greek Pausanias showed that all antiquity used as synonym the three terms Cyclops, Pelasgians, and Sicilians (or Sicels). "Sicily" took its name from "Sicels" who previously lived in central Italy. Homer (*Iliad*, book 16) says that Jupiter, the most powerful among the Uranides, Atlanteans, or Titans, was Pelasgus: "Zeus (Jupiter), king, (. . .) Pelasgian, (. . .) ruling high and cold Dodona." In Carinthia there is a temple erected to the Pelasgian Ceres. According to Homer, this people had common origins with the Phaeacians, the ancient inhabitants of Malta and builders of the megalithic temples of the island. According to Berosus, Plato, and Diodorus, the names Atlanteans and Italanteans, or Italians, were derived from Atlas, who was king of Italy, and Italy too. According to the traditions of Phrygia, he was more generally king of the West (Eusebius, *Evangelical Preparation*, chapter 6, "Of the theological statements of the Phrygians"). According to Diodorus, Atlas had children with his wife Titea, and they took the name Titans. Indeed, according to Homer, on several occasions the Titans were to erect the walls of Troy, just in Phrygia or Arzawa.

We call them "Cro-Magnon." Light-skinned, with light-colored eyes and blond or red hair, they *worshipped a single deity* and considered the snake a sacred animal, going so far as to assign this epithet to their greatest men. They were masters in navigation, geography, astronomy, and architecture, mapped the whole planet, and built huge monuments throughout. We can still come across their maps today, replicated by medieval copyists and exhibited in beautiful Renaissance villas and museum showcases. Their temples, constructed along riverbanks and ocean coastlines, were built with polished boulders weighing up to a thousand tons, brought from quarries that were hundreds of miles away, raised and aligned with systems that we fail to understand today.

Although Cro-Magnons belong to the *Homo sapiens* species they are distinguished by a different facial type consisting of a round cranium, high cheekbones, and wide, square orbits. On average taller than other *H. sapiens,* they do not present any other physical or mental difference. Some of their physical characteristics—beard, long and thin nose, light skin and eyes, blond or red hair—were transmitted to other *H. sapiens* generating the Indo-European kind. Cro-Magnon people suddenly appeared in Europe in 13,000 BCE, where they mixed with a previous race of *H. sapiens,* that of the man of Combe-Capelle, whose burial site in southern France is considered the earliest evidence of modern *H. sapiens* in Europe and who had come more than twenty thousand years earlier.[1] The absence of an evolutionary path traceable in any of the explored continents makes it necessary to seek its origins in the unexplored Antarctica.

After 13,000 BCE their diaspora split into two directions, Central and South America and Europe. In Europe they colonized the western Mediterranean, the Italian Tyrrhenian coast up to Sicily, Malta, and Algeria. Their knowledge easily made them "masters" of the primitive peoples inhabiting those places and, indeed, a mythical ruler was a sign of the advent of a Second Empire: Minos-Osiris, who subjected the eastern Mediterranean and later moved to India. A region of this vast empire went down in history as "Hyperborea": it extended from the Alps to Tuscany, and the Po River, then known as Eridanus, ran through its plain. The "Amber Route" crossed this area—birthplace of Dardanus, founder of the city of Troy—in a region called Arzawa, ancient western Turkey.

The empire lasted until 9600 BCE, almost three thousand years. During this long period some huge lakes had become trapped in ever-thinner ice dams. When these broke, with incredibly perfect timing, a catastrophe took place much like the one dating to 13,000 BCE. Once again Europe and the Americas were hit by floods and earthquakes. Everything was lost. The Earth shook again in 6700 BCE, the last dams collapsed, and the last lakes emptied.

Humans regressed to the state of hunter-gatherer and additional millennia were needed to regain advanced skills in farming and breeding, to rediscover techniques for building houses and cities, and to reorganize public life.

The chapters of this book will trace a map of those monuments and traditions that the ancient peoples inherited from the Pelasgians—territories, arts, myths, religions—revealing the connections that show common "cultural" origins.

The footsteps of the Cro-Magnon will lead us from the Mediterranean to the Indus River Valley, where their community lived displaced, carried so far by migration, disguised in the myth of Osiris or Minos as his Eastern military campaign. We will follow this god's footsteps, his long march that was inspiration for the dreams of conquest of Alexander the Great.

With the passing of the years, the language and ethnicity of the Asian colony will take on specific traits, which we call Indo-Europeans. We will see the Indo-Europeans returning to Europe 5,000 and 4,000 years before Christ, approaching the Middle East in 2600 BCE* at the head of the nomadic people of Gutei, which will cause the collapse of the Akkadian empire.

We will meet them again when, fleeing from the guerrillas of a Sumerian king, they will cross the sea and establish themselves on the Mediterranean coast that once belonged to their ancestors. They are called the "Peoples of the Sea," the same Peoples of the Sea that in 1200 BCE will create many inconveniences for the Near Eastern empires. We understand their distinction from those Pelasgians who lived in the "Old

---

*Recalibrated dating.

Europe," to whom they are connected by a thread leading back and forth from Europe to India over seven millennia.

Our project started three years ago as a utopian search for our past, a past that has been erased by a contagious amnesia. Today we are finally developing instruments that allow us to look underneath the Antarctic ice through the ruins of what we call Atlantis. This book represents only the first step. We'll write more as soon as we can open the still locked room inside the Pyramid of Cheops, which remains sealed by a small stone gate, filmed in 1993 by the German engineer Rudolf Gantenbrink and in 2002 by the iRobot Corporation. More rooms are waiting for us under the Sphinx and amid the ruins of a sacred well excavated in Italy by the unknown Sabines. How many rooms await, underneath the sand or water, maintaining the legacy saved by the great flood?

1

THE SLIDING OF EARTH'S CRUST

Hermocrates: *It is with shame that I here deny the time and place of which Critias spoke. Translating from Egyptian into Greek he was mistaken of as much as a tenfold.*

Instead of 3,000 as he wrote, they were perhaps 30,000 or even less than 300, the miles that separated the city of Atlantis from our shores. Likewise, it is possible that the age of the Lost Kingdom is more than 100,000 years or less than 1,000.

Socrates: *Even if a kingdom rose beyond any attainable limit, we would not know. We should accept the lowest amount.*

At the beginning of a research project you may believe you are alone, the only voice, far from common opinion and above all outside your own specific field. In fact, you soon find out that there are many potential classmates, if only you had lived in another time, or in another country. There are always a number of discredited, driven scientists, solitary researchers after the day's work was done, such as Albert Einstein until professors at the University of Bern noticed that this clerk at the patent office was not so ignorant as they initially thought.

On May 8, 1953, Albert Einstein took part in a debate on the origin of human civilization. In the first letter of a long correspondence, he congratulated Charles Hutchins Hapgood, professor of anthropology and the history of science at Keene State College in New Hampshire:

> I find your arguments very impressive and have the impression that your hypothesis is correct. One can hardly doubt that significant shifts of the crust of the earth have taken place repeatedly and within a short time.[1]

Hapgood's work had really impressed the scientist, so much as to induce Einstein to write a foreword to his book *The Path of Pole*:

> A great many empirical data indicate that at each point of the earth's surface that has been carefully studied, many climatic changes have taken place, apparently quite suddenly. This, according to Mr. Hapgood, is explicable if the virtually rigid outer crust of the earth undergoes, from time to time, extensive displacement.

Hapgood had proposed a geological theory that explained all climate changes and biological revolutions with one single cause. The ice ages, the concomitant global volcanic eruptions, the big mammals' mass extinctions, peoples' migration toward the Americas, the beginning of agriculture—everything was connected. Everything found its explanation in the movement of the Earth's crust: a quick, sudden, massive sliding of all continents and oceans as a single unit across the mantle of our planet. Lands would not have changed their relative position, and there would have been no relationship to the slow movement of individual continental plates.

At the time the professor advanced such a theory there were no instruments for practical tests, but we now know that something like this has happened at least once already. 535 million years ago such a crust sliding triggered a turmoil of earthquakes and volcanoes, provoking the subsequent differentiation in animal species: the "Cambrian explosion."*

In the mid-1960s Hapgood and his students examined a series of amazingly accurate ancient nautical maps, considering their antiquity, that fascinatingly included regions like China, the Americas, and Antarctica—the latter free from ice—still officially unknown to European explorers. The ancient maps could represent the Earth before the last displacement, when eastern Canada was covered by ice, whereas at least one-third of Antarctica was not.

That displacement changed human geography, with the decreased polar ice caps forced to melt down in the temperate area, thus swelling the flow of tsunamis. At that time the hunter-gatherers took refuge from the tide on high mountains, while the cities in the plains and on the seacoast were utterly destroyed. A herd or two of oxen and a few goats would be the only survivors in the animal world; shepherds pastured little herds, while that was hardly enough, it allowed them to survive.[2] The rise of agriculture, of which the breeding of the cattle is the basis, would therefore be no more than the revival of an activity that was known since long.

In 1886 Alphonse de Candolle was interested in the origins of agriculture. He wrote, "One of the most direct means of discovering the geographical origin of a cultivated species is to seek in what country it grows spontaneously, and without the help of man."[3]

The Soviet botanist Nikolai Ivanovich Vavilov (1887–1943) accepted Candolle's approach and in a few years gathered more than fifty thousand wild plants around the world, "identifying eight independent centers of origin of the most important cultivated plants."[4] He immediately noticed a direct relationship between these eight centers and the world's highest mountain ranges.

At the beginning, most cultivated plants in the Old World developed in an area between twenty and forty-five degrees north latitude, near the main mountain ranges: Himalayas, Hindu Kush, Caucasus, Balkans, and

---

*The Cambrian explosion, referring to the time when most groups of animals first appear in the fossil record, was a unique and unprecedented evolutionary burst of life forms that include almost all the lineages of animals alive today. This period, when most organisms evolved into more complex forms, is called an "explosion" because of the relatively short time over which the diversity of forms appeared.

Apennines. In America the same centers would run in a longitudinal direction, conforming to the orientation of the great mountain ranges. Thus Vavilov demonstrated that the most common crops derived from plants that would flourish in the mountains. The survivors of the flood—as we call the great catastrophe—terrified by the possibility of another flood, took refuge in the mountains, passing on ancient knowledge, especially farming (see the "seven wise men" of the Indian tradition, page 195).

Charles Hapgood's protégé, Rand Flem-Ath, demonstrated in an article published in *The Anthropological Journal of Canada* in 1981 that due to the crust displacement, some regions moved toward the equator and became warmer. Others were driven to the poles, while a few lucky ones remained climatically unchanged. Only three high-altitude regions, situated halfway between the current equator line and the previous one, maintained a stable climate. Tropical agriculture began 15,000 years ago in these places, more than five thousand feet above sea level.* In South America, agriculture flourished around Lake Titicaca. Indeed, it was only in this American region that plants and animals did not have to migrate in order to survive. Here, people cultivated potatoes for the first time and bred llamas and guinea pigs. Poles apart, for the first time, rice was cultivated in Spirit Cave on the Thailand highlands. On the Ethiopian highlands, near the Blue Nile's headwaters, millet was cultivated for the first time (figure 1.1). How could this happen simultaneously without the intervention of an external force?

The sliding of the crust made the ice caps shift to an area of warmer temperatures, provoking their progressive melting in three fast episodes that official geology establishes 15,000, 11,600, and 8,700 years ago. Afterward, it seems that agriculture was born—or reborn, presumably—in Egypt, Crete, Mesopotamia, India, and China, once again with amazing simultaneity.

Ancient peoples used to tell of an island that before the dislocation had hosted the first thriving civilization (the civilization of gods, also called Pelasgians or Viracochas), which developed over a dense network of canals that rose over its capital Atlantis, directly accessed from the bare rock and arranged in concentric circles. The outer ring housed mostly traders, while inland there were gardens, trails, walkways, and buildings,

---

*The Flem-Aths' theory dates the origins of agriculture to 11,600 years ago.

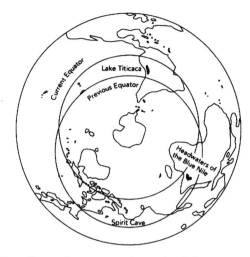

Figure 1.1. Seen from Antarctica, the path of the equator shifted with the last earth crust displacement. Lake Titicaca in the central Andes, Spirit Cave in the highlands of Thailand, and the highlands of Ethiopia were all midway between the current and former path of the equator. These favorable sites were climatically stable and supplied the survivors with raw crops that became potatoes, rice, and millet. From Rand and Rose Flem-Ath, Atlantis Beneath the Ice.

up to the city center with its majestic temples. Its collapse would be inextricably connected with the floods.

In Canada's province of British Columbia, the Okanagan Indians trace their origins back to "a remote island off the ocean. Its name was Samah-tumi-whoo-lah, meaning the White Man's Island, inhabited by a race of white-skinned giants."[5] Even Greek myth refers several times to the Pelasgians as "giants," and their light skin is a constant characteristic arising in any tradition that pertains to them, from one end of the planet to the other. The Okanagans believed that in some future age "lakes will melt the foundations of the world and rivers will untie it. Then, it will float and this will be the end of the world."[6] A similar prophecy has been handed down by the Cherokee of the southern Appalachian Mountains:

The earth is a great island floating in a sea of water, and suspended at each of the four cardinal points by a cord of solid rock hanging down from the sky vault. When the world grows old and worn out, the people will die and the cords will break and let the earth sink into the ocean, and all will be water again.[7]

This description well suits a sliding of the crust! The "cord[s] of solid rock" were—we'll talk about that—monuments that men had built according to a map of the stars, as if by copying the sky on the ground they were trying to anchor it, apparently to block its irregular motions, which would give the sensation of a movement of the crust.

Rand and Rose Flem-Ath indicate in *Atlantis Beneath the Ice,* a revised edition of the 1995 masterpiece *When the Sky Fell,* that

> American native mythology identifies four westerly mountains tied to the aftermath of a Great Flood. All four mountains are 1,800 meters or higher above sea level. . . . The native people of Washington and Oregon claim that their ancestors arrived in great canoes and disembarked on Mount Baker and Mount Jefferson. They believed that Mount Rainier was the refuge of those who were saved after the wicked of the earth were destroyed in a Great Flood. The Shasta of northern California tell of a time when the sun fell from its normal course. A separate myth relates how Mount Shasta saved their ancestors from the Deluge.[8]

From their reading of South American mythology the Flem-Aths' found that, "the 'gods' who brought agriculture to the vicinity of Lake Titicaca were said to have come 'out of the regions of the south' immediately 'after the deluge.'"[9]

At the time of Spanish colonization the Andean city of Vilcabamba the Old, better known as Machu Picchu (the name of the mountain on which it stands), was known to host the Virgins of the Sun. Despite attempts by the Spanish to discover its location, it remained secret until 1911 when it was discovered by the American explorer and historian Hiram Bingham. Several skeletons from the site were examined by George Eaton, professor at Yale University: "[T]here was not a single [skeleton] of a robust male of the warrior type. There are a few effeminate males who might very well have been priests, but the large majority of the skeletons are female."[10] The Flem-Aths concluded that the purpose of the refuge of Machu Picchu, situated on a pinnacle of rock and enclosed in an elbow-shaped bend of the sacred river Vilcamayu, was to ensure the repopulation of the world in case of disaster.

The town, characterized by an elegant terrace carved into the rock, must have once appeared as a beautiful mountaintop garden full of bright flowers. The houses are arranged in long rows and show very solid and functional architecture. Some ceremonial areas include huge blocks, similar to those of Sacsayhuaman (a walled complex of Cuzco, former capital of the Inca empire), one of which is about three meters high and one and a half meters wide and weighs about two hundred tons. There are dozens of blocks with such features, all set in puzzle-style walls with perfectly fitting, interlocking corners.

In the city we find authenticated facilities dating back to the period preceding the Incas,* particularly a megalithic cave dug into the rock known as the "Temple of the Three Windows" and the central hill-shaped pyramid.[11] The top of the hill is made of bare rock in the shape of a huge flattened fist with one finger pointing upward. Bingham called this object Intihuatana, which means "safety pilaster for the sun" (plate 3). At the foot of the Intihuatana, archaeologist and astronomer Ray White discovered basic representations of the four constellations that were supposed to dominate the four quarters of the Inca empire: the Southern Cross, the Summer Triangle, the "eye stars" of the Milky Way nebula, and the Pleiades.

Each winter solstice a rope was secured to the large "finger," magically anchoring the sun in the sky, thus impeding the mutation of its path.[12] Each day, as spring progresses and summer approaches, the sun rises slightly northward on the morning horizon; at summer solstice this shift stops to reverse its course the next day. Accordingly, every day it increasingly rises southward, till it reverses its course again at winter solstice. The priests of Machu Picchu tied the symbolic pillar Intihuatana to one of the stones arranged in the shape of a horseshoe. The Intihuatana was the observation point, and the sun would mark its annual march behind

---

*European universities date the construction of Machu Picchu back to the fifteenth century BCE. However, in the 1930s, Rolf Muller, astronomy professor at the University of Potsdam, dated the site between 4000 and 2000 BCE, basing his computations on the astronomical alignments of major structures.

the rocks, so the rope "forced" the sun to respect its path. A similar ceremony also existed among the ancient Egyptians and was known as "the stretching of the rope" (see chapter 5).

In *Atlantis Beneath the Ice,* the Flem-Aths explain that the story of the sun that deviates from its regular course, the sky that falls, and the Earth that's shaken by earthquakes and is submerged by large waves is found in the myths of all Native American peoples. In addition to those previously mentioned, others include the Utes of Utah, Kootenays of British Columbia, Washoes of western Nevada, Cahtoes of the Californian coast, A'-a'tam a'kimult (river people) along the Gila and Salt river valleys in Arizona, Ipurinà in the northwest of Brazil, Araucanians of Chile, and Anasazis of New Mexico. All these peoples are obsessed with the stability of the solar course because its deviation would signal a shift in the crust.

THE MECHANISM

The Flem-Aths tell the story of how, in the summer of 1799, the Tungus leader Ossip Shumakhov was searching for ivory along Siberian tracts when the frozen carcass of a mammoth, well preserved with remaining hair and flesh, appeared before his eyes. After this first accidental "meeting" the bones of thousands of these mammals were systematically discovered in the New Siberian Islands in the middle of the Arctic Ocean. How could these huge animals, which needed large amounts of vegetation, live on such desolate ice dunes and prosper in such numbers? And what devastating force could have killed them all?

The French naturalist Georges Cuvier (1769–1832) was persuaded by the idea that the world had suffered unimaginable disasters. He believed that mankind:

> might have inhabited certain circumscribed regions, whence he repeopled the earth after the terrible events; perhaps even the places he inhabited were entirely swallowed up and his bones buried in the depths of the present seas, except for a small number of individuals who carried on the race.[13]

These repeated eruptions and retreats of the sea have neither been slow nor gradual; most of the catastrophes that have occasioned them have been sudden; and this is easily proved, especially with regard to the last of them, the traces of which are most conspicuous. In the northern regions it has left the carcasses of some large quadrupeds, which the ice had arrested, and which are preserved even to the present day with their skin, their hair, and their flesh. If they had not been frozen as soon as killed they must quickly have been decomposed by putrefaction.[14]

Before this, eternal frost did not exist in the areas where these animals were found frozen, since they could not have survived at those temperatures.[15]

Cuvier bequeathed his ideas to Luis Agassiz (1807–1873), a Swiss naturalist and self-proclaimed pupil. Agassiz was the first to conjecture the theory of the ice ages:

A sudden intense winter, that was to last for ages, fell up on our globe; it spread over the very countries where these tropical animals had their homes, and so suddenly did it come upon them that they were embalmed beneath masses of snow and ice, without time even for the decay which follows death.[16]

In 1837 Agassiz's hypothesis provoked much skepticism in the scientific community. Although he could prove that the movement of glaciers would explain the location of the mountain ranges, the problem, the naturalist admitted since the beginning, was the lack of a trigger:

We have as yet no clew [sic] to the source of this great and sudden change of climate. Various suggestions have been made—among others, that formerly the inclination of the earth's axis was greater, or that a submersion of the continents under water might have produced a decided increase of cold; but none of these explanations are satisfactory, and science has yet to find any cause which accounts for all the phenomena connected with it.[17]

The first cause was advanced in 1842 by Joseph Alphonse Adhémar, a mathematician who taught in Paris, who observed that winter in the northern hemisphere comes when the Earth is at the closest point to the sun, so the winters are relatively mild. However, the inclined axis of the Earth rotates around a fixed point, slowly exchanging seasons in a cycle of about 26,000 years (the Precession of the Equinoxes). In this way, in a half cycle of 13,000 years, the northern winter will be more severe because the Earth will be at its farthest point from the sun.

In 1843 another French scientist, Urbain Le Verrier (1811–1877), found that in over 100,000 years the shape of the Earth's orbit changes from a nearly perfect circle, as it is today, to a more oval shape. So, the Earth is moving away from the sun, allowing the ice ages to tighten their grip on the planet.

The third and last cause was discovered by James Croll (1821–1890), a Scottish self-taught student who worked at the Andersonian College and Museum in Glasgow in order to take advantage of its library. The Earth's inclination angle determines the amount of sunlight that various parts of the globe receive. Croll found that although today the axis has an angle of 23.4 degrees, its slope varies from 21.8 to 24.4 degrees.

All three cycles are the result of the gravitational pull of the moon and planets. In *Atlantis Beneath the Ice,* the Flem-Aths explain how

> Milutin Milankovitch (1857–1927), a Serbian engineer who in 1911 was working as a professor of mathematics at the University of Belgrade, used these astronomical factors to calculate the amount of solar radiation that would reach the earth at any particular time in its history. He believed that ice ages resulted when winter ice did not melt the following summer because the earth was not receiving enough warmth from the sun. Over successive seasons the ice sheets would thicken, slowly smothering the land beneath. In 1976, Croll and Milankovitch's ideas were validated by James Hay, John Imbrie, and Nicholas Shackleton, who published a paper showing that the geological evidence of the ice ages matched the astronomical cycles.[18]

Usually, Hay, Imbe, and Shackelton affirm, "the earth is constantly wrapped in an ice age, whereas today we enjoy a mild climate compared to what the planet normally experiences. So this interglacial period, which began nearly 15,000 years ago, is intended to be of short duration."[19] Over the past 350,000 years there have been four interglacial periods, about 335,000, 220,000, 127,000, and 15,000 years ago. For an interglacial period to begin three astronomical cycles must coincide: the Earth's inclination must reach 24.4 degrees, the orbit must reach a more elliptical shape of at least 1 percent, and the Earth must be at the farthest point from the sun at the beginning of winter.

Apart from the inconsistency of this last statement—when the Earth is located at the farthest point from the sun, it is winter only in one hemisphere—it seems that the ice ages have not affected our planet globally, but have involved only some specific areas. One could say that, even today, the polar circles are in an ice age: if the crust moved, then new land would in turn come into the polar circles and would experience an ice age. According to Hapgood, the sliding of the crust is in fact due to the above-mentioned coincidence of astronomical cycles combined with the accumulation of ice at the pole. Einstein wrote:

> In a polar region there is continual disposition of ice which is not symmetrically distributed about the pole. The Earth's rotation acts on these unsymmetrical deposited masses, and produces centrifugal momentum that is transmitted to this rigid crust of the earth. The constantly increasing centrifugal momentum produced this way will, when it reaches a certain point, produce a movement of the earth's crust over the rest of the earth's body, and this will displace the polar regions toward the equator.[20]

MYSTERIES

Fifteen thousand years ago America was hit by massive extinctions: all the big bears, machairodonts, mammoths, and mastodons disappeared shortly after that date. In the same period the phenomenon was relatively mild in Europe and Africa, as a result of smaller changes in latitude produced by the shift.

> An imaginary circle drawn around the globe through the locations of the current and previous positions of the North and South poles reveals the area that experienced the largest latitude change, thereby

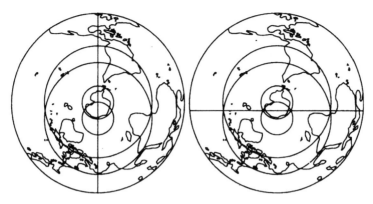

Figure 1.2. Line of greatest displacement (left) and line of least displacement (right). From Rand and Rose Flem-Ath, Atlantis Beneath the Ice.

suffering the greatest trauma. We call it the *line of greatest displacement* (LGD) or *ring of death*. This line runs through North America, west of South America, bisects Antarctica, travels through Southeast Asia, goes on to Siberia, and then back to North America (see figure 9.5). The ring of death corresponds directly with those regions of the globe that suffered the most extinctions. The *line of least displacement* (LLD) intersects with those climatic regions that remained relatively stable both during and after the catastrophe. It runs through Greenland, Europe, and Africa before cutting between Australia and New Zealand, passing Hawaii, and then returning to Greenland.[21]

This line perfectly corresponds to those areas where the extinction of animal species occurred on a small scale (figure 1.2).[22]

Rand Flem-Ath believes

An earth crust displacement randomly determines which species will survive and which will perish. The remnants of species that survive the destruction of an earth crust displacement represent smaller gene pools, increasing the probability of the development of new species because mutations can take a better "hold" within small communities. Ocean creatures stand a much greater chance because they can swim to climates to which they are already adapted. Land animals, however, have their mobility hampered by mountains, deserts, lakes, and oceans. With escape cut off they must adapt or extinction is inevitable. This explains why evolution appears to occur faster on land than within the oceans.[23]

Accordingly, nowadays, there is greater diversity between the genomes of two gorillas in neighboring communities than between two men born a thousand miles apart. This is a sign that, a few millennia ago, a catastrophe threatened to wipe out the human race.

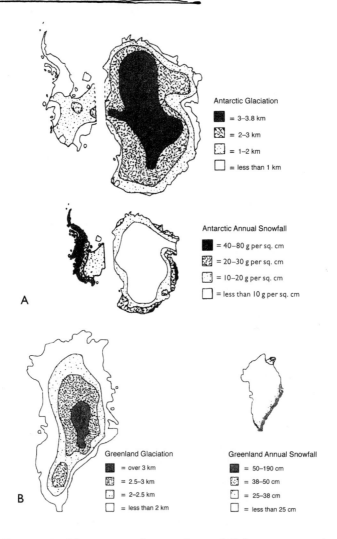

Figure 1.3. Glaciation and annual snowfall for Antarctica (top). Glaciation and annual snowfall for Greenland (bottom). From Rand and Rose Flem-Ath, Atlantis Beneath the Ice.

Before continuing with our considerations about extinctions, we will take a look at a geological problem that is closely related to them and will give us a better understanding of their occurence. It is a fact that the thicker the icy layers are—such as in Antarctica and Greenland—the less it snows. According to Hapgood's pattern, these areas were within the Arctic Circle before the displacement and remained there even afterward.

The Flem-Aths note the discrepancy between the ice sheets and snowfall patterns on Antarctica. Antarctica Minor (the tip that juts out toward South America) is characterized by mountains, thin layers of ice, and heavy snowfall. Antarctica Major (which is the continental part) contains most of the world's ice and today is a polar desert. Here, icy layers are over three miles deep, although it only snows a few times a year (figure 1.3a).

Central Greenland, like Antarctica Major, is largely covered with ice because, being at antipodes, it has always experienced the same climatic conditions. The layers of ice on both sides of the planet, however, are not symmetrical with respect to the Earth's axis, which means the lands have moved (figure 1.3b).

Up to 13,000 BCE, Antarctica Minor was outside the polar regions. Unfortunately, it has been little explored due to the fact that it is a land claimed by three countries (Chile, Argentina, and Great Britain), and because scientists usually prefer to work on Antarctica Major. An exception is the probing done using core drills by the Byrd expedition to Antarctica in 1949, whose goal was to extract sediment from the Ross Sea. The samples revealed several layers of fine-grained sediments, such as those brought to the sea by rivers flowing in temperate ice-free areas. The iodine dating (which uses three radioactive elements present in the seawater) indicated an age of no more than 15,000 years. Today the Ross Sea gathers the water melting from the Scott and Beardmore glaciers, which are more than one and a half miles thick.*

In 1893 the Norwegian captain Carl Anton Larsen, while on Seymour Island off the east coast of Antarctica's Palmer Peninsula, found about fifty balls of sand and "cement" on a set of columns of the same material.

---

*According to Oronzio Fineo's 1531 map compiled on the basis of earlier papers that were unfortunately lost, in this area are estuaries, inlets, and rivers. Similarly, the general profile of the southern continent and its physical features match information reported on maps made with the seismic method based on the reflection of the Antarctic subglacial earth surfaces.

According to Larsen the objects seemed to be made "by a human hand," but they were unfortunately destroyed in the fire of his house in Grytviken, a settlement on South Georgia (in the south Atlantic), and were never studied nor analyzed. Back from Antarctica, explorers of the caliber of Robert Falcon Scott brought fossils of trees and plants.

In 1999 the daring sailor Galileo Ferraresi retraced—on a sailing boat—Larsen's course, starting off from Genoa, navigating through the channels of Tierra del Fuego, then reaching the coast of the Antarctic Peninsula. Ferraresi was looking for a solution to the two mysteries of Seymour Island: the presence of fossilized plants, evidence of a temperate climate "perhaps even in historical times," and the presence of pillars topped with balls of gravel and sand. During the trip, he is thought to have found evidence of a geographic shift of the Earth, connected with the abrupt climate change in those remote regions. He brought new prehistoric trees to Italy, entrusting everything to the pages of the book *A Strawberry Amidst the Ice,* the account of that outstanding enterprise that is noteworthy even from a nautical point of view.

In 1975 Flavio Barbiero found a large amount of semi-fossilized logs in a moraine on King George Island (South Shetland) that could date back to 15,000 years ago.[24] Unfortunately, the scientific institutes tasked with examining these samples by carbon-14 dating have given no answer yet.

Finally, there is the mystery of the discovery of semi-fossilized marsupial mammals, like kangaroos, in Antarctica.

Let us return to the settlements and try to understand what may have happened in Antarctica, relying on the findings that emerged at the antipodes. The Flem-Aths report that

> In 1993, at a site 250 kilometers north of the Arctic Circle, Norwegian zoologists Rolv Lie and Stein-Erik Lauritzen discovered polar bear bones dating to the last ice age. The find was surprising because geologists assume that arctic Norway lies under a vast ice cap between eighty thousand and ten thousand years ago. . . . Carbon-14 and uranium dating confirmed that the remains must be at least forty-two thousand years old. Further excavations revealed the remains of wolves, field mice, ants, and tree pollen. "The wolf needs large prey like reindeer," said Lie. Reindeer, in turn, must be able to graze on bare ground. "The

summers must have been relatively warm and the winters not excessively cold . . . the area wasn't under an icecap as we believed."[25]

How could it be possible that a supposedly frozen area within the polar regions could present characteristics typical of temperate climates? Similarly, in 1984 off the northwest coast of Scotland two scientists' findings showed that the Isle of Lewis was not covered with ice during the period between 37,000 and 23,000 years ago: "Models of the last ice sheet showing Scottish ice extending to the continental shelf edge depict the north of Lewis as being covered by 1,000–1,500 metres of ice, but our evidence demonstrates that part of this area was actually ice-free."[26]

In 1982, R. Dale Guthrie of the Institute of Arctic Biology explained why he was so impressed by the variety of animal species that lived in Alaska in the period before 13,000 BCE:

> When learning of this exotic mixture of hyenas, mammoths, sabre-toothed cats, camels, horses, rhinos, asses, deer with gigantic antlers, lions, ferrets, saiga, and other Pleistocene species, one cannot help wondering about the world in which they lived. This great diversity of species, so different from that encountered today, raises the most obvious question: is it not likely that the rest of the environment was also different?[27]

In their reading about late Pleistocene extinctions, the Flem-Aths found that "of the thirty-four ascertained species that populated Siberia before 13,000 BCE, including mammoths, giant moose, hyenas, and cave lions, twenty-eight could survive only under temperate conditions."[28] In the New Siberian Islands, north of the Siberian Arctic shore, two Russian researchers unearthed the remains of some saigas, also known as antelopes of the steppes, typical only of the steppe. Charles Hapgood wrote:

> The remains of mammoths and other animals are more numerous than elsewhere. Baron Toll, the Arctic explorer, discovered there the remains of a saber-toothed tiger, and a fruit tree that, vertically, was twenty-seven meters high. The tree was well preserved in permafrost,

complete with roots and seeds. Green leaves and ripe fruits were still attached to its branches. . . . Nowadays, the only specimen of vegetation on the islands is a willow tree, two and a half centimeters high.[29]

As Darwin stated in *The Origin of Species*, such disruption "must have shaken the whole structure of the globe." In America more than seventy kinds of mammals became extinct, including the entire order of proboscideans. Such losses did not occur evenly over the entire melting period of ice caps but were concentrated between 11,000 and 9000 BCE. In Alaska, the organogenic deposit where animals' remains are buried looks like a fine, dark gray sand.

> Frozen and solidified here lie the twisted parts of animals and trees mixed with ice lenses, layers of peat and moss . . . bison, horses, wolves, bears, lions. . . . Apparently, entire herds of animals were killed simultaneously, overcome by the same force. . . . It is absolutely impossible that piles of dead animals and humans such as this is formed under normal natural causes.[30]

At various levels, stone artifacts were found "frozen in at extensive depth, along with specimens of fauna belonging to Glacial Period, thus confirming that man was already living in Alaska when the animals became extinct."[31]

Many of the Alaskan organogenic deposits are characterized by the presence of mammoths and bison torn and twisted by an unprecedented atmospheric turbulence; we exclude human intervention, since there was no trace of knives or other cutting tools.[32]

In conjunction with the extinctions the Earth was shaken by volcanic eruptions of extraordinary proportions. Thousands of prehistoric animals and plants sank in the mud of the famous tar pits in La Brea, Los Angeles. Similar discoveries of birds and mammals typical of the late glacial period were made beneath large piles of ash and volcanic sand in the valley of San Pedro, in the Florissant fossil beds in Colorado, and in other areas of America. Supposedly, there were frequent volcanic eruptions throughout much of the glacial period, not only in America but also in the North Atlantic Sea, Asia, and continental Japan.[33]

In order to imagine the impact that such widespread volcanic activity had on the people of that period, think about the eruption of the Indonesian volcano Krakatau in 1883: it was so violent that it caused the death of thirty-six thousand people and its explosion rebounded over a radius of more than five kilometers. Eighteen cubic kilometers of rock and huge quantities of ash and dust were driven into the upper atmosphere, and for over two years the clouds around the world were much darker and sunsets much redder. In this period the average temperature decreased as the particles of volcanic dust reflected the sun's rays back into space. For the glacial period we have to imagine many Krakatau volcanos erupting simultaneously, resulting in an outstanding temperature drop. Since the volcanos emitted huge amounts of carbon dioxide into the atmosphere—and carbon dioxide is a greenhouse gas—when the dust settled on the ground, the global temperature must have considerably increased.

Geologists agree that the complete withdrawal of ice caps of the last ice age took place by 7000 BCE. The previous six thousand years were characterized by geological and climatic turbulence on unimaginable scale. Europe and North America were buried under a layer of ice three kilometers thick, and it is estimated that 17,000 years ago the total volume of ice covering the northern hemisphere was about nine and a half million cubic kilometers. The great melting began so suddenly, and involved such a large area, as to be defined "a sort of prodigy."[34]

The speed with which the deglaciation occurred suggests a sudden event that happened some 15,000 years ago. The sea level rose rapidly by more than one hundred meters with the consequent destruction of islands and long stretches of coastline. In the United States marine characteristics typical of the glacial period have been found along the Gulf Coast east of the Mississippi at an altitude of more than 60 meters. On the Arctic coast of Canada marine deposits have been found containing walruses, seals, and five different kinds of whales. Finally, the bones of a whale were recovered north of Lake Ontario, about 130 meters above sea level, and another skeleton was found in the Montreal area of Quebec at an altitude of about 180 meters. In the period when life in the Siberian Arctic was lush and largely free of ice, two huge ice sheets were pressing on northeastern America. At its maximum extent, the ice sheet of the last glaciation, which pivoted in the Hudson Bay, was larger than the current Antarctic ice sheet: it took up most of Canada in addition to the states and provinces bordering the Great Lakes. Actually, the Great Lakes are what remain of it. Westward, the Cordilleran ice sheet ran along the Rocky Mountains, covering southern Alaska, almost all of British Columbia, a considerable slice of the province of Alberta, and the states of Washington, Idaho, and Montana. When these two layers of ice melted, Beringia, the corridor of land that joins Alaska and Siberia, was completely flooded. Notwithstanding, a corridor between the western and the eastern layers remained ice-free, thus serving as the eastern slope to the Asians who migrated to America (figure 1.4).

Now we are aware of a different former image of northern Alaska and eastern Siberia, much like the one for eastern Antarctica, one with green pastures eaten by mammals of all sizes, a sort of Eden. The sliding of the crust, subsequent climate change, and the relation of world mythology to these events have been thoroughly investigated by Rand and Rose Flem-Ath in *Atlantis Beneath the Ice*. Its pages offer a detailed report of our last 100,000 years:

> Prior to 91,600 B.C. the crust was situated in such a way that Canada's Yukon Territory stood at the North Pole. The Arctic Circle of this time encompassed most of the northwestern half of North America, as well as all of Alaska, Beringia, and much, but not all, of northeastern Siberia.
>
> This arrangement of the crust accounts for the Cordilleran Ice Sheet. During this era, passage from Asia to America was completely blocked. Europe was warmer than it is today and Greenland was without ice.
>
> An earth crust displacement at 91,600 B.C. moved the crust so that Europe fell within the Arctic Circle.
>
> From 91,600 B.C. to 50,600 B.C., Europe and Greenland were smothered under ice. Passage to America from Asia, across Beringia, was possible sometime after the old Alaskan ice cap melted. This means that people from Asia might have arrived in America before 50,600 B.C., an idea that has recently gained archaeological support.
>
> In the March 1994 issue of *Popular Science,* Ray Nelson reported on an important archaeological finding in New Mexico. Dr. Richard

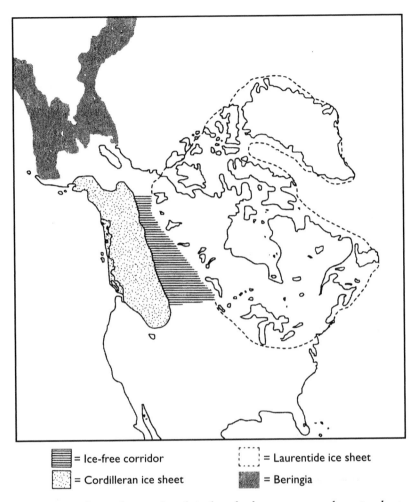

= Ice-free corridor   = Laurentide ice sheet

= Cordilleran ice sheet   = Beringia

Figure 1.4. Eleven thousand and six hundred years ago two huge ice sheets covered most of North America. The lower ocean level created an isthmus called Beringia, between a widely ice-free Alaska and a totally ice-free Siberia. Archaeologists believe that men moved from Asia to America by crossing this isthmus, then continued along the ice-free corridor between the surrounding icy areas. From Rand and Rose Flem-Ath, Atlantis Beneath the Ice.

S. MacNeish, along with his team from the Andover Foundation for Archaeological Research, excavated a site at Pendejo Cave, in southwestern New Mexico. They found eleven human hairs in a cave about 100 meters above the desert. Radiocarbon testing dated them at 55,000 years ago.

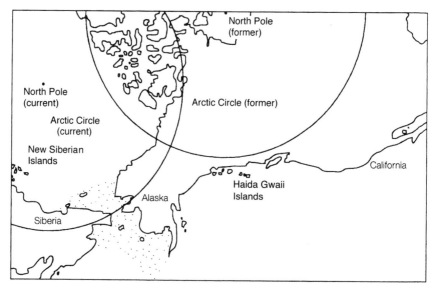

Figure 1.5. With each dislocation of the Earth's crust came a corresponding change in cardinal directions. Before the last catastrophe, the North American Pacific coast actually looked south, whereas the Arctic Circle was located on the shores of Hudson Bay. From this perspective, the migrations of peoples from Siberia through Beringia and along the coast of the Pacific Ocean meant moving from west to east. From Rand and Rose Flem-Ath, Atlantis Beneath the Ice.

An earth crust displacement at 50,600 BC moved the crust again, this time bringing North America into the polar zone.

The Arctic Circle now lay over Hudson Bay rather than the "Arctic" Ocean.

People and animals from Siberia could have crossed Beringia into Alaska and then moved east along the Pacific coast all the way to California. This Pacific waterway to America was open and inviting. It would have been possible for seafarers to travel along the coasts of Alaska and British Columbia to Washington without enduring many adjustments to their hunting and gathering way of life. And once they got to North America it would have been possible to get to South America and then to the ice-free Lesser Antarctica, in the antipodal areas to Arctic Norway, northern Alaska, Beringia, and

Siberia. They may have lived there anywhere from 50,600 B.C. to 9600 B.C. (or longer).

However, after the earth crust displacement of 9600 B.C., the people of Lesser Antarctica (Atlantis) would have had to flee their homeland as the Antarctic Circle encapsulated the whole island.

After the displacement of 9600 B.C., the ice sheet centered on Hudson Bay began to melt. Beringia was submerged by the rising level of the world's ocean as the old ice caps added water to the seas. Alaska and Siberia's climate took a dramatic turn for the worse.

It is assumed that people trapped in Alaska and unable to return to Siberia were forced south, and that these "first" Americans arrived through the "ice-free corridor" after 9600 B.C. There is very little archaeological evidence to support this theory. One possibility that is not considered is the tone the most closely matches the tales told by the people themselves: that they came from a white island destroyed by a great flood. They regarded their island as "white" because two-thirds of Antarctica was under snow.

The origins of the people of America are probably mixed. Some, no doubt, did arrive from Asia after 9600 B.C. Others, however, might have already been in America and Antarctica for forty thousand or even eighty thousand years before this time.[35]*

ISSUES OF LANGUAGE

On the Haida Gwaii Islands, off the northwest coast of Canada, lived the Indian tribe of Haida. According to recent studies made by some Russian researchers, the Haida language has strong affinities with ancient Sumerian.[36] Thirty-five thousand Sumerian tablets were unearthed in Mesopotamia between 1899 and 1900 at Nippur, the city of Enlil, god of the wind and floods. They tell us the origin of the Sumerian-Akkadian civilization, whose members were fugitives who escaped the waters of the flood on a large ship. Forced by fate, they left their homeland, the island-mountain

---

*It is our contention that the first destruction of Atlantis began in 13,000 BCE.

of Dilmun, lost southward in the ocean. The Flem-Aths make the following comparison:

Haida Myth*	Sumerian Myth*
Long ago, our ancestors lived in the world's largest village. Life was care-free until the great chief of the heavens decided to destroy mankind by changing the sky and bringing a worldwide flood.	Long ago, our ancestors lived on the island of Dilmun. Life was care-free until the sky-god and flood-god decided to destroy mankind by changing the sky and bringing a worldwide flood.
Survivors escaped in large canoes which took them to a new land where they landed on a mountain.	Survivors escaped in a large ship which took them to a new land where they landed on a mountain.
A new era began.	A new era began.

*From Rand and Rose Flem-Ath, *Atlantis Beneath the Ice,* 72–78.

Such a resemblance cannot by any means be just a coincidence; indeed, if we assume that the Sumerian language could be an artificial construct created by Akkadian priests—there is no other language in the world so similar to the Sumerian as Haida—its roots trace back again to the flood and Atlantis.

In 1984, the Bolivian mathematician Iván Guzmán de Rojas studied the language spoken by the Aymara, the aboriginal people inhabiting the shores of Lake Titicaca between Peru and Bolivia near the ancient city of Tiahuanaco, a place where there are numerous remains of the gods-Pelasgians-Atlanteans. Guzmán proved that the Aymara language could be used in the simultaneous translation of English into many other languages and developed a software for translations that experts from eleven European universities had not been able to create. The Panama Canal Committee made use of the IT-based interpreter to translate a commercial exam for Wang Laboratories.

The secret of his machine, which had solved a problem that was considered intractable by many specialists of computerized translation around the world, is the rigidly logical and unambiguous structure of the Aymarà language, which is ideal to be turned into a comput-erized algorithm.[37]

Aymara is simple and rigorous. Its syntax rules are always applica-ble and can be recorded concisely in the sort of algebraic shorthand understood by computers. Indeed, its purity is such that some histo-rians believe that this language has not evolved like other languages, but was invented anew.[38]

So can we really talk of an artificial language, a sort of ancient Esperanto?

THE ISLAND AT THE POLE

There are hundreds of legends all around the world about the island of Atlantis, yet the vast majority of fans learn of it through Plato's writ-ings, *Timaeus* and *Critias*, and do not go any further. Sometimes names change: an example is Dilmun, to which we must add the Egyptian's Ta-Neteru, the Mount Meru of the Hindu Mahābhārata, and countless others. Atlantis is always said to be a land rich in pastures and mines, crops and wildlife; it always is a mountain, an island, or rather an island-mountain. No coincidence that the name Atlantis derives from the ety-mon *atlas,* or *atlanta,* "to hold, sustain," which we find in the word of common use *atlas,* "mount, what sustains the sky."

According to Plato, at the beginning the gods split up rule of the land and Poseidon was given the island of Atlantis. In the center of the island:

> there was a mountain not very high on any side. In this mountain there dwelt one of the earth-born primeval men of that country, whose name was Evenor, and he had a wife named Leucippe. . . . [Poseidon enclosed the hill] making alternate zones of sea and land larger and smaller, encircling one another; there were two of land and three of water, which he turned as with a lathe, each having its circumference equidistant every way from the center, so that no man could get to the island.[39]

This description continues in another passage:

Some of their buildings were simple, but in others they put together different stones, varying the color to please the eye and to be a natural source of delight. The entire circuit of the wall, which went round the outermost zone, they covered with a coating of brass, and the circuit of the next wall they coated with tin, and the third, which encompassed the citadel, flashed with the red light of orichalcum. The palaces in the interior of the citadel were constructed on this wise: in the centre was a holy temple [. . .], which remained inaccessible, and was surrounded by an enclosure of gold. [. . .]All the outside of the temple, with the exception of the pinnacles, they covered with silver, and the pinnacles with gold. In the interior of the temple the roof was of ivory, curiously wrought everywhere with gold and silver and orichalcum; and all the other parts, the walls and pillars and floor, they coated with orichalcum.[40]

A comparison with the landscapes of the exotic Mount Meru as described in the Mahābhārata would be desirable, but to quote such a long epic poem would be probably tedious, so we rely on a short essay published on the Internet, which furnishes an excellent summary:

At the center of the cosmic ocean, at the time of creation, emerged Mount Meru, with the shape of a four-faced pyramid, each one composed of precious stones, where the Buddhist pantheon resides, where its inhabitants do not know either misery nor pain. The eastern part is made of rock crystal, the southern part of lapis lazuli, rubies compose the west, and finally the north consists of pure gold. The Meru is surrounded by seven concentric rings of golden mountains, interspersed with rainwater seas, enclosed in a circle of mountains of iron, and outdoors in four directions, there are the four continents.

Opening the heavy Hindu volume, we read that:

at Meru the sun and the moon go round from left to right (Pradakshinam) every day and so do all the stars. . . . The mountain, by its luster, so overcomes the darkness of night that the night can hardly be distinguished from the day. . . . The day and the night are together equal to a year to the residents of the place.[41]

In *Surya Siddhanta*, an ancient Hindu treatise on astronomy, the story changes very little:

Once raised, the gods, behold the sun for six months at a time.[42]

In the Avesta, a collection of sacred texts belonging to the Zoroastrian religion of pre-Islamic Persia, Airyana Vaejo is described as a fertile land with mild climate where

the stars, the moon and the sun are only once a year seen to rise and set, and a year seems only as a day.[43]

The seventh mandala of the *Rig-Veda* contains many hymns to the "Dawn." One of these (7.76) says that "the Dawns have raised their banner on the horizon with their usual splendor." Verse three refers to a period of "several days" that passed between the first appearance of the dawn and the subsequent rise of the sun.[44] Another passage states that "many days passed between the first appearance of light on the horizon and the uprising of the sun."[45] Usually these polar features are accompanied by contrasting images of a lush and sunny country, where arts and science reached unparalleled levels. However, there was an end to all this: in the Avesta, as well as the Norse Edda, and among the Toba Indians of South America, it is said that Atlantis was imprisoned in a terrible winter that forced its inhabitants to flee: the Pelasgians.

In the Avesta we read that in that period Airyana Vaejo enjoyed a mild and fertile climate with seven months of summer and five of winter but later became uninhabitable due to the onset of a sudden glaciation. Rich in game and crops, its lawns teeming with streams, this garden of delights was victim to the fury of Angra Mainyu, the Evil, and turned into an uninhabitable desolated land, with ten months of winter and only two of summer:

The first of the good lands and countries which I, Ahura Mazdah, have created was the Airyana Vaejo. [. . .] Then Angra Mainyu, who is full of death, created an opposition to it, a mighty serpent and the snow. Now there are ten months of winter, two months of summer, and these have cold water, cold land and cold trees. [. . .] All around there falls deep snow, which is the most terrible wound.[46]

In other passages, the author warns that "on the physical world will descend the evil of winter, so the snow will fall in great abundance" and Angra Mainyu will send "the intense and destructive freeze."[47] Indeed, all ancient peoples' traditions have memories of Earth cataclysms and upheavals. Among these, many speak of gods' lands and ancient paradises, all located in the south and suddenly caught by polar climatic conditions. In South America, the Toba Indians in the Gran Chaco, which reaches the modern borders of Paraguay, Chile, and Argentina, still tell an ancient legend on the advent of what they call "the Big Chill." The heroic god-like figure, named Asin, forewarned the people:

Asin told a man to collect all the wood he could, and to cover his hut with a thick layer of stubble, because it was coming a time of great cold. As soon as the hut was ready, Asin and the man locked themselves inside and waited. When the great cold came, shaking people came to them begging a firebrand. Asin was inflexible and gave the embers only to those who had been his friends. The population was dying of cold, and cried all night long. At midnight they were all dead, young and old, men and women . . . this period of ice and sleet lasted for a long time and all the fires went out. The ice was as thick as rawhide.[48]

Do we still have doubts about the location of Atlantis, the first and true one, in Antarctica? 15,000 years ago Antarctica Minor at least enjoyed a temperate climate, and then something happened that changed everything: geology and traditions inform us!

The Spanish conqueror Hernán Cortés had the undeserved honor of meeting the Aztec emperor Montezuma on the top of the Temple of the Sun in Palenque. Their conversation appears in a letter Cortés sent to the king of Spain that refers to a lost island of this tribe's ancestors: "Our fathers lived in a happy and prosperous place they called Aztlan, which means whiteness. A shining land, of a white candor and surrounded by water, consisting of seven cities at the foot of a sacred mountain."[49]

In Canada the Okanagan Indians of British Columbia link their origins to "a remote island off the ocean. Its name was Samah-tumi-whoo-lah, meaning the White Man's Island, inhabited by a race of clear-skinned giants."[50] Again, the term "giants" appears, along with "clear skin."

A scholar of the Vedas, Bal Gangadhar Tilak, the first in India to opt for a tactic of passive resistance against the British, published his most famous book in 1903, *The Arctic Home of the Vedas*, in which he demonstrated that the ruins of a lost paradise were kept on an island near the pole. Tilak summarizes a piece of an Iranian saga contained in the *Zend-Avesta:*

Ahura Mazda warns Yima, the first king of the men, about the approach of a severe winter, which will destroy all living creatures, blanketing the earth with a thick layer of ice, and advises him to build a "Vara," or fence, in which to preserve the seed of each plant and animal. The meeting, they say, took place in Airyana Vaejo, the Persians' Paradise.

The ideas of Tilak took inspiration from the book *Paradise Found: The Cradle of the Human Race at the North Pole* (1885), by William Fairfield Warren, founder of Boston University. The latter looked at how often the story of the fall of the sky and the flood was associated with the idea of a paradisiacal island, a lost place with pronounced polar character. Fairfield takes us back to Japan, 681 CE, when Emperor Temnu ordered Hieda no Are, the most respected voice of his company of storytellers, to gather the most ancient folk myths in a written collection. The compilation was completed in 712 CE and hereafter called *Ko-ji-ki* ("memories of ancient events"). Warren realized that the first part of the book contained the memories of a homeland on an island near the Earth's axis:

Standing on the bridge of heaven, [the deities] pushed down a spear into the green plain of the sea, and stirred it round and round. When they drew it up the drops, which fell from its end, consolidated onto an island. The sun-born pair descended onto the island, and planting a spear in the ground, point downwards, built a palace round it, taking that for the central roof-pillar. The spear became the axis of the earth, which had been caused to revolve by the stirring round."[51]

Warren understood that Onogoro-jima ("Island of the frozen drop," from the Shinto creation story) had to be located near the Arctic pole, and that the polar heaven was destroyed by a sudden drop in temperature, pursuant to a general geological upheaval:

Students of antiquity must often have marveled that in nearly every ancient literature they should encounter the strange expression, the Navel of the Earth. Still more unaccountable would it have seemed to them had they noticed how many ancient mythologies connect the cradle of the human race with this earth-navel. The advocates of the different sites which have been assigned to Eden have seldom, if ever, recognized the fact that no hypothesis on this subject can be considered acceptable which cannot account for this peculiar association of man's first home with some sort of natural center of the earth.[52]

Rand and Rose Flem-Ath evaluated Warren's work and noted that,

if Warren hadn't been so fixed on the northern view and had instead looked to the south, he would have seen that Antarctica represents a far more natural Navel of the Earth [figure 1.6]. Antarctica sits, like the mythological homeland of the Okanagan, in the "middle of the ocean." … Like the Aztec's Aztlan, Antarctica is "white." Like Iran's lost paradise, Antarctica is covered "with a thick sheet of ice." And like the first land of Japanese mythology, Antarctica is close to one of the earth's poles.[53]

The *Vishnu Purana* (about 2000 BCE), one of the oldest Puranas of Hinduism, speaks of "Atala, the white island." The terms "Atala" and "white island" are also used in the *Bhavishya Purana* (fourth century BCE). Here it is said that Samba, having built a temple dedicated to Surya (the sun),

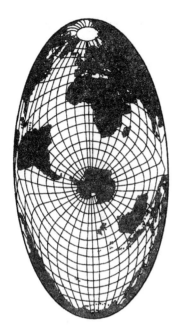

Figure 1.6. A world map from the U.S. Navy that, with Antarctica in the middle of the ocean, shows this continental island as the natural "navel of the world." From Rand and Rose Flem-Ath, Atlantis Beneath the Ice.

made a trip to Dwipa Saka "beyond the saltwater" in search of magicians and sun worshippers. During his trip, he was guided by Surya himself (or he simply headed west, following the sun) and riding Garuda (the flying vehicle of Krishna and Vishnu) finally landed among <u>the magicians of Atala.</u>

The Mahābhārata (ca. 600 BCE) also refers to "Atala, the white island," described as an "island of great splendor" inhabited by "white men who have never slept or eaten."[54] So, it is remarkable that the Greek historian Herodotus (450 BCE) described a tribe of Atlanteans that "never dream or eat non-living things."[55] Can this be just a coincidence?

By the way, in one of his books, Aristotle says, "Be careful, because in Sardinia there is a demigod that is able to deprive of dreams!"[56]

Sardinia? Why is he talking of Sardinia now? We were talking about Antarctica and its god Poseidon as a protagonist in the history of Atlantis. We expected to meet his counterpart, Varuna (the Hindu Poseidon), the protagonist in the Sanskrit accounts on Atala. We were going to talk about the capital of Atala, Tripura, with its circular shape and divided in three concentric parts such as Plato's metropolis. Should we now turn toward the direction Aristotle is suggesting?!

Indeed, in the next section we will see how Plato, in the fourth century BCE, created a link between the memories of Antarctica and the traditions encountered during the settlement of the Pelasgians on the western Mediterranean. Here Sardinia makes its appearance . . .

WHEN *OCEAN* MEANT *TYRRHENIAN*

In this section we rely on the studies of two main researchers about Atlantis: Plato, 428 BCE philosopher, and Sergio Frau, a journalist who has recently gained stage by brilliantly exposing the geography as it was conceived in classical Greece, with its toponyms similar—indeed almost identical—to ours, yet used with completely different meanings.

Sergio Frau's masterpiece, *Le Colonne d'Ercole: Un'inchiesta* (The Pillars of Hercules: An Inquiry), published in 2002 by Nur Neon Ltd., successfully demonstrates that the Pillars of Hercules were not located in Gibraltar until Eratosthenes, director of the library of Alexandria in the third century BCE, put them there by force. I had already suspected this when I read a passage of Diodorus and Cluverio, where Hercules was planting the mountain Pelorus near Messina, at the mouth of the ocean, to prevent a second inundation.[57] Unfortunately, due to the nomadic nature of Greek fables, as Pliny says (vol. 31), there is no specific location of these columns. By the way, the area of interest is the Strait of Messina, the Strait of Sicily, the Sardinian southern tip, and the portion of Libya in front of it. Mr. Frau has cleverly reinterpreted all of Hanno's peripli, Avienus, and Pseudo-Scylax* so that those trips, reminiscent of *Alice in Wonderland,* would now acquire seriousness and reliability thanks to a simple shift of the mysterious columns.

I will now briefly quote some extracts from Frau's book, though I highly suggest reading it:

Pindar (Nemean III): "It is not easy to cross the trackless sea beyond the pillars of Heracles, which that hero and god set up as famous witnesses to the furthest limits of seafaring. He subdued the mon-

---

*Hanno the Navigator, Carthaginian explorer (500 BCE) whose peripli (seafaring manuals) described the coast of Africa from current Morocco to the Gulf of Guinea; Avienus rewrote a poem by Dionysius Periegetes showing the limits of the habitable world from the perspective of Alexandria; Pseudo-Scylax is an ancient Greek periplus.

strous beasts in the sea, and tracked to the very end the streams of the shallows, where he reached the goal that sent him back home again, and he made the land known." [p. 82]

Eugenio Grassi (in a note from the Sansoni edition): "It seems that the passage refers to the victory of Heracles against Triton, [which] happened in the slums of Sirte [southeastern Tunisia]." [p. 82]

Polybius (*Histories,* **book 34, 6**): "As for Dicaearchus at least he says that the distance from the Peloponnesus to the Pillars of Hercules is 10,000 stades and that the distance to the Adriatic is more." [p. 270]

Aristotle (peri kosmos): "Up-country, Westward, making its way with a narrow passage through the so called Pillars of Hercules, the Ocean enters the inner sea as it entered a port and gradually widening, it extends embracing large bays connected with each other, now flowing in narrow openings, now widening again. In the first place, it is said that, on the right side if coming from the Pillars of Hercules, it forms two gulfs, constituting the so-called Syrtes, of which one is called the Great and the other the Small. On the other side, it does not form such gulfs, creating instead three seas, namely the Sardònion, the Galatikòn, and the Adriatic seas and straight after, slanted, the Sikelikon. Further on, it forms the Cretan Sea, and adjacent to this, on the one hand, the Sea of Egypt, the Sea of Pamphylia and the Sea of Syria, while on the other, the Aegean Sea and the Sea of Mirto [the part of the Aegean Sea closest to the east coast of Attica and Peloponnese]." The fact that the Sardinian Sea is located immediately eastward of the Pillars means that the latter are situated between Sardinia and Tunisia. [pp. 288–89]

Callimachus (Hymn to Delos): "And even as when the mount Aetna smolders with fire and all its secret depths are shaken as the giant under earth, even Briares, shifts to his other shoulder." Clearchus writes "Briares also called Hercules." [p. 260]

Timaeus: "The island of Sardinia is situated near the Pillars of Hercules." [p. 285]

Here it is: as someone has certainly noticed, the term Ocean has been inappropriately used to indicate the Tyrrhenian Sea, within the

Mediterranean. In fact, it is not a real misuse, because for the Greeks there was no other ocean than the Tyrrhenian Sea, and we have to keep that in mind while reading Plato.

Four centuries before him, Homer and Hesiod believed that the west coast of Italy marked the ultimate ends of the earth. Its coasts were washed by Ocean, "the last river that divided the kingdom of the living from that of the deceased," beyond which there was the underworld where Saturn and Janus had been exiled.

The witch Circe, Atlas's daughter, was Pelasgian since he himself was the father of all Pelasgians/Atlanteans. In the *Odyssey,* she advises Ulysses to visit the kingdoms of the deceased to consult Tiresias the soothsayer. He sailed in the morning and in the evening arrived at the freezing borders of the Ocean, where the Cimmerians or Cumans lived; here, he spoke with Tiresias and with his own mother, who is amazed that he has dared cross the border: "for between us and them there are great and terrible waters, and there is Oceanus, which no man can cross on foot, but he must have a good ship to take him."

Before sunrise he came back again through "the currents of the great river Ocean" and returned to Circe. Since the involved places were Cumae and Circeo, it makes sense that the Ocean started from the Tyrrhenian Sea and did not include the waters beyond the western Mediterranean. Borrowing a bit more from Frau:

Theopompus (about 300 BC): describes the position of Rome as not far from the Ocean. Timaeus (280 BC) positions Sardinia close to the Ocean and makes the Rhone flow in the Atlantic. [p. 87]

Timaeus: "Amber was believed to come from the Eridanus that, according to the period knowledge, then flew into the Northern Ocean."

Apollonius Rhodius (book 4, 630–31): "The Eridanus was identified with the Po. But in mythical geography, the river is symbolic of the northwest, representing at the same time both the Rhone and the Po and flowing" from the borders of the earth where are the doors and the houses of the night. [p. 87]

Herodotus (book 1, 202.3): "all that Sea which the Hellenes navigate, and the Sea beyond the Pillars, which is called Atlantis (that is burned, red) and the Erythraian Sea are in fact all one." [p. 150]

So, it is also the Atlantic, isn't it? Yes, the word "Atlantic" signified the waters north of the Tyrrhenian Sea, namely the Gulf of Liguria, and the waters along the west coast of Sardinia. Therefore, to have a better understanding of Plato, we need to acknowledge that in his period the Pillars would mark the border between the two "Mediterraneans," and considering that when Atlantis was flooded—in 9600 BCE according to the philosopher—the water level was much lower than today, we can assume that the Channel of Sicily was indeed a strait, supporting the idea of a Mediterranean divided into two basins. The ancient people remembered a terrible upheaval that had turned Italy upside down, divided Sicily from the Aeolian Islands, and submerged the in-between land. It was then that Hercules set his columns to stop future floods. For this reason the etymologic meaning for Eraklès is "dam digger."*

THE STORY

In *Timaeus*, Plato tells about the Athenians opposing the advance of the Pelasgians in the eastern Mediterranean in 9600 BCE. King Janus/Osiris had conquered Egypt and the situation seemed hopeless until Athens forced him back, a few years before the arrival of "violent earthquakes and floods; and in a single day and night of misfortune all your warlike men in a body sank into the earth, and the island of Atlantis in like manner disappeared in the depths of the sea."[58]

Philochorus, an ancient Greek grammarian, recalls the same event, when "a people invaded the ancient Greece and especially Athens; the Athenians were proud people with this struggle and, apparently, they succeeded in winning; these invaders were led by a king; they were indeed Tyrrhenians [which is a synonym for Pelasgians] and the Greeks, wishing

---

*Greek "era"; Semitic "heru"; Ugaritic "hr"; Akkadian "hararu" (to dig); Greek "klès"; Latin "cules"; Akkadian "kalu" (dam).

to induce horror for the royal name, called tyrants those Tyrrhenian kings that had invaded their land."[59]

<u>Plato plainly tells us that the island of Atlantis was located at the Pillars of Hercules (and not, as others wrote, "beyond" it)</u>. Given the ambiguous position of the latter, we should decide whether to look at Sicily or Sardinia, though our work develops on the latter. Take for example Locri's Timaeus with whom Plato dialogues: he could be Timaeus's great-grandfather, maybe Tauromenium's Timaeus, who places one pillar right in Sardinia. It was an island with many names, which the Greeks looked at with both admiration and suspicion, since they often fell into sandy Syrtes traps or the low muddy shallows of the channel of Sicily. The idea of *so far but no further* came about by reading Herodotus or Hesiod, or by getting frightened by the monsters that right there hamper Ulysses and Aeneas. In *Critias*, Plato remarks, "Even today, that sea remains impracticable and unsearchable, due to the muddy shallows that the sinking island produced." Plato himself says that the island was larger than Libya and Asia together. It is not implausible, if we consider that at that time they called Libya a territory a bit larger than the coast that goes from Egypt to Little Sirte, while the term Asia was used to identify a region of Turkey called Caria. It is Eratosthenes who says so, he who 2,300 years ago moved the pillars:

> Before the name Asia designated the whole continent, Eratosthenes observed, the Greeks just used it to distinguish their country from Caria, which was "in front of them" beyond the Aegean Sea.[60]

From Sardinia, one could reach the nearby Corsica and Balearic Islands, and from these islands reach the parts of the continent washed by the Ocean, namely the inner coasts of Europe and Africa west of Italy, which encircle the western Mediterranean:

> [There was] an island, where you call the Pillars of Hercules were, [. . .] from that you could go to other nearby islands, and from the islands to the whole opposite continent, which surrounds what can rightly be called Ocean.[61]

One can hardly think of tracking a continent that covers the Atlantic, or any of the other current oceans. Plato described Atlantis as rich in red, white, and black rocks, which perfectly corresponds to what the Egyptians wrote about the island of Shardanas "coming from Basilea, a high island with red, white and black rocks, and rich in copper."[62]

So, this is all? Sardinia, which in ancient times was called Tartessos and Espera, was also Atlantis? Plato speaks of abundant mineral resources, and undoubtedly Sardinia has been the capital of the "Mediterranean mining industry" from the third millennium BCE up to 1800, when the island became the stage for a silver rush comparable to the American gold rush. The philosopher also speaks of many high mountains, and although Sardinia is 80 percent mountainous or hilly, its peaks barely reach 1,500 meters. Something doesn't quite fit: Plato's understanding of history came from Critias; Critias, in turn, had heard it from his grandfather, also named Critias, son of Dròpide, friend of the legislator Solon, who learned history in Egypt from the priests of Sais. As for us, we have knowledge of the Egyptians' tradition through their own papyri found in their temples, and always Atlantis—better known as Ta-Neteru—was located southward, while they identified Sardinia to the north, in the middle of Ouadj-our (the Great Green, the Mediterranean). If we look at the name "Atlantis," we will note it is very similar to the Native American name "Atala," or the Aztec name "Aztlan," and it is hard to believe that Native Americans or Aztecs could be worried about a disaster that affected the Mediterranean.

In *Timaeus,* the sea surrounding this island compared to the sea beyond is considered "similar to a port," which does not match a description of Sardinia, and do not forget the strong analogy with Meru and other mythical islands, which would place Atlantis at polar latitudes.

My idea is that a real disaster—the second flood—did sink large coastal areas of Tyrrenhid, composed of Sardinia and Corsica, splitting it into two islands after the sea level rose back. Geology dates this disaster back to 9600 BCE, just like Plato does. This is such a perfect coincidence that one cannot question its authenticity, even if many would like to exchange those 9,000 years with 9,000 months. Sardinian folktales still remind of that disaster:

Suddenly, one night, the ground began to shake, shaken by terrible upheavals, and the sea was convulsed by a terrible fury. The waves were so high that they almost touched the sky and struck on Tyrrenhid ruinously, shaking the coast, flooding the fertile plains. Tyrrenhid was about to be swallowed up entirely when God ceased from his wrath. Because a small portion of dry land still emerged, he put a foot over it and managed to keep it down until the sea had swallowed it completely. It was thus that from the great Tyrrenhid detached that lone footprint in the middle of the large expanse of water, from which it took its name Ichnusa ("footprint," Sardinia's ancient name).*

It's possible that Plato or Solon took possession of the traditions relating to <u>two separate floods (13,000 and 9600 BCE)</u> and interpreted them as parts of a single story, then mixing Tyrrenhid with Atlantis and Antarctica with Sardinia. Plato reminds of a sudden change in the solar course, such as happened in 13,000 BCE. Rand and Rose Flem-Ath note that the high mountains mentioned in the story are located in Antarctica well above sea level and represent the world's highest continent. The average heights of the continents are listed in the following table:

Continent	Average Height
Antarctica	2,100 meters (6,500 ft.)
Asia	1050 meters (3,200 ft.)
South America	650 meters (2,000 ft.)
Africa	650 meters (2,000 ft.)
North America	600 meters (1,900 ft.)
Europe	300 meters (940 ft.)
Australia	260 meters (800 ft.)

So the priest told Solon: "To begin with, it is said that the entire region was well above sea level, from where its peak was visible . . . [and the moun-

---

*A narrative from one of the stories collected by the Pangea Association during numerous interviews with residents, especially the elderly, during our visit to Sardinia.

tains] were famous because higher, and more beautiful and numerous than those that exist today."[63]

THE WAR

Unlike the previous section, here we will observe the events prior to the sinking of Tyrrenhid. It had been about three thousand years since the Atlanteans/Pelasgians had abandoned the Antarctic, and most probably they did not know how to get back. Those who had been saved and reached the western Mediterranean found it easy to dominate the indigenous peoples who worshipped them as gods because of their knowledge.* Eventually, they re-baptized Tyrrenhid as the "Second Atlantis."

It is appropriate here to wonder how in that period Athens could stand up against the Pelasgians. Probably Athens did not exist yet at all, and perhaps that name was just given as a geographical indication, a sort of "more or less, where Athens is." The Greek men were hunter-gatherers, or cavemen, and therefore unprepared for war.

We spoke earlier of the exiled gods, Saturn and Janus. Some believe they were father and son, while others called them Baal and Osiris, kings of Atlantis; according to Evemerus da Messina they would have ousted the legitimate king Titan, brother of one or the other. It was 10,500 BCE and the Pelasgians dominated from Gibraltar to the Gulf of Messina, including Spain, France, Libya, and the Italian peninsula. Only Tyrrenhid was beyond their control, defended by women warriors known as Amazons or Gorgons. Diodorus Siculus describes those years, when Osiris (Menes) included Egypt in his kingdom, and drove the Amazons out of Tyrrenid,† while Titan (Danaus) fled away, but with a private army was able to colonize Pontus, Saudi, Syria, and finally Greece (plate 4).[64]

---

*Those primitive people looked with admiration at the newly arrived and remembered their deeds with devotion, until future poets made the most famous into gods. Herodotus expressly says that "Hesiod and Homer are those who brought to the Greeks the 'generation of gods,' gave them names, conferred honors and attributes and drew the figures," mixing Pelasgian doctrines with their stories.

† *Some Greek traditions to which archaic historians attributed a Pelasgian origin relate that Bacchus, an Oceanite or Atlantean or Pelasgian, conquered Lydia. Bacchus/Dionysus is the Greek-Latin name for Osiris: it is none other than Menes/Minos himself (see chapter 5).

Once his conquests were steady, the war broke out that ended with his victory and the exile of his relatives to Tartarus (or Tartessos), on the Ocean. This story is insistently repeated in Greek and Egyptian myth but with different actors: Aegeus equals Danaus, Seth, Titan, or Minosse,* and Janus equals Osiris or Menes.

Greek stories tell us about Danaus, also calling him Inachus, but now they are possibly even more confusing, mixing up the family trees as far as to make Inachus the grandfather of himself. It is said that the natives of Greece had accepted a stranger named Inachus who had arrived from the sea and founded the first colony near the present Argos, then moving from there to sow the seeds of civilization. In Aeschylus's *Prometheus Unbound* Io is Inachus's daughter, while elsewhere she is mother of Danaus and Minos, described as an Oceanite woman (a Pelasgian). Inachus is called both "Oceanite" by Sophocles in a fragment of the tragedy preserved by Dionysius of Halicarnassus, and "King of the Tyrrhenian Pelasgians." He was named "Son of the Ocean" by Hyginus, and "son of Ocean and Thetis" by Apollodorus (*Library*, book 2, chapter 1). Inachus is yet to be presented by Acusilao as Pelasgian, who also states that Pelasgus was the son of Inachus, first king of Argos (*Acusilaus Fragments*, Sturz, Lipsia, 1824; *Suidae Lexicon* tells how he had derived genealogies from some metal ancient inscriptions collected by his father).

According to Plato, the war was won by Greece, and Osiris/Menes paid with his life. That was not all, however, in fact there was still Horus, son of Osiris, brought up by his uncle like a Shakespearean Hamlet: Horus avenged his father, tore off Seth's testicles, and unified the country,

---

*Regarding law, as the Greeks remembered Spartan Lycurgus had founded the oldest and most famous code of laws based on those of Minosse (Minos). In this regard, Diodorus describes Menes/Minos as the greatest king among the Pelasgians and says that his wife Pasiphae was a Pelasgian of Sicily, daughter of Hyperon and sister of Circe—whom Hesiod says is Oceanite. It is interesting how, in another passage, the poet describes Hyperion in the guise of Menes himself, making him, like Danaus-Inachus, father-in-law of himself.

going down in history as the king of the Upper and Lower Kingdom, the epithet later given to the Egyptian pharaohs.

THE PLANETARIUM

The capital of Atlantis was derived from its own white, black, and red rocks, a masterpiece of engineering that also showed in the towers and gates that protected the access roads made of the same rock. It was structured in a sequence of walls of concentric rings, alternating land and sea. The outer wall was "sea-made" and appeared as a kind of internal harbor. A wide canal 90 meters wide and 890 meters (five stades) long connected it with the ocean (figure 1.7).

In *Timaeus* Plato refers to the belts' widths in stades (1 stade = 177.6 meters):

- Acropolis, radius = 2.5, from 0 to 2.5 stades from the center
- First belt of water, width = 1, from 2.5 to 3.5 s.f.c.
- First belt of land, width = 2, from 3.5 to 5.5 s.f.c.
- Second belt of water, width = 2, from 5.5 to 7.5 s.f.c.
- Second belt of land, width = 3, from 7.5 to 10.5 s.f.c.
- Third belt of water = 3, from 10.5 to 13.5 s.f.c.
- Total radius of the city = 13.5
- Outer wall = 18.5 s.f.c.

The story takes place in the form of a dialogue during which Critias reports the words that Solon had heard from the priests of Sais, in Egypt. Suppose they reported to Solon the total radius of the city and the radius of the acropolis, and the widths of the first four walls. Using this data, Solon or Timaeus could have reconstructed the width of the external wall, although they may have performed the computation without taking into account the width of a plectrum (= $^1/_6$ stade) that was occupied by each single wall. By adjusting the error, you get:

- Acropolis, radius = from 0 to 2.5 stades from the center
- First belt of water = from 2.67 to 3.67 s.f.c.

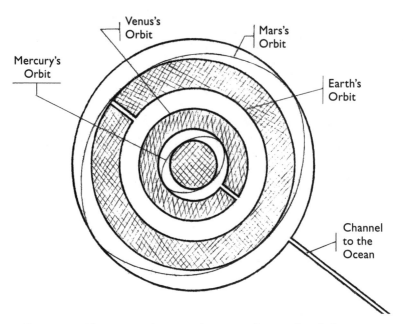

Figure 1.7. Planetary orbits in relation to the canal and the ocean.

- First belt of land = from 3.83 to 5.83 s.f.c.
- Second belt of water = from 6 to 8 s.f.c.
- Second belt of land = from 8.17 to 11.17 s.f.c.
- Third belt of water = from 11.33 to 13.33 s.f.c.
- Total radius of the city = 13.5
- Outer wall = 18.5 s.f.c.

Now compare these values with the distances from the sun of the planets closest to it: for the planets with eccentric orbits, we report the values of both the perihelion (the closest point) and the aphelion (the farthest point).

- Mercury, perihelion 0.3075 astronomical units
- Mercury, aphelion 0.4667 a.u.
- Venus 0.7233 a.u.
- Earth 1 a.u.
- Mars, perihelion 1.381 a.u.
- Mars, aphelion 1.666 a.u.

When placing the wall radii in the ordinate and the distances of the planets from the sun in the abscissa on a graph (figures 1.8 and 1.9), the result does not change significantly when taking the radii of the walls from the inside or the outside of the walls:

Quite a perfect correlation! Without considering the miscalculation.

In this last case we notice the slight displacement of Mercury's perihelion and Mars's aphelion. Consequently, the wall system of Atlantis could serve as a model for the solar system. The outer wall could correspond to the asteroid belt (the fifth planet, which exploded—it is said—300,000 years ago).

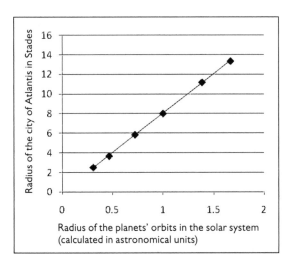

Figure 1.8. Graph of the wall radii compared with orbital radii of planets in the solar system.

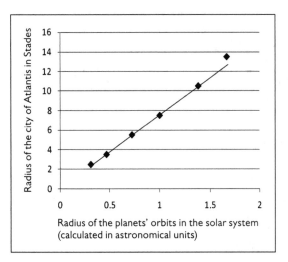

Figure 1.9. Graph of the wall radii without considering the miscalculation.

THE JEWISH GROVES

On the central island, around the temple, was the "Grove of Poseidon." It started a religious tradition that we will find millennia later among the Hebrews, heirs to the Pelasgian's monotheism. Actually, in old Judaism there were places of worship called "sacred woods," referred to in chapter 21 of Genesis: "And Abraham planted a grove in Beersheba, and called there on the name of the LORD, the everlasting God." The sacred groves were usually located upon hills known as "bamoth," which contained stone pillars used in the sacrificial practices called "massboth." The trees were decorated with strips of colored fabric, as one can read in the second book of Kings: "the women wove arrases for the wood." These practices were suppressed by the elite priesthood in the days of Josiah in the seventh century BCE, but the prohibition never arrived in Ethiopia, where the Qemant Hebrews still use them.

MAGNETIC FIELD

Some lava rocks contain ferromagnetic minerals that magnetize upon solidification under the influence of the Earth's electromagnetic field. The result is that the rocks are turned into real magnets oriented along the magnetic axis of our planet.

The polarity of some volcanic rocks formed in ancient times appears "reversed" with respect to the direction of the geomagnetic field, a sign that at the time of solidification they were in the opposite hemisphere and not, as many have argued, the consequence of a reversal in the Earth's magnetic field. The latter, though subject to variations in intensity, is generated by the rotation of the outer nucleus of liquid iron, and there is no "pump," natural or artificial, capable of reversing its motion.

Lava rocks also allow recording of the intensity of the field in different eras. In figure 1.10 are the approximate times of the most significant variations in intensity over the past 800,000 years, a period known as the "Brunhes Normal Polarity Chron," to indicate how the rocks formed therein show the correct polarity. On the abscissa we report the strength of the field (or rather of the virtual axial dipole moment or VADM) in units of 10^{22} amperes per square meter.

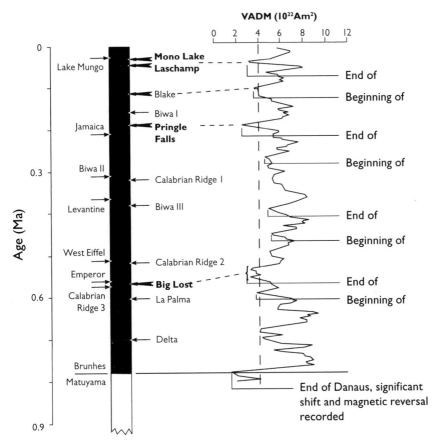

Figure 1.10. Intensity levels of Earth's magnetic field during the Brunhes Normal Polarity Chron.

The negative peaks in intensity correspond to little deviations between the direction of the geomagnetic field currently recorded and the one recorded by the rocks formed during the equivalent time. In particular, the vertical dotted line indicates the critical value below which, according to Yohan Guyodo and Jean-Pierre Valet (1999), the deviation is unquestionable. So, the negative peaks tell us that the lava rocks that formed in those periods were located some degrees more northward or southward than their current latitude, and allow us a recording of the corresponding sliding of the crust. This fact is of high relevance because the peaks are negative at the beginning (see figure 1.10) as well as at the end of a glacial period, confirming the hypothesis that these phenomena are indeed the cause of deviation. Thus, it goes without saying that the motion of the crust can also disturb the flow of materials within the Earth. The transition from a linear motion into a turbulent one, within the nucleus, leads to a decrease in the magnetic field on the surface, which explains the correspondence between negative peaks and directional deviations. Thus, a significant decrease in magnetic field is an indicator that the next sliding of the crust is near.

ANTIQUE MAPS

After the decline of the Roman Empire (476 CE) and Alexandria (642 CE) all knowledge, and especially all old maps, were kept in Antioch and Constantinople along with all the material saved from the burning of the libraries. In the ninth century, while western European countries were still immersed in the Dark Ages at the mercy of the Vikings' plundering, the Islamic world was prospering and favored the perpetuation of knowledge. Much of the success of this age can be attributed to the golden Muslim caliph Abu-l-Abbas Abd-Allah al-Ma'mun, who ruled over a territory expanding westerly from Baghdad, throughout North Africa, up to the Iberian Peninsula and easterly up to India. Al-Ma'mun maintained a correspondence with the Byzantine emperor and once asked permission to receive a selection of old scientific manuscripts preserved in Byzantium (Constantinople).

In 833, al-Ma'mun gave order to build a library that he would name "House of Wisdom." The headquarters was in Baghdad, which became for the Arabs what Alexandria used to be for the Greeks. Here they continued and deepened the ancient studies: Muslim scholars copied many works that had been handed down and introduced new mathematical concepts, giving birth to the science of alchemy, mother of modern chemistry.

Some centuries later, in 1559, an Arab map was found. The "Hadji Ahmed Map" (figure 1.11) outlines the North American profile, highlighting areas that the Europeans would be able to locate only two centuries later, including the unexplored northwest coast. The precise calculation of longitude shown by this map was only reached and recorded on a map after 1735, with the invention of the marine chronometer by John Harrison (1693–1776), and a remarkable correspondence appears between the continental profiles of both maps and the actual continental profiles as they were in 13,000 BCE (note the absence of the Persian Gulf, which was actually dry).

Until the middle of the twentieth century it was not possible to confirm the existence of the ancient subcontinent called Beringia, even though it appears very clearly in the map of Hadji Ahmed.

Arab maps have appeared in Europe since 1200. Pope Innocenzo III, elected in 1198, was obsessed with the idea of unifying the Catholic

Figure 1.11. The Hadji Ahmed map.

Church with the Greek-Orthodox and hoped to organize a Fourth Crusade in order to free Egypt and Palestine from Muslim rule and so regain the Holy Land. The expedition was led by Boniface, Marquis of Monferrato, and sponsored by the Doge of Venice, Enrico Dandolo, entrusted to provide the fleet, logistics services, and food supplies for the Crusaders in exchange for 85,000 silver marks. Having naively accepted a price that they would have never been able to pay, the Crusaders had to accept from time to time the Doge's deviations, first to capture Zara (in Dalmatia) again, torn by the Venetians from the king of Hungary. Then it was the turn of Byzantium, which was occupied in retaliation against an adventurer named Marzufflo, who was heading a conspiracy against Dandolo. When on April 13, 1204, the city surrendered, maps, manuscripts, marble statues, and four bronze Alexandrian horses were confiscated and taken to Venice.

When Marco Polo returned from the East, at the end of 1200, in addition to silks, spices, and precious stones, he brought a map that showed a large continental island located at the south of the world. The idea of the large island in the southern hemisphere had appeared in our culture for many centuries and then disappeared into thin air. Pythagoras had already mentioned it in the sixth century BCE, and priest Sonchi described it in detail to Solon.

The only Latin book of geographical subject, written by Pomponius Mela, a famous Roman geographer living in 43 BCE, stated that the globe was surrounded by a "hot" climatic belt separating the northern and southern regions. Later, the inability to cross the so-called torrid zone laid serious doubts. If you could not communicate the word of Christ to those poor people, how could they be saved? To solve this theological problem, devotees destroyed all maps including the lands in the southern hemisphere.

In the fifteenth century, at Sagres on the southern coast of Portugal, Prince Henry of Portugal established a study center where some scholars and he had gathered all the globes, world maps, and exploration diaries they could buy. In 1428, his older brother Pedro was received with great honor in Venice and, upon return, brought two precious gifts for Henry, a copy of *The Travels of Marco Polo* and a collection of world maps. Henry ordered the captain Gil Eannes to set sail southerly and once and for all refuted the notion of an inaccessible torrid zone. In 1432 Henry ordered Goncalo Velho to sail west to occupy the islands that the maps indicated in that direction. Velho returned without having sighted the Azores, declaring that there was no trace. Then the prince commanded the reluctant browser to sail that course again: "There, there is an island, go and find it!"[65] The tenacity was rewarded and, by discovering the Azores, Henry could open the ways to the west and the south.

In 1453 Constantinople fell to the Turks and the last scholars sought refuge in the west. Upon hearing that the prince of Portugal would receive them, they went to Sagres, literally flooding Henry with projects for potential discoveries. Thus, Portugal became the world center for the collection of ancient maps. Columbus's father-in-law was a close friend of Henry, and it was said that his mother-in-law had given him some valuable maps that her husband left her at his death.

Ferdinand Magellan was a Portuguese navigator, and once appointed page by the Portuguese queen in 1496 he found employment in the Portuguese Royal Navy, where he could access all offices. Here he could examine the collection of maps belonging to Henry. Before leaving for Spain, where he offered his services, he was given permission to enter the chart room, where he found a globe that precisely showed a strait (which would be later named after him) south of the yet unexplored South America. Arriving at the Spanish court, Magellan spoke of his plan to sail to the Indies by going west. Here is how a witness explains his advocacy to the Spanish monarchs: "Magellan had a colored globe which traced the whole globe, he pointed to the sea areas where he intended to go, deliberately omitting to mention the strait for fear that someone could precede him."[66]

A map of Atlantis was discovered by the German Jesuit Athanasius Kircher (1601–1680) who was a teacher of physics, mathematics, and Oriental languages at the prestigious Collegio Romano, and the first to conceive that diseases are caused by microbes. In 1665 he published the first volume of his encyclopedic work, *Mundus Subterraneus*, which republished the map of Atlantis that, according to him, was taken from Egypt to Rome (figure 1.12 on p. 56).

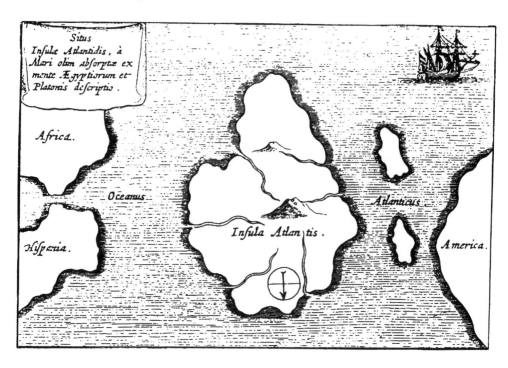

Figure 1.12. The position of the island of Atlantis.
From Rand and Rose Flem-Ath, Atlantis Beaneath the Ice.

The Latin inscription says: "Site of Atlantis, now beneath the sea, according to the belief of the Egyptians and the description of Plato." The Flem-Aths were the first to recognize that Kircher's map of Atlantis was a remarkably accurate map of an ice-free Antarctica. They explain in *Atlantis Beneath the Ice* that

at first glance, the map seems odd to modern eyes because north, as indicated by the downward-pointing compass, is at the bottom of the page. But the ancient Egyptians believed that the most important direction was south, toward the headwaters of the sacred Nile. Therefore south must be "up." Kircher reproduced this belief. The map appears much more familiar to us if we look at it upside down. What looks like America then appears on the left, with Spain and North Africa on the right—where we are accustomed to seeing them in twentieth-century maps. However, if we lift a modern globe off

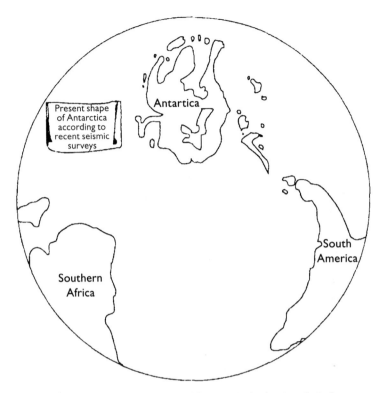

Figure 1.13. Rotated modern world map with the South Pole on top. From Rand and Rose Flem-Ath, Atlantis Beaneath the Ice.

its hinges and roll it about like a beach ball so that the South Pole faces us, placing South America on our right and South Africa and Madagascar on our left, we can immediately see that the Egyptian map of Atlantis represents an ice-free Antarctica in size, shape, scale, and position.[67]

2

GLACIAL MELTS AND GLOBAL FLOODS

Hermocrates: *The glorious Atlantis founded two colonies, a*
Minor one 360 miles northwest of the City and a Major
450 miles southeast.
The Gates of the Kingdom opened only with special stones.
The Sunstone was in many outposts if the morning light
burned the high horns.
The Major Colony also needed the Moonstone, with the
setting sun when the new moon was rising.
To access the true Atlantis, also the Worldstone was necessary,
with the crescent moon, the only answer of the sky to the
fires beneath.
Access will be given only to opposing minds.

The air was full of dust and the sky, covered with ash, appeared red, streaked with black, showing a bloody sun. Birds turned in circles, disoriented, alighting on the ground only when fatigue overcame terror. The land was covered by lava that flowed on the carcasses and twisted bodies of humans and animals. The plains, flattened by the waves that uprooted trees and piled stones, were lavish banquets for the vultures. Ice fell down where magma did not flow, and it shattered, feeding the flood. There was neither prey nor hunter anymore—it was the end of the world, the ice age was beginning.

In Europe and northeastern America the so-called ice age started 125,000 years ago when ice sheets began advancing. They reached their peak 21,000 years ago and then slowly withdrew, returning water to the oceans. Up until 17,000 years ago the change in shorelines can be considered irrelevant: the era of the "real" fast melting began soon after, concluding 9,000 years ago. Another 2,000 years passed before completion of the slow melting of the residual mass of ice and the final sea level rise.

Seventeen thousand years ago sea level oscillated between 115 and 120 meters lower than the current level, and of course the antediluvian world looked very different from today:

- Alaska and Siberia were connected by a land bridge crossing the Bering Strait.
- In the Mediterranean, many more islands were present, and Corsica and Sardinia were greatly expanded, forming, with Malta and Sicily, one single island.
- In India, the Gulf of Kutch and the Gulf of Cambay were above sea level, Sri Lanka was a peninsula, and the coastal plains were larger everywhere, up to one hundred kilometers on the west side and on the tip south of the Tamil Nadu.
- Between Malaysia, Indonesia, and the Philippines, up to northern Japan, stretched a vast plain called the Land of Sonda.
- In the Pacific, thousands of small islands were incorporated into larger single islands; Japan itself formed an uninterrupted large island.
- The large bank of the Bahamas, which currently is a shallow bed in the western Atlantic, formed a vast plateau 120 meters above sea level, along with the plateaus of the Yucatan, Florida, and Nicaragua.

These lands reached their present form only 7,000 years ago. Before then, the areas that are now densely populated—like most of North America and northern Europe—were uninhabitable, covered with kilometers of ice. By contrast, many areas now uninhabitable, situated in a hostile desert or submerged by the sea, were once places that could support a high-density population, such as the Sahara, which flourished for 4,000 years near the end of the ice age. Geologists estimate that an area of twenty-five million square kilometers, about 15 percent* of the Earth's surface, was submerged by the rising level of the sea,[1] equaling a surface area three times the size of Canada, or the sum of the United States plus South America.

These missing lands are important because they represented the coastal regions of the warmer latitudes, at that time the best ones available to humanity since most of northern Europe and North America were inaccessible.

In textbooks, at universities, and through media, archaeologists make historical reconstructions that do not take into account the twenty-five million square kilometers lost at the end of the ice age. Only in recent years have underwater archaeologists begun a systematic investigation of potential sites submerged in these areas.

AUSTRALIA

Seventeen thousand years ago New Guinea was fully integrated into the Australian continent through the Torres Strait and the Arafura Sea, and Tasmania was connected to Australia southward by the Bass Strait, which was then above sea level. Jim Allen[2] and Peter Kersha[3] estimated that "Great Australia" would have extended almost exactly from the equator to about 44 degrees south and from the 112th to 154th east meridian.[4] With the melting of the ice, Australia lost three million square kilometers, a much wider area than Mexico.[5] The width of the coastal plains was

---

*The value of 15 percent is calculated on *all* emerged land. The value of 60 percent reported in the introduction is calculated only on the lands that were habitable at the time, taking into account the lands canceled by the rising sea as well as those made uninhabitable by the climate change.

reduced by some hundreds of miles, and melting ice flooded many sites of the last Pleistocene.[6]

The human history of Australia is covered in mystery due to the antiquity of its early settlers, dating back to 50,000 years ago. Some aspects of Aboriginal culture are ambiguous, although there is no archaeological evidence that agricultural, crafts, or urban societies have ever existed on this continent before the modern era. We find, however, sophisticated astronomical ideas from a very early period, and the use of a particular astronomical terminology similar to the one used by other, faraway regions of the world.

Boris Frolov, Russian expert in prehistoric times, finds a similarity between the indigenous tribal peoples of North America, Siberia, and Australia: all refer to the constellation of the Pleiades as the "Seven Sisters." According to the scholar, this would relate back to a remote antiquity that would give a common heritage to all the peoples involved. And according to the anthropologist Richard Rudgley, a tradition that could be handed down by the sky had existed for more than 40,000 years.[7]

So far, archaeologists of the Australian sites on land have no evidence confirming the existence of infrastructures associated with the spread of a global astronomical tradition. On the other hand, we must consider that with over three million square kilometers of Australia submerged between 17,000 and 7,000 years ago and still unexplored, no one is sure what is likely to be found.

ISOSTATIC MOVEMENTS

The 120-meter increase in sea level dramatically changed the distribution of habitats suitable for human settlement and deserves more interest among archaeologists. Underwater archaeology has been practiced very little along the continental shelves, instead focusing on the discovery of shipwrecks or sites submerged in recent historical periods. The only exception was the study done by Robert Ballard on the Black Sea on behalf of the National Geographic Society, which has been investigating a massive incursion of the Mediterranean that happened 7,500 years ago through the Bosporus Strait.

Archaeologists assume that 17,000 years ago the population on Earth was uniform, at the same level of social and economic development, that of hunter-gatherers, and the first cities were built only 7,000 years later. On the other hand, should the cultural development of that period not have been uniform, and one or more cultures been concentrated along the coast, then postglacial flooding would have had a decisive role in the history of civilization. Moreover, the rise in sea level would have been able to flood entire cities and destroy all evidence of their existence.

This increase did not provoked uniform changes to the coastlines: in some areas, the flooding of certain places was more disastrous than expected, but in others the coastlines have remained the same for several millennia. These differences lead back to local phenomena of subsidence or uplifting, followed by earthquakes or volcanic activity.

The Earth's surface can bend and distort when subjected to pressures of some significance. For a better understanding, let's take a rubber ball as an example: exerting pressure on a point results in an indentation in that area. "Isostasy" is the technical name used by geologists to define this phenomenon, and it has had an important role during ice ages and for thousands of years after the melting of the ice. The weight of the ice caps is capable of crushing the crust of the Earth in a great depression—when ice melts, the pressure is suddenly removed and the bottoms of the basins rebound. 17,000 years ago the ice sheet of North America and northern Europe was about two to four kilometers thick and applied a load of thousands of billions of tons over the continental masses.[8] Geologists say that, on average, a load of one hundred meters of ice makes the continental crust twenty-seven meters lower.[9] Such a pressure is exerted by the ocean, with greater specific gravity, so that thirty meters of water make the crust get thirty meters lower.[10]

The ice on the land surface formed from seawater taken from the oceans, so while the crust was crushed beneath the continents, it rose (rebounded) beneath the oceans.

According to Professor R. C. L. Wilson of the Open University in Great Britain, the formation of ice sheets during the ice age took a layer of 165 meters of water away from the oceans. At the same time the sea level dropped to "only" 115 meters. This discrepancy is easily explained: the reduced load of water on the oceans allowed the seabed to rise more than fifty meters.[11]

Briefly:

1. 125,000 years ago the most recent glacial wave took place: North America, Greenland, northern Europe, South America, and the Himalayas were buried under ice caps thousands of meters high.

2. The maximum extent of ice formation was reached 21,000 years ago and was maintained up to 17,000 years ago, so the continental crust sank in huge basins almost a kilometer deep.

3. With the levels of seawater lowered, the ocean floor rose fifty meters.

4. After the last glacial peak the ice began to melt and moved back as liquid into the oceans, completing the process in 10,000 years.

5. 165 meters of water were diverted from the oceans and became ice; of course, when the ice broke up, 165 meters of water returned to the oceans. The speed at which the crust and mantle respond to loading and unloading is "much slower than the formation and melting of ice caps. This is why areas that were buried under several kilometers of ice 18,000 years ago are still raising."[12]

6. As a result, the fifty-meter bounce of the ocean floor would require thousands of years to be brought back to zero by the pressure of the "new" water from melting ice.

7. The sea level today is very close to a final equilibrium in the equation that references the seas rising on one side and on the other side the sinking of their seabeds.

Currently, segments of continental crust are still rising due to the isostatic rebound: the Scottish Highlands, the Gulf of Bothnia seabed in the present Baltic Sea, Denmark, Norway, parts of southern Chile, the northeast coast of Canada, and portions of coasts and continent in Sweden.

Returning to our example of the rubber ball, the indentation in the point of pressure also causes a corresponding elevation of the surrounding area, or outer swelling, called "forebulge," which is always larger than the area affected by rebound.[13]

Once the pressure ceases, this area lowers, giving birth to not-so-unusual phenomena like the raised beaches of the Scottish Highlands (areas that once formed an ancient coastline, but later on hoisted well above it), or areas of the British Isles that are on the verge of being submerged by water. The layer of ice on the continental crust of northern Europe on its last glacial peak raised an enormous area of forebulge hundreds of kilometers beyond the ice margin. Now this area is collapsing, and as a consequence the English Channel is sinking, whereas during the last glacial peak it was completely dry.

Similarly, the "Little Sole Bank," a vast underwater plateau known as the "Celtic platform" or "Hy Brazil," 200 kilometers southwest of Ireland, suddenly tilted upward at the approach of the last glacial peak, then collapsed around 11,600 years ago, the same date suggested by Plato for the submersion of Atlantis.

THE THREE FLOODS

Romuald Schild from the Polish Academy of Sciences talks about the onset of sudden warming in the North Atlantic that occurred about 12,700 years ago, which ended abruptly, leading to a cooling 10,800 years ago, followed later by another warming up about 10,000 years ago. According to Robert Scoch, professor of geology at Boston University, the first main phase of warming took place 11,600 years ago,[14] and there was a clear synchronism between the sudden heating in 9600 BCE and the date of the sinking of Atlantis according to Plato. The science publisher Paul LaViolette says:

> There may be much truth to the many flood cataclysm stories that have been handed down to modern times in virtually every culture around the world. In particular, the 9600-B.C.E. date that Plato's *Timaeus* gives for the time of the Deluge happens to fall at the beginning of the Preboreal at the time of the upsurge in the rate of meltwater discharge.[15]

Scientists agree on the amount of approximately 120 meters of sea-level rise during the 10,000 years of postglacial melting. However, many do not accept that these phenomena were indeed "floods" in the true sense of the word. The majority of scholars, after calculating an average time of seas rising, said that it was a gradual and not catastrophic process, in the order of one meter per century.

This theory is unacceptable for Cesare Emiliani, professor of geology at the University of Miami and pioneer of isotopic analysis of deep-sea sediments used for the study of land climates of the past. In the 1970s Emiliani's findings cast doubt on the theory adopted by the majority: indeed, the increased research showed how the melting ice caps could result in a real disaster. In short, the work of Emiliani has unearthed evidence of three catastrophic global floods happening within the time bands from 15,000 to 14,000 years ago, from 12,000 to 11,000 years ago, and from 9,000 to 8,000 years ago.[16] Nearly half the meltwater was released during these three quick and violent episodes.

ICE DAMS

Emiliani was one of the first to calculate the precise mechanism responsible for the global flood: meltwater would form a reservoir behind a dam of ice, and when the dam collapsed, the result was a huge wave of water. The weight of the ice on the Earth's surface created cup-shaped depressions one mile deep. The heat inside the Earth was trapped under ice sheets that melted on the bottom, forming large freshwater lakes. Breaking their margins of ice, these lakes generated enormous floods, sharply raising the sea level around 15,000 years ago, 11,600 years ago, and again 8,700 years ago.

Such a flood leaves its mark: in the northwest of America, Lake Missoula burst into "a 600 meters high wall of water over the Columbia Plateau in eastern Washington State."[17] Two thousand kilometers of water and muddy debris ended up in the Columbia River and dug the Channeled Scablands; other floods beat down on the Mississippi Valley, which served as a drain for the Gulf of Mexico; the same happened along the valleys of the Siberian rivers up to the Arctic Ocean.[18] Furthermore, with the melting of the ice cap in Canada, Lake Agassiz merged with Lake Ojibway, creating an inland sea of gigantic proportions with an area of 700,000 square kilometers, suspended behind a dam of ice on Hudson Bay at an altitude of 450 to 600 meters above sea level.[19] When the dam broke, a mass of water equal to between 75,000 and 150,000 cubic kilometers poured into the North Atlantic almost all at once. This single episode could have raised the global sea level about half a meter. The water came out from all sides, with the exception of the east side of the Hudson Strait, where a huge amount of ice impeded the outflow; instead, it flowed southward and crossed the St. Lawrence River, through the Finger Lakes, along the Red River, the South Winnipeg and Winnipeg lakes, and then out through the Saskatchewan River and the Milk River (the Continental Divide south of Alberta). The Milk River overflowed northerly up to the Arctic, easterly to Hudson Bay, and southerly to the Gulf of Mexico. Almost simultaneously, with the collapse of the ice sheet on Laurentia,* the northeastern side of Great Britain was affected by a devastating flood, with a twenty-meter rise in sea level. Recent evidence suggests that there were also large basins of ice in northern Asia and northern Russia.[20]

Huge amounts of glacial melt water held for thousands of years behind ice dams in continental Europe and Continental North America were then released into the ocean all at once.[21] According to the studies of Charles Fletcher and Sherman Clark, of the department of geology and geophysics at the University of Hawaii, each event added at least four thousand cubic kilometers of water to the oceans. These prehistoric floods have apparently generated the legends about "The Flood" shared by many civilizations.[22]

John Shaw, professor in earth sciences at the University of Alberta, is one of the world's leading experts on the last ice age and the catastrophic melting of its ice. Shaw describes this period:

---

*Laurentia, a large continental craton made up of present-day North America and Greenland, forms the ancient geological core of the North American continent. In its past it has been a separate continent (as it currently is in the form of North America), although originally it also included areas of Greenland and northwestern Scotland.

It seems that the great ice sheets that covered Canada, most of Scandinavia and much of northern Russia, instead of being formed by ice and rock, turned out to be formed, at a late stage, by a first basis of rock, then by a lake or reservoir of sub-glacial water, and finally by ice. It is possible that with the heating up, the highest part of the ice began to melt and the ablation zone and the amount of sub-glacial water started to increase, even though logically the ice should have sealed around the margins.[23]

The kind of flooding we are talking about would have had the capacity to move at ten million cubic meters per second, so about 15,000 years ago the sea level would have been raised by at least ten meters. It is no wonder, then, that this would have had an important influence on oral traditions and myths.

For each of the three major floods the existence of validating evidence suggests a change in global sea level in the order of five to ten meters. According to experts, however, several temporary increases in sea level during that time would have passed the said order beyond measure. An important role was played by the high walls of hundreds of meters of water coming out of ice domes* when the dams broke and the glacial lakes emptied from below. Stephen Oppenheimer claims that earthquakes, caused by isostatic rebalancing toward the end of the ice age, could have caused "great waves as tall as a mountain" in the northern regions of the Atlantic and the Pacific.[24]

VOLCANISM AND EARTHQUAKES

The end of the ice age must have appeared to the survivors as a real apocalypse, worth St. John's visions: the continental plates moved up because they were no longer held down by the weight of the ice, while destructive earthquakes and intense volcanic activity accompanied this rebalancing of the crust on a large scale. To make things worse, there was the murky

---

*An ice dome is a major component of an ice sheet or ice cap. It has a convex surface and symmetrically formed parabolic shape, and it can be as thick as 3,000 meters or more.

atmosphere of the sky, burdened by the presence of volcanic dust and black bituminous rain.

One of the geoclimatologic mysteries of the melting period, from 17,000 to 7,000 years ago, relates to the simultaneous increase in volcanic activity. An article published in *Nature* in 1997 puts great emphasis on what seems at first a strange correlation between the rate of change in global sea level and the frequency of explosive volcanic episodes in the Mediterranean area.[25]

> In areas where active volcanism and glaciation coincide, the correlation between the events can be explained by the effect of changing ice volumes on crustal stresses. In contrast, the effect of ice-sheet volume changes on unglaciated volcanic areas remains problematical.[26]

Researchers for *Nature* analyzed the layers of tephra (the solid matter ejected during volcanic eruptions) taken during deep core studies carried out in the bottom of the Mediterranean:

> The frequency of tephra-producing events and, by proxy, notable explosive eruptions at Mediterranean volcanoes, can be related to rapid variations in sea-level change. In particular, we draw attention to the quiescent phase centered at 22,000 years ago and corresponding to the last low sea-level stand, and to the most intense period of tephra layer formation between 15,000 and 8,000 years ago, which accompanied the very rapid rise in post-glacial sea levels.

Fifteen thousand years ago a phase of volcanic inactivity that lasted 7,000 years came to an end, whereas a period of very violent eruptions began in coincidence with the first global overflood; similarly, the intense volcanic activity ended around 9,000 years ago simultaneously with the third and last overflood. The authors of the article argue that changes in ice pressure over the continental margins and insular arcs may have had a large-scale influence able to facilitate the ascent of magma in volcanoes. Moreover, the increase of regional seismicity related to the redistribution of the weight of the ice would have encouraged the destabilization of already weak volcanoes.

The current spatial distribution of active volcanoes shows 57 percent on islands or coastal towns, while 38 percent are located within a radius of only 280 kilometers from the coastline. Of the fifteen hundred volcanoes that were active during the last ice age, fourteen hundred have probably suffered the most direct consequences of a rapid change in the sea level.[27] As Graham Hancock observed in his book, *Underworld*:

> The studies described in *Nature* suggest that the process of isostatic rebalancing of the Earth, caused by the sudden melting of ice sheets and the rapid rise in sea level at the end of the last Ice Age, must have been what ignited the volcanoes. The implication is that the isostatic adjustment does not always proceed at a regular speed, but must sometimes cause violent movements that convey a sort of shock wave through the Earth's crust, powerful enough to reawaken the volcanoes around the globe.

Such rapid and intense changes made the ground "collapse." At the time of the third great flood (about 9,000 years ago), the stress and earthquakes became so strong that the ground formed huge waves, one of which, in northern Sweden, was 150 kilometers long and 10 meters high. It has been described as a "tsunami rock"[28] caused by "earthquakes with unimaginable magnitude."[29]

The Parvie ("wave in the ground") fault, with its winding course in the barren Swedish landscape, looks like a tsunami made of solid rock three floors high. This part of northern Sweden is an area of low seismicity and is located on top of what seismologists call a "stable continental region" of the tectonic plate,[30] yet the evidence of a catastrophic earthquake that lifted the Parvie is unmistakable:

> Researches of the last two decades show that it was generated all of a sudden by an earthquake that created the fault line in the last Ice Age or in the early post-glacial epoch of the Finno-Scandinavian

great ice sheet (roughly 8,000 to 8,500 years ago), and suggest a generic relationship between the two phenomena.[31]

"Postglacial faults" like Parvie have been studied by Ronald Arvidsson of the department of seismology, University of Uppsala, who demonstrated how they frequently cut through the Earth's crust up to forty kilometers in depth. These faults were caused by huge earthquakes that occurred within a period of one thousand years, between 9,000 and 8,000 years ago. According to Arvidsson's estimates, the earthquake that originated Parvie measured 8.2 degrees on the Richter scale.[32]

Another scholar, Arch C. Johnston of the Center for Earthquake Research at the University of Memphis, notes that such strong earthquakes usually occur *only* along the margins of the tectonic plates. Therefore, the strength of the wave that blew the ground of Parvie must have been enormous.

Finno-Scandinavian postglacial faults are a consequence of the extraordinary rapid relief due to crustal melting of ice sheets in the last Ice Age. Parvie along with other postglacial faults represent fractures of induced earthquakes, events that would happen without some conditions created by human manipulation of the external environment.[33]

Postglacial earthquakes are the most popular examples of induced seismicity: extraction of stones from a quarry may cause earthquakes from two to four degrees on the Richter scale, deep drilling and waste disposal in wells can cause events of five to six degrees, and the creation of large reservoirs induces tremors of six and half degrees. Except for the postglacial faults, induced earthquakes greater than seven degrees are impossible. The magnitude of the earthquake varies with the intensification of the crustal stress: the melting of large ice sheets may induce wide earthquakes.[34]

The Richter scale is calibrated so that the increase of one unit represents a tenfold increase in the magnitude of the earthquake: two is ten times more severe than one and so on. The earthquake that hit Kobe in

Japan in 1995, killing more than five thousand people in twenty seconds, measured 7.2 degrees on the Richter scale.[35] A magnitude of 8.2 means the earthquake that generated Parvie was ten times more violent than the one in Kobe.

According to Arvidsson and Johnston, the rebound of the crust and the rebalancing of the crustal forebulge* occurred very quickly when the ice caps melted, causing disastrous earthquakes and huge fractures. Arvidsson argues:

> More than 9,000 years ago the Earth had almost reached isostatic equilibrium because of the depression of the lithosphere due to the ice. After a quick disappearance of the ice sheet, a non-isostatic condition caused compressive stress within the crust that generated earthquakes.[36]

According to what we have read the history that archaeologists have reconstructed today is based on analysis carried out in areas that are too narrow. Ignoring the submerged areas, perhaps the most populated during the ice age, would be like talking about our present world by observing only the Amazon or Australian rain forests—in which case we would find that people in the twenty-first century are primitive, nomadic, and illiterate! And, of course, what archaeologists believe they have discovered about inhabitants of 17,000 BCE is that they were primitive hunter-gatherers.

From now until the end of the chapter we will provide a curious series of overwhelming evidence on the existence of three famous overfloods based on data obtained from the analysis of deposits where ice moved into the sea or was shaped inside valleys.

The subject can indeed be a little boring, due to its nature. So, if you are not interested in such information, you can go directly to the next chapter and see what was going on in South America.

---

*A forebulge is a flexural bulge on the Earth's rigid, outermost shell, comprised of the crust and part of the upper mantle.

DRUMLIN

John Shaw's interest in overfloods began with drumlins*—long or oval hills formed by non-stratified soil and rock fragments deposited under a glacier in motion—which he worked with daily at the University of Alberta.

Most geologists believe that the formation of drumlins is the result of a rather slow subglacial process that initially saw the filling up of a great mass of "till" on the rocky substratum beneath the glacier, followed by later shaping into a "tapered hill" due to the sliding of the ice.[37] Shaw gradually verified a convergence of evidence that led to a different explanation in which drumlin formations would be generated in different ways, by different types of floods, *and not* by the shaping of the ice. He argues that the drumlins of Livingstone Lake in northern Saskatchewan were generated by running water pushing a flood of great volumes of sediment that filled cavities eroded from under the base of the ice. The sediments could range from fine-grained clays up to huge stones or rocks.[38] Indeed, the sediments of some drumlins supplied a filling from below as a result of flooding.

According to Shaw, at some point during the period of melting, parts of the mass of ice that moved slowly must have come to a stop *not* on the rocky bottom substrate, but on a deep layer of meltwater moving at high speed and under enormous pressure. The sediment deposit pushed from below would have taken the characteristic shape of a tapered and elliptical hill that was then sealed inside the ice, which would have carried it forward until the final melting brought it to light.[39]

---

*A drumlin is described in *Micropaedia* (volume 4) of the *Encyclopaedia Britannica* as "an elliptical hill formed by till (non-stratified glacial deposit consisting of moraine deposits and rock fragments of various kinds) deposited under the ice of a glacier in motion." Drumlins are grouped with the long axis more or less parallel to the direction of the ice movement. They have steep slopes in the direction of the glacier's origin and softer slopes in the direction toward which the glacier shifts. They range in height from six to sixty meters and can reach up to several kilometers in length. Drumlin fields may contain up to ten thousand drumlins; one of the largest drumlin fields is situated in the northwestern plains of Canada.

Shaw thinks other fields of drumlins in Canada have been created by meltwater (rather than ice) that acted as an agent of erosion on the underlying rock and deposit formations: "The drumlins around Peterborough and Trenton, Ontario are mostly erosive and their internal stratigraphy is relatively non-deformed. Irish drumlins contain complex glacigenic sequences. The shape of these drumlins in Ireland is almost entirely due to erosion."[40]

Among the drumlins of this type Shaw focuses on the groups of Beverly Lake (northwestern Canada) and Georgian Bay (Ontario). According to him, they would have been sculpted by exceptional floods whose stream must have submerged them, thereby reaching a minimum depth of twenty meters. The signs of erosion in the underlying rock substrate show extended subglacial meltwater streams 160 kilometers wide.[41] Only floods of such scale could have carved drumlin fields: "The volumes of water needed to replenish such floods would be about a million cubic kilometers, meaning a several meters rise of sea level for a period of weeks."[42]

ICEBERG

Meltwater filtrating under glaciers causes their separation from the soil and their consequent shift; "layers of melt water, several tens of meters thick, formed over large areas of the Laurentian ice sheet. The posting of glaciers from their bed, as a result of the increased water pressure, is a cause that is increasingly used to explain their shift speed."[43]

There is evidence of some massive "surge" (a short period of rapid shifts) at the end of the last ice age contemporary to waves of meltwater and peaks in sea level rise. These are reported in the underwater barriers of *Acropora palmata* in the Caribbean-Atlantic region, near Barbados Island. *Acropora* is a light-loving coral that dies at depths of more than ten meters and a hard-hitting indicator of the increase in sea level. Barbados's barriers were flooded three times at the end of the last ice ages (15,000, 11,600, and 8,700 years ago): in each of these episodes there formed a distinct terrace so that at the end of the three floods there were three terraces. Paul Blanchon and John Shaw, in a

1995 article in *Geology*, argue that research data confirms the cliff:

> [There were] three catastrophic sea level rises, on a meters scale, during the deglaciation. By delivering the events that occurred at sea and in the layer of ice dated by radiocarbon to a sidereal chronology, we can demonstrate that the timing of these three catastrophic risings coincides with the collapse of the ice sheet, the reorganization of the oceanic atmosphere and the conspicuous release of melt water.[44]

Geologists Dean Lindstrom and Douglas Macayeal, in an article in *Nature*, have argued that meltwater would raise the ice from the ground and release it into the sea, thus increasing the stream of water, which would have removed further ice in a sort of snowball effect:

> Sudden and significant changes in sea level due to floating ice sheets, once resting on the ground, and the consequent fall of ice domes, may have accompanied the flood waves of melt water and these "gaps" in sea level may have not been taken into account while drawing the data on the barrier's growth. Therefore, there is a logical mechanism for which the sea level has risen more quickly and perhaps to higher levels than those described in the history of the Barbados barrier's growth.[45]

According to Shaw and Blanchon a hike in global sea level of between eight and sixteen inches, in a period of several weeks, would be "sufficient to clean the stranded ice and encourage further destruction of the ice sheet and, in addition, to raise the sea level from five to ten meters or more."[46]

This sudden rise in sea level caused the separation of fleets of giant icebergs. In 1988 the German oceanographer Hartmut Heinrich was the first to detect geological evidence of this process of iceberg detachment during the last ice age. By analyzing samples taken in deep sea in different parts of the North Atlantic he was able to demonstrate the existence of layers of scattered "debris of glacial transport." Millions of tons of rock and debris once on the mainland had been eroded and transported to the sea as giant icebergs:

When they melted, they released rock debris that ended up in the fine-grained sediments of the ocean floor. Most of the debris transported by ice consists of limestone, similar to that which today appears on the surface over large areas of eastern Canada. Heinrich layers, such they have been named, extend over 3000 km across the North Atlantic almost up to Ireland.[47]

These layers show at least six episodes in which fleets of icebergs have detached and finished in the North Atlantic; we call them "Heinrich events" and they are thought to have occurred in less than a century.[48]

By studying the location of the Heinrich layers geologists have concluded that much of this floating ice originated from the Laurentian ice sheet.[49] Also, other debris has been found—mixed with some Heinrich layers—coming from different ice sheets that covered not only Canada but also Greenland, Iceland, the British Isles, and Scandinavia.[50] The meltwater would mix with the water of the oceans, multiplying the effects and causing the glacier basins to detach from the continents and float in the sea. Stephen Oppenheimer calculated that the ice that broke in through the Strait of Hudson had a thickness of 1.6 kilometers and a surface area equal to one-third that of Canada.[51]

Research on ice sheets in the Southern Hemisphere, the Andes, and New Zealand has shown that they also collapsed simultaneously with the recurrent waves of glacial transport in the North Atlantic.[52]

Researcher Paul LaViolette argues that in the melting period any civilization that settled on the edge of partially closed seas—areas serving as drainage for large ice sheets—would undergo rapid and massive changes in sea level. LaViolette focuses on the Mediterranean:

> The glacial meltwater would have entered the Mediterranean much more rapidly than it could escape through the Straits of Gibraltar, and, as a result, the temporary rise in Mediterranean sea level would have been much greater than in the surrounding oceans. According to one estimate, this meltwater surge could have temporarily raised the Mediterranean by some 60 meters, flooding all coastal civilizations.[53]

Avalanches of rocks and ice must have been knocked down several times over the oceans during the melting as a consequence of the isostatic effect on continental margins and of the collapse caused by the detachment of the huge ice sheets. Floods generated by the leakage of glacial lakes may have had more destructive effects than we can imagine.

During periods of intense climatic warming, the Earth's ice sheets were melting extremely rapidly, with most of this melting taking place on their upper surfaces. Consequently, large quantities of meltwater would have collected on the ice sheet surface to form numerous supraglacial lakes perched at elevations of up to 30 kilometers. In cases where the impounded waters were restrained by ice jams and where mounting pressures caused these jams to give way, large floods of glacial meltwater would have poured out over the ice sheet surface. As one such glacier burst swept forward, gradually descending the ice sheet's surface, it would have incorporated any impounded meltwater that lay in its path, triggering these supraglacial lakes to discharge their contents and add to its size. Through this snowballing effect, a single initial glacier burst would have progressively grown in size and kinetic energy during the course of its downhill journey, eventually becoming of mountainous proportions. . . . [W]aves of greater height travel faster. Accordingly, as a glacier wave proceeded across an ice sheet to lower altitudes, gaining in height and kinetic energy, it would have accelerated to higher speeds. By the time it had journeyed thousands of kilometers to the edge of the ice sheet, it could have attained heights of 600 meters or more, a cross-sectional breadth of as much as 40 kilometers, and a forward speed of several hundred kilometers per hour. . . . Upon entering the ocean, the wave would have continued forward as a tsunami to cause considerable damage on the shores of distant continents. Because of its immense energy, a glacier-wave tsunami would be far more destructive than any tidal wave observed in modern times.[54]

What is the point in studying the origin of civilization if we ignore all this? Can we ignore the constant references to the people that personally experienced the end of the ice age—the people of Antarctica, the Pelasgians?

> **Athenian:** *Do you consider that there is any truth in the ancient tales?*
>
> **Cleinias:** *What tales?*
>
> **Athenian:** *That the world of men has often been destroyed by floods, plagues, and many other things, in such a way that only a small portion of the human race survived.*
>
> **Cleinias:** *Everyone would regard such accounts as perfectly credible.*
>
> **Athenian:** *Let us consider one of them, that which was caused by the famous deluge.*
>
> **Cleinias:** *And what are we to imagine about it?*
>
> **Athenian:** *That the men who then escaped destruction must have been mostly herdsmen of the hills, scanty embers of the human race preserved somewhere on the mountain-tops.*
>
> **Cleinias:** *Evidently . . .*
>
> **Athenian:** *Such survivors would necessarily be unacquainted with the arts and the various devices which are suggested to the dwellers in cities by interest or ambition, and with all the wrongs which they contrive against one another.*
>
> **Cleinias:** *Very true.*
>
> **Athenian:** *Shall we assume that the cities situated in the plains and near the sea were totally destroyed at the time?*
>
> **Cleinias:** *Let us assume it.*
>
> **Athenian:** *Would not all implements have then perished and every other excellent invention of political or any other sort of wisdom have utterly disappeared?*
>
> **Cleinias:** *Why, yes, my friend; and if things had always continued as they are at present ordered, how could any discovery have ever been made even in the least particular? For it is evident that the arts were unknown during ten thousand times ten thousand years. And no more than*

a thousand or two thousand years have elapsed since the discoveries of Daedalus, Orpheus and Palamedes—since Marsyas and Olympus invented music, and Amphion the lyre—not to speak of numberless other inventions which are but of yesterday.

PLATO, *LAWS,* BOOK 3

3

ANCIENT
CIVILIZATIONS OF
MEXICO AND PERU

Hermocrates: *It is said that in Atlantis duelists had no horses nor needed them.*

> *Orichalcum, the metal that shines like fire, they had. They melted it into glittering gems that they used as coins, paying statues for their work as for an enchantment.*

> *When their colonies started declining, the wise men created strange devices made of amber in order to search for metal, but never the proud Atlantis would grant supply.*

Socrates: *You have defined the kingdom as "rich," but this is really absurd.*

It was March 3, 1972, when German journalist Karl Brugger met Tatunca Nara, head of the Ugha Mongulala Amazon tribe in Manaus, Brazil. Tatunca Nara talked at length about an evolved civilization that would have landed in South America at the end of the ice age and helped the people there get out of barbarism.

> Within centuries they formed a sort of great civilization, a great "Empire of Stone" that dominated different regions of the Earth some of which still exists, some other have disappeared, erased by a [second] huge global catastrophe. The people of Mongulala managed to survive this disaster hiding in tunnels and underground cities. Afterwards, the Mongulala were able to create a real Amazon Kingdom, which could survive a third cataclysm, reaching its maximum power at around 2500 BC, when they started having regular relations with the Egyptian civilization. Since then, the civilization of Mongulala began undergoing a slow but steady decline, up to the present day, when its people live isolated from the rest of the world in the underground city of Akakor. Before the next end of the world the guardians of 13 crystal skulls will gather in Akakor, where they will meet "the one" . . .[1]

Antarctica had been imprisoned and buried in the ice forever, and the Pelasgian survivors had sailed their ships in search of a new home. The shortest and most accessible route led to South America. It is really difficult to reconstruct what happened due to both the time gone by and the conquistadores, who looted treasure and murdered people beginning in that fatal year of 1532. We found that a universal form of writing had appeared at the end of the last ice age, including symbols such as the labrys, the ankh, and the tanith (figure 3.1). Someone had brought it from a distant homeland and spread it throughout the Mediterranean and Central and South America. Here we find it engraved in Pedra Pintada's cave paintings dating back 11,200 years (plate 5), in Tarame (on the border between Brazil and Venezuela), in the oval find and in the "cat table" of Cuenca (Ecuador, plate 6), and in the petroglyphs of Pusharo (Madre de Dios, Peru). This is the mother of Linear A, the Cretan hieroglyphic, the Tifinagh and the Etruscan alphabets, and other similar alphabets differentiated in the Mediterranean during the Bronze Age.

The writing arrived with the Cro-Magnon, a new human race with a higher-than-average stature, light skin, blue eyes, and blond or red hair.

Labrys   Tanith   Ankh

*Figure 3.1. Universal form of writing used after the
end of the last ice age.*

Could they be the Pelasgians? Or, borrowing the name the Incas used for them, the Viracochas?

Fortunately, many other travelers in addition to the conquistadores arrived from Spain and were prodigal in documenting native beliefs and traditions. As the last guardians of the treasures of Peru the Incas play an important role: their stories tell us about the ancient lost civilization of Viracochas, which thousands of years earlier had colonized the lands of Peru.

The Incan empire was the largest in the pre-Columbian Americas. At the time of its maximum expansion at around 1532 CE it included a significant part of the current-day South American countries of Colombia, Ecuador, Peru, Bolivia, Chile, and Argentina. We're talking about an area encompassing more than two million square kilometers, nearly nine thousand kilometers long, linking distant places with a sophisticated road network and with a wide range of works featuring high standards of engineering and design such as bridges and tunnels dug into the rock along the coast. This empire, whose existence goes from the thirteenth to the sixteenth century, had its capital in Cuzco, current-day Peru, whose name in Quechua means "navel of the world." In this city there is a gigantic building with a huge monolith known as "the stone of the twelve angles" (plate 7), along with megalithic ruins that are astronomically aligned. According to legend it was founded by Manco Capàc and Mama Oqllo, the two sons of Inti, the Sun God.

Until the advent of the Spaniards in the sixteenth century the Incas practiced the already ancient "Cult of the Sun," which dated back to the mysterious Tiahuanaco empire, whose center was located in the highlands south of Lake Titicaca. The South American ancient civilizations believed that Lake Titicaca was the place of creation: from an island in the middle of the lake* emerged Viracocha, the human shape of the sun, described in the myths as <u>a tall man, with light skin and beard</u>.[2]

Apparently, according to available documentation, the god Viracocha was revered by all the civilizations that marked the history of Peru before the Incas integrated him into their religion and dedicated one of the most beautiful temples in Cuzco to him.

PERU

Cuzco and the Coricancha

After choosing Cuzco as the capital, the Incas occupied a sacred site that had already existed in the city center and there built the Coricancha, the temple dedicated to Viracocha. The main entrance was completely covered with thousands of foils of pure gold (each weighing two kilograms) and led into a courtyard of corn ears forged from gold. Right in the center of this area, known as Cuzco Cara Orumi ("the undiscovered navel of the Earth"), there was an octagonal shrine of gray stone, once also covered with gold.

Often, when the Spanish conquerors were faced with an indigenous sacred site, they built a church on top. Here they built the church of Santo Domingo, fortunately leaving intact much of the Incan masonry. Due to an earthquake in 1951 the church was destroyed, but the superstructure of the original temple, surfaced with its earthquake-proof walls made of immense blocks of stone, wedged like pieces of a puzzle, survived. The joints between the blocks were executed with great skill so as to be almost invisible. The foundations and walls that formed the temple have been

---

*In Italy the Vie Cave ("hollow ways"), dug into rock up to thirty meters deep near Lake Bolsena, is where the Etruscans worshipped their sacred Water Goddess, who was honored along with the Earth Goddess Uni. At the center of the lake are two important islands that legend said were connected to the mainland by tunnels. According to Incan myth the two islands on Lake Titicaca were also connected to the mainland by tunnels, and there too was a cult dedicated to the Earth Goddess and the Water Goddess. A similar tradition is found in the *Odyssey,* relative to Lake D'Averno near Cumae: from one of these islands came the white civilization, a sign that the legend of Atlantis was transposed into local geography.

INTERESTING

preserved intact to this day thanks to an architecture that combined an ingenious system of interlocking robust polygonal blocks, as well as more sophisticated features. Noteworthy are the niches carved in the hollow of single megaliths.

Garcilaso de la Vega, who knew the Coricancha before and after it became a church, provided further evidence to reconstruct the original features of this Temple of the Sun:

> The high altar was placed eastward; the carpentry of the roof was very high to allow enough fresh air, the roof was thatched. . . . All four walls of the temple were covered from top to bottom with golden foils and plates. On what we call the high altar there was the image of the Sun, represented by a golden plate twice bigger than the one covering the walls. The figure's face was round and was surrounded by rays and flames. . . . It was large enough to fill the entire back wall of the temple, in all its largeness. . . . On both sides of the Sun there were the bodies of the dead Kings . . . who had been embalmed and looked alive. They sat on seats of gold placed on the plates of the same metal . . . they would look toward the people. . . . These bodies were hidden by the Indians along with the remaining treasures and, to date only some of them have reappeared.[3]

It would be a "cosmological temple" dedicated to the Sun God, equipped with a solar alignment, a vantage point having a "target" of the top of near Mount Pachatusan ("fulcrum, the crossbeam of the universe"). An observer who found himself in the courtyard of Coricancha would see the sun rising behind Pachatusan at the dawn of the solstice in June. Around the central courtyard there were five square rooms, not adjoining, with a still visible structure made of smooth blocks of gray granite. It seems that these rooms had a pyramid-shaped roof: one was consecrated to a high priest and his assistants, while the others were dedicated to cosmological and astronomical phenomena. Citing Garcilaso, one room was

> dedicated . . . to the Moon, wife of the Sun . . . the whole . . . was lined with plates of silver . . . here was placed the image and picture

of this night star like those of the Sun in the temple; it consisted of a silver plate with an embossed portrait of a woman's face. . . . Another of these dwellings, the closest to the Moon's, was dedicated to Venus and the Pleiades and to all the other stars. . . . This dwelling was lined with silver, just like the Moon's: the ceiling was dotted with stars* . . . as a kind of night sky. . . . The other adjacent house . . . was dedicated to the thunder and the lightning.† . . . Another dwelling (the fourth) was dedicated to the rainbow because they saw that it proceeded from the Sun. . . . It was all covered with gold. . . . Above the golden plates a rainbow was painted . . . with all its lively colors . . . so big as to occupy the entire space from one wall to the other.‡. . . The fifth and last dwelling was reserved for the High Priest and officiants, in charge of the temple service; they must all be Incas of royal blood. . . . Like the others, this dwelling was also adorned with gold from top to bottom.[4]

The high priest of Coricancha, called Uilac-Umu ("the one who speaks of the divine"), was supported by a caste of priests called Amuatas that included a group of astronomers. They studied the astral bodies, monitored the progress and retreat of the sun, decreed solstices and equinoxes, and predicted eclipses. For this purpose they used monoliths known as sucanas, raised in past times on the horizon of the valley of Cuzco in crucial points observable from Coricancha, which indicated the meridian of winter and summer solstice. Archaeo-astronomer William Sullivan believes that the Coricancha served as a model for the ecliptic trajectory, considering the elliptical shape of its outer wall. In support of this argument, Sullivan points out that one of the names given to Viracocha was

---

*Tombs of Egyptian pharaohs also have ceilings dotted with stars.

†It is a hypothesis that the dedication to lightning and thunder has more to do with astronomy than meteorology, seeing that these phenomena were used as symbols to indicate the meteorites in other parts of the ancient world. There is evidence that long ago a cult of the meteorite flourished in the Andes similar to one that existed in Egypt for the Benben. Moreover, in both cases, the meteorites were associated with the creative power of the universe, fertility, and rebirth.

‡The Incas conceived the rainbow as an emanation of the sun. Indeed, the Khmer of Angkor considered rainbows as bridges connecting the world of the gods with the world of men.

"Intipintin Tiki-Muyo Camac," which literally means "the sun in its central core creator of the circle."[5]

The Incas saw the valley of Cuzco as a reflection of the sky and considered the Vilcamayu River as the counterpart of the Milky Way.*

Before the arrival of the Spaniards it seems that in the Coricancha's "Holy of Holies" there was a marble statue representing the god Viracocha. A text of the period, *Relacion anonyma de los costumbres antiquos de los naturales del Piru*, describes it as resembling the representations of the apostle St. Bartholomew, and other descriptions compare its appearance with that of St. Thomas. Both saints are described in the manuscripts of the Church as lean white men with a beard, elderly, with sandals at their feet, and wrapped in long cloaks. It is evident that the appearance attributed to Viracocha by his worshippers was that of a Cro-Magnon, and certainly not of a relatively dark-skinned Indian with sparse facial hair.

The physical aspect of Viracocha is repeated in most of the legends and religious traditions, so the Spaniards were welcomed as the disciples of their god. Viracocha had indeed prophesied his return, and the conquistadores of Francisco Pizarro took advantage of this psychological influence to facilitate Incan compliance.

Viracocha was described as a "master of science and magic," brandishing terrible weapons and coming from the south† in a period of chaos in order to reorganize the world. It was a scary time: lands had been submerged by a terrible flood and darkness was everywhere; society was falling into disarray and the population was experiencing great difficulty.[6]

Viracocha, with his magnificent architectural and scientific knowledge, taught the people he encountered on his journey northward how to build houses and live in a community. He urged them to be good and kind, to love each other and be charitable to each other. One story tells that when Viracocha arrived in Cacha the people rose up against him and

---

*In Egypt, the Nile was the earthly counterpart of the Milky Way; the June solstice rites were celebrated along the banks of both the Nile and the Vilcamayu. In both places, these rites were conducted by king-gods, namely the pharaohs and the Inca, and took place among ancient megalithic structures.

†Legends divide between those claiming his origin was from the south, and those asserting he originated from an island in Lake Titicaca.

threatened to stone him, but by invoking his hands to the sky he threw a fire that encircled them. Terribly frightened, they bowed to him and asked for mercy. Immediately, the fire extinguished and he went away, reached the nearest coast and, clutching his cloak, stepped into the waves, leaving no trace behind him. For this reason the people who saw him moving away gave him the name of Viracocha, which meant "sea foam."[7]

All of this information was gathered by ancient chroniclers who traveled region by region, transcribing Andean traditions told to them by the indigenous people. Though far apart, they all identified Viracocha as a "tall, bearded man, wearing a white cloak reaching to his feet, tied at the waist by a belt."[8] In other legends he was a "bearded man of medium stature, wrapped in a long cloak, lean and gray-haired, who walked with a cane and spoke all tongues even better than the natives,"[9] or he was "a white man with lofty presence, blue-eyed and bearded, without headgear and wearing a cusma, a doublet or a sleeveless shirt, that reached to the knee."[10] All these features were typical of the Pelasgian people!

Viracocha is described as a "master." Before his coming, people lived in chaos, walked naked like savages, and lived in caves—he is credited with having changed everything and given birth to the golden age, lost a long time ago. He succeeded in civilizing all the lands he crossed with great kindness, without ever using force; the teaching and careful examples he gave of himself were the most effective ways to help the Andean people. He taught medicine, agriculture, cattle breeding, the art of writing (later forgotten), and a keen knowledge of engineering and architecture.

Viracocha was accompanied by two types of messengers, the "loyal soldiers" (huaminca) and "shining soldiers" (hayhuaypanti), who had the task of taking the message of their lord all over the world. Indeed, many Andean masonry works cannot be attributed with certainty to the Incas: it was not their work in the advanced road network that ran parallel twenty-four thousand kilometers from north to south along the coast and along the Andes. Even today, experts are unable to date these roads or determine who might have built them. The mystery deepens upon listening to local traditions, according to which the road network and other sophisticated architectures were built by a civilization older than the Inca, an evolved population of "white men with auburn hair" who lived thousands of years earlier.[11]

The Inca were not keen on working the stone (although many monuments in the area of Cuzco are definitely their work), <u>and we believe that
most of these extraordinary works in the Andes were erected by earlier
civilizations that lived in the so-called golden age.</u> This resplendent era
had come to an end when Viracocha moved away from the lands of Peru
along with his helpers: "when Viracocha reached the District of Puerto
Vejo, he was approached by his followers who, after having joined him,
took the sea with the same ease with which they used to walk on the
ground."[12]

Sacsayhuaman

In the ancient fortress of Sacsayhuaman ("satisfied hawk") north of Cuzco
there are more than a thousand stone blocks. Many are of the order of
two hundred tons, and there is even one—8.5 meters high—estimated
to be 361 tons (plate 8). Every stone has a different size and shape. These
rocks appear to have been cut and machined with ease, perfectly overlapping and interlocking.

In the sixteenth century Garcilaso de la Vega described it as follows:

The grandeur of [Sacsayhuaman] would be incredible to anyone
who had not seen it, and even those who have seen it and considered it with attention imagine, and even believe, that it was made by
enchantment. . . . Indeed the multiplicity of stones, large and small, of
which the three circumvallations are composed (and they are more
like rocks than stones) makes one wonder how they could have been
quarried, for the Indians had neither iron nor steel to work them
with. And the question of how they were conveyed to the site is no
less difficult a problem, since they had no oxen and could not make
wagons, nor would oxen and wagons have sufficed to carry them. . .
. And if one went on to wonder how such large stones could be fitted together so that the point of a knife could scarcely be inserted
between them, there would be no end to our pondering. . . . If you
think about it, this is an incredible job without the help of a single
machine . . . how can we explain the fact that these Indians of Peru
have been able to cut, excavate, transport and lift and lower these

huge blocks of stone, more similar to pieces of a mountain than parts of a building? It is an exaggeration to say that they represent an even greater mystery of the Seven Wonders of the World?[13]

Sacsayhuaman is too large to be visible in a single glance; it belongs to a larger design that with the oldest districts of Cuzco draw a huge puma. The Tullumayu River follows the spine of the feline, while the body is recognizable in the strip of land between the Tullumayu, eastward, and the Huatanay River, westward. The head of the puma is Sacsayhuaman itself. Southerly, the gigantic zigzag walls represent the teeth of the lower jaw. Northerly, the jaw is bordered by a rocky hill. The long strip of land between the jaws is the open mouth of the beast.*

Many chroniclers of the early colonial period were puzzled before this extraordinary masonry and considered it a demon's job. Indeed, it is difficult to attribute these operations to the Andean people, who according to the orthodox opinion did not even know the wheel.

An interesting episode related by Garcilaso de la Vega and recorded in the *Royal Commentaries of the Incas* tells of a king who had tried to emulate the deeds of his ancestors, the constructors of Sacsayhuaman. The attempt was to deliver there a block of granite of enormous size from a remote location several miles away, to finally add it upon the other masses. It was drawn by twenty thousand men across mountains and steep slopes, but the enterprise failed because of the loss of three thousand men, killed by a huge boulder that had escaped from their hands and crushed them. This record suggests their inexperience.

Modern technology cannot identify the construction date of Sacsayhuaman, but many indications suggest that the Incas had settled in already existing buildings. We cannot exclude the theory that these works had been built by another race that lived thousands of years before and only later had been acquired by the Incas. Moreover, we are not sure that there was any continuity between these two civilizations: the Incas could have simply adopted the traditions and knowledge of those

---

*The giant puma faces west, the direction of the equinox sunset, just as the Great Sphinx of Egypt faces east, the direction of the equinox sunrise.

who preceded them, trying to imitate on a smaller scale their gigantic works.

Their myths say the original constructors were the "Viracochas," foreigners with "beard and white skin," whose coming is associated with a disaster, a terrible flood that submerged the lands and destroyed much of the human race.

In his book, *Natural and Moral History of the Indies*, the friar José de Acosta reports "all that the Indians themselves say about their origins"—that for some serious crime ancient peoples had been annihilated by the Creator with a great flood, and the Creator had appeared from Lake Titicaca in human form in the likeness of Viracocha, stopping in Tiahuanaco, where today there are still old buildings such as the "Pumapunku" and the "Kalasasaya." Here they say he created the stars and the moon and regenerated the human population on Earth.

A legend also hands down the memory of a race of prehistoric master builders called "Huari." These are described as "white giants, bearded men who had been created on Lake Titicaca, where they had started to civilize the Andes."[14]

In another myth we read about some giants who, having disobeyed the Creator, were destroyed by a great flood; similarly, in the Hebrew Old Testament, especially in the sixth chapter of Genesis, it is said that in ancient times the Earth was inhabited by the Giants, before God unleashed the Great Flood. It then comes naturally to wonder why a Jewish source and a Peruvian source tell the same story of an angry God, who unleashed a great flood on the Earth as a punishment, killing all life forms, including the Giants.*

Father Molina described the flood in a story handed down in his *Account of the Fables and Rites of the Incas*: according to his report, the flood had killed all humans and living creatures, and the water had risen over the highest tops of mountains all over the world. No living creature survived, with the exception of a woman and a man closed in a box who,

---

*"Giants" was used by Greek and Latin historians as a synonym for Pelasgians or Atlanteans, and Pelasgians were invariably described as bearded and white-skinned, with light hair and eyes.

once the water had receded, were carried by the wind to Tiahuanaco. Here the Creator gave rise to the new peoples and nations that populated those regions.

All scholars confirm that the Incas would have absorbed and passed down the traditions of civilized peoples during the widening of their empire: in the words of Graham Hancock, "their role as perpetrators of the ancient beliefs is doubtless."[15]

An original tradition of Lake Titicaca tells of a divine civilized hero, called "Thunupa," probably Viracocha himself. He is described as a white man, of noble presence, with blue eyes and a beard, who appeared on top of the plateau in ancient times. He created a peaceful reign and taught the arts of civilization, until a group of conspirators attacked and seriously wounded him, placed him on a reed boat, and drove it to the lake. He moved away so quickly that all present were paralyzed, considering that the lake had no currents. The boat touched land at Cochimarca, and the river Desguardero would be born as a result of the violent collision with the boat. This story appears to be incredibly similar to that of Osiris— both he and Viracocha were great civilizers and both were victims of a conspiracy. In addition, both were closed in a container or vessel before being thrown into the water and dragged away to the sea by the current of a river.[16] Last, they both were the first to make their peoples desist from cannibalism.[17] At this point, it's reasonable to wonder whether they are the same person.

At Siriqui, a small village near the shores of Lake Titicaca, there is still a tradition of building boats with bundles of reeds as a means of transportation. This type of boat is similar to those made of papyrus on which pharaohs sailed the Nile thousands of years before.

Ollantaytambo

Sixty kilometers northwest of Sacsayhuaman is the hill-temple Ollantaytambo, a huge, terraced amphitheater that extends on the side of a concave hill. The lowest levels are built with small to medium dry stone, but as they go up, their size increases. We come to a height of at least two hundred feet where all around are megaliths of granite weighing between fifty and seventy tons. From this place, we walk along a ledge under a wall of well-connected trapezoidal blocks that houses a row of ten niches (plate 9). The far south of the ledge goes through a megalithic door surmounted by a lintel that leads to an observation point located on the side of the mountain. Going back we climb a staircase carved into the trapezoidal wall and emerge on top of Ollantaytambo—half mountain and half temple. Here there are several megaliths between one hundred and two hundred tons and, on the highest point, an impressive structure whose facade has six huge megaliths (plate 10). Perhaps these stones originally formed the back wall of a room. The front and side walls were located both on the side of a higher hill and on the top, and all around are other megaliths. It is curious that blocks of pink porphyry have been found up here, and we wonder how they could have come to this place considering that the caves that are their source are located about eight kilometers away and about nine hundred meters above on the opposite bank of the Vilcamayu River. These blocks reproduce the architecture of Tiahuanaco: massive, straight-edged megaliths, with knobs, protrusions, and indentations joined together with skill and precision. In this regard, a stepped pyramid—found in Tiahuanaco—appears in relief on one of the vertical blocks of Ollantaytambo's megalithic wall. Graham Hancock points out that "in ancient Egypt the same sign was used as a hieroglyph and symbol of the Benben stone, emblem of eternal life. In Egypt and at Tiahuanaco as well as at Angkor, one label of the builders was a particular construction technique in which double T-shaped metal clamps—I—were used to hold the blocks together."[18]

The Misunderstood Code

In his study of Andean cosmology William Sullivan pointed out that both the Inca and their predecessors had explained the Precession of the Equinoxes by using the same "mythological technical language" as we find throughout the ancient world. According to Sullivan the Incas had forgotten or misunderstood the original teachings, taking the symbolism of the rites of initiation literally. This mistake led to human sacrifice, drifting away from the teachings of Viracocha that were based on the principles of "compassion, kindness, and mercy."

Sacrifices of the Inca took place along a system of straight lines called "ceques," orientated depending on the rising and setting of certain stars and constellations. This network of sacrifices, spreading in all directions from the "Navel of the World," would create invisible links between sacred monuments distant from each other. In *Heaven's Mirror*, Graham Hancock explains that in Egypt and Angkor they believed that the souls of initiates went up to the sky and became stars not through human sacrifice but through the understanding of "astronomical wisdom." In Mexico and in the Andes the astronomically aligned pyramidal monuments were used as devices for human sacrifices, while in Egypt and Angkor they served a Gnostic search for immortality. It is possible that Egypt, Angkor, Mexico, and the Andes have inherited the same legacy of ideas on the dualism of sky and ground, yet with very different interpretations. One of the ancient ceque lines revered by the Inca passes through or near Machu Picchu, Ollantaytambo, Sacsayhuaman, and Cuzco. The alignment extends across Lake Titicaca, on the island of Suruqi, and up to the city of Tiahuanaco for a total distance of over 800 kilometers.

Tiahuanaco

Located about 3,800 meters above sea level between Peru and Bolivia, with an area of over 5,000 square kilometers and a depth of over three hundred meters, Lake Titicaca is characterized by a puzzling geological history.

Although it is at a high altitude, the area around the lake is dotted with a myriad of marine fossil shells, leading us to believe that at some point in history, probably about a hundred million years ago, the whole Andean plateau was pushed up from the seabed. It is believed that the plateau of the lake is still rising slowly and unevenly, as is proved by a still visible though ancient shoreline, which is ninety meters higher than the current shoreline to the north and eighty-three meters below the lake level at the far south.

In 1910 the historian Clements Markham dedicated one of his works to the mysterious existence of the ruins of a large city on the southern shore of Lake Titicaca. We are talking about Tiahuanaco, formerly known as Taypicala, the Stone in the Center. Experts do not agree about its dating; some date it back to the second millennium BCE, while others believe it is far more recent, between the second and ninth centuries CE.

Tiahuanaco was an ancient port with several piers on the shore of Lake Titicaca, but now it is about twenty-five kilometers south of the lake and more than thirty meters above the present shoreline. All this puts the date of the founding of the city into serious doubt; the astronomical calculations of engineer and archaeologist Arthur Posnansky (1873–1946) and astronomers Ralph Muller and Nel Steed agree it was about 10,500 BCE. If this theory is correct—while universities continue to say it is not—the city, after having joined the shore, would have been separated again by a natural catastrophe at around the eleventh millennium BCE and then drifted away.

The builders of Tiahuanaco used spectacular, gigantic megaliths, with some scattered around the city, so well cut as to appear to be the job of superhuman beings. The early sixteenth-century Spanish travelers were amazed by both the incredible size of its buildings and the Indians' stories that set the building of the city at the time of their predecessors, sent from heaven to Earth by the god creator. Accordingly, Tiahuanaco emerged in the span of a single night, its stones miraculously raised from the ground and transported through the air to the sound of a trumpet.[19]

Now we must say a few words on the great and almost incredible buildings of Tiahuanaco. There is an artificial hill, very high, built on a foundation of stone so that the earth does not slide down. There are giant stone carved figures . . . these are eroding, which demonstrates that they are ancient. There are walls made of stones so huge that it is difficult to imagine what human force was able to place them. And there are the remains of strange buildings, among which the most exceptional are some stone portals, hewn in the bare rock; such stones are located on basements about thirty feet long, fifteen feet wide, and six feet thick, and the base and the portal are made of one piece. . . . How and with the use of what instruments or tools, it was possible to create such massive works are questions that we are not able to answer yet. . . . Nor can you imagine how it is possible to carry up here huge stones like these.[20]

The city is composed of the following basic elements: the Underground Temple, the Akapana Pyramid, Kalasasaya, the Gate of the Sun, and Pumapunku (see figure 3.2).

The Underground Temple

The Underground Temple, a semi-subterranean enclosure open at the center of the city, is a large rectangular pit 1.8 meters deep with a gravel floor about 12 meters long and 9 meters wide. In the middle stands a column of red rock 2.1 meters high (plate 11). There is a carved portrait of a man with a high forehead, large round eyes, a straight nose, and full lips, with an elegant and impressive beard. On the sides of the head are carved images of strange animals, similar to large prehistoric mammals, with large tails and deformed legs.

The stone figure that the scholars identify with Viracocha is carved

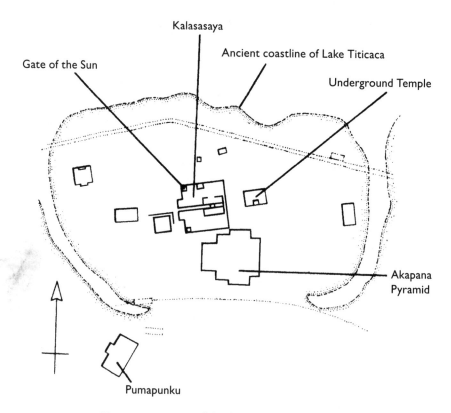

Figure 3.2. Map of the layout of Tiahuanaco.

with arms and hands crossed over a long dress, standing next to a snake (the universal symbol of wisdom and spiritual power) that rises from the ground, zigzagging up to the shoulders. The figure looks southward, with Viracocha's back to Lake Titicaca; it is placed as a central obelisk in the temple, along with two other smaller columns, most likely representing his legendary companions. Along the walls of the temple emerge several human heads carved in stone, which protrude from the walls in three dimensions.

The Akapana Pyramid

South of the Underground Temple is the Akapana Pyramid, a sacred stepped mountain—210 feet from the side at the base—covered with large blocks of andesite. Its layout resembles a tree drawn on a computer monitor with only a few pixels, its edges precisely following the cardinal directions.

Archaeologists discovered this pyramid in the heart of a complicated network of tunnels that run in a zigzag pattern, lined with beautiful ashlar stone, angled and artfully fitted. Water piped down through these tunnels starting from a large reservoir at the top of the structure flowed up to a moat that completely surrounded the monument and lapped the base of its southern side. Such a complicated hydraulic structure makes Akapana a great mystery, although there are theories that assign lethal purposes to the pyramid: In ancient Aymara, the words *hake* and *apana* mean "men who are perishing," probably because of the water. Another theory holds that the running water was used to wash minerals. The research group headed by Dr. Oswaldo Rivera, director of the National Institute of Bolivian Archaeology, is looking for the entrance to a room said to be inside the pyramid and is convinced that the original sacred city is twelve or twenty meters beneath Tiahuanaco.*

---

*Researchers identified some rooms under the Sphinx in Giza in the 1990s and a camera exploring the Queen's Chamber southern channel filmed a closed gate door that apparently led to a never-opened room. It is surprising that both Giza and Tiahuanaco date back more than 12,000 years and both sites have been built upon deep underground labyrinths and rooms. In both places we expect to soon find messages from a lost civilization.

Kalasasaya

North of Akapana coming east from the Underground Temple is Kalasasaya ("vertical stones"), an impressive geometrical portal with large slabs of red sandstone, four meters high, embedded in a perimeter wall at regular intervals, surrounding a square area of approximately 150 meters per side. Oriented to the cardinal points, the giant trapezoidal blocks lodged in the wall convey the effect of a large fence. The function of this place was that of a sophisticated astronomical observatory where the Inca could observe the equinoxes and solstices and predict the seasons with mathematical precision. Certain structures within its walls, aligned according to particular groups of stars, seem to be designed to facilitate the measurement of the sun amplitude* through the different seasons.

The German-Bolivian scholar Arthur Posnansky has devoted fifty years of his life to the study of Tiahuanaco's ruins, dating the founding of the city based on astronomical calculations.

Each day of the year the sun rises at a different horizon. Looking from an observation area (a portal) west of Kalasasaya toward the west on the first day of spring the sun rises exactly in the middle of the gateway. On the first day of winter or summer the sun should rise behind the markers at the corners of the east side of the fence, but this is not so. We cannot attribute this to a mistake of the constructors of the temple (who built it with rocks of one hundred tons completely devoid of commissures): in fact, in 10,500 BCE the angle of Earth's axis was different, influencing winter and summer solstices; so the sun would have risen exactly over the angular stones† (plate 12).

---

*The amplitude is the horizon's arch between the cardinal points east or west and the points of the rising and setting of the sun. It is measured from zero to ninety degrees from east or west toward south—in the first case we say north, in the second case south.

†The Earth rotates around an axis passing through its center and the poles. The axis is inclined in respect to the surface of the Earth's orbit around the sun: this inclination is called the "obliquity of the ecliptic," which changes cyclically from a maximum of 24.4 degrees to a minimum of 21.8 degrees and can be calculated using simple equations. During the 1911 Ephemeris International Conference in Paris a graph was shown that reported on a curve of the angles of the ecliptic according to the historical dates.

Establishing the solar alignments of some other constructions, Posnansky showed that the obliquity of the Earth at the time of the construction of Kalasasaya was 23° 8' 48", which, on the Ephemeris graph, corresponds to 15,000 BCE.[21] Later on more precise measurements made by Nel Steede moved the date to 10,500 BCE, which perfectly fits, we'll see, with the astronomical alignments of the pyramids of Giza and the temples of Angkor.

Between 1927 and 1930 several scientists, including Hans Ludendorff, at the time director of the Astronomical Observatory of Potsdam; astronomer Arnold Kohlshutter, University of Bonn; Dr. Rolf Muller, University of Potsdam; and Dr. Friedrich Becker, Specula Vatican, meticulously checked the archaeological-astronomical research of Posnansky for accuracy. After three years of work these scientists corroborated his thesis. In 1997 Dr. Rivera confirmed the dating of 10,500 BCE:

We are realizing that Tiahuanaco is much older than we ever thought before. After 21 years of excavations and studies in Tiahuanaco I can say that every day we remain open-mouthed because Tiahuanaco is unbelievable, even for the archaeologists who work there. Every day we discover new things.[22]

Presuming that this city dates back to the eleventh millennium BCE implies accepting its link with a lost civilization.

Inside the southwestern corner of the Kalasasaya is El Fraile, a large statue about 1.8 meters high carved from a block of sandstone, representing a kind of androgynous humanoid with huge eyes and lips (plate 13). In his right hand he brandishes a wavy bladed knife, in the other he holds a bound book with hinges. An unidentified object bends out of the top of the book. From the waist down the figure is clothed in a garment of fish scales, each scale designed with rows and rows of very stylized, small fish heads. The statue wears a belt carved with images of large crustaceans.

A second idol is located in the eastern part of the fence, facing the main entrance: carved in gray andesite, this very thick monolith is about two meters high. The figure is similar to El Fraile in the scaled clothes and in his hands holding unidentified objects. In this case the object in his right hand has a roughly cylindrical shape: it is narrow in the middle up to the handle and larger on the back and at the base, narrowing again upward. It appears to consist of several overlapping parts stuck one inside the other. The object in the left hand is a sheath from which a curved handle comes out.

These "fish men" are linked to an ancient local tradition that tells the story of the "gods of the lake with fish tails," called Chullua Umantha.[23] The legend seems to have connections to the Mesopotamian myths that tell of strange amphibious beings endowed with wit that visited the land of Sumer in a remote prehistory.[24]

The leader of these creatures, called Johannes,* had the body of a fish with a human head and feet attached to the caudal fin. When the sun was setting, he would dive back into the sea and abide all night in the depths, just like an amphibian. According to the Chaldean scribe Berossus, Johannes was primarily a civilizer.

> During the day he used to converse with men, but no food was consumed during that period; he enabled them to understand letters and sciences, and all kinds of art. He taught them how to build houses, found temples, compile laws, and taught them the principles of geometrical knowledge. He explained how to distinguish the seeds of the earth and showed how to collect fruits, in short, instructed them in everything that could serve to soften manners and humanize mankind. Since then, his teachings were so universal that nothing essential has been added to make them better.[25]

Images of fish men found in the Babylonian and Assyrian bas-reliefs have many similarities with El Fraile, such as fish scales covering their clothes or unknown instruments in their hands. One wonders whether the appearance of the Mayan "feathered" Quetzalcòatl was not the result

---

*The probable derivation of "Iohannes" is from "Iani," which we will find out is one of Osiris's several names.

of confusion between feathers and scales, made by those who based Quetzalcòatl's description on statues and bas-reliefs (plate 14).*

The Gate of the Sun

Located northwest of Kalasasaya is the Gate of the Sun, a monolithic block of andesite about three meters tall and four meters wide, weighing ten tons. It seems a kind of miniaturized triumphal arch, one of the archaeological wonders of the Americas for its exceptional quality of stone workmanship, especially the "Calendar Frieze" carved across the top of the eastern facade. In the center the frieze is dominated by the representation of Viracocha with a stern face, the royal diadem surmounted by nineteen rays, with an arrow in each hand.

Every nineteen years at summer solstice, looking through the arch of the Gate of the Sun from first one side and then the other, you can see the sun setting in the northwest while the full moon rises in exactly the opposite direction over the summit of Mount Illimani to the southeast. It seems as if "the door acts as a fulcrum in a kind of cosmic balance between sun and moon."[26] William Sullivan argues that the rays on the head of Viracocha are not related to the sun but "show the knowledge of the nineteen years metonic cycle of the moon, that is the number of years that a particular phase of the moon takes in a given solar date."[27]

On the right and left side of the image of Viracocha there are three rows, each consisting of eight figures wearing bird masks with very sharp noses. They're marching in regimented files toward Viracocha, who also holds a thunderbolt. The base of the frieze is decorated with a design known as the "maze," a series of uninterrupted geometric stepped pyramids arranged alternately upside down and right side up. On the third column from the right and the third from the left you can distinguish an elephant head, which is unusual given that these animals did not exist in the New World. However, in prehistoric times there were some species of elephant called *Cuvieronius* in the southern Andes—proboscideans

---

*The Mayan people inhabited the Yucatan peninsula for more than a thousand years, sharing a common culture, religion, and unique form of hieroglyphic writing. The Incan culture, located in the highlands of the Andes in present-day Peru, lasted for less than two hundred years.

that became extinct around 10,000 BCE. You can also find carvings of another stylized animal species, the toxodon, a three-toed amphibious mammal about 2.7 meters long and 1.5 meters tall, which became extinct at about 12,000 BCE.[28]

These indications would confirm the astronomical and archaeological data that date Tiahuanaco back to the end of the Pleistocene, cutting off the orthodox historical chronology, which gives the town just 1,500 years. Forty-four toxodon heads are carved in the frieze of the Gate of the Sun and others are depicted on numerous fragments of pottery found in Tiahuanaco. Even more convincingly, the same animal has been portrayed in various sculptures.[29] Representations of other extinct species have been found, such as *Scelidoterium*, diurnal quadrupeds, and *Macrauchenia*, a horse-like animal, with three-toed feet.[30]

These images show that Tiahuanaco was a sort of illustrated book of the past; unfortunately its drafting was abruptly interrupted because the Gate of the Sun was never completed.

Tiahuanaco was originally built as a port city on the shores of Lake Titicaca. The large harbor structures with docks and quays, and the numerous canals and water works, currently dry but corresponding to the ancient lake bed, show that at around 10,500 BCE the lake reached Tiahuanaco.

Pumapunku

About a hundred meters southwest of Kalasasaya is a place called Pumapunku (literally "gate of the puma"). Excavations managed by Posnansky surveyed two artificially dredged basins on both sides of a "quay or slope, where hundreds of ships could simultaneously disembark and embark their heavy loads."[31] Terraced, with three levels of retaining walls, the platform covers an area measuring fifty by sixty meters, and one of the blocks weighs 470 tons. Many other blocks weigh between one and two hundred tons and are joined by metal staples in the shape of an I or double T (see figure 3.3). Studies of these devices have demonstrated that they were poured into the notches while molten, which assumes the use of a portable furnace and a level of technology certainly much higher than that of a pre-Columbian civilization. The staples were made of an uncommon mix of elements: 2.05 percent arsenic, 95.15 percent copper,

0.26 percent iron, 0.84 percent silica, and 1.70 percent nickel. This type of metallic alloy does not exist in Bolivia and would have required a furnace that could reach very high temperatures. A double cross frequently appears on these blocks and other works in Tiahuanaco: according to orthodox history, this symbol dates back at least a thousand years before the arrival of the Spanish missionaries.

One wonders how the builders of this work could carry boulders of such size, especially when considering that the quarries were about sixty kilometers away, and that Tiahuanaco is 4,115 meters above the sea level!

Dozens of blocks were scattered everywhere in Pumapunku due to a natural disaster that surprised Tiahuanaco in the tenth millennium BCE

Figure 3.3. Metal staples joining megalith blocks. On the left, starting from the top: Pumapunku, Ollantaytambo, Angkor Wat (Cambodia), Dendera (Egypt). On the right: two Achaean examples.

(in conjunction with the second flood). It might have been the case of a terrible flood, triggered by the same seismic movements that caused the flooding of Lake Titicaca.

The discovery of lake vegetation and fragments of human beings and animals in the same flood debris (amidst a chaotic disorder of polished stones, tools, equipment, and an endless variety of other objects) proves how destructive the power of water is when combined with abrupt movements of the Earth.

A series of earthquakes caused the lake level to grow and overflow the banks; with the passing of years the opposite effect reduced the lake level inch by inch, causing the water to recede from the port city. At the same time the climate became colder and Tiahuanaco much less favorable for the growth of crops. It appears that the seismic activity was interrupted by a period of calm, followed by a climatic worsening that urged the Andean people to migrate to places where the struggle for life was less arduous. Disconcerting evidence shows that the highly civilized inhabitants of Tiahuanaco—perhaps the Viracochas—tried to deal with the situation by conducting scientific agricultural experiments. This means that, in ancient times, someone made a sophisticated analysis of the chemical composition of a large number of tubers and high-mountain poisonous plants, detoxifying them and making them harmless, nutritious, and edible. As David Browman, professor of anthropology at the University of Washington, admits: "There is still no satisfactory explanation as to how these detoxification processes have been developed."[32]

At the same time someone built elevated fields on the recently emerged land, a process that gave rise to characteristic alternating high and low land strips, with the latter—at certain periods of the year—spontaneously transformed into low channels. These fields, still visible today and called *waruwaaru* by the inhabitants, facilitated the growing of crops without modern cultivation techniques. Many archaeologists and agronomists tried to rebuild some elevated fields, with amazing results: the harvest tripled compared to the most productive traditional land, and in periods of cold and drought the crops survived with no loss.[33]

The Strange Discovery of
a Royal Air Force Cartographer

A cartographer of the Royal Air Force, Jim M. Allen, has found some features of Atlantis as described by Plato in a zone 200 kilometers south of Tiahuanaco in a part of the Andean plateau adjoining Poopó Lake in Bolivia, whose basin is connected to Lake Titicaca by the Desaguadero River.* Here there is a flat area of 2,000 by 3,000 Andean stade, surrounded by mountains. Prolonged rains in this kind of closed basin certainly would have caused a flood capable of erasing every trace of an ancient city.

According to Allen, Plato could have confused Andean stade with Greek stade, as he described a plain with dimensions of 2,000 by 3,000 Greek stade. A Greek stade (177.6 meters) corresponds to one-tenth of a prime degree of Earth's circumference. Andean populations, which use not a decimal numbering system, but instead a numbering system based in twentieths, would have adopted a stade corresponding to one-twentieth of a prime degree of Earth circumference (88.8 meters). So the plain discovered by Allen has lengths that are one-half of what would be expected from a literal translation of Plato.

The name "Andes" comes from an incorrect pronunciation of "Antis." In the language of the Incas (Quechua) it means "copper," and it is also the name of a population that settled along the eastern slopes of the Andes.

Before the Spanish conquest, a quarter of the Incan empire (note: the Incan empire was organized in four regions called "quarters") was called "Antisuyo": kingdom of Antis. By joining the word "atl," which in the Aztec language (Nahuatl) means "water," we obtain "Atl-Antis." During the rainy season large areas of the Amazon basin are under water, reaching levels of up to nine meters deep. As the first inhabitants of the Amazon lived on stilts, such a name would be appropriate for South America. According to Plato the plain (of Atlantis) stood in the middle of the long side of the continent, as the plain discovered by Allen does.

Four kilometers from the southwest margin of Poopó Lake but still inside what was once its ancient basin, a hill rises (once an island) with

*All of Allen's studies can be found at www.atlantisbolivia.org.

the remains of concentric walls that are reminiscent of the image given by Plato for the capital city of Atlantis. Allen has also detected a canal one stade wide that surrounds the plain, just as Plato said. Maybe the Pelasgians replicated their capital city near Tiahuanaco?

MEXICO

Chichén Itzá

On the way to the past of Central America, in the Mexican state of Yucatán we find ourselves in a white and black checkered corridor, with a series of light and shadow, yin and yang, all inexplicably coexisting.

When in the light, the philosophical, cultural, scientific, and artistic expressions of high spirituality are apparent. On the contrary, trampling the shadows, we see that from the sixteenth century—in the Valley of Aztec*—acts of inhuman atrocities were carried out, degenerating into over a hundred thousand human sacrifices per year. We are faced with a schizophrenic culture, devoted to slaughter, which shocked the first conquistadores and Catholic priests who arrived in these lands.

The conquistador Bernard Diaz de Castillo was almost traumatized during his first visit to an Aztec temple:

> In that narrow space one could see many demonic things, horns, trumpets and knives and many hearts of Indians who had been burned to incense their idols, and everything was so soaked in blood and there was so much as I curse it, and because it smelled like an abattoir, we hastened to take away from the stench and such a horrible sight.[34]

The hearts of sacrificial victims, usually captured in battle, were ripped out, and then, during the ceremony, the celebrants would flay and dismember the prisoners.

In Chichén Itzá a ziggurat (pyramidal structure with outside staircases and a shrine at the top) stands about 30 meters high: it is the Temple of

---

*The Aztecs dominated northern Mexico at the time of the Spanish conquest and had created an empire surpassed in size only by that of the Incas in Peru.

Kukulkan. Each staircase consists of ninety-one steps and, including the top platform, the pyramid contains a total of 365 steps, the exact number of days in the solar year. The geometric design and orientation of the old buildings were created to accomplish a particular goal: during the spring and fall equinoxes, triangular patterns of light and shadow combine to create an image of a giant snake rising from the north staircase (plate 15).

Continuing eastward you come to the Temple of the Warriors, on top of which is the immense figure of the idol of Chac-Mool. Its total length is 240 centimeters and it was forged half lying and half sitting in a strange and rigid position. On his abdomen he holds an empty tray that once served to contain the newly extracted hearts. A sixteenth-century Spanish observer reported that the sacrificial victim was grabbed by four men, two for the arms and two for the legs, splaying them all; the executioner made an incision between the ribs with a firestone knife and drew out his heart, putting it on the tray.

The Altar of Child Sacrifices

In Villahermosa, in the state of Tabasco, there is the Altar of Child Sacrifices, made by the Olmecs. It is a single block of granite about 120 centimeters thick, its sides carved with bas-reliefs of four men in strange hats, each holding a child who squirms, visibly panic-stricken. The back of the altar is not decorated, while the front shows a man holding a lifeless baby.

The Olmecs were the first civilization of ancient Mexico to encourage sacrificial practices, and about 2,000 years later, at the time of the Spanish conquest, the Aztecs were the last people to continue a tradition by now very ancient and deeply rooted.

Ahuitzotl, the eighth and most powerful emperor of the Aztec dynasty, celebrated the consecration of the Temple of Huitzilopochtli in Tenochtitlàn by sacrificing four rows of prisoners accompanied by teams of priests who took four days to kill them all. On this occasion, in the course of a single rite, eighty thousand people were killed. It was calculated that at the beginning of the sixteenth century the average number of sacrificial victims in the Aztec empire was around 250,000 a year. The Aztecs destroyed millions of lives because they were convinced that only human sacrifice would delay the end of the world.

These people believed that the universe operated in great cycles. According to a collection of Aztec documents called *Codex Vaticanus,* since the creation of humanity four ages or "suns" had passed. At the time of the conquest the Fifth Sun was dominating. Five suns compose a cycle of 25,625 years. Humanity has recently surpassed the end of the Fifth Sun and so it has re-entered the first.

Another witness that survived the depredations of the conquest is the Stone of the Sun of Axayacatl, the sixth emperor of the royal dynasty. This monolith, weighing about twenty-four and a half tons, was carved from basalt in 1479. It features concentric circles, each of which has complex symbolic inscriptions concerning the belief that the world had already gone through four suns. The era of the Fifth Sun is depicted with the face of Tonatiuh the Sun God himself. This god's tongue is described as an obsidian knife that protrudes noticeably, as if to indicate his desire of blood; the wrinkled face indicates his advanced age, and appears within the Ollin symbol, which means movement. According to the ancients, the Earth will be violently rocked and we will all be destroyed. Human sacrifices were a hopeful attempt to postpone the impending catastrophe. This belief, though with slight variations, was shared by all the great civilizations of Central America. Unlike the Aztecs, some people had calculated the precise day of such an event that would lead to the end of the Fifth Sun. According to Mayan teachings, the Fifth Sun was said to end on December 21, 2012.

Quetzalcòatl and Tezcatilpoca

Quetzalcòatl was the most relevant deity of the ancient Mexican pantheon, the "Sovereign Plumed Serpent," or the god king of the golden age, who had died, but was prophesied to return at some point in the future.

Quetzalcòatl was credited with the invention of the advanced mathematical formulas and calendaring that the Maya used to calculate Judgment Day. He was described in a very familiar way: a white large-built man, with broad forehead, large eyes and a flowing beard. He wore a long white robe that reached to the foot; he condemned the sacrifice, except those of fruits and flowers and was known as the "god of peace." According to an ancient pre-Columbian myth, Quetzalcòatl was "a ruddy-skinned and blond man with a long beard."[35]

We note that Quetzalcòatl was a bearded and white-skinned deity, similar to Viracocha, the pale Andean god who came to Tiahuanaco bringing the gifts of light and civilization. A Central American tradition says that Quetzalcòatl came from the sea, on a boat that moved by itself (like the boats of the Homeric Phaeacians), taught men how to use fire for cooking, and built houses in order to teach them how to live together peacefully.

In some areas of Central America Quetzalcòatl was called "Gucumatz," while at Chichén Itzá he was "Kukulkan." These two words were translated, obtaining the same meaning as "Quetzalcòatl," namely "feathered serpent."

There were other deities directly related to these: the first was Votan, a civilizer also described as a fair-skinned man, covered with a robe. Scholars have failed to translate the name of this deity, but his principal symbol, like Quetzalcòatl, was a snake. The second god was Itzamana, the Mayan god of healing, a bearded man wearing a long robe, whose symbol was a rattlesnake. All local legends claimed that without a doubt Quetzalcòatl/ Gucumatz/Kukulkan/Votan/Itzamana had come to Central America from far away, beyond the eastern sea, to which he returned after a few years. Traditions seemed to indicate that the stranger with pale skin and beard was not an isolated person: in many Mesoamerican traditions Quetzalcòatl/Kukulkan/Itzamana is accompanied by some "helpers" or "assistants."

Some religious texts, known as the Books of Chilam Balam, report that "the first inhabitants of Yucatán were the people of the serpent: they had come from the east on boats, along with their leader Itzamana (Eastern Snake), a healer who could resurrect the dead."[36]

According to the Spanish chronicler Las Casas, "The Indians said that in ancient times twenty men came to Mexico, headed by their leader Kukulkan, who instructed the people in the arts of peace, and erected several important buildings."[37] Quetzalcòatl introduced the art of writing and the invention of the calendar, and he taught architecture and wall art in Mexico. He was the father of mathematics, astronomy, and metal-lurgy, established agriculture, and introduced corn. During his presence in Central America human sacrifices were forbidden, as happened with Osiris in Egypt, but soon after his departure, they were reintroduced with great ferocity.

Why did Quetzalcòatl depart? Mexican legends describe the arrival of Tezcatilpoca, an evil god, whose name means "smoking mirror," who interrupted the government of the "Feathered Serpent." It seems that in ancient Mexico there was a struggle between the forces of light and darkness, and the latter triumphed. A fight that echoes the conflict in Egypt between Osiris and his evil brother Seth! Everything would have taken place at Tollan (now known as Tula), where Tezcatilpoca forced Quetzalcòatl to leave Mexico on a raft of serpents. (Another echo of the fight between Osiris and his evil brother Seth.) A legend says that he "burned his houses made of silver and shells, buried his treasure, and sailed the Eastern sea preceded by his assistants, who had been transformed into beautiful birds."[38] It is believed that Quetzalcòatl left from Coatzalcoalco, which means "shrine of the serpent," with the promise to return and defeat Tezcatilpoca, thus inaugurating an era in which the gods would accept sacrifices of flowers and stop claiming human blood.

Tezcatilpoca, the eternal rival of Quetzalcòatl, was associated with the night, the darkness, and the sacred jaguar—often described as a glowing skull, he was said to possess a mysterious object, the "smoking mirror" he needed to observe the activities of men and gods.

Along the base of the pyramids of Tula, north and east, were murals depicting jaguars and eagles banqueting with human hearts. On the platform of this pyramid were four columns and four fearsome granite idols, two meters and sixty centimeters high: their sculptor had created them with stern faces, blank eyes, and beaked noses.

The objects they are holding are most interesting: in the right hand they hold tools to launch spears, called *atlatls,* and in the left they have arrows or rods and bags of incense. Some legends say that the gods of ancient Mexico were armed with *xiuhcoatl,* "fiery serpents," instruments that would apparently emit fiery rays, capable of piercing and dismembering a human body.

Yet what were these fiery serpents? <u>Both tools looked like technologi-</u> \
<u>cal devices,</u> and both recall the items held by the idols of Kalasasaya in
Tiahuanaco.

Cholula

Cholula, in central Mexico, is where we meet Tlachihualtepetl, a majestic
building that seems to have bloomed from Mother Earth in the vastness
of the forest. It is referred to as the "artificial mountain" in Nahuatl, language of the Aztecs. With a perimetral area of 183,000 square meters and
a height of 64 meters it is the largest human-made monument by volume
in the world, three times the size of the Great Pyramid of Giza. Its con-
tours are now covered with grass, but that cannot hide what the monument used to be: <u>an impressive four-stepped ziggurat, whose sides come</u>
<u>close to half a kilometer in length.</u>

Once upon a time it was <u>dedicated to Quetzalcòatl, but</u> when the
conquistadores arrived in Cholula the temple that stood on top of it
was desecrated and pulled down, and in its place they built a Catholic
church.

With their beards and their white skin, dressed in shining armor,
they seemed the realization of a prophecy: hadn't Quetzalcòatl promised
to return with his followers? Indeed, it was with this mental attitude that
the people of Cholula let the conquistadores into the garden of the temple, where waiting for them there was a banquet of bread and meat cooked
with care. The Spaniards, however, were not at all so friendly: they closed
and controlled all the revenue and murdered about six thousand people,
equaling in ferocity the most bloodthirsty in the fierce rites of the Aztecs.

How many written testimonies of the ancient peoples of Central
America have been passed down to us? The answer, thanks to the
Spaniards, is less than twenty of the original codices and scrolls. The
Spaniards themselves, however, realized that prior to the Aztecs there had
existed a really great civilization in Mexico, and so some Franciscans tried
to reconstruct the past. Diego de Landa became a collector of oral stories and traditions of indigenous peoples of the Yucatán. Bernardino de
Sahagùn would track down the most learned, older natives and ask them
to describe everything they remembered of Aztec history, religion, and

legend. Diego de Duran was another Franciscan who fought to recover the lost knowledge of the past: in 1585 he visited Cholula, where he interviewed a venerable old man whose age was said to be more than one hundred years. The story of this native has come down to us:

> Before light was created, Cholula was immersed in darkness and gloom. Immediately after the sun had risen east and gigantic men appeared taking possession of the earth. They loved sunlight so much so that, using very adhesive clay and bitumen, they built such a high tower that its top touched the sky. When they had raised it, the Lord of Heaven irated because they had dared go up there; immediately, the inhabitants of heaven rushed as lightning and destroyed the building, and scattered its builders all over the earth.[39]

This story is reminiscent of the biblical Tower of Babel, but also it shows differences far too significant to be ignored. We wonder if the two versions of the legend were developed separately for thousands of years, and if, before then, they both originated from the same ancient ancestor.

The galleries of the Great Pyramid of Cholula are not very ancient. Archaeological excavations revealed that it was not the work of a single dynasty (like the pyramids of Egypt) but was built over a period of about two thousand years. The extended construction of this ziggurat was a collective project of different cultures, such as the Olmec, Toltec, Teotihuacan, Zapotec, Mixtec, Cholula, and Aztec. The main building is the oldest one and consists of a high conical pyramid with a flat top, where once stood a temple. Much later another conical pyramid was built over the top, raising the platform of the temple more than sixty meters above the surrounding plain. Then, after about fifteen hundred years, four or five other cultures broadened the base in various stages without increasing the height. Today, its sides measure 460 meters at the base, about twice that of the Pyramid of Giza, and its volume is three million cubic meters, making it one of the largest buildings ever built on Earth.

According to archaeologists only a handful of Mexican monuments date back over two thousand years ago, and Cholula is definitely one of them. Indeed, no one can say with certainty what remote epoch saw the raising of its ramparts. Apparently, for thousands of years before the town truly began to develop and expand (about 300 BCE), where the great ziggurat now stands was another, much older building.

More of the remains of ancient civilization scattered throughout Central America still await discovery. Just south of the University of Mexico City in Cuicuilco, beside the main road linking the capital to Cuernavaca, stands a highly complex circular, stepped pyramid with four galleries and a central staircase (figure 3.4). There are visible traces of massive paved roads that allowed easy access to the site. It was not until the 1920s that the blanket of lava that had completely buried three sides of the pyramid (and continue covering about ninety-five square kilometers of the surrounding area) was partially removed. Geologists who intervened on the spot carried out a thorough examination and dated the lava emitted by the volcano Ajusco—to their great surprise, they concluded that the volcanic eruption must have happened at least seven thousand years ago.[40]

Figure 3.4. Circular, stepped pyramid found in Mexico City in the twenties.

Historians and archaeologists who deny the possibility of the existence of an ancient civilization capable of building such a pyramid in Mexico are apparently ignoring this geological data. However, it is worth noting that Byron Cummings (the American archaeologist who initially excavated the area on behalf of the National Geographic Society) was convinced by the clearly demarcated layers above and below the pyramid that this is "the oldest temple ever discovered in the Americas." He categorically stated that this temple "tumbled down about eight thousand years ago."[41]

Olmec Centers

One of the oldest and most mysterious civilizations of the New World, the Olmecs inhabited the area between Veracruz and the Gulf of Mexico. Their name in Nahuatl means "people of the rubber," and that is how the Aztecs referred to the population of this area when it fell under their control. Here they extracted latex from *Castiglia elastica,* a type of rubber tree. We do not know, though, if the Olmecs called themselves the same name.

The Olmecs flourished during what is called the pre-classical period between 1400 BCE and 100 CE. Then, mysteriously disappearing, they were absorbed by later cultures. The Aztecs recalled the Olmecs in their hunting legends and found many of their ritual objects, which they gathered and placed in prominent places in the temples.

The Coatzacoalcos River flowed through the Olmec lands, ending up in the Gulf of Mexico near the homonymous town whose name means "shrine of the snake." According to tradition, it was at the mouth of Coatzacoalcos that Quetzalcòatl and his companions landed in Mexico. They arrived by sea on ships "whose sides shone like the scales of the snakes' skin" and would set sail from the same place at the time of leaving Central America.[42]

Many Olmec sculptures have been unearthed in Tres Zapotes, one of the last Olmec centers located southwest of Santiago Tuxtla and west of Coatzacoalcos, as well as in San Lorenzo and La Venta, respectively southward and eastward. Some of these monoliths made of basalt and similar resistant materials represent giant heads and weigh up to thirty tons. Others are huge scenes of battle between two different races of men, neither of them native. Besides these works, there is nothing from which one can infer the characteristics and origins of their craftsmen.

At the center of the park in the *zócalo,* the main square of Santiago Tuxtla, in the state of Veracruz, Mexico, a monumental sculpture is exhibited that is three meters high and weighs over thirty tons. Representing an African head covered by a helmet, this sculpture depicts a person with unmistakable Negroid features of fleshy lips and a flat nose (figure 3.5). His proud expression is the enigma of its origin, because Africans were not known to have lived in America until the advent of the slave trade!

Figure 3.5. Olmec head.

Tres Zapotes flourished between 500 BCE and 100 CE. Before 1940, when this site was excavated, it was commonly thought that the Mayan civilization was the oldest in the Americas. The news caused a sensation because it showed that <u>the Olmec, and not the Maya, were the "mother culture" of Central America</u>: they were the inventors of the calendar, with its system of annotation points and bars, and its start date August 13, 3114 BCE, and its "catastrophic" end after 2012 CE.

Also in Tres Zapotes some toys emerged in the shape of small dogs "on wheels," which contradicted the academic thesis that the wheel was unknown to pre-Columbian Central Americans.

Carbon-14 dating tells us that the current San Lorenzo houses the oldest Olmec site on the mainland, but this city *cannot* be the site of development of their civilization, <u>because in the city's early days this civilization was already fully developed and evolved</u>. Archaeologists have not yet found evidence of Olmec development—it is as if this population appeared out of nowhere!

In 1966, Michael Coe discovered over twenty reservoirs in San Lorenzo connected by a network of ducts lined with basalt. Water flows there during the rainy season, but we still do not understand their purpose.

In the same site there were found five huge Negroid-featured sculptures buried along specific alignments. Within these "tombs" there were more than sixty precious objects, artifacts, and figurines, some of them mutilated before burial. The only clue to the age of the findings is suggested by the presence of carbon (C-14) dated to around 1200 BCE. Unfortunately, the coal tells us about the burial date but says nothing about the age of the objects' production.

Another city symbol of the Olmec civilization is La Venta, excavated by Matthew Stirling between 1940 and 1943. According to carbon-14 dating the Olmecs settled in this city between 1500 and 1100 BCE and remained there until about 400 BCE. Then, suddenly, construction activity was halted, all buildings were destroyed as part of religious ceremonies, and enormous stone heads were buried at San Lorenzo.

La Venta graves, carefully arranged and very elaborate, were lined with thousands of tiny blue tiles and filled with layers of colored clay. Three

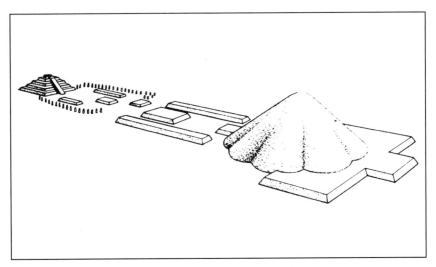

Figure 3.6. Reconstruction of La Venta: note the unusual grooved, cone-shaped pyramid that overlooks the site. Courtesy of Graham Hancock, Fingerprints of the Gods.

mosaic floors have also been found buried beneath several alternating layers of clay and adobe. The main pyramid stands at the southern end of the settlement: roughly circular at the base, it has the shape of a grooved cone with a rounded surface consisting of ten vertical layers separated by gullies (figure 3.6). The pyramid is thirty meters high with a diameter of sixty meters and a total mass of ninety thousand cubic meters.

The rest of the settlement extends for almost half a kilometer along an axis that points eight degrees northwest—on this line there are other smaller pyramids that in all cover an area of five square kilometers. La Venta is classified a "center of Olmec worship," but with many uncertainties since nothing is known about Olmec traditions. From what we've seen, it seems that even the enigmatic giant heads are not their work, but that of a previous population. These huge heads depicting men with typically African traits—broad, flat nose, full lips, and square denture—are just like the face of the Sphinx. Some men, however, appeared to be Cro-Magnon: tall, with delicate facial features, long noses, straight hair, and bushy beards. They would have been identified as "Mediterranean" rather than indigenous.

Next to the Great Pyramid of La Venta, at ground level, we can see a fence about a foot high that defines a rectangular area as large as a quarter of an average block. When archaeologists began to dig up this thread, it was discovered that it was the top of a wall made up of more than six hundred columns three meters high placed so close together as to form an impenetrable fence. The columns, made of basalt boulders weighing about two tons each, were transported to La Venta from quarries more than ninety kilometers away. The fence must have provided protection for something that was very important!

Matthew Stirling's research discovered here a huge stele (carved or inscribed stone slab or pillar) four meters high, two meters wide, and almost ninety centimeters thick. The reliefs depict the encounter between two tall men, both wearing elaborate clothes and stylish shoes with upturned toes. One of the two figures is completely disfigured, while the other clearly depicts a Cro-Magnon male with high nose line and long beard. The racial likelihood is too precise to be due to the artist's creativity.

Following in the Olmecs' footsteps, we head southeast and arrive at the artificially flattened top of a hill overlooking Oaxaca: Mount Albàn, a site dating to around 1000 BCE, consisting of a huge area bounded by groups of pyramids and other buildings arranged in precise geometric terms. Next to the pyramids is an observatory: the arrow-shaped building inclined at an angle of forty-five degrees to the main axis contains several tunnels and steep stairways that open up to view different areas in the sky.

At the side of a pyramid a dozen carved steles depicting men with Cro-Magnon or Negroid features are stacked. The Olmecs' fall is reflected in the stone: compared to those of La Venta, indeed, here the steles are more approximate and less worked, and yet they try to portray the same subject. One stele is engraved with a text of undeciphered glyphs, considered the oldest form of writing in Mexico.

Some researchers want to see in them the Phoenicians—even though not really faithfully depicted—who passed from the Mediterranean through Gibraltar and into the Atlantic Ocean at the end of the second millennium BCE, bringing Negroid slaves who were later portrayed in the huge heads. It is a shame that in all places where Phoenicians had been there are abundant examples of their crafts, with the unique exception of Central America.

More accountable is the theory of the "hypothetical third element," which says ancient Mexican civilization could not have been born without an external impulse, nor have risen without the contact of peoples of the Old World. It is likely that cultures of the Old and New Worlds, in ancient times, inherited ideas and traditions from a third element.

If so, we would expect to find similarities between different cultures affected by the same influence. Both Egyptians and Olmecs were particularly interested in dwarves, considered as directly related to the gods. In the Early Dynastic Period of Egypt (more than 4,500 years ago) priests celebrated the cult of nine deities, the Ennead, and similarly, both the Aztecs and Mayans believed in a system of nine gods. Another common presence is the concept of "astral rebirth," namely the reincarnation of the dead into stars, which required the use of ritual magic spells. According to the ancient peoples of Central America the afterlife consisted of nine stages that the dead had to cross in four years, overcoming obstacles and dangers. The dead in late Egyptian religion had to face the same obstacles: once cleared, those who got through were allowed entrance to the next "division" of the underworld. In both the Americas and Egypt it was believed that the soul was transported from one stage to another on a boat, accompanied by rowers. In both civilizations, the king enjoyed a privileged status that allowed him to skip the tests in hell and go straight to the sky thanks to a ceremony presided over by a priest and his four assistants. In Egypt, to ensure the resurrection of the pharaoh, a priest opened the mouth with a ritual cutting tool called *peshenkhef*, often in a gathering in an inner chamber of the Great Pyramid. In Mexico human sacrifice inside a pyramid was rather widespread—here the victim's body was struck with a sacrificial knife to allow the soul to ascend directly to heaven. The most amazing coincidence is that the generic term for "sacrifice" in all Central America was *p'achi*, literally "to open the mouth." Excluding the direct contact between these peoples, it is arguable that these similarities are the remains of a common heritage received from a single ancestor.

Palenque

The Mayan temple of Palenque, in the state of Chiapas, has three rooms and rises above a pyramid with nine steps, thirty meters high. Next to this temple is the palace, a vast complex sitting on a triangular base characterized by a narrow four-story tower that was probably used as an observatory by Mayan priests. Entering the main room of the temple, on the back wall are two gray slabs with 620 Mayan hieroglyphs depicting faces, both human and monstrous, together with a bestiary of mythical creatures.

WHY IS IT CERTAIN? No one knows for sure what they mean because they have not yet been completely deciphered; what is certain is that they refer to epochs of thousands of years ago and tell of gods and people who had taken part in prehistoric events.

To the left of the hieroglyphics, among the huge stones that pave the floor, is a steep staircase that leads into the core of the pyramid—the tomb of King Pacal. The narrow stairs made of limestone blocks, dangerously wet and slippery, remained inaccessible from the time they were sealed in 683 CE until 1952, when the archaeologist Alberto Ruz lifted the huge plates that covered the floor. The space had been intentionally filled with rubble by its builders, and it took the archaeologists about four years to empty it and reach the bottom, where they were faced with five or six skeletons of young sacrificial victims strewn across the floor of the room. In the back of the room they discovered another triangular stone slab—when Ruz moved it, he found a tomb that he himself called extraordinary: "A huge room that seemed carved in the ice, a sort of cave in which the surfaces of walls and ceiling had been completely leveled, or an abandoned chapel with dome draped with curtains of stalactites, while from the floor rose stalagmites likewise the candle dripping."[43]

The room's walls were adorned with stucco bas-reliefs depicting an ennead of nine deities watching over the night hours. At the center, guarded by these figures, was a huge, carefully carved monolithic sarcophagus covered with a slab of stone weighing about five tons. Inside a tall skeleton ascribable to Pacal, ruler in the seventh century BCE, was surrounded by ornaments of jade, and fixed to his forehead was a funeral mosaic mask composed of two hundred pieces of jade. The engravings say that the monarch had died at the age of eighty years, but the body found by archaeologists belonged to a man of about forty.

The sarcophagus of the monarch has a typically Egyptian form, considerably expanding at the base. The Egyptian versions, however, had this shape because they were placed vertically, whereas the Mayan types were made of massive stone and therefore could only be placed horizontally. Yet why did Mayan artisans bother with broadening the bases if there was no utility? One possible answer suggests again that the Maya had acquired an earlier tradition without understanding the real reason and use of it.

Do we still need to whisper, afraid of being laughed at, the name of Atlantis? Or can we now speak loudly, or even shout? Well, I suggest following all the Pelasgian's routes, even those addressed to the other side of the Atlantic. Moreover, I would recommend going beyond the Pillars of Eratosthenes, well established in Gibraltar. We are moving there, in any case, because in Crete I will introduce the greatest of the kings descended from Atlantis, and let you admire his palace and his maze, but beware, do not enter disarmed—it could be still awake, the Minotaur . . .

4

THE KINGDOMS OF THE MEDITERRANEAN AFTER THE FIRST FLOOD

Brothers will battle to bloody end,
and sisters' sons their kin betray;
woe's in the world, much wantonness;
Axe-age, sword-age—sundered are shields—
Wind-age, wolf-age, ere the world crumbles;
Will the spear of no man spare the other.

THE PROPHECY OF THE SEERESS—
VǪLUSPÁ, VERSE 45

THE KINGDOM OF MINOS

Today we know a multifaceted hero, someone who is far more powerful than Superman or Spider-Man!

His nom de plume is Minos, as they knew him in Crete, where he reigned as king.

During the Victorian era, an Englishman called Arthur Evans did the first excavations of the great Cretan palaces and discovered the palace of Knossos and its inhabitants, baptized "Minoans," supposedly in honor of their personal king. Indeed, these Minoans had not always lived in Crete, and before 2300 BCE—when they arrived on the island—perhaps they would have said that Minos reigned elsewhere, in their old land.

Where exactly we do not know, but at that time there were two peoples hurrying into a forced exile. The Ichnusians were leaving Sardinia* in those years, while the Sicels were leaving the lower Lazio: the Peoples of the Sea had arrived! The Shardanas, the first invaders, gave their name to Sardinia, the "old" Ichnusa; the second were Sabines, a people who were the basis of the foundation of the future Rome. The former occupants were cast out and so took the sea route: the Ichnusians arrived in Tuscany, and we bet *they* were the Etruscans' ancestors!

The Sicels were divided between Umbria and Sicily, but we also know that someone reached up and came to mingle with the Illyrians on the Balkan Peninsula, leaving clear traces in the Illyrian and Albanian languages. We now focus on the Ichnusians in Crete, due to the statues of mother goddesses produced by both peoples, so similar to each other, even if rougher among the first and more sophisticated during the Minoan period (figure 4.1).

It seems Ichnusians used the universal form of writing, Iberian, which we mentioned at the beginning of the previous chapter. That writing would have arrived in Crete and with minimal modifications become the written language of the Minoan people, Cretan Linear A.

Figure 4.2 shows a list of Iberian signs extracted from Pozzomaggiore pottery, the engraving on the tomb of Perdu Pes (Paulilatino), Pallosu's ring seal, the pot of Arzachena's "meeting hut," Norbello Stone, Allai's pendant, and many more. We invite you to look at chapter 8, page 240, where you can read a comparative chart between Iberian and other writing systems.

According to the Cretans, Minos ruled over the island of Crete and the Cyclades from the palace of Knossos, and he was so bold as to

---

*The island of Sardinia was known as Ichnusa by the Greeks and the Romans.

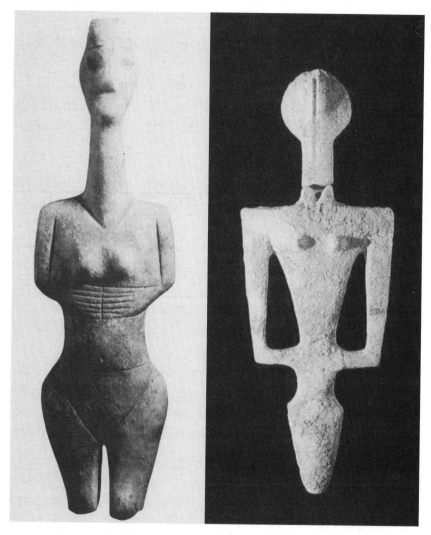

Figure 4.1. Ichnusian mother goddess (right), compared to a mother goddess of the Cyclades (left).

betray the sea god, Poseidon. Actually, many have betrayed this god, like Homer's Ulysses, who, for having taken him in, wandered for ten years throughout the Mediterranean and smashed his fleet. Perhaps the doom of Minos was even worse—at least most humiliating—because Poseidon made his wife Pasiphae fall in love with a sacred bull, thus conceiving the terrible Minotaur.

The Minoans had set Minos's deeds in their new land, but those

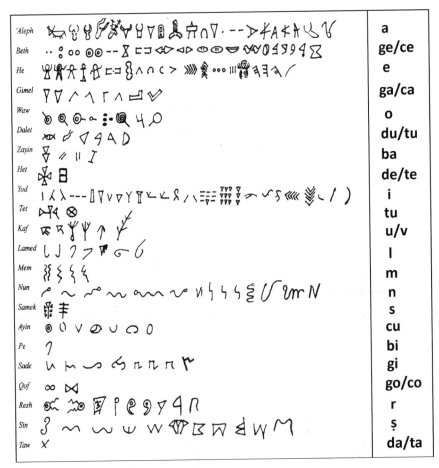

Figure 4.2. Iberian writing characters found in Sardinia on over sixty items including bronzes, seals, and pendants, as well as engraved on the stones of nuraghes and holy wells. (The nuraghe, an ancient megalithic building found in Sardinia, developed during the Nuragic Age between 1900 and 730 BCE.) On the left the letters correspond to the Aramaic alphabet.
Source: L. Melis, Shardana Jenesi degli Urim.

deeds take us back thousands of years, when the Pelasgians had passed Gibraltar and slowly reached out eastward.

Minos had grown up with his mother, Europe, and his stepfather, the Pelasgian king Asterius, son of king Tectamus, who first pushed the Pelasgians to Crete around 10,500 BCE.[1] It is said that Minos built a vast maze to hide the Minotaur and the work was commissioned to an architect named Daedalus.* When the fame of Daedalus arrived in Egypt, King Menes commissioned him to build a maze that served as a tomb in the "city of crocodiles," now a heap of ruins at the oasis of El Faijum.†2

A temple, still visible at the time of Diodorus (Herodotus, book 2, 99; book 1, in the end), was dedicated to Daedalus in the territories nearby Memphis. According to Plato (Alcibiades), Daedalus was the son of Vulcan and therefore of Pelasgian race. Remember that the expression "sons of Vulcan" indicated the Cyclops, which we have already identified with the Pelasgians. After leaving Crete he lived in Sicily at the court of King Kokalos, for whom he erected numerous works. In the territory of Megaride are the remains of a basin that has been attributed to him, called the Colimberta; in the area surrounding Agrigento there are memories of a fortress that was considered impregnable due to tortuous access defensible by three or four persons. Daedalus was credited with creating a thermal bath in Selinunte as well as the Temple of Venus Ericina in Erice, and many buildings in Sardinia (see Diodorus Siculus, *Library*, book 4).

Are we really talking about *that* Menes, the first pharaoh of Egypt? Certainly not: the real name of that pharaoh was Narmer, and "Menes" was used only as a pharaoh's title, as it was for Osiris.

Now, it is clear that King Menes and Minos had to be contemporaries, belonging to the same period as Daedalus. Might it be the same

---

*According to Diodorus and Herodotus, the oldest monument in Egypt was the shrine of Sokar, a god who was known by Greeks as Vulcan, built at Memphis by Daedalus in the same period. The architect was considered one of the oldest and most famous visitors of Egypt and was revered as a god. According to Plato, Daedalus was the son of Vulcan and so of Pelasgian race (the expression "sons of Vulcan" indicated the Cyclops, which we have already identified with the Pelasgians).

†Right in Crocodilopolis the Shardana mercenaries held their strongholds during Ramses' reign (Frau, 441). This is probably no coincidence.

king who dominated the Mediterranean thousands of years before Rome? In book 19 of *The Odyssey,* Homer writes:

> *In the city of Knossos*
> *between Pelasgians and the magnanimous Cretans*
> *the illustrious wisdom of Menes reigns*
> *inspired by God every nine years*
> *mysteriously and with thundering voice . . .*

Here Minos is precisely called the name "Menes" and the term "Pelasgians" is explicitly used. The fourth verse refers to the myth:

Androgeus, son of Minos, he went to Aegeus, king of Athens, and won all Panathenaic games. Out of jealousy and suspecting a friendship between Androgeus and his brother Pallas's fifty rebel sons, Aegeus assassinated him. This was the cause of the war Plato writes about, between the Pelasgians and Greece. Minos gathered fleets from every corner of the Mediterranean, defeated Athens, and asked, as a ransom of war, the delivery of seven boys and seven maidens to feed the Minotaur, every nine years. It was Aegeus's son and successor Theseus who reversed the tide of the war. He himself went to Crete, killed the Minotaur, and put an end to the sacrifice, handing the domination of the seas to the city of Athens.

Let's now open *Suda* or *Suidas,* a Greek historical encyclopedia of the tenth century relating to the ancient Mediterranean world with thirty thousand entries, many taken from ancient sources now lost, relevant to geography, history, literature, philosophy, science, grammar, and customs. We find further information on Menes directly drawn from the Etruscans' sacred books—Acherontic, Augural, and Tagetic texts. Here we read that Menes was also called Mestre as well as Egypt, and that the country was indeed named after him.*

---

*Correspondence with Genesis's Mizraim can be explained by Mizraim and Egypt having identified the same territory, but with different languages.

According to tradition, Egypt/Menes had a twin brother, Danaus.

When his father Belo* died, Menes inherited the kingdom and conquered the land of the Melampodes ("black, trampled-mud-colored feet") called Egypt. The brothers quarreled over the inheritance, and Menes proposed to a reconciliation marriage between his fifty sons and Danaus's fifty daughters (the Danaides).† The latter, however, suspected a trick that was confirmed by an oracle, so he fled to Greece with his children, where he completed an omen and became king of Argos. His daughters took to Greece the mysteries of Isis (Demeter), and Danaus became so powerful that from then on all Greek Pelasgians called themselves "Danais."‡

Menes's fifty sons came to Argos with the intent to punish Danaus, hiding behind the pretext of marriage. Danaus seemed to fall into the trap but gave his daughters a needle to pierce the heart of the bridegroom during the wedding night. So the children of Menes were murdered and Danaus arranged a running competition to choose the new spouses from among the natives. Meanwhile, Menes arrived in Greece, but once he discovered his children's fate, he fled to Aroe, where he died.

We cannot help but notice the recurrence of certain themes: in both cases there are fifty children who undermine the reign of a Greek king (as the fifty sons of Pallas, King Aegeus's brother) and both involve the assassination of the royal progeny connected to sporting events (Androgeus, son of Minos, went to Aegeus, king of Athens, and won all the Panathenaic games but was assassinated, and Danaus arranged a running competition to choose the new spouses from among the natives, the result of which was the murder of Menes's fifty sons).

---

*The name "Belo" goes back to the Baal of the Old Testament and to the Bel of the Apocrypha Gospels, assuming the name of the Sumerian goddess of the moon, called Belili.
†The number fifty is symbolic because there were fifty priestesses of the lunar goddess Danae. Danae is considered the daughter of Danaus and is identified with the Akkadian goddess Daminka and with Dinah from Genesis, thereafter masculinized into Dan.
‡In other traditions we read that "Dana" was the title given to the grandchildren generated by the union of the fifty native daughters with their indigenous husbands.

Let us now look at Menes and Minos's mothers. The traditions collected in Egypt by Herodotus, Diodorus, and Strabo say that Menes was the son of the Pelasgian Io (Isis), which corresponds to the Mizraim of chapter 10 of Genesis, the name by which the Egyptians called their homeland.

> Io was the princess of Argos and Litto nymph in Crete, her name for the Argives meant "Moon." Zeus fell in love with her and transformed her into a white cow to hide her from his wife Hera. Yet, the latter managed to imprison her; Zeus freed her with the help of Hermes, but Hera sent a gadfly to sting her which urged her to an erratic flight which ended in Egypt, where Zeus restored her human form.[3]

Diodorus Siculus shows a second version, according to which Menes was born of an unknown daughter of the king of Memphis who was in love with the Nile River, which had assumed the form of a bull.[4] Here again we find Crete, Egypt, and the story of Io, which resembles very much the story of Europe, Minos's mother, whose Greek name is synonymous with full moon: Zeus turned into a white bull and asked Hermes to help him lead Europe on a beach in Crete and rape her. As a result of the violence, she gave birth to Minos, Rhadamanthus, and Sarpedon.

Although there is certain confusion between the cities of Athens and Argos we believe that at this point we can consider Menes and Minos as the same person. Since these are events that occurred at around 10,000 BCE, it is reasonable to assume that upon hearing the story of a big city's feats both the natives of Argos and Athens wanted to be assigned such inheritance.

So the murder of Minos's royal progeny at the hand of his brother Danaus (or Aegeus) sparked the war between the Pelasgians of Atlantis and Athens, ending with the temporary subjection of the latter. In *Timaeus* Plato tells us the same story, with Theseus's Athens redeeming itself by stopping Menes's Pelasgians who had just occupied Egypt and were waging war on Greece:

> This vast power, gathered into one, endeavored to subdue at a blow our country and yours and the whole of the region within the

straits; and then, Solon, your country shone forth, in the excellence of her virtue and strength, among all mankind. She was preeminent in courage and military skill, and was the leader of the Hellenes. And when the rest fell off from her, being compelled to stand alone, after having undergone the very extremity of danger, she defeated and triumphed over the invaders, and preserved from slavery those who were not yet subjugated, and generously liberated all the rest of us who dwell within the pillars.[5]

Some authors argue that the name "Danais" was used by Atlanteans before the rise of Danaus; in this case, it would seem that the name was likely affixed to the crown prince. Menes would thus be an illegitimate sovereign, which would force the true king to flee to Greece. With Danaus taking power and organizing the resistance, the victory in Athens would in fact have been the victory of the legitimate royal descendant.

Tradition has it that by the next generation the kingdom had passed to Deucalion, son of Minos, the "survivor" of the flood in the Greek myth.

In other traditions, Deucalion is the son of the Pelasgian Prometheus, who along with Atlas was one of the ten kings of Atlantis Plato has described. We do not really need a DNA test because Prometheus does look like Menes.

Prometheus had lived at the time of the revolt of the Pelasgians (Titans) against the gods, which went down in history as Minos's revolt against Danaus. Chroniclers remember with awe his behavior when, conscious of the battle result, he left the Pelasgians and sided with the gods! Let's imagine that the reporters have had some confusion between father and son; perhaps it was Deucalion who moved onto the side of his uncle Danaus. A link between Prometheus and Minos can be found in the episode of the sacrifice of a bull:

Prometheus was invited to act as arbiter. He therefore flayed and jointed a bull, and sewed its hide to form two open-mouthed bags, filling these with what he had cut up. One bag contained all the flesh, but this he concealed beneath the stomach, which is the least tempting part of any animal; and the other contained the bones, hidden beneath a rich layer of fat. When he offered Zeus the choice of either, Zeus, easily deceived, chose the bag containing the bones and fat [. . .] but punished Prometheus by withholding fire from mankind.

This saga of punishments ended with the opening of Pandora's Jar.[6]

Minos was instead punished by Poseidon for not having sacrificed the sacred bull, which had appeared from the sea as a sign of his right to the throne, deceptively replacing it with another bull from the pen.[7] The exchange of roles between Poseidon and Zeus is of little interest here since the Pelasgians worshiped a single god whose characteristics were shared among various entities only in historical times. Paula Philippson, in *Origini e forme del mito greco* (Origins and Forms of the Greek Myth), proves clearly that in the original, more ancient cult, Zeus and Poseidon were identified as one and the same.

During Deucalion's kingdom the second major episode of ice melting of the last ice age, and the beginning of the decadence of the Pelasgians, took place. This was around 10,000 BCE and the episode is described in *Timaeus:* "But afterwards there occurred violent earthquakes and floods; and in a single day and night of misfortune all your warlike men in a body sank into the earth, and the island of Atlantis in like manner disappeared in the depths of the sea."[8]

Meanwhile, we have removed one of Menes's masks, or should we say Minos, or Prometheus, king of Atlantis. Patiently, we will remove one after another, recognizing in him Osiris, Hercules, Janus, Dionysus, and Bacchus.

THE WAR AFTER THE ETERNAL WINTER

In the era immediately following the first flood (13,000 BCE) an empire would extend on the Mediterranean coasts, overwhelmed toward its end by a dynastic war between the brother "princes" Menes and Danaus; the end will be marked by the second flood, in about 9600 BCE. In the myths of Egypt, such a war is fought between the brothers Seth and Osiris, the first playing the role of Danaus, the second the role of Menes, with the

latter's son, <u>Horus, in the end—just like Deucalion—getting the throne.</u>
Further north, the story is remembered with more details from the Norse
people and the war is called <u>"Ragnarök."</u>

The version that came to us was not written until the ninth century, during the Christianization of northern Europe, whose influence
has affected it considerably, especially in the similarities with the book of
Revelation of St. John the Evangelist. Like the former it is written in the form
of a vision and revelation of the future. Its composition is lost in the mists of
time: it is difficult to say whether we should trace it back to the Pelasgians,
the first settlers of northern Europe and possible builders of the stone circles, or to the Germanic peoples who settled in those areas in 3000 BCE.

The Ragnarök is the final battle between the bastions of light and
order, the Aesir (the gods of Greek myth), against the powers of darkness and chaos, the Giants (the Titans of Greek myth). French mytholo-
gist Georges Dumézil has highlighted the strong similarities between
the Ragnarök and the battle between Pāndava and Kaurava in Hindu
mythology, as it is narrated in the Mahābhārata. While the Ragnarök
is set in the future, the similar epic battle of the Mahābhārata is set in
the past.

After the fight the whole world will be destroyed—by the 9600 BCE
flood, we assume—*and later it will be regenerated.* The name is composed
of *ragna,* the genitive plural of *regin* (gods, organized powers), and *rök*
(fate, destiny, wonders)—later confused with *røkkr* (twilight)—which
means of "the fate of the gods." The French historian Claude Lecouteux
suggests the translation "judgment of the divine powers." *Ragnarøkkr,*
however, means "twilight of the gods," a mistranslation made famous by
Richard Wagner's opera *Götterdämmerung.* The story has come down to
us mainly through three Norse poems:

- *Völuspá* ("The Prophecy of the Seer")
- *Vafþrúðnismál* ("Vafþrúðnir's Sayings")
- *Gylfaginning* ("The Deception of Gylfi")

<u>*The Ragnarök will be preceded by Fimbulvetr, a terrible winter.*</u> We
have seen such a climatic event in Greek myths, the Indian *Vedas,* and

in Antarctic geology describing a paradisiacal land trapped in an "eternal winter." Under those circumstances human nerves must have ceded because <u>the Fimbulvetr appears to be the cause of the collapse of social and family ties in a whirlwind of blood and violence beyond every law and rule.</u>

After the Fimbulvetr, Sól and Máni disappear. Sól is the goddess of the sun: every day she rides in the sky on her chariot pulled by two horses called Alsviðr and Árvakr and is constantly chased by Sköll, a wolf that wants to devour her. John foresees the sad fate of Sól in his Revelation (12:1–4)*:

> In the sky there appeared a great sign: a woman clothed with the sun, the moon under her feet and on her head a crown of twelve stars. She was pregnant and cried out in her pangs and pains of childbirth. Then another sign appeared in heaven: an enormous red dragon with seven heads and ten horns, and seven diadems on his heads, his tail swept down a third of the stars of heaven and cast them to the ground. The dragon stood before the woman who was about to give birth, to devour her new born child.

The twelve stars represent the zodiac and the woman in labor is the Sun, which is about to be devoured (by a dragon instead of a wolf) upon the birth of a new zodiacal era (specifying which era it was). Máni is the moon, also chased by a wolf, Hati (note the link between the name Máni/Menes and the moon, or the bull, whose horns simulate the scythe).

Preceding Ragnarök the two wolves will reach the two stars and devour them, depriving the world of the natural light. Even the stars will turn off. The poets have certainly implied a little fantasy in this story, yet the sky was really obscured by the abundant emission of volcanic ash at the end of the ice age.

---

*Revelation is believed to have been written by St. John the Evangelist during his confinement on the island of Patmos (94–95 CE), at the time of Christian persecution by Emperor Domitian. However, in its 405 verses, we find at least 219 quotations from the Old Testament, especially Isaiah, Zechariah, Ezekiel, and Daniel, so that one can assume that the information encoded herein may come from a distant past.

Yggdrasil, the cosmic tree, the axis of the earth, will shake, and all boundaries will be dissolved: earthquakes, floods, and natural disasters will follow. The creatures of chaos will attack the world: the wolf Fenrir will be released from his chain, while the snake Miðgarðsormr will emerge from the depths of the waters. Here we find the story of a beast coming from the sea as told by John. The ship Naglfar raises anchor to take the destructive powers to war; at the helm is the god Loki. Heimdallr, the white guardian god, blows his horn, the Gjallarhorn, to call Odin to the final battle together with the Eihnerjar, the other gods and warriors of Valhalla (the residence of the gloriously dead in battle).

The plain of Vígríðr will be the scene of the great final battle: each deity will face up to its nemesis, in a mutual destruction, until Surtr, the giant of fire from the land of flames, will fire up the world with his flaming sword. It is curious that Genesis (3:24) also talks of a flaming sword: located east of Eden after the expulsion of Adam and Eve, it preserved the gateway to the "tree of the Knowledge of Good and Evil." Despite the difficulty in supposing a link with the events of the world, there are other texts about world mythology where the association is obvious. We always talk about a beast corrupting the first couple, which lies between the fronds of the cosmic tree, which is the same as Yggdrasill.[9]

When the combat of Vígríðr ends the world will rise from its ashes. Baldr, the god of hope, and Hodra, his brother, will return to Hel, the realm of death. On the grass of the new meadows they will find the chess pieces with which the disappeared gods used to play. Here it is possible to spot a remarkable similarity with the second coming of Christ as described in John's Revelation. The rebirth of the world, however, is overshadowed by the high-flying Níðhöggr, a mysterious serpent—a European Quetzalcòatl—that will carry dead bodies among its feathers.

As promised, we now unhinge the Revelation (4:2, 4:4, 4:6–8), keeping an eye to figure 4.3, and find the exact zodiacal era during which the Fimbulvetr occured:

Immediately I was in ecstasy. And there was a throne in the sky, and on the throne sat one. Around the throne there were twenty-four seats and on the seats were twenty-four elders, clothed in white robes with

Figure 4.3. The evangelists combined with the corresponding constellations, clockwise from top left: Marcus (Leo), John (Eagle-Scorpio), Matthew (Man-Aquarius), and Luke (Calf-Taurus).

golden crowns on their heads. Before the throne there was a transparent sea like crystal. In the midst of the throne and around the throne there were four beasts full of eyes before and behind. The first beast was like a lion, the second beast looked like a calf, the third had the look of a living man, the fourth beast was like a flying eagle. The four living creatures, each having six wings, around and inside are full of eyes; day and night they shall not cease repeating: Holy, holy, holy Lord God Almighty, Who was and Who is and Who will be!

The twenty-four elders represent the binary subdivisions of the twelve houses of the zodiac, and the four living creatures are the constellations that "govern" the world at a given time, or better the constellations preceding the sun, rising a few minutes before sunrise at the equinoxes and solstices. The many eyes they have, in front and back, represent the stars. The wings are the subdivisions of the houses: these are important, as a house of the zodiac corresponds to thirty degrees on the ecliptic, which the sun crosses in 2,160 years during the precession's apparent motion.* One-sixth of the house corresponds to 360 years, a numerical value that returns to the complete ecliptic, 360 degrees; it is for this similarity that such a time takes on a symbolic meaning.

The first "beast" is certainly the constellation of Leo, and the second is Taurus. The third can be traced to the constellation of Aquarius, which has always been represented with a man carrying a pitcher of water and associated with an angelic creature by archaic and classical iconography. The fourth is Scorpio, which, from time immemorial, bears the double name of Scorpio and Eagle.[10] The same four "beasts" can be found in the twenty-first tarot: The World (plate 16). These constellations were later adopted as symbols of the four evangelists, but they were also the constellations that would hold the world between 8500 BCE and 10,700 BCE: an age that bridges the second flood and is subsequent to the eternal winter that trapped Antarctica. These are the years involved in the astronomical alignments of Giza, Angkor, Tiahuanaco, Mnajdra (in Malta), and Dashur and the geological dating of megalithic temples of Egypt such as Osirion, the Valley Temple of Chepren, and the Sphinx Temple. What an amazing coincidence! Egyptians call this epoch Zep Tepi, which means "First Time," and it represents the starting point from which to calculate the dates of subsequent prophecies.

---

*Every year on a specific date the sun rises in a slightly different position from the previous year, moving one degree every seventy-two years (2,160 years, 30 degrees) from one zodiacal house to another, or changing the constellation that forms the background to its rising. The passing of the constellations along this cycle is reversed with respect to the flow of the annual zodiac signs. Over 25,920 years the sun passes through all twelve constellations, completing the cycle of precession.

Let's look now at the sixth era (1-Leo*, 2-Cancer, 3-Gemini, 4-Taurus, 5-Aries, 6-Pisces): it began in the first century BCE and perhaps it is for this reason that the first Christians used the symbol of a fish in place of the cross.

We start from here to comprehend the number of the beast, 666, which should be explained as "he who has understanding." The first 6 is the era we are already looking at, begun in the first century BCE and now running out of time; to obtain the second 6 we should look for the sixth of the aforementioned division (each of 360 years) which is the Pisces era. So, at the beginning of the sixth, we have 5 × 360 years = 1,800 years, and counting 1,800 years from the first century BCE we are between 1700 and 1800 CE. For the last 6 we need to repeat the division in sixths, not of the whole era, but of a portion of it, so 360 ÷ 6 = 60 years, and among these parts of 60 years we search for the beginning of the sixth one. So, we let 5 parts out of 6 pass in order to arrive at the beginning of the sixth: 5 × 60 years = 300 years. Last but not least, adding up these 300 years to those previously obtained (1,800), we get between 2000 and 2100 CE. Is it only a coincidence that the fateful 2012 falls within this time space?

A similar prophecy can be found in the Book of the Dead of Ancient Egypt: "Calculating and taking into account the days and the propitious hours of the stars of Orion and of the Twelve Gods that govern them, here are they joining hands palm to palm but the sixth between them hangs on the brink of the abyss in the hour of the devil's defeat."

This inscription was engraved on a block of bronze found at the foot of the statue of the god Osiris in the city of Khemenu (Letopolis), in Egypt, dating back to 2700 BCE. Here too we find mentioned the "twelve gods," representing the twelve houses of the zodiac, who, "joining hands palm to palm" (24 palms as the 24 elders), are combined to form the precessional period of 25,920 years (2,160 × 12). In Revelation, as well as in the Book of the Dead, we find the number six, namely the "sixth Divinity that hangs on the brink of the abyss." We already know what this represents: walking backward in the houses of the zodiac we

---

*During the Zep Tepi, Leo preceded the sunrise of the vernal equinox. By convention, in fact, the name of a zodiac era is given by the spring equinox constellation.

arrive again to our present time, to the ending of the Age of Pisces, "on the brink of the abyss."

At this point in the investigation, the time has come for us to look for answers under the sand in the land of the gods par excellence, the Egypt of Menes. First stop: Giza.

There are unpleasant tales of the Sphinx: whatever its original features were, a monarch ordered that they be replaced with his own in such a way that men might look at the colossus without fear. . . . It was then that the smile of the Sphinx vaguely displeased us, and made us wonder about the legends of subterranean passages beneath the monstrous creature, leading down, down, to depths none might dare hint at—depths connected with mysteries older than the dynastic Egypt we excavate . . .

H. P. LOVECRAFT, *FROM THE PYRAMIDS*

5

MEGALITHS AND GODS AMONG MEN IN THE TIME OF OSIRIS

Hermocrates: *As the waters rose around their city, the kings of Atlantis, one after another, sought to hold off fate. Knowing mortal men would never rule the sea, they planned a huge colossus, which by use of orichalcum, ten beads at a time, would make them like the gods themselves. Nur-Ab-Sal was one such king. He it was, say the wise men of Egypt, who first put men in the colossus, making many freaks of nature at times when the celestial spheres were well aligned.*
Socrates: *I doubt it. We're hearing a fairy tale.*

In front of the pyramids of Giza H. P. Lovecraft felt his dark imagination drawing him to the time of Queen Nitocris, who lived during the Sixth Dynasty and was buried alive in the pyramid of Menkaure. She had been punished for having organized a feast for her enemies in a temple on the Nile before opening the floodgates and drowning them. The Arabs carefully avoid approaching the pyramid during certain phases of the moon, scared by strange voices, while the boatmen of Memphis sing a lullaby:

> *The subterranean nymph that dwells*
> *between lightless gems and occult splendours*
> *The lady of the pyramid!*

We are in the furthest northern region of the two that naturally divide the country. Upper Egypt is a fertile valley about nine hundred kilometers long and five kilometers wide, where trading occurs and which is the "rich" area of the country. Lower Egypt, the floodplain, is a swampy area on the Nile delta that the Egyptians were able to turn into one of the most arable lands of the ancient world.

Narmer, a king of Upper Egypt called the Scorpion King and the first pharaoh to rule over Egypt, unified the country around 3100 BCE and founded the First Dynasty.*

Egyptian popular culture takes us back to previous millennia, telling of a time before the Pharaonic age when the country was ruled with great wisdom by "living gods" who came from the sea and brought civilization and knowledge.¹ In our studies we identify these "gods" as an ancient people of navigators who were the Pelasgians. In this chapter, we'll uncover the *fil rouge* (guiding thread) that connects this ancient civilization with the pharaohs' kingdom.

THE FIRST RULER

In spite of what Egyptologists claim, according to Egyptian popular culture the first ruler of Egypt was Osiris: together with his wife-sister Isis

---

*According to Mario Pincherle, Narmer would be the same Akkadian king called Naram-Sin who unified Egypt and Mesopotamia during his reign and in whose tomb seven hundred amphorae (large two-handled jars) were found that contained Canaanite-Mesopotamian wine. Another indication comes from the Book of the Dead discovered by Prince Herutataf (grandson of Menkaure) on a bronze plate at the foot of the statue of Osiris in the city of Letopolis. The inscription was unintelligible to the prince but quite clear to his helper, who had an Akkadian name, Nekhte. Hence we are perhaps looking at an Akkadian inscription in early Egypt.

he ruled with authority and wisdom over the country, <u>teaching the people</u> <u>agrarian techniques, vine cultivation, hunting, and writing.</u> Moreover, he required the Egyptians to learn and <u>encouraged them to study astronomy</u> <u>and architecture.</u>

According to the classic storytellers, Osiris was seen as the personification of the sun, the first inhabitant of Egypt together with its counterpart the moon, his sister Isis. <u>The two would arrive in Egypt from a</u> <u>distant land, along with other survivors of an ancient advanced civiliza-</u> <u>tion destroyed by a sudden flood.</u>

In acknowledgment of the great gifts that they gave to Egypt, the people decided to remember them after death by assigning them two figures depicted in the sky: Osiris in the constellation of Orion and Isis in the star Sirius.

After Osiris's death the Egyptian people remembered him on Earth as well, worshipping him as a "black oxen with a white spot on the head and on the back the figure of an eagle, thick-haired tail and a white mark on the right flank."[2] They would search for such an animal all over the kingdom and revere him until his death, after which a new example was found to succeed the previous one, continuing this endless cycle of life aimed at celebrating the immortality of Osiris.

A GREEK OSIRIS!

Leafing through the pages of a masterpiece such as the collection of myths by Robert Graves, we found an interesting Greek version of the story of Isis and Osiris. It is said that <u>the god-child Dionysus had been conceived</u> <u>by a loving relationship between the goddess Io (native of Argos and lover</u> <u>of Zeus) and the father of the gods himself.</u> Unfortunately, Zeus was married to a goddess, Hera, capable of killing out of jealousy, so that Io had to wander throughout the known world in search of a safe place to give birth to her son.

She crossed Dodona (in Epirus*), the Caucasus, Minor and Middle

---

*Epirus was in present-day southeastern Europe, shared between Greece and Albania; Bactria was in present-day northern Afghanistan.

Asia, Bactria, and India. Upon returning she crossed Arabia to arrive in Ethiopia, beyond the Strait of Bab El Mandab, the Red Sea. At the end of her long wandering she took refuge in Egypt, where she gave birth and founded the cult of Isis.[3]

In the Egyptian myth Isis had to seek shelter in the delta of the Nile near Heliopolis to give birth to her son Horus, far from the evil Seth.

The Argives had baptized the goddess "Io" because this was the name of the moon. The Egyptian Isis was connected with Sirius, but also with the moon, and often was represented as wearing horns whose shape resembled the crescent moon.

Diodorus Siculus[4] suspected that the two were in fact the same goddess and asserted that the birthplace of Isis had been "moved" to Argos by the Greeks. In another passage,[5] by invoking the ancient mythographers Eumolpus and Orpheus, he identified Osiris with Dionysus, who was dressed in a cloak of fawn skin whose stains mimicked the variety of the stars.* The same writer affirmed[6] that Dionysus was Io's son, while Apollodorus[7] and Apollonius Rodhius[8] reported that he was the son of the moon.

This overlapping of roles, Io/Isis in the role of mother of Dionysus/Osiris, must not stagger us: in fact, divine parenthoods are easily exchanged even within the same culture. And in the Egyptian tradition the figures of Horus and Osiris overlap and confuse.†

In the previous chapter Io appeared in the role of "mother of Egypt" or mother of Menes and Danus, two brothers involved in a dispute identical to that of the brothers Osiris and Seth. Menes died in the clash with Danaus (likewise Osiris), but at any rate the kingdom had passed to his son Deucalion (just like it was passed to Horus, son of Osiris).

The same collection of myths[9] informs us that, by order of Hera, the Titans had taken Dionysus, a horned and snake-haired boy, and although he would mutate continually, had torn him to pieces.

---

*This particular concept is also found in the Mayan tradition in which priests use a jaguar's leather coat with spots imitating the stars.
†The Greek tradition says that the son of Osiris, Horus or Phaethon, was thrown into the river Eridanus, while the Phoenician version tells of the head of Osiris (here Tammuz/Adonis/Orpheus) thrown into the sea or river of the Milky Way.

A similar thing happened in the Egyptian myth to Osiris (depicted with horns), who was cut into pieces by his brother Seth's followers, so there is a parallelism between the followers of Seth and the Titans. Let's go back to the Greek myth: His grandmother Rhea rushed to the aid of Dionysus and restored him to life. The Greeks identified Rhea with Cybele, the evolution of the mother goddess, while in Egypt the mother goddess was Isis, who reassembled the remains of Osiris and brought him back to life. The parenthood similarities do not correspond perfectly, but it is still hard to ignore the correspondences between the two myths.

> As an adult [Dionysus] sailed to Egypt, bringing with him some wine; once in Faro, king Proteus received him hospitably. Among the Libyans of the Delta of the Nile, opposite the island of Faro, there were queens of the Amazons and Dionysus invited them to march with him against the Titans, who had driven King Ammon off his kingdom. The defeat of the Titans and the rendering/restitution of his kingdom to King Ammon was one of Dionysus' many successes.[10]

So the Titans had overthrown the ruler of Egypt just as Danaus-Seth did before being defeated by the son of Menes-Osiris. At this point there is an apparent identification of the Titans-Seth-Danaus with the gods-Osiris-Menes.

The Greek myth tells of Dionysus's journey to the east, the same trip toward India that Osiris did with the Amazons that we'll see later on.

> He then headed east, towards India. . . . He thus reached India, after facing many opponents along the way, and conquered the entire region, teaching the inhabitants the art of viticulture, establishing laws and founding cities.[11]

A confirmation of the highlighted correspondences comes from the ancient use of the names "Egypt (Menes)" and "Danaus" as names of the Theban co-kings of the Seventeenth Dynasty (1650–1550 BCE),[12] while in the entire history of Egypt the pharaoh was labeled as "Osiris."

So, ultimately, it can be schematized as follows:

Io = Isis

Danaus = Seth

Menes = Dionysus = Osiris

The record of Menes or "Meni" as the first pharaoh, acknowledged through the inscriptions of the New Kingdom (1550–1070 BCE), was then aimed at replacing the name of Narmer, by now forgotten, with the name of Menes-Osiris.

The name "Danaus" was also used by Hyksos (Sabian) invaders during their period of domination in Egypt (see page 258). In 1550 BCE the Hyksos were defeated and enslaved, along with those Habirus who had entered Egypt with them. They were citizens of the Canaanites who fled from Palestine to prevent debt bondage. These were the Jews that four years later flee from Egypt, led by Moses: there was an unidentified tribe to help them, whose name was "Dan," the same name that had belonged to both a son of Jacob and a daughter of Danaus.

THE FIRST TIME

There was once a time for the Egyptian people when the gods fraternized with humans. This period was called Zep Tepi, "First Time." During this government of gods a system of cosmic order was established in the country to be maintained even after power passed on to the mortal pharaohs. The pharaohs together with the priests represented the link with the gods and First Time, guarding the laws of wisdom and knowledge.

Every earthly event and all natural events (from the movement of the celestial bodies to the flood of the Nile) would be justified in relation to First Time, seen as a sort of "royal bond" that even the pharaohs had to maintain.[13]

The First Time was called the Time of Osiris and for the Egyptians represented a historical reality of prosperity and nobility. Then followed a period called the Time of the Followers of Horus, the keepers of the lost knowledge of the First Time.

MILLENARY MONUMENTS

Found along the routes of the Egyptian desert are countless buildings and many signs of the ancient inhabitants of those places. Some of these are dated or have inscriptions bearing the name of the owner, or at least the builder. In others there is no explicit reference to the monument's builder, and everything is dated back to a certain historical period by assumptions based on the monumental context.

The oldest and most enigmatic monuments of ancient Egypt are the pyramids, identified by most academic Egyptologists and historians as the ancient tombs of deceased pharaohs.

Let's step back, trying to figure out why these monuments, of such a great size, should have been built as tombs only. Is it true?

According to documented Egyptian history the first tombs built in the arid desert areas were the so-called mastabas, the simplest and most common of these consisting of a "large step" of truncated pyramid shape. The structure contained one or more ritual chapels, a false door (through which the deceased could leave the hereafter to receive the offerings left by the living), and a well (closed by stones and debris, sometimes more than twenty meters deep) that gave access to the proper tomb. The mastabas were used as tombs for kings of the First and Second Dynasties, and it is commonly thought that they influenced the subsequent construction of the pyramids. Later they served as burial sites for members of the royal court (viziers, scribes, priests, and nobles).

Before the dynastic period the dead were buried in pits dug in the sands of the desert, where mummification took place as a natural process, but the body was often prey to jackals or grave robbers. Then there was a shift, and the Third Dynasty inaugurated the greatest works of the Egyptian people: the pyramids. According to historians the first pyramid to be erected was the tomb of King Zoser at Saqqara, known as the "stepped pyramid." Structurally it was like a mastaba; the difference was that it was designed to be viewed from far away (it rises sixty meters above its rectangular base). The proponent of this great innovation was the brilliant vizier architect Imhotep, one of the wisest figures of his time, who was also high priest and general astronomer ("Chief of Observatories") at the time of King Zoser. After Zoser pyramids appeared in various places in Egypt until this building culture reached its apex in the Fourth Dynasty.

Afterward the construction of pyramids suffered a steady decline in the number of erected buildings and, especially, in their quality and size.

THE PYRAMIDS OF GIZA

The Fourth Dynastic Period represents the highest building quality of the pyramids. The most perfect and enigmatic ones are located in Giza, not far from Cairo.

Although the pyramids at Giza have no inscription inside and none among the discovered texts indicates the name of the builders, scholars have classified the three pyramids as tombs of some of the most important pharaohs of the Fourth Dynasty: Khufu, Khafre, and Menkaure (Cheops, Chefren, and Mykerinos in Greek).

The entrance to the pyramid of Mykerinos is at the center of the northern side, about four meters from the base, in the fifth course of masonry (figure 5.1). An access tunnel covered with granite up to ground level goes down about thirty-one meters to a vestibule carved into the rock and covered with slabs from which another passage—protected by three sluice gates—leads horizontally to an underground chamber located more or less at the center of the section. In the latter, at the dawn of the Christian era, a wooden sarcophagus was discovered. Near the top of the room's wall, though, there is another "access tunnel" that proceeds northward but stops after only a few meters. Generally, it is identified as the entry of an original core pyramid, and consequently its end indicates the position of the northern facade of that ancient pyramid.[14] The Egyptian historian Manetho claims that only the core pyramid was built during the reign of Mykerinos, while the big cover would be an addition by the last pharaoh of the Fifth Dynasty, Queen Nitocris.

From the western edge of the underground room a ramp goes down westward and leads to another passage lined with granite. A staircase leading from the right wall of the latter gives access to a room dug into the rock whose walls contain six deep niches. The same passage, how-

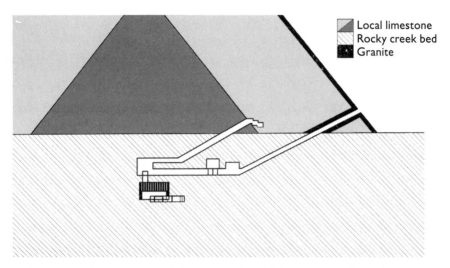

Local limestone
Rocky creek bed
Granite

Figure 5.1. The passages of the Pyramid of Mykerinos seen from the east.

ever, leads to a large room of north-south orientation, entirely covered in red granite, with massive embossed ceiling gables that form a barrel vault. Originally, this room hosted a beautiful basalt sarcophagus, decorated in the style typical of the Old Kingdom. Unfortunately, the English lost it at sea in an attempt to purloin it from its homeland.[15]

Ascribed to Pharaoh Chephren and far more imposing, the Second Pyramid has two northern entrances, both shifting about thirteen meters to the left with respect to the center (figure 5.2). The highest, located about eleven meters from ground level, gives access to the usual descending passage, lined with red granite. Underground the tunnel leads into a long horizontal passage protected by granite shutters. The lowest entry, also shifting to the left, opens not on the northern facade of the building, but from the ground a few meters away from it. From there, a second entrance tunnel descends into the underlying bedrock, although this time with an inclination rather inferior to the first. This passage leads, in turn, to a horizontal underground passage protected by a sluice gate, to the right of which opens the access to an underground chamber dug into the rock. Skipping the access, the same passage leads to a second sluice gate, followed by a tunnel that reaches the bottom passage a little further than the point where we had left it.

Hence the horizontal passage reaches a point slightly deviated from

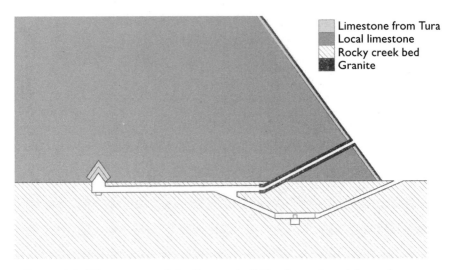

Limestone from Tura
Local limestone
Rocky creek bed
Granite

Figure 5.2. The passages of the Pyramid of Chephren viewed from the east.

the center of the pyramid and enters into a room with an east-west orientation partially embedded in the rock; the gables of the limestone chamber emerge a little from the ground level. On top of the northern and southern walls are two small rectangular cavities, about thirty centimeters deep, which seem to correspond to the mysterious "ventilation shafts" of the King's Chamber in the Great Pyramid. Two red squares drawn on the walls about one and half meters below the two openings appear to suggest alternative positions. At the western edge of the room on the floor is a void sarcophagus in polished granite, along with its cover.

Now we are ready to face the mute yet untruthful giant, the highest and oldest of the three pyramids: Khufu's supposed mausoleum, officially built during his reign, apparently between 2551 and 2528 BCE.

The first archaeologist to explore the Pyramid of Cheops in modern times was Sir Flinders Petrie between 1880 and 1882. He was the one who discovered that the faces of the pyramid are aligned to the cardinal points with great precision (the discrepancy does not exceed three minutes of arc, equivalent to 0.06 percent error). Petrie also measured the sides of the base (230.25 meters north, 230.44 meters south, 230.38 meters east, 230.35 meters west). The ratio between the base perimeter (921.42 meters) and the original height (146.7 meters) is 6.28, equal to the ratio between the radius and circumference of a hemisphere.

Let's assume that the Great Pyramid could represent Earth's northern hemisphere to scale. Calculating the latter it corresponds to 1:43,200—a sacred number and the exact duration of twenty zodiacal ages that appears in countless mythological texts. Moreover, the same proportions also work for the other two pyramids, this time calling into question Mars, Venus, and the moon (see figure 5.3).

The Pyramid of Cheops (Khufu) is not at all hollow, and its 2.5 million blocks of limestone have an average weight of 2.6 tons, with a total of 6.3 million tons.

Before being plundered for the construction of Cairo, the Great

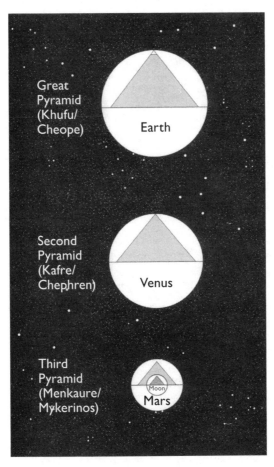

Figure 5.3. The Pyramids of Giza and corresponding planetary hemispheres.

Pyramid was covered on all four sides by smooth white stones from the quarries of Tura, on the opposite bank of the Nile. Apparently the cover blocks weighed about fifteen tons each and were linked tightly enough so that it was not possible to get a knife blade between them.[16] Since the thirteenth century CE Arabs removed them in order to build their mosques. It is said that when the pyramid was still intact it seemed like a glittering jewel in the sunlight.[17]

Venturing inside the pyramid, there is initially a corridor with a low ceiling and a steep gradient (no more than 1.19 meters high per 1.04 meters wide, with an inclination of 26° 32′ 23″ with respect to the horizontal plane). The tunnel dips down through the heart of the pyramid for a total of 105.15 meters, then continues horizontally for a distance of 8.83 meters before arriving at a roughly carved room whose purpose is not yet clear. Inside, a large empty sarcophagus takes up the space. Some Egyptologists believe this underground chamber was built by others at an earlier time than the pyramid (figure 5.4).

Eighteen meters from the entrance there is a junction on a second corridor (ascending with a gradient of twenty-six degrees and continuing for forty meters) running in the north-south direction on the building midline like the previous one. At the top is the heart of the pyramid, the Grand Gallery, and, before its climb, there is a short hori-

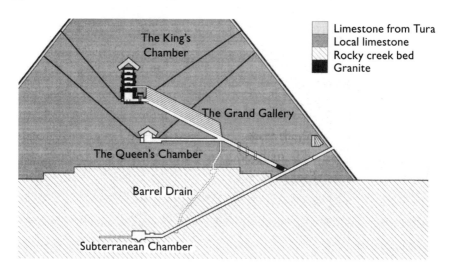

Figure 5.4. The system of passages of the Cheops (Khufu) Pyramid.

zontal corridor leading to the Queen's Chamber (this room also remains a mystery).

The Queen's Chamber is not very large (5.74 meters from east to west and 5.23 meters from north to south with a ceiling that reaches a maximum height of 6.22 meters). In the east wall there is a niche similar to a mihrab.* Interesting elements in the Queen's Chamber are two ducts, which have their counterparts in the King's Chamber. These ducts are square in shape, twenty centimeters per side, and inclined 45° upward. Like in the King's Chamber, one duct points southward and the other northward, although the ducts of the Queen's Chamber do not lead outside of the pyramid, while those of the King's Chamber do.

The Grand Gallery is the most elaborate and mysterious of the entire complex, with a height of 8.53 meters and walls equipped with niches (plate 17). Going up the tunnel is the King's Chamber: 10.46 meters wide from east to west, 5.23 meters from north to south, and 5.81 meters high. Unlike the Queen's Chamber, which is entirely made of limestone, this room's walls are black granite from Aswan (Upper Egypt). The blocks weigh seventy tons and have been linked and smoothed without the use of any mortar. Two ducts, measuring 20 centimeters on each side, rise from the northern and southern walls and reach the outside of the pyramid. No such tunnels have been found in any other pyramid.

At the western end of the room is the alleged sarcophagus, actually a "simple" cube of granite that is finely carved with sharp corners and where the volume of the void is equal to the volume of the full. This seems to be more a tank than a coffin, the more so since no traces of embalming products or any pieces of treasure have ever been found.

In the Pyramid of Cheops have been found some engravings reproducing Iberian, the universal form of writing that we had already found in South America. Some signs are visible in the underground chamber. At least one is carved on the ceiling; four more signs are in front of the entrance of the descending corridor, discovered by Robert Schoch and Colette Dowell. Actually, they are the only writings found in the Great Pyramid.

---

*A prayer niche, typical of Arab mosques.

THE MYSTERY OF THE GREAT PYRAMID

One of the biggest puzzles concerning the Great Pyramid concerns the channels, or so-called air ducts, in both the King's Chamber and the Queen's Chamber. In the former room they have an outside escape, while in the second they do not exit from the pyramid. According to scholars the reason for this anomaly is that the builders were not able to finish those channels. However, this thesis does not seem plausible considering that in 1993 a German engineer in robotics (Rudolf Gantenbrink) sent a tiny robot (Upuaut 2) into the southern duct of the Queen's Chamber. After traveling sixty-five meters along the channel it sent a surprising video image showing a door with two copper handles and with a distinctive-looking slit below, probably indicating that the ancients did not cease construction of the well but voluntarily blocked the access. It seems plausible to assume that there is a continuation after this obstacle, perhaps another secret room. On September 16, 2002, a robot called Pyramid Rover (designed by iRobot, of Boston) was sent back into the southern duct with the task of breaking through the barrier in order to see what was on the other side. Unfortunately, there was a second door that barred the way to the research. In this regard, it is interesting to quote the Italian engineer Mario Pincherle, who performed a smoke test in the 1970s:

> Flammable smoke material was burnt at the duct's mouth [southern duct of the Queen's Chamber]. Instead of being conveyed into the room where I was, the smoke penetrated the hole in the wall and dispersed! The duct was not so blind but "breathed." The air moved backwards as regards the air ducts of the sarcophagus' crypt [namely, the King's Chamber]: from the "Queen's Chamber" it entered a mysterious place situated a few meters beyond the wall.[18]

The Pyramid Rover was also sent also along the northern shaft. The movement was difficult because of the four sharp corners, and at the end of the shaft was discovered another "stone of division, or door," again with two copper handles.

Let's look at what the purpose of these channels really was. In 1984 a building engineer of Belgian origin, Robert Bauval, made a sensational discovery. On the assumption that the Egyptian priests were excellent observers of the sky and, as we shall see, the whole Egyptian mythology is probably derived from a "religion of the stars," he drew a possible correlation between the "air ducts" and some well-defined star constellations.[19] Bauval tried to penetrate the tunnels through virtual reality, to see what part of the sky they pointed at when the Great Pyramid was allegedly constructed. Thanks to an astronomical simulation program, he was able to go back to the period of construction of the monument: 2500 BCE.

He noticed, with a stir, that a sort of "cosmic plan" connected the ducts with some of the main stars that the Egyptians identified with the most important deities: the southern duct of the King's Chamber pointed directly toward the star Al Nitak (the star of Orion-Osiris that corresponds to the pyramid on the Earth), while the northern duct looked at the star Thuban (the once pole star in the constellation of the Dragon).

More references were hidden in the Queen's Chamber, where the wells are still closed; yet, by virtually pointing at the sky, Bauval noted that their trajectory crossed south to the star Sirius (in the constellation of Canis Major) and north to the star Kochab (the Ursa Minor star tied to the rebirth of the soul). In this case also, the first reference is essential, because the star Sirius was worshipped in antiquity as the goddess Isis.

We do not know exactly the reasons why they "point" at the stars, but we assume that they are a sort of a "passage" enabling the deceased pharaoh's soul to achieve immortality—this happened at the end of a journey to the stars, specifically to a region of the sky called the Duat where the god Osiris reigned after having ascended to heaven. This is not an abstract place, but the region of the southern sky containing Orion, Sothis (Sirius), and the winding waterway that is the Milky Way:

Walk to the Water Way. A ladder to the Duat can be ready for you in the place where you find Orion.[20]

For decades Egyptologists have continued the false belief that the three rooms of the pyramid were a sign of projects started and then abandoned: First Khufu/Cheops wanted to rest in peace in the down-stairs room. During construction he changed his mind, opting for a half-height room: the Queen's Chamber. But poor Cheops was hard to please and blocked the work of the air ducts before they could reach the pyramid's surface, finally wanting an even higher room: the King's Chamber.

Instead, according to Peter Lemesurier's *Gods of the Dawn: The Message of the Pyramids and the True Stargate Mystery*:

> Even today in the rock that is located one hundred meters east of the Great Pyramid there is a series of works called "trial passages," known almost exclusively by specialists in pyramids. Perhaps dug as a sort of prototype before they would begin the work of the pyramid, they contain all the main sections of tunnels (except the section made for the King's Chamber) in their correct lateral dimensions, albeit with some differences. This shows that a coherent plan existed at the beginning, although at that time some of its details were not completely included, or had not yet been definitely established.[21]

The author also shows the section of the trial passages (figure 5.5).

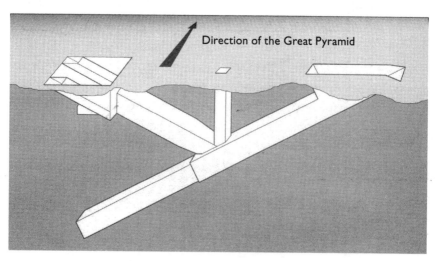

Figure 5.5. The trial passage. The Great Pyramid is located 100 meters eastward.

THE GIZA COMPLEX: BEFORE AND AFTER

Bauval was able to discover an even stronger relationship with the stars, a plan that covered all the plain of Giza. In the Pyramid Texts and the subsequent Book of the Dead it is explicitly stated that Egyptians considered the necropolis of Memphis as the Duat on Earth. Therefore, Bauval's idea was that the three pyramids or even the whole complex of Giza were the Egyptians' attempt to represent the sky on their land.

The first step was to reconstruct the night sky as it appeared when the pyramids were built, and to do that he had to consider the Precession of the Equinoxes.

The precession is a movement of the Earth that slowly but continuously changes the position of its axis of rotation in regard to the ideal sphere of the fixed stars. The axis undergoes a precession—a rotation around the vertical axis of Earth's orbit (similar to that of a spinning top) that takes over 25,920 years to complete. In this cycle the apparent position of stars on the celestial sphere changes slowly. As a result of the precession each constellation reaches its lowest point and its highest point of elevation. To reach the highest peak it takes 12,960 years, which is equivalent to half the precessional cycle. An equal amount of time is needed to reach the lowest point again.

Let's look at the positioning of the three pyramids on the Giza plateau. They form an angle of forty-five degrees with the Nile and the north-south axis, with the western pyramid (Menkaure) slightly shifted east of the diagonal. Looking south, this axis extends to the southern celestial meridian. In the sky the stars of Orion form an angle of forty-five degrees with the Milky Way, recording the same slight shift toward east from the westernmost star of this constellation. But the angle with the meridian varies through the ages.

It is known that the Egyptians' most important period of the year was the dawn of the vernal equinox, when day and night have equal length. Bauval's question: Precisely when was the belt of Orion in the sky perfectly traced upon the Earth by the pyramids at the equinoctial sunrise, with the Milky Way* and the Nile on the same line, parallel to both the north-south

---

*Ancient texts confirm that the Egyptians considered the Milky Way to be the celestial counterpart of the Nile, and it was often called the "Celestial Nile."

axis and the meridian? Going back in time, thanks to technology, we can see that there was such a moment and that the last time was March 21, 10,500 BCE (figure 5.6). This same date corresponds with the one indicated by the Kalasasaya in Peru and the Temples of Mnajdra in Malta.

At that moment, before sunrise, the constellation of Orion was in the lowest point of its precession cycle (about 9° 20' elevation when passing on the meridian), which suggests that the positioning was not a coincidence. On the same date the star Sirius appeared for the first time in the Egyptian sky: the celestial image of Isis, whose rise during the dynastic era meant the beginning of the fertilizing floods of the Nile.

Apparently, this day was Zep Tepi, the First Time, the day of birth. In Dashur (twenty kilometers south of Giza), there are two other considerable pyramids, 105 meters high, built by Snofru, father of Cheops, known as the

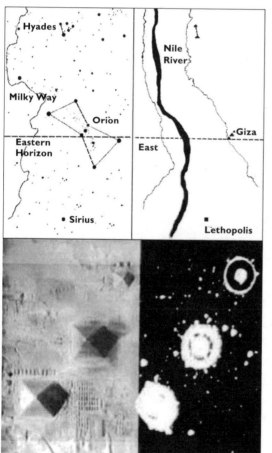

Figure 5.6. Correspondence between the stars of Orion's belt and the pyramids of the Memphite necropolis. The scheme is completed by the city of Letopolis further north, "overlapping" the star of Sirius.

Red Pyramid, and the Bent Pyramid. They are added to the design of the 10,500 BCE sky and represent two stars of the Hyades,* the bull's head to the left of Orion. Fifteen kilometers north, a tower that rose in the city of . Letopolis completed the drawing, it being the counterpart of the star Sirius[22] as it was in the sky of 10,500 BCE—but why a tower?

The pyramid complex at Giza represents the Duat, the region of the southern sky containing Orion, Sirius, and the Milky Way as it was in a much earlier period than the date of their construction and alignment of the channels in the Great Pyramid.

Consider the hypothesis that, where now there are the pyramids, once there were towers. Also, it was customary to build new monuments in the places made holy by previous, older buildings. Here follows a list of evidence supporting this theory:

- C. Plinio[23] reports that the construction of the towers was due to the Cyclops, a race that was identified with the Pelasgians. Dionysius of Halicarnassus writes that the Pelasgians, the first inhabitants of Italy, lived in high, fortified places surrounded by walls and ditches. He added that these houses were known to the Greeks as Tyrses and to the natives as Turses, and that they gave name to Tyrrhenians or Tyrsenians. In his *Il Gello* (1546), P. F. Giambullari explains that the name Etruria had its origin in the shape of the houses of the first civilized people who lived in Italy: they were all towers, from which derived the name of Eturria or Etursia. The above-mentioned writer shows that the transition from Etursia to Eturria and the transposition in Etruria is not a new phenomenon. The "r" and "s" often exchange one with the other, as it happens for example in Valerius, Furius, Decor, and Honor, which first were Valesius, Fusius, Decos, and Honos.

- In Enoch, chapter 22, we read: "From there I proceeded to another spot, where I saw on the west [with respect to Syria] a great and lofty tower, of strong granite. And there was in it four empty cavities, deep, spacious and very honed: three of them were dark and one bright and in it there was a bathtub full of water right in the middle. . . . These are the delightful places where the spirits,

---

*According to mythology, the Hyades were the daughters of the Pelasgian Atlas.

the souls of the dead, will be collected; for them were they formed; and here will be collected all the souls of the sons of men. . . . They are divided one from each other." If we compare this passage with a section of the Pyramid of Cheops we note its similarity with the King's Chamber: bright with a tub in the middle, the alleged sarcophagus, and with overlying dark rooms so-called of discharge (figure 5.7). All these rooms are smooth and made of granite blocks weighing from twenty to eighty tons, while the rest of the structure is limestone blocks of two to four tons. Drillings carried out on the walls of the chamber showed the existence of a gap of sand between the granite and the limestone, suggesting the pyramids are the cover of the tower of the dead.

- The ancient Egyptians celebrated the Feast of the Tower of the Dead, during which they threw invocations to the four corners of the Earth—the cardinal points formerly called Artus, Disi, Anatol, and Mesembria. They shouted loudly the name of "ADAM," formed

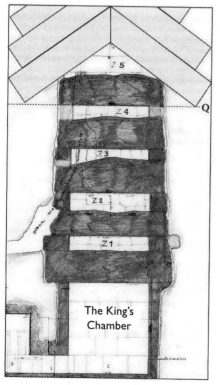

Figure 5.7. The King's Chamber and overlying dark rooms.

by the initials of those points, and, soon after, a sacred archer threw four arrows in the direction of the four cardinal points.[24]

- The Zed, symbol of Osiris's power, was a tower identical to that of the dead and was used as a hieroglyph for the word *djed,* meaning power. According to our reconstruction, <u>Osiris lived around 10,500 BCE,</u> the period in which the pyramids of Giza and Dashur reproduced the exact constellation of Orion and the Hyades on the ground. In spite of this correspondence, the pyramids' channels pointed toward stars that were sacred during the Fourth Dynasty, a sign that at least the pyramidal covers must have been built in this period. In the representations of the Zed we see the scepter and the rod coming out from underneath the rooms and tilted upward, symbols of power representing the two kingdoms, Upper and Lower Egypt (figure 5.8). The rod is closer to the vertical in a way that the scepter and the rod find a perfect match with the northern and southern air ducts in the King's Chamber of the Pyramid of Cheops. The channels come out horizontally from the granite of the King's Chamber and lean into the limestone, so their construction must coincide with that of the cover during the Fourth Dynasty.*

Figure 5.8. Representation of the Zed.

---

*The exact alignment of channels with the pole star Alpha Draconis (North King), the Orion Al Nitak (South King), Kochab (North Queen), and Sirius (South Queen) occured in 2450 BCE.

- In Enoch, chapter 89, we read: "A tower lofty and great was built on the house for the Lord of the sheep, and that house was low, but the tower was elevated and lofty, and the Lord of the sheep stood on that tower and they gave him offerings of all kinds." Although this passage refers to the temple of Jerusalem, we note a striking coincidence: When the Bible speaks of a physical presence of the Lord, it refers to the Ark of the Covenant. So the passage says that the Ark of the Covenant was inside a tower, while in the temple of Solomon, it seems, there was no tower worthy of note. Curiously, the internal measurements of the so-called sarcophagus, or bathtub, in the King's Chamber equal the ark's measurements of 68 by 87 by 198 centimeters.

- Inscriptions on the walls of the Temple of Edfu on the west bank of the Nile mix fragments of several lost stories. Among them, the "Offering of the Lotus," set in the First Time (10,500 BCE) when the divine race of the "Ancients" emanated from the "earthly god," also known as the "nameless snake." The Ancients would have raised an island built with water-grown reeds, called "Land of the Beginning" or "Rostau," surrounded by water and crowned by the column Zed. According to Egyptologist Eve Reymond the bundles of tied reeds would have been the method of construction of religious shrines in prehistoric Egypt. If the natives of Egypt had observed the construction of a granite structure such as the Zed, they could have interpreted its "miraculous" raising as a "spontaneous and magic" work of the papyrus reeds. According to Edfu's story, the Zed became the roost of the earthly god who at that time took the form of a hawk and became Sokar. According to Andrew Collins, researcher for the ARE (Association for Research and Enlightenment) and the ARCE (American Research Center in Egypt), the Zed would correspond to the Benben* of Memphite theology. Some lines forward on we read of the Seven Sages emerg-

---

*An upright stone topped by a capstone of meteorite iron found in the temple of Heliopolis. According to Egyptian creation myth when the world arose out of lifeless waters a pyramid-shaped mound, the Benben, was the first thing to emerge.

ing from the primordial waters, who in the form of hawks perched on reeds surrounding the Zed columns. This step is important, because for the first time we talk about columns, using the plural, and not about a single Zed. Millennia later, the Seven Sages (or their descendants) erected the first edified structure in the world, a square refuge (the pyramid?) created to hold the Zed column. Inside the refuge were placed powerful objects belonging to the nameless god, including a sacred mace called "Great White," and something called "Image of God's Face." Continuing the reading we discover that Rostau became <u>a field of battle between the original inhabitants and a population of newcomers.</u> During the fight something called the "Deep Eye" was demolished and the primordial waters were plunged into darkness during a storm that destroyed the sacred land, killing most of its divine inhabitants. The survivors were to go and live in a hidden structure underneath the island, the burial place of the earthly god.[25]

- The original Egyptian name of Cheops is Medjedu (Mezedu), composed by the consonant clusters "m djd(zd) w." In his *Guardians of Immortality*, philosopher Piero Magaletti writes: "Let's analyze the composition of the name: *w* means *place*; *m* indicates *to stay*; *djd(zd)* indicates the *Zed*; so the result is: *the place where the Zed stays*, a rather bizarre meaning to be the name of a pharaoh."[26]

With this new interpretation everything takes on a different meaning and the alignment of the three pyramids really does not seem a coincidence.

According to Herodotus, the Egyptians were not proud of the coverage work of the towers done by the pharaohs of the Fourth Dynasty:

They calculate that the Egyptians suffered extreme hardships for all of the 106 years and that for this length of time, all the sanctuaries were shut down and remained closed. The Egyptians hate the very memory of these two kings [Cheops and Chephren] so intensely that they will not even speak their names. Instead they call another man the pyramid builder—one Philitis, who pastured cattle in these regions at the time.[27]

"Philitis" is a corruption of "Pelastoi" (read "Felastoi"), as found in several texts in place of the more common "Pelasgians," and the word "shepherd" might have the figurative meaning of "guide."

THE SPHINX

We have seen the correlation between the three pyramids of Giza and the southern sky at the vernal equinox in 10,500 BCE, but there is another enigmatic monument, anonymous indeed, which seems to be born in the same date: the Sphinx.

According to archaeologists, the Sphinx was built during the reign of Khafra (Chephren, 2500 BCE, Fourth Dynasty). Composed of a crouching lion allegedly with the head of the pharaoh Khafra, it overlooks the plateau of Giza, turning its ancient face toward the east.

Studies conducted in the early 1990s on the face of the Sphinx by Lieutenant Frank Domingo, a reshaper of disfigured and mutilated faces for the police department of New York City, have shown that the immense sculpture does *not* have the physical traits of Khafra, or at least not those in his black diorite statue. Indeed, the three-dimensional graphic reconstruction of the face points to the interesting finding that the characteristics of the Sphinx are Negroid.

Additional important work on the monument, independently executed by Egyptologist John Anthony West with the help of geologist Robert Schoch, examined the furrows left by the corrosion of the limestone on the body and the face of the Sphinx. According to classical Egyptology, the natural damages that can be seen on the monument are due solely to the arid wind of the desert. Schoch has instead shown that such special signs of erosion (from top to bottom) can only have been caused by a slow and continuous exposure of the stone to rain and weathering. If we follow the traditional view, this could not be possible, as in 2500 BCE Egypt was as dry as it is today. To find a temperate climate with abundant rainfall, one must go back of at least four thousand years. According to Schoch, then, the Sphinx would date to at least 6000 BCE, maybe earlier.

If we consider the plateau of Giza as a ground reproduction of the night sky, we must consider the Sphinx as part of this mapping. And it feels rather natural to associate the constellation of Leo, its celestial counterpart, with this monument.

We now use the same astronomical date we have assumed for the First Time and, through computer processing, go back to 10,500 BCE during the vernal equinox: at that time the Sphinx looked east, exactly toward its stellar counterpart, the Lion. The face, quite out of proportion, was presumably re-sculpted from the earliest dynasties of black pharaohs.

THE PYRAMID TEXTS

In the ancient Pyramid Texts we find the largest number of references to the origin of the Egyptian people, the First Time, and the Duat. These extended inscriptions on death and rebirth are carved on the walls of the tombs of a number of pyramids of the Fifth and Sixth Dynasties at Saqqara, fifteen kilometers south of Giza. The most ancient texts were found in the pyramid of Unas, dated between 2375 and 2345 BCE, but their compilation is based on older sources.

Together with other archaic and mysterious texts, like the Book of the Dead, the Book of the Imminent Coming, the Book of Two Ways, the Book of Gates, the Book of What Is inside the Duat, and the Coffin Texts, the Pyramid Texts were meant to guide the journey of the deceased.

In the Egyptian religion the pharaoh embodied Horus on Earth and after his death he would take the form of the god Osiris in the realm of the Duat. The name Osiris-Unas, which the texts use to refer to the pharaoh, suggests the king was ready to become a soul whose home is a star in the celestial region of Orion.

According to the Egyptologist Selim Hassan, "The Egyptians believed in multiple, perhaps superimposed heavens."[28] He drew attention to a papyrus preserved in the Louvre[29] with the expression "the Two Heavens, it means the earth and the Duat."[30] Hassan writes that "these heavens were laid one over the other."[31] The Coffin Texts talk of a "high" and a "low" sky, associating them respectively with Upper and Lower Egypt:

Open! Oh Heaven and Earth, open your temples of the Upper and Lower Egypt.[32]

The same concept is repeated in the Pyramid Texts:

When his name was Orion, Horus comes, Thoth appears. They lift Osiris from where he is and raise him, when came into being this name of Orion, long-legged and long-stepped, who presides over the Upper Egypt. Rise up Osiris, the sky is given to you, the earth is given to you.[33]

Following the constellation of Orion during its transit along the meridian we see that since 10,500 BCE, when it was at the lowest point, it slowly began to rise until reaching its highest point in the present day. The Pyramid Texts reproduce the movement of Orion from the bottom (Giza, Lower Egypt) to the top (Abydos, Upper Egypt):

They found Osiris when his name became Sokar [Memphite Necropolis]. Walk toward Water Way, traveling upstream [south], travel toward Abydos in this spirit-form of yours; follow a [street] uphill to the Duat, which is ready for you in the place where Orion is.[34]

The expression "when his name became Sokar" implies a correspondence between the body of Osiris and the land of Sokar, namely Giza and the three pyramids.

The Pyramid Texts speak of the pharaoh searching for the astral body of Osiris, not as it was at the time of the pyramids, but as it used to be at the First Time. This is a path in the opposite way, from top to bottom, symbolically represented by a journey from Abydos to Giza. The stele of Shabaka summarizes the religious beliefs developed in Memphis during the early dynasties: we read that the lifeless body of Osiris is dragged by the water from his temple in Upper Egypt in Abydos toward his temple in Lower Egypt in the "Land of Sokar," the Memphite necropolis.*

---

*The Memphite necropolis, burial ground for the city of Memphis, includes the sites of Giza, Saqqara, and Dahshur.

The body is described as "gigantic" and we suspect that this adjective refers to the three great pyramids, as earthly image of the body of Osiris-Orion.

In another passage the pharaoh refers to an astral double of himself, says the Duat of Orion was the double of the Land of Sokar, and explicitly states the pyramid is Osiris:

> Here I come with my astral essence. This pyramid and temple be built for me and my double, and that this pyramid and temple be enclosed for me and my double. . . . This pyramid of the king is Osiris. Live, be alive, be young next to Orion in the sky. . . . Oh king Osiris, you are this great star, the companion of Orion, who traverses the sky with Orion, who navigates the Duat with Osiris.[35]

The search for the First Time is insistently proposed by the Pyramid Texts, according to which the soul of the pharaoh would travel through the heavens from the vernal point of the sun (this is the area of the sky where the sun rises at the spring equinox) near the Hyades—the "Bull of Heaven"—and cross the Milky Way until joining with Regulus, the brightest star of Leo.[36] Here he would meet Rwty, the "lion-looking divinity."[37] It's a trip back in time to the First Time, when the vernal point was precisely in Regulus. The Coffin Texts refer to some words or magic formulas that would allow the deceased to use the path of Rostau (another name indicating the necropolis of Giza) on Earth and in heaven in order to "walk any sky he wanted."[38] According to Egyptologist Jane B. Sellers these formulas would be "precessional numbers": "Is it possible that early man encoded in his myths special numbers; numbers that seem to reveal to initiates an amazing knowledge of the movement of the celestial sphere?"[39]

Sellers shows that the particular sequence of precessional numbers (12, 36, 54, 72, 360, 432, 2160)* occurs in the ancient myth of Osiris, where seventy-two conspirators were involved, along with Seth, in the assassination of the god-king.[40]

---

*The number of years of astronomically relevant periods contained in the cycle of precession.

A passage of the Coffin Texts invites us to look for a secret sealed under the monuments of Giza-Rostau:

> This is the sealed thing, which is kept in darkness, with fire all around, that contains Osiris' emanation, and has been placed in Rostau. It has been hidden because it fell from him and from him descended on the sandy desert; this means that what belongs to him was kept in Rostau.[41]

If we watched a computer simulation of the sky above Giza in 10,500 BCE we could see the constellation of Leo while it rises slowly to the east in the pre-dawn of the vernal equinox—at five o'clock in the morning it rose exactly at the real east. In the same moment the sun, indicating the vernal point, was twelve degrees below its hind legs. By overlaying this image on the figure of the Sphinx, the lion on Earth, the sun can indicate the location of the hiding place of "the sealed thing," about thirty meters below the hind legs (figure 5.9).[42]

In 1991 the seismographer Dobecki Thomas, helped by John Anthony West and Boris Said (a filmmaker from Los Angeles), conducted acoustic

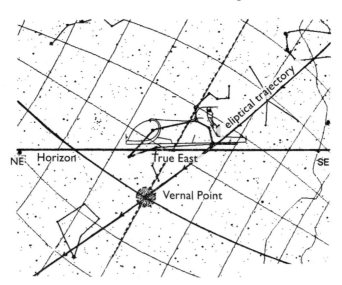

Figure 5.9. Location of the secret sealed beneath the Giza-Rostau monuments, based on the stars. Courtesy of Robert Bauval and Graham Hancock, Keeper of Genesis.

tests around the Sphinx and identified a large rectangular anomaly under the right foreleg. Dobecki describes it as "a rather large space, nine by twelve meters large and less than five meters deep. The regular shape of the anomaly distinguishes from the cavities of natural origin, and there are indications that it is of human nature."[43]

THE VALLEY TEMPLE OF CHEPHREN AND THE TEMPLE OF THE SPHINX

The pyramids and temples of the main monuments of the plateau of Giza are anonymous and contain no inscriptions. In none of these monuments has the body of a pharaoh been found. The Sphinx belongs to a complex including the Temple of the Sphinx and the Valley Temple of Chephren. The former is located immediately east of the Sphinx, towering above it, while the latter is located slightly south of the Temple of the Sphinx, separated by a narrow corridor (figure 5.10).

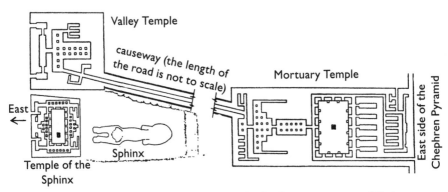

Figure 5.10. Temples and monuments of Chephren. Courtesy of Robert Bauval and Graham Hancock, Keeper of Genesis.

The Valley Temple, largest of the two, is forty meters per side and almost square. The Temple of the Sphinx is more markedly rhomboid with sides about thirty meters long.

Originally about twelve meters high, both monuments are made of massive blocks of limestone, and at one point they were covered with granite both inside and outside. These coatings and much of the central core of masonry were removed from the Temple of the Sphinx, leaving it somewhat deteriorated. The Valley Temple, however, is still largely intact. Both monuments are roofless, missing the original beams of the ceiling. In the Valley Temple, however, sixteen original interior columns and lintels are still in their place in the T-shaped central room, creating pleasant alternations of light and shadow.

The common elements of these structures are the rigorous austerity devoid of decoration and the constant use of huge stones, many of which weigh about two hundred tons (roughly equivalent to three hundred cars each). The smallest one weighs fifty tons. Such weights could not be lifted by the classic building cranes that normally can raise up to twenty tons at the "minimum extension"—the minimum distance from the tower along the crane jib. The maximum extension limit is around five tons. Loads exceeding fifty tons require a special crane, called a gantry crane, like those seen in factories and industrial ports. In the U.S. a "jib-and-counterweight" crane was taken to a site on Long Island to raise a 200-ton boiler in a factory. The crane had a 67-meter-long jib with 160 tons of counterweight at the end to keep it from capsizing. A team of twenty workers took six weeks to prepare the ground so that the boiler could be lifted.[44] The technician responsible for lifting was shown photos and provided with all technical details related to the blocks of the Valley Temple. When asked if he would be able to place similar blocks with his crane, he replied:

> Looking at these photos, my first thought goes to the travel distance. I am not sure if we would be able to lift 200-ton blocks starting from where they are positioned. . . . When we work with very difficult loads, we try to understand how similar weights have been raised by others who have done it before us. But looking at these huge blocks of 200 tons, displaced thousands and thousands of years ago, I have no idea how it was possible to accomplish such a feat. It is a mystery for me and probably will remain so for all of us.[45]

A technical study has never been undertaken regarding the logistics of the construction of the Sphinx and annexed temples, although the pyramids have been studied by a rather large number of highly qualified architects and engineers.[46] These studies have established that the maximum gradient for a building ramp onto which heavy loads can be driven by men on foot is 10 percent.[47] In the case of the Great Pyramid, which originally reached a height of 146.7 meters, it would have needed a ramp over 1,460 meters long and at least three times more massive than the pyramid itself.[48] A problem of this kind does not arise for the Temple of the Sphinx and the Valley Temple, which are much lower than the pyramids and therefore likely to be built with relatively short ramps. However, the incredible mass and weight of the numerous blocks weighing two hundred tons each found in these temples excludes the use of any ramp made of materials less stable than the limestone blocks used to build the temples themselves.[49]

We can deduce that ramps of compact stone were used, dismantled, and taken away. The question now is how many men were required to transport hundreds of blocks of two hundred tons over these ramps?

The engineer Jean Leherou Kerisel, consultant for construction of the underground of Cairo, studied a technique by which blocks of seventy tons could have been used to build the King's Chamber. According to his calculations the work could have been done, although with great difficulty, by teams of six hundred men lined up in rows on a very large ramp leaning against the side of the pyramid.[50] It follows that in order to move the blocks of the Valley Temple teams of eighteen hundred men would have been required. But could eighteen hundred men actually harness such dense and relatively compact loads with a maximum size per block of approximately 9 by 3 by 3.5 meters? More precisely, since the walls of the temple do not exceed a length of forty meters per side, was it possible to organize such numerous teams in order to make them work efficiently, or simply work, despite the scarce available space?

The Sphinx was built by digging a deep horseshoe-shaped ditch in the bedrock of the plateau of Giza, leaving a central core to be shaped later. Geologists have shown that the megaliths of limestone used for both the temples came from the ditch and were built at the same time as the Sphinx.[51] The temples' megaliths show the same traces of rainfall found on the Sphinx. The blocks of granite cladding appear to have been carved on the inner side in such a way to adapt them to the central blocks of limestone, which at that time were already heavily marked by erosion. The coating seems to belong to a typical architecture of the Old Kingdom (unlike the internal blocks of limestone), which can be considered evidence for the theory that an ancient, revered, and very corroded structure was restored and renovated by the pharaohs of the Old Kingdom. Robert Schoch, professor of geology at Boston University, has said, "I remain convinced that the backs of the Old Kingdom granite facing stones were carved to match or complement the earlier weathering features seen on the surfaces of the core limestone blocks of the temples."[52]

The only written evidence of the Valley Temple, found on the Inventory Stele,* tells us that the monument could not (at least initially) have had anything to do with Chephren for the simple reason that it was built before his reign. The stele dates the construction of the temple back to the First Time at the hands of the gods who settled in the Nile Valley in that period. It explicitly states that the temple is the "House of Osiris, Lord of Rostau."[53]

10,500 BC ?

THE OSIRION OF ABYDOS

Located at Abydos, twelve miles west of the Nile, is a temple preserved in excellent condition with its roof still intact and a range of reliefs adorning its walls. This monument has been attributed to Seti I, who ruled the Nineteenth Dynasty from 1318 to 1298 BCE.

Seti I is famous not only for being the father of Ramesses II (pharaoh of the Exodus in the Bible), but also as a commander of large military campaigns beyond the borders of Egypt. He erected numerous buildings and restored many oeuvres.

His temple at Abydos, also known as the House of Million Years, was dedicated to Osiris, "Lord of the Eternity."[54] Inside the temple everything is reminiscent of King Osiris, the greatest civilizer whose role was god of the dead, installed in the throne and accompanied by Isis. There are many reliefs depicting this figure.

---

*Discovered at Giza in the nineteenth century, the Inventory Stele claims that pyramids were there before the advent of Cheops.

In this place we find other interesting information, such as the list of 120 gods of ancient Egypt combined with their main temples. In addition the names of the seventy-six pharaohs who had preceded Seti I on the throne are inscribed within oval cartouches ("List of the Kings of Abydos"). This table covers a period of nearly seventeen hundred years, from about 3000 BCE (date of the reign of Narmer) to the real realm of Seti I himself, approximately 1300 BCE.

Behind the temple a large underground construction, a hypogeum, was found. The structure opens at the front through a huge stone door made of gigantic blocks of granite and sandstone. The interior of the hypogeum is very large, about sixty meters long and twenty-two meters wide, and was built with huge stones. Along the four walls are seventeen cells as high as a man with no decoration at all. They have no floor and are instead full of increasingly wet sand and soil. The structure was once filled with water, and probably the cells were reached by boat.[55]

The building itself is divided into three naves, the central one wider than the two on the sides. The division is made up of two colonnades composed of huge granite monoliths supporting architraves of similar magnitude. The stone lintels are almost eight meters long (plate 18).

According to John Anthony West, Osirion presents as many signs of rain erosion as the temple of the Sphinx and therefore should also be dated to the eleventh millennium BCE.[56]

The architecture of this temple, contiguous to the monument erected by Seti I, makes us believe it is much older than the scholars claim. Also, since monoliths were used as they were for the Valley Temple and the Temple of the Sphinx, it is natural to ask why they used blocks of granite more than seven meters long instead of smaller and more manageable blocks. Were they meant to endure over time as evidence of a lost civilization?

THE TEMPLE OF EDFU
AND THE SEVEN SAGES

The Edfu monument is one of the finest preserved temples in Egypt. The beginning of its construction is dated around 237 BCE.

Long rows of hieroglyphics engraved on the walls of limestone say that the present temple is a copy of an original, earlier temple and speak of several reconstructions. These Edfu Building Texts say that the initial construction of the temple was determined by a preexisting entity of mythical nature during the First Time. The tradition says also that a group of divine beings—here named the "seven wise men" or "seven sages" instead of the usual appellation of "followers of Horus"—had moved to Egypt to build "sacred hills" in various points. These hills would serve as both foundation and reference for the orientation of temples that were to be erected in the future. The aim was to promote the "resurrection of the former world of the gods," an area that stood on an island in the middle of primordial waters far away in time that was completely and suddenly swept away by a great flood. In this tragic event the majority of its "divine inhabitants" perished.[57]

ANCIENT CIVILIZATIONS

We can now try to summarize what happened from the end of Atlantis to the construction of the first Egyptian monuments. The whole human race had risked extinction due to a cataclysm. The Pelasgians had fled from Atlantis to explore the globe and had built an empire in the Mediterranean millennia before Rome was born. In 10,500 BCE they arrived in Egypt, led by Osiris/Menes, and joined the local people, who were indigenous Negroid such as the image engraved in the Sphinx.

The first inhabitants of Egypt considered the Pelasgians as gods because of their extraordinary knowledge. They brought the universal writing, Iberian, mixing it with the Nubians' ideograms, thus developing the Egyptian hieroglyphic.[58]

Among these men-gods, besides Osiris, stood out Isis-Io, Seth-Danaus, and Thoth. Thoth, as the Etruscan Tages, was attributed a corpus of texts containing the knowledge necessary to understand human destiny and obtain life after death. Diodorus Siculus tells us "he was the first who distinguished the articulation of words, thus creating the common tongue, assigned to many things their names, found the letters and organized the worship and sacrifices."[59]

To this period we collocate the construction of the Sphinx and the Pillars of Osiris (the megalithic towers) in order to reproduce heaven on Earth. In a medieval manuscript preserved at Oxford, drawn up by the Arab writer Al-Masudi, we read:

> The Great Pyramid is not a tomb. It hides an older part built by Surrid (Osiris) before the flood, to preserve for posterity the memories of the civilizations he founded.[60]

It was during these same years that Osiris usurped the throne of his brother Seth/Danaus and then conducted a military campaign in the East.

In 9600 BCE there would have been another flood, and again mankind risked extinction and returned to the primitive state. According to the myth, elites of wise men called the Followers of Horus would have survived in Egypt, which would have maintained and perpetuated over the years the mysteries and secrets of the ancient civilization that brought the knowledge to this land.

In 6700 BCE they fled to the current Nubia to shelter from the third and last flood, marking the end of the ice melting. The spreading of agriculture and livestock farming followed, thus encouraging the development of settled villages. There followed a period of "climatic optimum" in which the melted glacier water had not yet solidified in the new poles, maintaining a higher overall temperature on the Earth.

This phenomenon, which ended around 3500 BCE, was followed by a cooling of the Earth: the average temperature was lower, rain fell, Sahara's lakes drained, and Nubian peoples migrated to the Nile in search of water and cultivable land. The migration from the east of Akkadian peoples caused them to mingle with the Nubians, leading to an increase in the population that allowed—thanks to the knowledge perpetuated by the Followers of Horus—the birth of the Egyptian Pharaonic civilization.*

---

*This migration is confirmed by the ankh (the Egyptian symbol of life) that the Akkadian high priests used for the blessing of couples getting married. See Mario Pincherle, *I Mandei* (Diegaro di Cesina, Italy: Macro Edizioni, 2003).

Under the Fourth Dynasty pyramids were built in the sacred sites of the towers, covering the remains or, in the case of Cheops, incorporating them into the new structure.

JOURNEY TO THE EAST OF OSIRIS: HYPERBOREA

The historian Diodorus Siculus tells us that Osiris, desirous of fame, put together an army to visit all inhabited lands to teach the populations how to plant the grapevine* and sow wheat and barley in order to cancel the "human stupidity" that prevailed in that chaotic time.[61]

He organized the Egyptian state and gave supreme power to his wife, Isis, to whom he provided the wise counselor Thoth.

He went initially to the lands of Ethiopia and from there, like Alexander the Great, through the Middle East, and he was worshipped as king because of his knowledge. Evidence of his arrival in India was collected by western reporters in the fourth century BCE.

Some writers followed Alexander the Great in his conquests in the East from 334 to 324 BCE. Among these, Onesicritus and Nearchus shipped down the Indus River and from its estuary skirted India up to the mouth of the Persian Gulf, and then from here back up to Susiana. Megasthenes then went via land past the places conquered by Alexander and further into India. All the works of these authors are lost, but the memories they collected were preserved by Strabo in *Geography* and by Arrian in *Anabasis Alexandri* (a history of Alexander's campaign and a journal detailing Nearchus's voyages), and in *Indica*. Thanks to these writers we know Indians of that period used to tell of a conqueror called Bacchus or Jacco or Iano coming from the West who brought them the first seeds of civil life. We have already identified Osiris with Bacchus or Menes, and it is easy to think

---

*The interest in the planting of the vine associated Bacchus with Osiris/Dionysus/Janus. The ancient Greeks called Italy "Oenotria," that is, mother or homeland of wine; this epithet indicated the western origin of the vine. Janus himself is often named "Oenotrio" and Aristides and Lucian call him "king of Italy." Apollodorus wrote that the first vine was brought to Greece by Ceres and Dionysus, strangers of the Atalantean people (Apollodorus, *Bibliotheca*, book 3, chapter 14).

that the Hindus referred to the same person when talking about a civilizer named Manu, whose assonance with Meni or Menes is undisputed.*

The Nisaean ambassadors, inhabiting current southern Turkmenistan on the eastern shore of the Caspian Sea, and belonging to the Arimaspian people, came to Alexander to plead for the preservation of their liberty. They told him that Nisa, their capital, was founded by Bacchus on the banks of Cofene (ten kilometers from Ashgabat) in collaboration with the disabled soldiers returning with him from the expedition in India.[62] The ambassadors of other Indian peoples, the Malloi (or Malla) and the Hydrakes (or Oxydrakai), reported of preserving their freedom and independence since the days when Bacchus came to India.[63] Diodorus adds:

> In ancient times, the Indians being divided into small villages with no union, Osiris or Bacchus arrived from the West. He gave the Indians seeds and shoots of fruit, and told them how to produce wine, and use many things; he taught to worship the gods, founded cities, gave laws, established the courts, and for all these benefits he was believed to be a God. They add that there also arrived Hercules, who left progeny.[64]

Indeed in the Indian traditions there is mention of one man who survived a deluge named Pramathesa, which sounds not far from Prometheus/ Osiris, Deucalion's father.[65]

For his eastern campaign, Osiris gathered many soldiers from a region of his empire known in history as Hyperborea, the current Po Valley and northern Tuscany, birthplace of Apollo. It was one of the Hyperboreans, Dardanus, the son of Electra and grandson of Atlas, who founded the city of Troy on the Hellespont and conveyed the cult of Apollo.†

---

*Tibetan traditions give Manu the epithet "king of the world" due to its connotation of the king of the underworld. It is curious to note how in the Jewish tradition the same epithet refers to the Pelasgian Sataniel, later called Satan, king of the underworld, or hell.
†We find an echo of the transit of Osiris in this land in the legend of the construction of Turin. The Turins claimed the city was founded by the Great Civilizer and were said to keep an "Iseion" (temple dedicated to Isis) underneath the neoclassical temple of the Great Mother. According to what Filiberto Pingon of Savoy wrote in his *History of Turin* (1577) this happened when the giants, namely the Pelasgians, inhabited that place. Perhaps the city of Mantua derives its name from Apollo himself, whom the Etruscans called Manth.

Pliny, in his *Naturalis Historia,* places Hyperborea beyond an inhospitable region:

> for the frequent snowfalls, in the likeness of feathers, a part of the world condemned by nature and immersed in a thick darkness, occupied only by the action of frost. . . . It is believed that in that place [Hyperborea] are the hinges of the world and the extreme limits of the revolutions of the stars, with six months of light and a single day without sunshine . . . for them the sun rises once a year . . . and sets once. . . . It is a bright region with mild climate, devoid of any harmful scourge.

The passage is largely contradictory, speaking first of polar conditions such as frost, darkness, and six months of continuous light without ever seeing the sun go down, and then describes a bright region with a mild climate. In fact, these are reminiscences of what happened to their native land, Antarctica, when the sliding of the crust imprisoned a once temperate land in a freezing cold. Such a passage has commissioned the most brilliant brains to seek Hyperborea all around the world, starting from the Baltic Sea, although the vast majority of the materials was passed down to us by the Greeks, while the Latins clearly placed it in northern Italy. To justify this assertion, we have verified some of this material.

Phaethon, or Horus, was the son of Osiris. It is told how one day Phaethon had stolen his father's solar chariot, yet unable to drive it, he fell from the sky into the Eridanus. On the border of that river he was buried by his sisters, who wept over him tears of electro, then transformed into poplars. This story originally intended to describe a disaster in heaven (meaning the sky), and Eridanus was perhaps the homonymous constellation of the celestial river. In this regard in *Timaeus* Plato tells of Solon (640–560 BCE), who, having gone to Egypt, received the following explanation from an Egyptian priest:

> There is a story, which even you have preserved, that once upon a time Phaethon, the son of Helios, having yoked the steeds in his father's chariot, because he was not able to drive them in the path

of his father, burnt up all that was upon the earth, and was himself destroyed by a thunderbolt. <u>Now this has the form of a myth, but really signifies a deviation of the bodies moving in the heavens around the earth, and a great conflagration of things upon the earth, which recurs after long intervals.</u>

Mythology remembers the Eridanus as the river crossing Hyperborea. Hesiod[66] places the Hyperboreans "at the falls of the deep-bedded Eridanus." The quote might suggest the re-baptism of a river hit by frequent falls of meteorites, such as the areas of Cremona and Bergamo in the Po Valley (see box).

Antonia Bertocchi in *Hera,*
February 2009

Aristotle has left us the memory of a pool of warm water from the pestilential exhalations located near the Po, where the locals thought the struck Phaeton had fallen. (See De *Mirabilibus Auscultationibus* [On Marvelous Things Heard], chapter 81.) I think it is identified with the legendary Gerundo Lake that once stretched from Bergamo, to Crema and Lodi, up to the confluence of Adda with Po', near Cremona. It did in fact possess the characteristics described by the philosopher and also responded to other characteristics specified by Apollonius Rhodius* such as the flammability of those poisonous waters and its being in a forward position along the course of the river. . . . The first, the hot and poisonous water, is the result of the phenomena of decay, whose grandeur is connected to the second clue: the flammability of such poisonous waters. The most likely hypothesis is that, after the processes of eutrophication, some large fires have occurred that triggered other processes of demolition of the organic matter under anaerobic conditions. That is, in the absence of oxygen, there developed the methane gas which is toxic and flammable. We have an example (microscopic) in the ignis fatuous that appear in the tombs of buried corpses. Methane gas is a hydrocarbon, a highly flammable organic chemical compound with a high calorific power, discovered by Alessandro Volta in 1778 who called it "inflammable air native of the wetlands." In support of this hypothesis, it is worth remembering that in these places there are still some active deposits of methane gas, for example in Cortemaggiore, on the right side of the Po, 15 kilometers south of Cremona and in Bordolano, about 15 kilometers northwest, in the direction of Cremona toward Bergamo. In 1952 a fire broke out in Bordolano: gas at 200 atmospheres burned for more than thirty days causing hot flashes that were seen from afar. As we all know, the most acclaimed monsters that produce poisonous "fire throwers" breath are the dragons. And in fact there was a terrifying one in Gerundo Lake: the dragon Tarantàsio or Tarànto, metaphor of such a landscape and protagonist of Lodi's legends.[†] Gerundo Lake was of meteoric origin, as proved by the findings of mammoth's ribs inside of it, brought to light by the impact of geological upheaval, still preserved in the churches of Cremona and Bergamo as the ribs of dragon Tarànto. Even today, the lake area has experienced a number of impacts of meteorites, from the smallest, fallen in Acquanegra Cremonese in 1937, to the largest ones, described by the historian of the seventeenth century Pietro da Terni, who wrote the history of Crema 1470 to 1557 on the basis of an anonymous 1500 text.

---

*The ship, Argo, went so far forward due to the sails that it entered the Eridanus's upper course—where Phaeton was once struck at the heart by a flame of lightning and from the chariot of the sun fell half burned in the water of the deep swamp. Today a heavy steam still rises from the burn wound and birds cannot cross the water expanse by stretching their spread wings, but fall, burned mid-flight (see *Argonautica*, book 4 by Apollonius of Rhodes).

†Antonia Bertocchi, "Inferni e paradisi nella Padania atlantidea," *Hera* (February 2009).

In *Theogony* Hesiod says that the Eridanus flows into the Mediterranean. At the time of Herodotus, when knowledge of the Earth was widening, merchants began to talk of a sea situated in the direction of the north wind from where amber was exported to the south. Believing that the amber was the electro (which now means an alloy of gold and silver) mentioned in the myth, they began to think that the Eridanus was the earthly river that led into that sea, namely the northern Adriatic. We are obviously talking about the Po. In *Talia,* certain of his knowledge on the celestial river, Herodotus wrote, "I do not allow that there is any river, to which the barbarians give the name of Eridanus, emptying itself into the northern sea, whence (as the tale goes) amber is procured."

It is not really important to understand when the Eridanus was "moved" from heaven to Earth; rather it is useful to clarify that when the Po was baptized Eridanus it flowed into a sea that the Greeks said was windward of Boreas (god of the north wind).* So, speaking of Hyperborea, which is the land of the north (with regard to Greece), they clearly spoke of the land beyond that sea where the Po flowed: the Padan Plain or Plain of the Po.†

In two passages of *Attica* Greek geographer Pausanias informs us that the Eridanus flowed through the campaigns of the Gauls (Celts). Also, Pausania writes, "Swan was king of the Ligurians beyond the Eridanus in the country of the Celts."[67] According to ancient tradition gathered by Catullus and Lucian, Swan was located on the hillside overlooking Brescia, whose inhabitants are referred to as Celts and Ligurians by Pausanias.

---

*Timaeus makes the Eridanus flow into the Ligurian Gulf: "The amber was thought to be coming from the Eridanus, which, according to the information they had, flows into the Northern Ocean." It is no mistake, because as Apollonius of Rhodes says (book 4, 630–631), the Eridanus was identified with the Po, but in mythical geography it is the emblematic river of the northwest, representing at the same time both the Rhone and the Po "gushing from the ends of the earth, where are the portals and mansions of Night."

†Reading Herodotus, it is not difficult to understand that the idea that Eridanus would be found in the countries on the Baltic Sea relies on the belief that the amber came from there. According to Herodotus the name Eridanus (Great River) was not barbarian but had Greek origins and was imposed on the Po by the Pelasgians themselves, while in the Greek territory the generic phrase "great river" indicated the river that received the waters of all the rivers of half the Italian territory.

Lucian located the tales of Phaethon in Italy since he was convinced that they referred to someone who "showed the paths of sky with great diligence, and who died leaving the science imperfect" (see Lucian's *Astrology*, volume 3). The connotation of Phaethon as a master astronomer, then, more likely places him within the family of Osiris. At Altino (Chieti, Italy) there is a forest of poplars called "Forest of Phaethon," and in his *Epigrams*, Martial spoke of this forest as a renowned place. In his works, Lucian repeatedly says he arrived in Lombardy and, sailing up the Po, mocked the poets who were questioning the boatmen on the electro, the swans, and the adventures of Phaethon. He amazed them by telling them that the mad Greeks thought that their poplars poured such rich tears (see Lucian's *Amber or the Swans*). The story simply highlights that the Greeks had always attributed these traditions to the river Po.

In classical Greek "atlas" was a general term for mountain; "Hyperborean Atlas," for example, would indicate the Alps,[68] although today it is only used to describe the Libyan Atlas. Plutarch, in *Life of Camillus*, quotes the words of Heraclides Ponticus and reports how an army of Hyperboreans had taken Rome. He was referring to the Gauls, who at that time did not live beyond the Alps, but in that part of Italy called Cisalpine Gaul. At the time of Heraclides Ponticus, the Hyperboreans were the contemporary inhabitants of Lombardy, if not of Istria, situated on the sea toward Boreas, namely the Adriatic Sea. Pherecydes told that the Hyperboreans were of a titanic race, and that the Pelasgians were firstly named Hyperboreans.[69]

Now we can better comprehend ancient traditions that say the first roots of wild olive "have been introduced in Greece by Heracles from the land of the Hyperboreans," and that Heracles "crowned the winner [of the Olympic Games] with a branch of wild olive";[70] "the first-fruits of the Hyperboreans had sent to Delos their gifts hidden in wheat straw";[71] "the most ancient temple of Apollo was made of laurel. . . . This temple must have had the form of a hut made by bees from bees-wax and feathers, and that it was sent to the Hyperboreans by Apollo";[72] "Abari, coming from the Hyperboreans, had erected in Laconia, at Scias, a temple to Proserpine," and many others are scattered in the books of several Greek writers. This is because the olive tree grows wild along the shores of Garda Lake, the first culture of bees was Italian,* and Proserpine and Ceres, who spread to the world the first seeds of wheat, were born in this country.[73]

Hecataeus of Miletus (seventh century BCE) placed the Hyperboreans between the Ocean (the Tyrrhenian Sea; see chapter 1) and the Riphean Mountains. These mountains appear, along with the river Ister, in Hyperborea's geography, as reported by authors such as Virgil, Strabo, Pindar, Hellanicus of Lesbos, Damastes of Sigeo, and Hecataeus of Abdera, and seem to be identifiable with the Alps. The Ister would be the Po or another river of the Padan Plain. In a passage of *Prometheus Unbound* the Greek playwright Aeschylus, who lived between 525 and 456 BCE, asserted that the sources of Ister are situated in the Hyperboreans' country and in the Riphean Mountains.

Some reporters of the classical era went against the tide, identifying the Ister with the Danube and the Riphean Mountains with the Urals. Apollodorus told that Hercules would have come to the Caucasus to free Prometheus and remove the apples that were in the Hyperboreans' Atlas.[74] Such confusion leads us to suppose that the geographical names of the Hyperboreans were copied (transposed) in Asia, including the same name "Hyperborea." Indeed, this is more than plausible, <u>since the Hyperboreans had taken part in Osiris's campaign.</u>

This new "Asian Hyperborea" inspired a passage of Herodotus that summarizes a poem by Aristeas of Proconnesus[75] (sixth century BCE):

Then there is Aristeas son of Kaystrobios of Proconnesus, who composed verses in which he claims to have been inspired by Phoibos Apollo and to have visited the land of the Issedones. Above the Issedones, he says, live the Arimaspians, one-eyed men; above

---

*Atistéo, the first inventor and teacher of dairy, the culture of bees, and olive trees, was Italian. For more on this see Diodorus Siculus, *The Historical Library*, book 4, and Angelo Mazzoldi, *Delle Origini Italiche* [Of Italic Origins], chapter 8.

them dwell the gold-guarding griffins, and above the griffins, the Hyperboreans, whose land extends all the way to the sea. With the exception of the Hyperboreans, all these peoples, beginning with the Arimaspians, attacked their neighbors in successive waves, so that the Issedones were pushed out by the Arimaspians, the Scythians by the Issedones, and the Cimmerians living along the sea to the south were forced by the Scythians to leave their country, too.[76]

According to the story by Aristeas of Proconnesus, among the Greeks and the Hyperboreans were allocated at least three Asian peoples: the Scythians, the Issedoni, and the Arimaspians.

The Scythians, also known as Saka, occupied the shores of the Black Sea, the Caucasus, and northeastern Turkey earlier than the fifteenth century BCE, when they were a scourge for the Hittite empire. Aristeas places a Cimmerian people along the Black Sea, just west of the Scythians, while other authors (including Homer) indicated with "Cimmerians" the inhabitants of Cuma, a region of Campania, in southern Italy. This may indicate a name shared between two populations or a displacement of the Cimmerians from Italy to the east, due to the same campaign.

Apart from Herodotus's summary we have received only a few quotations of the poem of Aristeas from the Byzantine Tzetzes. In Chiliades[77] a verse recalls the Issedoni were proud of their long hair,[78] and five other verses introduce the Arimaspians as brave warriors on the northern border who were breeders of horses, sheep, and oxen, with one eye only, thick hair, and extraordinary vigor.[79] Ptolemy speaks of a city named Issedon Serica situated in the country of the Seris (most likely identifiable with the current Khotan in Uygur, Kazakhstan), where they once spoke an Iranian dialect called Khotanese, a variant of Sogdian. The name Arimaspians can be interpreted by the sum of two Iranian words, *ariama* and *aspa,* meaning "those who love horses," which is well suited to the Central Asian nomadic peoples on horseback. We saw in the previous paragraphs that they inhabited the present Turkmenistan on the eastern shore of the Caspian Sea, and among their cities they counted Nysa, founded by Osiris with the disabled soldiers returning from the campaign. The invalidity of the soldiers led to the connotation of "monocle Arimaspians." Therefore, we can assume that the Hyperboreans of the Po Valley had founded a colony in the Indus Valley, or at least in Asia. This would explain why Pliny in *Historia Naturalis* placed Hyperborea in the direction of the aquilonis (north wind) blowing from the northeast. Likely the passage reported by Pliny about Indian traditions—which will be studied more deeply in the next chapter—also becomes clearer when interpreting it as a reminder of the original Pelasgians, in particular when it tells of a homeland where day and night lasted six months and the stars traced circles in the sky instead of rising in the east and setting in the west.

TRAILS OF CIVILIZATION IN THE DESERT

Egyptologists date the beginning of the dynastic age at around 3100 BCE, while an earlier period was marked by the advent of Osiris/Menes in Egypt and the civilization of the Mediterranean. We also know two floods (9600 BCE and 6700 BCE) wiped out the civilization and the surviving Pelasgians constituted the Followers of Horus, an organization responsible for preserving antediluvian knowledge. They sought a safe land, moving toward up-country Africa in western Nubia and in the current eastern Sahara Desert, where thousands of years ago there was a thriving atmosphere suitable for the development of agriculture and livestock. Here the "livestock people" developed—the first spark of Pharaonic civilization.

In ancient times the Nile Valley was not a warm and fertile place but a swampy and inhospitable land, infested with reptiles and diseases. It was therefore an ominous atmosphere for the birth and development of any human settlement. Since 12,000 BCE, with the end of the last ice age, the situation changed drastically due to sudden floods that poured into the Nile from the lakes of central Africa, swollen by the arrival of the monsoon. This phenomenon led to a "cleansing" of the whole valley. Slowly, there came a warmer climate and swamps gradually withdrew, leaving huge spaces and green valleys on the borders of the desert. The heavy rainfall considerably marked the profile of the Sphinx, built in 10,500 BCE, which was initially the sculpture of a "simple" lion. From 6700 BCE the rain stopped abruptly and the desert walked in, reducing the fertile areas (around 3500 BCE) to a thin strip at the edge of the Nile, where Pharaonic Egypt was. To the west was the Sahara, where some organized rural communities lived at that time, some of which were Followers of Horus. Tall, lean, and dark-skinned, they have been termed by anthropologists "the cattle people" because after periods of floods they were the first to domesticate animals (especially cows). They would also develop the cultivation of cereals, navigation, time calculation, the creation of calendars, and the study of the sky (carefully recording positions of the sun and stars) and were the first to bury their dead in ceremonial graves.

These people traveled great distances in the desert in search of lakes that were formed inside dry depressions in the month of June after the passage of the monsoon rains. When these dried up they went to other places in search of water.

One of the temporary lakes (which became a permanent settlement in 5000 BCE), now known as Nabta Playa, is located about one hundred kilometers west of the Nile. Here they began the excavation of wells that were used to collect water in the dry season. No longer needing to travel the desert in search of water, they now had more time available and slowly began to transform their knowledge of navigation by the stars in a true "religion of the sky" with complex rituals and ceremonies. They knew the first rising of the constellation of Orion and the star Sirius at that time during the summer solstice; watching the circumpolar northern stars (especially the Big Dipper) they could predict the duration of both the night and the seasons.

Since 6500 BCE in Nabta Playa the development of a huge ceremonial complex linked to a kind of astronomical calendar began that consisted of a circular array of a twenty-eight vertical stones driven into the ground, more or less variable in size, with two sets of "doors" or "viewfinders." The first is aligned with the north-south cardinal axis, while the second is parallel to an axis stretching from southwest to northeast, toward the point of sunrise at the summer solstice.

In addition to this circle enormous blocks of stone were found, including one driven almost three meters below the ground, machined and polished by man, and carved with an irregular shape of a cow. Moreover, to the west of the circle there were found ten mounds of earth covered with stones beneath which there were some cows' bones, their heads turned southward. One of the mounds hid the complete skeleton of a young cow along with a few small bones and stone amulets. South of these mounds have been found about thirty megalithic structures arranged in oval shapes, each containing a horizontal slab in the center, with almost all the slabs oriented to the north. With regard to the discovery of human skeletons, we have no feedback on the site of Nabta Playa. However, about twenty miles away, in a place called Jebel Ramlah, there were found sixty-seven human burials that, thanks to carbon-14, have been dated to around 4360 BCE: probably the remains of the people who built the ceremonial complex of Nabta Playa.

These findings reveal three fundamental characteristics of this population:

1. They were great observers of the solar cycle and the movement of the stars.
2. Like the ancient Egyptians, they worshipped the cow.*
3. They were the first (Mediterranean) people, after the floods, to bury their dead in burial mounds.

After 3400 BCE Nabta Playa was abandoned forever—with the sudden disappearance of the monsoons the area became barren and dry. Therefore, the people of the stars, along with their livestock and knowledge, migrated east to the Nile Valley.[80]

THE STONE CIRCLES

Let us now examine in detail the meaning of the circle of stones of Nabta Playa. It has been named the Calendar Circle or the Cromlech, and apparently it served to observe and determine various astronomical aspects,

---

*During the Pharaonic age they worshipped the goddess "Celestial Cow Nut," believed to be the bearer of the stars, and the cow goddess Hathor, who represented an evolution of the figure of Isis and thus was associated with the star Sirius.

including the arrival of summer solstice, the change of the seasons, and the length of the day.

According to a study by astronomer Kim Malville and anthropologist Fred Wendorf, six rows of megaliths extend through the establishment of Nabta Playa, and like the spokes of a wheel they fan out across the eastern portion of the Calendar Circle, extending to the east beyond. These lines coincide with the rising position of three preeminent stars in the period between 4800 BCE and 3700 BCE: Sirius (in 4820 BCE), Dubhe (the brightest star in Ursa Major, from 4742 BCE to 4199 BCE), and the stars of Orion's belt (in 4176 BCE and 3786 BCE).

Enough has been said about the value of Sirius and Orion for the Egyptians, but not enough regarding Dubhe, who actually is the protagonist in the ceremony of the astral alignment called "stretching the cord." In this ceremony the pharaoh, assisted by a priestess (who played the role of the goddess Seshat, Thoth's wife), checked the axes of pyramids or temples, using as a reference the stars of Ursa Major.

Other studies done by Thomas Brophy, a former NASA astrophysicist, with the help of high-resolution satellite images of the site of Nabta Playa, have established a further alignment of stones oriented toward the belt of Orion as early as 6270 BCE.

It seems that the complex of Nabta Playa is the oldest astronomical calendar of the world, perhaps older than Stonehenge.

THE BLACK MUMMIES

Another piece of evidence supporting the theory of at least a partial origin of the Egyptian people from the African strain can be found in the discovery of black mummies in some tombs of ancient Egypt. In 1792 anthropologist and German physiologist Johann Blumenbach discovered such tombs, where he found the remains of mummies belonging to two different families, one white Semite and another one more numerous and morphologically very different: big lips, prominent cheeks, flat nose. These parameters clearly identify a Negroid people, precisely, Nubian.

In 1840 Professor Angelo Mazzoldi wrote:

As to the population, consider true the ancient Nubians' tradition reported by Diodorus, that the Egyptians were a colony that came from their town, located south of Egypt. Blumenbach, who had to unwind and dissected several mummies extracted from the catacombs of Egypt, proved without a doubt how their skulls belonged to two separate and distinct large families: in one he had seen all the signs of Nubian race with its thick lips, prominent cheeks, flat nose, whose type is repeated in the famous Egyptian sphinx; in the other, instead, there were all the tracts of the white race he called Caucasian. In this regard, see the *Dissertation* on these mummies Blumenbach published at Göttingen in 1794.[81]

THE END AND THE BEGINNING

Now, a quick summary and then we'll leave the black mummies and run back to that irreverent 10,500 BCE . . .

10,500 BCE

ATLANTEAN Pelasgian colonization of Egypt under the illegitimate king Menes/
Osiris and mingling with the indigenous blacks (Nubians).
- Birth of the hieroglyphics by contact between the Pelasgian alphabet and the Nubian ideograms.
- Beginning of the building project of the Sphinx and of other structures (Zed or Pillars of Osiris) reproducing the sky of Orion-Sirius and of Hyades.
- War against the legitimate king Danaus/Seth and victory of the latter, later deposed by the son of Osiris, Deucalion/Horus.

9600 BCE
- Second flood.
- Beginning of decline; the civilization reverts to the primitive state.

6700 BCE
- Third flood.
- End of the ice melting.

- Agriculture and livestock take on a new life, and settled villages are reborn.
- The "climatic optimum" begins and a phase of global warming starts due to the abundant amount of water in the oceans, which has not yet become ice at the new poles.
- The Followers of Horus find a safe land in Nubia; old ideas and cults come back to life.
- Construction of stone circles in the Sahara lakes (also at Nabta Playa).

3500 BCE

- End of "climatic optimum"; the global temperature drops and rain-fall stops.
- The Sahara lakes become dry and the Nubians move to the Nile.
- Akkadians coming from the east migrate and mingle with the Nubians.
- The population increase stimulates the growth of the Pharaonic Egyptian civilization.
- The head of the Sphinx is re-sculpted by one of the first black pharaohs.
- The new adopted language is Hamitic-Semitic and hieroglyphs are adapted and used to write it.

2500 BCE

- Under the Fourth Dynasty pyramids are built where the Pillars of Osiris once were.

Such fascinating things were whispered about lower pyramid passages not in the guide-books; passages whose entrances had been hastily blocked up and concealed by certain uncommunicative archaeologists who had found and begun to explore them.

H. P. LOVECRAFT,
UNDER THE PYRAMIDS

The Earth was . . . subject to many violent revolutions of nature. By one of such revolutions, that portion of the upper world inhabited by the ancestors of this race had been subjected to inundations, not gradual, but rapid and uncontrollable, in which all, save a scanty remnant, were submerged and perished. . . . A band of the ill-fated race, thus invaded by the flood, had, during the march of the waters, taken refuge in caverns amidst the loftier rocks, and, wandering through these hollows, they lost sight of the upper world forever. In the bowels of the inner earth, even now, I was informed as a positive fact, might be discovered remains of human habitation—habitation not in huts and cavers, but in vast cities whose ruins attest the civilization of races which flourished before the age of Noah, and are not to be classified with those genera to which philosophy ascribes the use of flint and the ignorance of iron.

EDWARD BULWER LYTTON,
THE COMING RACE

This story inevitably takes us to India in the wake of Osiris and his army . . .

6

PELASGIAN MIGRATION TO THE INDUS VALLEY

Archaeology is the search for fact. Not truth. If it's truth you're interested in, Doctor Tyree's Philosophy class is right down the hall. . . . So forget any ideas you've got about lost cities, exotic travel, and digging up the world. We do not follow maps to buried treasure and "X" never, ever marks the spot. Seventy percent of all archaeology is done in the library. Research. Reading. We cannot afford to take mythology at face value.

HENRY JONES JR. (INDIANA JONES),
INDIANA JONES AND THE LAST CRUSADE

In 10,000 BCE there was a great march: tens of thousands of soldiers, thousands of wagons and horses, spears, shields, and swords, under the fast-paced rhythm of metallic roar. Osiris had recruited the largest army on Earth, and had also obtained the alliance of the Libyan Amazons. They moved to one side, shy of the curious glances of the soldiers; they

188

moved together, men who could not conceive of women in battle and women who would have never wanted to fight for a man, together, toward the unknown East.

The Amazon soldiers would be rewarded with Scythia on the Caucasus: Diodorus Siculus had said so and proof is the recent discovery of the tombs of the "warrior queens." The human river got further than Alexander, up to Indochina. There Osiris built some towers, pillars in the form of the Draco constellation, whereas in Asia he built several cities, like the already mentioned Nisa.

The soldiers from Hyperborea (the Po Valley and northern Tuscany) founded in Asia another homonymous jurisdiction: it is the Hyperborea narrated by Herodotus, Aristeas of Proconnesus, and Pliny the Elder, just to name a few, and was situated northeast of the aquilonis, beyond the village of monocle Arimaspians.

We can divide the legacy left by the passage of Osiris through India into three strands: the four compilations of Hinduism's sacred hymns, known as the Vedas ("knowledge"); the Indus-Sarasvati civilization; and finally a nonquantifiable number of underwater sites off the coast of India.

A MYSTERIOUS CIVILIZATION

It was a mysterious civilization that left a legacy of over two thousand sites between the Indus Valley and, farther east, along the river Sarasvati that has been dry for more than four thousand years. Mostly these places were cities, planned and built according to a project, complete with urban sewage, areas for public garbage cans, and tidal basins. The towns were mostly built with baked mud bricks using molds of standard size,[1] so exceptionally made as to have been widely used by builders in the nineteenth and early twentieth centuries. The settlements were designed based on a grid, with streets and buildings aligned along the cardinal directions, under the direction of expert astronomers. It is reasonable to assume that this civilization regarded astronomy as a science and linked it to religion.[2]

At its peak around 2500 BCE this civilization, called Indus-Sarasvati, could boast at least six cities in the hinterland counting more than thirty thousand inhabitants. These cities were linked to hundreds of smaller towns and villages and many key ports like Lothal and Dholavira, along the coast and navigable rivers. There were overseas outposts, including a thriving colony in the Persian Gulf, and an extensive sales network supported by a large merchant fleet.[3]

The writing of their inhabitants has not been completely translated: from 4,200 artifacts, including crockery and seals of steatite (soapstone) and clay, emerges a fully formed system of signs called "graphemes," for a total of about four hundred signs.[4] Writing, in its mature form, suddenly appeared around 2600 BCE. The reasons that may explain its appearance from day to day are manifold: maybe it was invented and introduced all at once, or its use was previously reserved for commercial and bureaucratic purposes, or this civilization may have chosen not to use its own writing to spread information of great cultural importance.

Non-Indian archaeologists claim that the Vedic hymns were encoded around 1200 BCE, which is paradoxical considering that it was quite a poor intellectual period in India.

Protagonists in the Vedas are the "Aryans" or the "noble or learned people." The similarity among the different European languages had already demonstrated the existence of an "original" people, speaking a "mother" tongue from which the others were derived. The accounts of travelers and merchants who visited India in the sixteenth century kindled interest and curiosity about the unexplained similarities within European languages and Sanskrit, of which the Vedic language is an archaic version. Thomas Stephens, Filippo Sassetti, and Bonaventura Volcano discovered a remarkable number of similarities in the fields of numbers and kinship terminology despite numerous and profound differences in climate, religion, and culture.* In 1790 the first grammar of Sanskrit appeared in Europe, written by the Carmelite Paulinus a Sancto Bartholomaeo and published in Rome. It was later improved by H. T. Colebrooke (*A Grammar of the Sanskrit Language,* Calcutta, 1805).

---

*Examples of numerals: εἰσ, unus, ékas; δϕο, duo, dvau; τρεῖσ, tres, tràyas; ζξ, sex, sas; ζπτά, septem, saptà; ὁχτω, octo, astau; ζννζα, novem, nàva; δζχα, decem, dasa. Parental examples: πατήρ, pater, pitàr; μάτηρ, mater, matàr; ϕράτηρ, frater, bhratar; νυόσ, nurus, snusà; vidua, vidhàva.

Londoner and Orientalist Sir William Jones, judge at the Supreme Court of Calcutta, founder and president of the Royal Asiatic Society of Bengala, was born in 1746. During the company presidential speech in 1786 he made a pronouncement that is generally regarded as the first scientific view of the origins of Sanskrit and the European languages:

> The Sanskrit language, whatever be its antiquity, is of a wonderful structure; more perfect than the Greek, more copious than the Latin, and more exquisitely refined than either, yet bearing to both of them a stronger affinity, both in the roots of verbs and the forms of grammar, than couldn't possibly have been produced by accident; so strong indeed, that no philologer could examine them all three, without believing them to have sprung from some common source, which, perhaps, no longer exists.

In the nineteenth century Europeans were certain that their languages and Sanskrit had descended from the same source, the language of the "original people," and naturally identified with the Vedic Aryans. Of course, their origin was believed to be European: "The European intellectual and moral superiority was a foregone conclusion for most of the scholars of the nineteenth and early twentieth century."[5]

According to European history and the cultural development of its peoples the Aryans could not have invaded India—starting from Europe—before 1500 BCE: archaeologists say the Vedas began collecting their stories a few centuries later. By contrast, in the 1920s and 1930s, the excavations in Harappa and Mohenjo-Daro on the Indus River proved that these cities were much older than 1500 BCE and belonged to an ancient and evolved civilization dating back to 3000 BCE, or even earlier. Toward the middle of the third millennium BCE, the inhabited area of Mohenjo-Daro exceeded 250 hectares and it is possible that the population had increased up to 150,000. With the Indus-Sarasvati civilization in the middle, the Aryan invasion in India should have left a clear sign!

Today we know with certainty that the "mother" language was born in the east, and if ever there was an invasion from Europe, it should have taken place before the birth of both this language and the Indus-Sarasvati civilization. Anyway, the dismissing of an "Aryan invasion" was not yet deemed enough to reassess the accepted dating of the Vedas—non-Indian scholars do not even consider the possibility that these texts belong to the Indus-Sarasvati civilization. If they did, due to their proven antiquity, the Indus-Sarasvati civilization would be the ideal candidate as the civilization of the "mother" tongue, a language that from now on we will call "Indo-European."

The people who wrote the Vedas had probably lived in India, and in the Indus Valley, for several millennia since the displacement of peoples occurred during Menes's eastern campaign. The Pelasgians could be identified with the Aryans because of the unmistakable physical characteristics of the Cro-Magnon: light skin and eyes, blond or red hair. Once on the Indus, the Pelasgians became isolated from each other after the second or third flood that coincided with the development of the first settlements in that area. As a consequence, their language took a new course, evolved, and became the so-called Indo-European. A few thousand years later, some groups would migrate back to Europe, bringing the new language.

Upon some seals of steatite, decorated terra-cotta artifacts, and a clay tablet of Harappa appears a figure in the act of strangling two tigers with bare hands. The same pattern is observed in some carved Mesopotamian seals, in the notch of the grip of an ivory knife found at Gebel el-Arak (Egypt) from the Gerzean period (3500–3300 BCE), and in a wall painting of a Gerzean tomb in Hierakonopolis. The story of the strangling of wild animals is found in both the Sumerian Epic of Gilgamesh and Vedic stories, and surprisingly also in the art of Tiahuanaco in Bolivia, an example of which was found embossed on a bronze breastplate.

Indian academics immediately grasped the direct link between Indus-Sarasvati civilization and the Vedic texts. Dr. R. S. Bisht, director of the Archaeological Survey of India, has argued that the hierarchical arrangement of urban districts in the city of Harappa was organized by the *Rig-Veda* system called *trimeshthin* (from the oldest *Rig-Veda*), which includes three different areas of settlement: upper town, middle town, and lower town. He also reported that the city of Dholavira in Gujarat, dating back to the third millennium BCE, measured 771 meters from east to west and 616.8 from north to south, with a ratio of five to four. The upper city measured 114 meters from east to west and 92.5 meters from north to south, with the same ratio of five to four, in conformity with the ancient texts that define the criteria for the construction of the Vedic fire altar.[6]

S. P. Gupta, professor of art history at the National Museum Institute, New Delhi, points out that the main features of Rig-Vedic religion and culture can already be found in the ancient cities along the Indus and Sarasvati rivers. Unlike the old interpretation, according to which the Vedas represent a nomadic and pastoral way of life, everybody now agrees that in the Vedas cities are often referred to as houses of the Aryans. Moreover, excavations have confirmed the presence of livestock and domesticated horses, the use of fire altars, widespread international trade, and deep-sea navigation. According to Gupta:

> Once the Vedas have been demonstrated to contain enough material to assert that the authors of the hymns were fully aware of the city, urban life, business relationships with overseas and distant lands, etc., which were typical of Indus-Sarasvati urban and cultural elements, it becomes easier to understand the theory according to which the features of both Indus-Sarasvati and Vedic civilizations may simply be complementary aspects of a single previous civilization.[7]

THE SEEDS OF KNOWLEDGE

The oldest elements of the oral tradition of India are contained in the Vedas and consist of four *samhita* (compilations of hymns): *Rig-Veda* (the oldest and most revered), *Sama-Veda*, *Yajur-Veda*, and *Atharva-Veda*. The language used for writing these hymns is a very archaic form of Sanskrit. The *Rig-Veda* has 450,000 words in 1,028 hymns formed by 10,589 verses.[8]

For a long time these texts had no written version; it is believed that the priests of the Vedic religion, which later evolved into Hinduism, wanted to keep them alive only in memory.*

---

*It is not, however, that we believe there was nothing at all written. See David Frawley's *Gods, Sages and Kings* (Salt Lake City: Passage Press, 1991).

Writing is never mentioned in the *Rig-Veda*. Indeed, even after writing spread in ancient India there was a strong objection to the transcription of the Vedas. The content of the four books was entirely memorized by the *sruti* and the Brahmins, a priestly Hindu caste, initially by adding or modifying the hymns from generation to generation. At some point, however, the priests themselves decided the texts were immutable, impossible to modify in even a single word or syllable, and even the slightest inaccuracy of pronunciation would have been considered a sacrilege. Gregory Possehl, one of the world's leading authorities on ancient India and the Indus-Sarasvati civilization, says:

> The Indian Brahmins took very seriously the memorization of the Vedas. . . . The scrupulous and even exact oral reproduction of the Vedas was part of the Hindu faith, institutionalized during the learning process and maintained through observation and peers' pressure during a Brahmin's life . . . the deviation from the . . . way of the exact reproduction caused the censorship of powerful forces against the guilty. . . . [Thus, there are] a number of reasons to believe that this oral tradition is different from most others, and that the texts that we read today can be very similar to the remote ones.[9]

According to the generally accepted period of the oldest written versions, it is assumable that it was only one thousand years ago that the ban on transcription was abolished.

MANU AND THE SEVEN SAGES

Manu was the first, and greatest, patriarch and lawmaker of the Vedic people, described as the preserver and father of humanity and of all living creatures.[10] Ralph Griffith, translator of the Vedas, describes him as "the representative man and father of the human race and the first founder of the religious ceremonies."[11] It is said that Manu was one of the greatest devotees of yoga and sacred hymns.

Manu arrived in India accompanied by "Seven Sages" whose main objectives, like the Egyptian Followers of Horus, included the preservation of all known seeds. Together they would survive the flood and preserve the Vedas from destruction by memorizing them in order to hand them over to the human race following the disaster.

After the flood, Manu committed himself to restoring agriculture, using a small hidden treasure of seeds and plants he had brought for this purpose. So Manu and his followers moved to the Himalayas, where they retired to meditate and practice asceticism. They played a decisive role in the management and direction of secular affairs and the appointment and guidance of sovereigns, just like Heliopolis's Egyptian priests.

The name Manu sounds like Menes or Minos, who, in the previous chapters, we have followed in his campaign to India in 10,500 BCE. In the Indian version, Manu survived the flood with an ark on which he sailed with seven wise men upon indication of a fish, which will turn out to be an incarnation of Vishnu. As a reward for having saved the seed of humanity and all living creatures, the gods allowed Manu the understanding of the "mystery of the soul,"[12] mastery of "all knowledge,"[13] superhuman powers, and a millions-of-years lifespan, allowing him to reign for a *manvantara*,[14] sixty-four million and eight hundred years, equal to seventy-one cycles of four *yugas* (epochs or eras). Is it pure coincidence that a similar lifetime of one million years is achieved by Osiris/Menes after his resurrection? And what about the Akkadian version, where Zisudra, who survived the flood, gets eternal life?

> *Life as that of a god they gave him;*
> *Eternal breath as a god, they fell for him,*
> *. . . Zisudra the king.*
> *He who has preserved the names of plants and seeds of*
> *the human species.*[15]

Both Vedic and Akkadian traditions speak of the Seven Sages; in the latter they are described as amphibious creatures, "in the shape of fish," emerged from the sea in the train of Iohannes the civilizer in antediluvian times to teach wisdom to humanity. During the floods both Mesopotamian and Vedic groups were instructed to preserve the gifts of civilization, particularly the seeds of plants, and to appoint and advise the king.

We can assume that the myth of fish suggesting to Manu what to do could be an echo of the amphibian semblance of the Seven; likewise, the Seven Wise Men, followers of Viracocha in Inca traditions, were described as feathered beings, perhaps because of confusion between feathers and scales. We believe they are members of the same institution, and that the number seven is in fact a symbol. Perhaps their amphibious representation was chosen to commemorate their coming from the sea and, accordingly, statues and paintings have been carved in this likeness. The appearance of these handiworks may have caused confusion between feathers and scales.

The similarities between the Mesopotamian and Indian versions cannot be explained by mutual contact between the two civilizations—there are too many differences between the two traditions to make them a result of direct transmission. As highlighted by Graham Hancock in his book *Underworld,* the archaeological evidence shows that the two civilizations "did not exchange cultural ideas, themes and motifs—even at a cultural level as trivial as the style of jewelry, much less a religious and historical concept as fundamental as that of the Seven Sages." The most plausible conclusion is that both share a legacy left by an ancient common ancestor.

Often referred to as those who composed the Vedas, the Seven Sages were called Riksha ("the bears")[16] in ancient times. Later, the term *rksa* ended up meaning "star," which leads us to believe that it once referred to the seven stars of the Ursa Mayor.[17] The identification of the Seven Sages with these stars resonates with the Egyptian belief of the stellar fate of the soul—in the Pyramid Texts it is said that if during his lifetime the spirit of the pharaoh has been perfected, upon his death he will become a star.[18] Two areas of the sky welcomed this revival: the region of Orion in the southern sky and the region of the circumpolar stars that never set, the "Undying Stars," in particular Kochab, within Ursa Major. The epics of the Ramayana and the Mahābhārata speak of how one of the Seven Sages, Visvamitra, transferred King Trisanku to heaven in bodily form "where he shines as the constellation of Orion."[19]

Like the priests of Heliopolis, the Vedic Seven Sages had the task of guiding, shaping, and indefinitely maintaining a society in perfect balance with itself and the universe, respecting what the Egyptians called *maat* (terrestrial and cosmic harmony, truth, balance, "the right way") and the Hindu called *dharma,* with the same meaning.[20] Both in Egypt and in India the presence of a king was considered essential to ensure the cosmic balance, and when there was no king, it fell to the Seven Sages to seek an appropriate one.

THE DAWN OF THE VEDAS

It is not easy to trace the origins of Vedic rites, but one useful source to temporally locate them is the *Rig-Veda,* which repeatedly speaks of the Sarasvati River. This mighty river began to dry up at the end of the third millennium BCE, ceasing to flow at the beginning of the second millennium BCE, detected only in modern times thanks to satellite technology.

Gregory Possehl, professor of anthropology at the University of Pennsylvania, admits that the image created by the *Rig-Veda* of the Sarasvati is that of a mighty river with an extensive stream, implying that those who composed the *Rig-Veda* were in the region of the Sarasvati before the river dried up![21] According to Graham Hancock,

> The "chronological implications" of Vedic Aryans in the Punjab by
> 2000 BC are . . . potentially devastating for the academic edifice of
> Indian literary history founded on the date for the *Rig Veda* of around
> 1200 BC—and thus for every assumption about Indian prehistory
> that has ever been based on such a date for the *Rig.* At the very least,
> if this is what the references to a full and powerful Sarasvati mean,
> then the possibility of a connection between the Indus-Sarasvati civi-
> lization and the Vedic religion must be greatly enhanced.[22]

More precisely, in the *Rig-Veda* it is said that the Sarasvati ran unbroken from the mountains to the ocean: "The stream Sarasvati with fostering current comes forth, our sure defence . . . the flood flows on, surpassing in majesty and might all other waters. Pure in her course from the mountains to the ocean . . ."[23]

In an article in the journal *Remote Sensing,* S. M. Ramaswamy, P. C. Bakliwal, and R. P. Verma argued that the era when the Sarasvati stopped flowing to the Arabian Sea—leaving in its place the Indian desert—was about 12,000 years ago, which backdates at least part of Vedas.[24]

The same date was suggested by Bhimal Ghose, Anil Kar, and Zahrid Jussaid in a study they did for the Central Research Institute for Arid Zone, in Jodhpur, and by Ghose and others in the *Geographical Journal*.[25]

Two of the most respected late-nineteenth-century scholars of Vedic culture, H. Jacobi and Bal Ganghadar Tilak, believed the *Rig* contains ancient astronomical observations. On the basis of astronomical references Jacobi argued that the most prolific period for the composition of the Vedas had been between 4500 and 2500 BCE.[26] Tilak also endorsed this date, calling this era "the period of Orion" because of references to "the time when the vernal equinox was in the constellation of Ardra (Betelgeuse in Orion) when it withdrew towards the constellation of Krittika (the Pleiades)."[27]

But he also identified a substrate of the oldest Vedic hymns in what he called "the Aditi or the pre-Orion period," roughly between 6000 and 4000 BCE.[28]

David Frawley has reported other references that might bring us further back than 6000 BCE (at least to 7000 BCE), when the winter solstice occurred for the first time in the constellation of Ashwini (Aries).[29]

In support of this date is the Saptarishi ("the era of the seven rishis"), a calendar belonging to the Vedic culture[30] still in use in Kashmir. It calculates a series of recurring cycles, each lasting 2,800 years, with a precise start date of 6676 BCE.[31]

According to scholar John Mitchiner the works of Greek and Latin authors contain historical evidence of the beginning of Indian chronology in the seventh millennium BCE. Some examples are Solinus and Pliny the Elder (23–79 CE), the latter asserting that Indians, from the time of their founding father to Alexander the Great, "count to have had a number of 154 kings and a time of 6,451 years and 3 months."[32] Alexander the Great entered the Punjab in 326 BCE and left the same year. Therefore, they believed that the figure of a father (associated with the Bacchus of Onesicritos, Nearchus, and Megasthenes) "had been king in India 6,451.25 + 326 = 6777 years before Christ."[33] Pliny and Solinus drew on reports sent to Rome by ambassadors of the Mauryan court, and their chronology is considered to be firsthand.

The date of 6700 BCE, in addition to being coincidental with the third flood, fits the astronomical references contained in the Vedas and is close to the dating of the Indus-Sarasvati's first settlement at Mehrgarh in Balochistan, as well as the introduction of systematic cultivation of cereals, vegetables, and livestock in India.

The information on the Sarasvati, and the identification of Manu with Osiris, bring us back to at least 10,500 BCE. Even if Menes/Manu had brought civilization to India at that time, it is known that it decayed a few centuries after the flood in 9600 BCE to rise again only after the third flood in 6700 BCE with the reintroduction of agriculture. All knowledge was preserved by the Seven Sages, and in 6700 BCE, the first sovereign reigning in the Indus Valley was renamed Bacchus or Menes as a sign of good omen.[34]

In support of this dating we will look at some of the *Rig-Veda* hymns related to the legend of Indra and Vritra (or Vrtra) the dragon. According to the Vedic myth, Vritra is a demon in the form of a dragon or serpent that enwraps the snowcapped mountain ranges surrounding northern India and strangles seven major rivers. The story tells of how it is killed by the god Indra, and how the seven rivers are released.

> I will declare the manly deeds of Indra, the first he made, the One who controls the Thunder. He killed the dragon, then parted the waters and cut off the channels of the mountain's rivers. He killed the dragon lying on the mountain; his heavenly bolt of thunder was forged by Tvastr (the smith of gods). Like bellowing cows coming down rapidly, the waters slipped into the ocean. . . . Indra with his great and deadly thunder tore Vrtra to pieces. . . . There he lies like a river that bursts its banks, and the waters, taking on courage flow above him. The Dragon lies beneath the feet of the torrents which Vrtra with his greatness has contained. . . . Tumbled down in the midst of constant currents that incessantly flow out, the waters carry away the nameless body of Vrtra. . . . O Indra . . . you set the Seven Rivers free to flow.[35]

Many foreign scholars and Indian commentators, including Horace Wilson, considered Vrtra as an allegory of large and dark rain clouds, which Indra splits with his thunder. Despite the *Rig* describing Vrtra as "the one that blocks the rain," linking its destruction with the beginning of the floods, Wilson's symbolism does not explain all aspects of this myth. For this reason, other researchers have interpreted it more literally: the rivers would be the seven geographical rivers of ancient northwestern India, remembered as the "Land of Seven Rivers" (namely the Indus, the Sarasvati, and the five rivers of Punjab). According to this interpretation Indra would be the god of the rainy season recalling the rivers alive and Vrtra the demon of the summer drought.[36] The "Enterprise of the Rivers" appears, however, as a unique and unrepeatable event, not annual or seasonal. So it seems strange that the ancient sages spoke of events that occurred annually when describing an epic conflict that ended with the victory of Indra "forever." We have to remember that the dragon is described as "extended" and "stretched against the seven prostrate rivers," a metaphor apt to represent the Himalayan ice cap. If we start from this assumption we can easily interpret the passage "Tumbled down in the midst of constant currents that incessantly flow out, the waters carry away the nameless body of Vrtra." It describes the dome's blocks of ice being thrown off the water. Massive earthquakes follow due to the burden reduction caused by the ice sheet on Earth: "The mountains shook in turmoil."[37]

GEOLOGY CONFIRMS THE DATING

We look for the time when throughout the chains of the Karakoram and the Himalayas gigantic glaciers penetrated the valleys, blocking the course of the seven major rivers. Probed sediments taken in the Arabian Sea off the southwest coast of India contain traces of pollen that enable a view of the vegetation that grew on the subcontinent and, ultimately, of the climate. It seems that after the first flood the Indian climate underwent a rapid reversal from "cold and dry" to "hot and humid" due to the increased amount of water in the oceans—not yet solidified into new poles—with a significant increase in monsoon rainfalls.[38]

Around 11,000 BCE the long period of uninterrupted heating was stopped abruptly by a period of global cooling known as the Younger Dryas.[39] Weather conditions passed inexplicably from hot and humid to dry and cold, and in many areas conditions were restored to full ice age. The temperatures dropped within a few decades eight to fifteen degrees centigrade and the monsoon rainfalls reduced considerably.[40]

A report published in *Nature* by a group of Australian scientists,[41] based on further probing off the Indian coast, reveals a strong contrast between the salinity values before and after 10,000 BCE. After a thousand years the Younger Dryas ended, abundant fresh water was suddenly released in the Arabian Sea and Bay of Bengal, and the Himalayan ice had freed the seven rivers. At the same time the monsoons returned, which explains why in other passages of the Vedas, Vrtra the dragon is depicted as a demon that holds the rain.

In conclusion the geological evidence, combined with the historical, brings us back to 10,000 BCE—the approximate date when Manu, and presumably the Pelasgians, arrived in India.

MEHRGARH

Above the western edge of the Indus Valley is the steep part of the Bolan Pass, the site of Mehrgarh. Its inhabited layers extend continuously from 6700 BCE until the decline of Indus-Sarasvati civilization in the second millennium BCE.

The period of 6700 BCE coincides with the third flood and the worldwide rebirth of agriculture and farming: the people of Mehrgarh, like Nausharo and a good number of ancient sites, were made up of farmers and ranchers who had a developed architecture based on mud bricks. These people appeared suddenly, without any trace of evolution—it is likely they possessed the knowledge preserved by the Seven Sages, whose task was to protect the seeds of the plants during the floods.

DWARKA: THE CITY OF KRISHNA

Hindu legends speak of an ancient city founded by Krishna (human avatar of the god Vishnu) and swallowed by the sea immediately after his death. It was off the coast in front of current Dwarka, in the state of Gujarat northwest of the Kathiawar peninsula overlooking the Arabian Sea. Indian archaeologists from the National Institute of Oceanography led by S. R. Rao dove about one kilometer from the coast and discovered a huge underwater site. The dates for this site—which contains remains of massive walls and underwater fortifications built with megalithic blocks locked together by means of dovetail joints the same as in Egypt and Peru—have not yet been determined.

According to the city map (figure 6.1) the ruins cover a large area bounded northeast from the Gomati's mouth and southwest by a submerged pier, which is twelve meters deep* and extends for about a kilometer. Holes found on the outer side of the pier, dug in various parts of the bare rock, were probably used to accommodate the mooring of vessels. Nearby huge megaliths are scattered on the sea floor in a depth of up to eighteen meters. Continuing eastward along the pier you can see other smaller blocks, similar to big square tiles, arranged in a grid pattern amidst chaotically scattered boulders. This pattern seems to continue even under the rocks.

Inside the pier the remains are presented as rectangular buildings and are located much closer to the shore, concentrated mostly between five and seven meters away from the beach.[42] Among these ruins are twelve "citadels" protected by massive ramparts, six on each side of a submerged section of Gomati's channel.

> The ancient city was divided into six blocks: all these areas are provided with defensive walls made of large well squared sandstones (some of these measure from a meter and a half in length, from fifty to seventy-five centimeters in width, and from thirty to fifty centimeters in thickness). The commissures, obtained with an L-joint, suggest that a strong cohesion between the blocks was necessary to resist the action of waves and currents. In the walls of the fortresses, circular or semicircular bastions were placed at small intervals, used to divert the current and offer a good view of the ships arriving or

---

*Actually a rocky ridge that had been transformed into a pier before it was submerged.

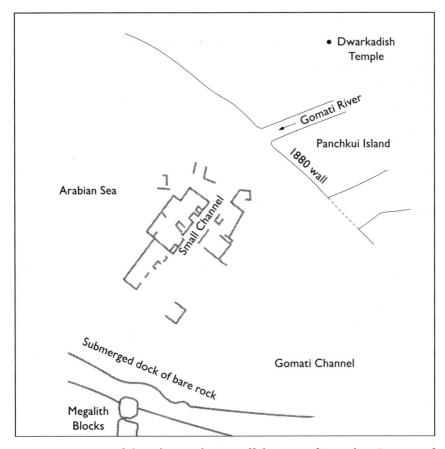

Figure 6.1. Map of the submerged ruins off the coast of Dwarka. Courtesy of Graham Hancock and Santha Faiia, Heaven's Mirror.

departing. . . . In all areas there are doors, as shown by the presence of slabs acting as threshold. The citadels' walls and ramparts, made of large blocks too heavy to be stirred up by waves and currents, are found *in situ* a few meters above the submerged foundations. In some points, one can see up to five courses of blocks, while in others the walls and ramparts have collapsed.[43]

These findings are in shallow water, seven meters deep or even less—such areas may have been submerged in relatively recent times because of the bradyseismic movements following the colossal earthquakes that periodically hit these regions.

Reported in both the epic poem Mahābhārata as well as the Puranas' collection of myths and genealogy, the story of the submerged Dwarka straddles two world ages or *yugas*. Toward the end of the latest Davapara Yuga, Dwarka was a fabulous city on the northwest coast of India. Built and governed by Krishna, it was a place of ritual and magic, praised for its gardens and its beauty.

Years later in 3102 BCE, while the Davapara Yuga was ending, Krishna was killed. "The same day that Krishna left the earth, the mighty Age of the dark-bodied Kali* fell down. The ocean rose and submerged the whole Dwarka."[44]

Dwarka was built on the site of an earlier city, Kususthali, on land reclaimed from the sea: "Krishna asked the ocean a space of twelve furlongs (two thousand four hundred meters) and there he built the city of Dwarka, defended by high towers."[45] The most reliable dating for a flood due to the rising of the waters in the region of Dwarka seems to be around 1700 BCE. Yet if Dwarka is the city of Krishna, according to the Mahābhārata and the Vishnu Purana, an exploration further offshore and in deeper waters should reveal the site's oldest submerged Kususthali, destroyed by the floods!

MAHABALIPURAM AND THE VISION OF THE "SEVEN PAGODAS"

In the southern part of the Indian east coast, fifty kilometers south of Madras, is the city of Mahabalipuram (figure 6.2), which has a square stone temple by the seaside. According to an anthology of diaries and accounts of travelers (*Descriptive and Historical Papers Relating to the Seven Pagodas of the Coromandel Coast,* edited by Captain M. W. Carr in 1869) it turns out that "Seven Pagodas" is the old name sailors used for Mahabalipuram, and Coromandel is the coast of the Bay of Bengal from the mouth of the Krishna River northward to the tip of Calimere

---

*Kali's age is indeed the current age of the Earth, a period when "people will be greedy, ill behaved and merciless, and they fight one another without good reason. Unfortunate and obsessed with material desires . . ." (*Srimad Bhagavatam*, chant 12).

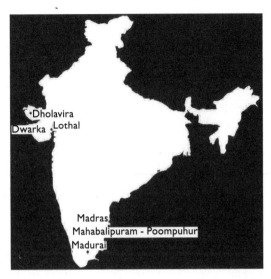

*Figure 6.2. Map of India showing Mahabalipuram
in relation to other significant Indian cities.*

southward. The reports tell of a stone mountain coming out of the sea, a hill where monuments would be carved, on top of which seven pagodas would be visible.

Brahmin lore tells of Vishnu deposing a corrupt raja, replacing him with the kind Prahalad, who was then succeeded by his son and grandson Bali (Baal/Belo), considered the founder of the city of Mahabalipuram ("the city of Bali the giant").[46] His dynasty continued with his son Banasura (Danaus/Aegeus), also depicted as a giant (which is synonymous with Pelasgian). In Greek myth a war broke out during the reign of Aegeus/Danaus due to the assassination of the sons of Menes (or son of Minos, depending on the version). In India, the motivating factor is the imprisonment of Krishna's grandson, Aniruddha, who attended the court of Banasura to seduce his daughter—like the children of Menes who came to ask to marry Danaus's daughters.

Later on, in Mahabalipuram, Raja Malecherem (whom we can identify with the Greek Atis/Horus/Deucalion) ascended the throne. He befriended a creature from the kingdom of heaven and was taken "in disguise, to see the divine court of Indra."[47] The raja returned with new ideas of magnificence and Mahabalipuram was soon praised more than any other city on Earth, until a report was read at the court of Indra where the gods were meeting. Driven by jealousy, they ordered the God of the Sea to devastate and submerge the city.[48] In the Akkadian version of the flood and its later variants—including the Babylonian versions as well as in Plato's history of Atlantis—the gods, angry and jealous of men, also convene an assembly.

Vast areas of the Indian subcontinent were subject to violent oceanic floods near the end of the ice age, particularly between 13,000 and 6700 BCE. In the Arabian Sea and the Bay of Bengal they were amplified and fed by the melting of the Himalayan ice cap, which during the ice age was much thicker and more extensive than it is today. Two hundred kilometers south of Mahabalipuram, along the coast of Tranquebar-Poompuhur near Nagapattinam, marine archaeologists have identified a large U-shaped structure built by man, flanked by a semicircular structure and an oval-shaped mound. These submerged ruins, where you can see layered rows of well-distinguished, adjoining blocks (with visible separation lines), are located five kilometers offshore at a depth of twenty-three meters,[49] almost double the depth of the ruins of Dwarka.

Sea level is likely to rise and fall for a variety of reasons. Glenn Milne, from the University of Durham, one of the leading experts in the mapping of floods, has collaborated on models of the ancient coastal profile, taking into consideration the more complex variables, including ground subsidence. From his account we learn that the areas that are currently twenty-three meters deep were submerged 11,000 years ago. It follows that the structures must go back at least to this period.[50]

Despite the inaccuracy of the models we can deduce that these structures were submerged by the second flood of 9600 BCE, and they were presumably built by the Pelasgians who perhaps were already in India nine hundred years before that date.

Leafing through Milne's models it is clear that up to the first flood's date in 13,000 BCE the coastal plains of India were larger everywhere than they are today (figure 6.3). Look at Tamil Nadu, the southern tip of the subcontinent, also known as "Dravidian peninsula"—here some areas were much more extended, especially toward modern Sri Lanka.

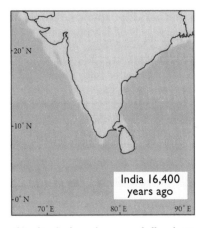

Figure 6.3. Map of India before the second flood. Courtesy of Graham Hancock and Santha Faiia, Heaven's Mirror.

The same applies to the areas around Gujarat, in northwest India. According to Milne's calculations, Dwarka would have been 150 kilometers from the sea, Mahabalipuram 50, and the Poompuhur site would have been almost 100 meters above sea level.

After the second flood the coast of Tamil Nadu was reduced to almost the current surface (figure 6.4). Five kilometers offshore, Poompuhur's structures were flooded. In Mahabalipuram the coastal plain widened for

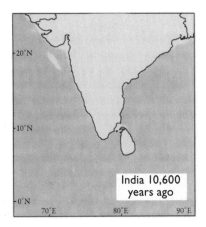

Figure 6.4. Map of India after the second flood. Courtesy of Graham Hancock and Santha Faiia, Heaven's Mirror.

two or three more kilometers, entering the Bay of Bengal (enough, in theory, because the mythical city of Bali could be built later than that date).[51] Ten thousand six hundred years ago the gulfs of Cambay and Kutch were still entirely above sea level and Dwarka was located at least 140 kilometers from the sea.

After the third flood sea level was higher than it currently is due to the deglaciated water not yet having solidified in the new poles, so all sites were submerged.

More increases in the level slowly followed, as underwater explorations off Poompuhur confirm. Only three meters deep and very close to the shore the ruins of the port city of Kaveripumpattinam have been identified—archaeologists place them between 300 BCE and the year zero.

THE FABULOUS LAND
OF KUMARI KANDAM

Tamil traditions speak of wisdom schools or academies (*sangam*), dating back 10,000 years, founded to "promote the golden age" in a territory that stretched far to the south of the current Cape Comorin.[52] This lost land was called Kumari Kandam and was swallowed by the sea in two different floods that occurred thousands of years apart from each other. It is said that the survivors fled inland to Madura.

The myth of Kumari Kandam can then be placed in a remote stage of prehistory between 10,000 and 12,000 years ago. According to the scholar V. Kanakasbhai, the Tamils of the first millennium of our era would have handed down an ancient tradition according to which:

At the period of which I now write, the people remembered that *in former days the land had extended further south, and that a mountain called Kumarikkodu, and a large tract of country watered by the river Pahruli had existed south of Cape Kumari.* During a violent irruption of the sea, the mountain Kumarikkodu and the whole of the country through which flowed the Pahruli had disappeared.[53]

The historian informs us that before the flood the lands between the Prahuli River and Kumari were divided into forty-nine districts, which covered about fifteen hundred kilometers.[54]

The *Manimekalai* (one of five great Tamil epics) speaks of a city located off Poompuhur, older than Kaveripumpattinam, swallowed by the waters as a divine punishment for the king who had not celebrated the festival of Indra.[55]

According to the model of Milne, in the period between 10,000 and 12,000 years ago the Dravidian peninsula and surrounding islands had to be larger than now; however, they were about to be submerged by the rising sea at the end of the ice age.

The myth of Kumari Kandam, with its stories about cities submerged by the waters and lost lands, prophesizes the discovery of ruins plunged in prehistoric times off the coast of Tamil Nadu more than 10,000 years ago.

Extensive structural remains consisting of processed sandstone blocks, heavily corroded and scattered on the seabed to a depth of about seven meters, have been identified off Poompuhur. At the same depth a number of circular mounds have also been discovered, some of which are ten meters in diameter, made of rounded stones together with some small standing stones. At a depth of twenty-three meters is a U-shaped structure, submerged by the waters long before the sinking of the coastal structures. It is an anomalous structure in which one can clearly see the courses of masonry, proving it is an artificial work. Consisting of walls made of huge stones deeply eroded and corroded, the U-shaped structure rises a couple of meters from the seabed, forming the outer edge of a rather extended platform. The side walls are oriented east to west, and its length—from the open end (defined as the entrance) to the U's curved base—is about thirty meters. On either side of the entrance gate the massive retaining wall (elsewhere two meters high) increases in height by at least one meter, almost forming the jambs of a door. In addition it has an accentuated edge protruding by almost half a meter with respect to the internal conglomerate, thus suggesting that the U structure served not as a platform but as perimeter wall—it cannot be a natural rock formation. Along the southern wall of the structure, at the height of one meter on a narrow section, you can see an ordered pattern of small blocks arranged in four different courses, together with the tail of a possible fifth course, only partly visible below the sea vegetation. These blocks are brick-sized even though they have an irregular section and seem embedded in a matrix.

The U-shaped structure is part of a complex that includes other large structures scattered about a fairly large area: forty-five meters away and at the same depth we find a second structure formed by well-cut blocks scattered on the seabed.[56]

THE REVELATION OF SHIVA

At eight hundred meters above sea level, in the region of Tamil Nadu, lies Arunachala, a mountain sacred to the Tamil Indians inhabiting these lands. According to local tradition this hill is the revelation of the god Shiva, who appeared here in ancient times in the form of an "infinite column of dazzling light* and burning fire that penetrated the sky and pervaded the entire universe"[57] to resolve a dispute between Brahma and Vishnu. They begged him to weaken his brightness, intolerable for their eyes, and as an answer "Shiva lessened the blinding splendor of his luminous appearance in the column, becoming this opaque mountain,"[58] which is Arunachala's "Red Hill." Brahma and Vishnu, in order to adore and worship him, asked Shiva to take the form of a lingam (phallic symbol) and on the eastern side of the mountain appeared a stone pillar (the Shivalinga or phallic symbol of Shiva). As a token of thanks, Brahma and Vishnu kept it in a temple commissioned to Vishwakarma, architect of the gods.

The Red Hill is also mentioned in the *Tolkappiyam,* the oldest text of Tamil literature ever found, which in turn referred to a previous lost work belonging to a library of archaic texts whose compilation was initiated more than ten thousand years earlier. This was the first library of the legendary Sangam ("academy") of the Kumari Kandam's Tamil civilization, now lost. It seems that among the first members of the Sangam was Shiva himself,[59] the god of the red mountain, the god of

---

*Yahweh, the god of the Jews, manifests himself in the same manner in the presence of the Ark of the Covenant.

yoga who practiced asceticism, the god of cosmic knowledge inhabiting the lingam.

The city of this first cultural center was called Tenmadurai (southern Madurai) and was in the southern part of Kumari Kandam. When the waters swallowed it, the site of a second Sangam became a town called Kapatapuram, which was located further north. This lasted for several thousand years, but eventually this one also sank: the *Tolkappiyam* was written during the second Sangam. When Kumari Kandam disappeared under water, the third Sangam was founded in the city of Madurai, which at that time was called Uttara Madurai (northern Madurai).

THE IMPORTANCE OF SANGAM

Retracing the history of Sangam: in less than 10,000 years the Pandya (Tamil dynasty of kings, partly historical, partly legendary) founded three Sangams in order to foster love for culture, literature, and poetry among the subjects. These institutions, the primary source of Tamil civilization, shared the goal of reaching perfection in Tamil language and literature.[60]

As we have seen, the first two Sangams stood in what was once the land of Dravidian in the southern Indian peninsula and were later submerged by the flood. In ancient times these lands were called Kumari Kandam (literally "land of the virgin" or "the virgin continent").[61]

The first Sangam had 549 members, including Agastya (patron saint of southern India), plait-haired Shiva, Murugan (the hill's god), and Kubera ("lord of treasure").[62] With eighty-nine sovereigns, the first Sangam lasted 4,440 years, during which many literary works that are now lost were produced, including *Agattiyam, Paripadal, Mudunarai, Mudukurgu,* and *Kalariyavirai.* These works are still respected and revered by Tamils.[63]

Following the flood the survivors were forced to move further northward, saving some of the books of the first academy and founding the second Sangam in Kapatapuram, which was protected by fifty-nine sovereigns. This Sangam lasted 3,700 years, after which the city was swallowed by the waters together with all its texts with the exception of the *Tolkappiyam,* according to some.[64]

The survivors of this second disaster retreated further northward in the Indian peninsula, and the third Sangam was founded in current Madurai. This Sangam was protected by forty-nine sovereigns and survived for 1,850 years.[65]

The Sangams, as the seven Rishis of the Vedic culture, were institutions or "brotherhoods" of scholars who had survived the periodical "scourge of the flood" and rose again after the withdrawal of water with the purpose of promoting knowledge in the new era. This correlation between Vedic and Tamil reality is further underlined by the presence of Agastya among both the Vedic Seven Sages and the members of the first Sangam.

A PLATONIC PARALLELISM

The generally accepted date for the end of the third Sangam is between 350 and 550 CE.[66] If we accept this date, which seems to have a semblance of historical reality, we can count on a fixed point for anchoring the chronology of the myth. If we take 350 CE and subtract 1,850 years, representing the duration of the third Sangam, we go back to 1500 BCE, about 3,500 years ago. Now, taking away from the obtained date (1500), the second Sangam's duration, which is 3,700 years as mentioned in the myths, we arrive at the date of 5200 BCE (7,200 years ago). Last, removing from this date the period of the first Sangam, 4,400 years, we get 9600 BCE (11,600 years ago). As Graham Hancock observes, "The date 9600 BCE obtained for the founding of the first Sangam suggestively matches the date Plato indicates for the flood that submerged the land of Atlantis."[67]

Studies conducted by the International Association for Research on Tamil Civilization have confirmed the existence on the Indian peninsula of three great and distinct episodes of flooding that occurred in the millennia prior to the foundation of the historical (third) Sangam. The second of these floods (dated 9600 BCE) occurred around the time of the foundation of the first Sangam, when a vast region of Kumari Kandam was swallowed by the waters![68]

CEYLON

During the ice age ancient Ceylon, current Sri Lanka, was united with the Indian peninsula by an isthmus located near Poompuhur (part of Kumari Kandam).

Some Sinhalese texts, based on ancient historical sources (the *Mahavamsa, Dipavamsa,* and *Rajavaliya*) written by Buddhist monks around the fourth century of our era, "speak of three floods that destroyed a large portion of territory, as well as Ceylon."[69]

They tell of a flood that hit Sri Lanka in an earlier epoch when the giant Ravana, king of the demons, incited the wrath and punishment of the gods because of his wickedness:

> The citadel of Ravana, which included twenty-five palaces and four hundred thousand streets, was swallowed by the sea. . . . The submerged land extended from Tuticorin (southeast coast of the current Tamil Nadu) to Mannar (northeast coast of the current Sri Lanka) and the island of Mannar is all that remains of what was once a very extended territory.[70]

In fact, Glenn Milne's maps show that about 16,000 years ago there was a vast expanse of land between Tuticorin and Mannar. In confirmation of the information contained in the Sinhalese texts, the maps show a raised area that has never been submerged that corresponds to the current island of Mannar.

THE REDINS

In the Maldives, south of the Indian peninsula, ancient myths and legends tell of a mysterious people, the Redins. Local traditions passed down by the elders from generation to generation testify to the feeling of a primordial grandeur of the archipelago, with this ancient group of people described as follows: "They were very tall, with brown hair and light skin, sometimes with blue eyes. And they were very, very skilled in sailing."[71]

The Redins came long before the Maldivians. Between the Redins and the current inhabitants there were other peoples, but none as powerful as the Redins, who were very numerous. They not only sailed but also used oars, which enabled them to move in the sea at great speed.[72]

This idea of men with superhuman or divine powers flying on the sea at incredible speeds on board boats is reminiscent of Homer's Phaeacians, as well as the *Rig-Veda*'s Asvins, two "intermediaries divine" or "guardian angels" to whom the Vedas frequently refer who are often praised for having carried out a daring rescue in the depths of the Indian Ocean.[73]

Archaeological evidence on Maldivian ground offers interesting ideas: from the bush of the numerous islands of the archipelago stand dozens of pyramids reaching up to ten meters high, partially collapsed, with their sides oriented to the cardinal points. The function and origin of these structures, called *hawitta,* has never been confirmed, although radiocarbon dating places them between 500 CE and about 700 CE.[74]

Curiously, there are no traces of an evolution of architectural and symbolic ideas behind the oldest of the Maldivian structures. Indeed, the hawitta make their appearance suddenly, already fully formed, which leads us to presume their builders had knowledge of basic construction techniques. We wonder at this point whether it is plausible that the early stages of the history of the Maldives could have been destroyed and erased by the sea. In the few archaeological excavations carried out in the Maldives several phallic sculptures were brought to light that, according to scholars, would be merely Shivalinga.

MUMMIES OF THE GOBI DESERT

It was 1978 when the arid plains of eastern Taklamakan revealed to the world thousands of perfectly preserved mummies. Chinese archaeologists, digging along the Silk Road among the ruins of the oasis city of Loulan, made the discovery. The team was impressed by the bodies' physical features, which were definitely *not* Eastern—white skin, red hair, long narrow noses, spiral tattoos, and long braids.

Taklaman forms the western sector of the Gobi Desert, one of the most inhospitable places in the world, with an expanse of steppe sand covering 1,295,000 square kilometers in the Xinjiang region between China and Mongolia.

An even more dramatic discovery occurred in 2005 at the site of Xiaohè on the western shore of Lop Nor Lake in Taklamakan, a recent site for Chinese nuclear testing, where white mummies were found buried under a mound on top of which many poles were driven corresponding to the different burials. The bodies were kept in sarcophagi shaped like canoes, and the skin of the deceased was covered by a layer of latex rubber to protect them from the process of putrefaction. The rubber tree could only have come from the Pacific or South America, suggesting a great dynamism and knowledge of sea sailing, like the Vedic Aryans.

Today we know that the Gobi's ancient white men were worshipped as gods by their neighbors and were admired for their metalworking, domestication of the horse, and inventions such as the wheel and the chariot. Contact with the Pelasgians, master builders of tunnels, is indicated underneath the Taklamakan Desert, where a circuit of tunnels cut into the rock (now used for water supply) emerges. Also in Tunhwang, at the southeastern extremity of the Gobi, about sixteen kilometers north of the city, we find many caves carved into the rock known as the Caves of the Thousand Buddhas.[75] Iconographies in this site represent Buddhist monks with white beard and red hair, long ears and noses, and an onion-shaped hairstyle—a style that recalls Easter Island's *moai* statues (plate 19).

Chinese tradition tells of a remote epoch when Taklamakan was not a desert but part of the Gobi's internal sea: we would have seen an island inhabited by "white men with blond or red hair and blue eyes"! These men built a fortress and a city connected to the mainland by undersea tunnels.

This takes us to the work of Pyotr Kuzmich Koslov, archaeologist at the Institute of Oriental Studies of the Russian Academy of Sciences in St. Petersburg. From 1908 to 1916 Koslov oversaw excavations of the city of Khara Khoto along the river Ejin in the interior of western Mongolia, near the edge of the former Lake Gashun. The city dates back to the Tangut empire, founded in 1032 CE by the Xi Xia Mongolian-Tibetan dynasty.

The excavation revealed an underlying layer where they discovered an older city called Uighur that contained a tomb dating back 12,000 years. On the walls is a representation of the ruling married couple who are buried there, and a curious symbol consisting of a circle divided into four sectors and overwritten by the letter μ. Not too far from there, in the caves of Kohistan, ancient celestial charts represent the sky from about 12,000 years ago with some mysterious lines connecting the Earth to the planet Venus.

Nearly a thousand kilometers north from Uighur is the city of Ukuk in the Altai Mountains. Here, in 1993, on the border between Russia and Mongolia, was found the body of a white woman of about fifty years of age under the ice, completely covered with tattoos: a shaman of the Pazyryk people. These Cro-Magnons, descendants of Osiris's cortege, had buried their "chief warrior" in the neighborhood, the flowing blond hair still intact, mummified by permafrost. Not too far from here they say a deep cave leads to an underground and still inhabited kingdom, enlightened and directed by a clan of initiates to the orders of the "King of the World"—it is Agharta!

THE LEGEND OF AGHARTA

In an article published in the *Journal of the Brazilian Theosophical Society*, Professor José Henrique de Souza showed how the city of Atlantis was located above or at the entrance to an underground world.

> Among all races of mankind, back to the dawn of time, there existed a tradition concerning the existence of a Sacred Land or Terrestrial Paradise, where the highest ideals of humanity were living realities. This concept is found in the most ancient writings and traditions of the peoples of Europe, Asia Minor, China, India, Egypt and the Americas. This Sacred Land, it is said, can be known only to persons who are worthy, pure and innocent, for which reason it constitutes the central theme of the dreams of childhood.
>
> In ancient Greece, in the Mysteries of Delphos and Eleusis, this Heavenly Land was referred to as Mount Olympus and the Elysian Fields. Also in the earliest Vedic times, it was called by

various names, such as Ratnasanu (peak of the precious stone), Hermadri (mountain of gold) and Mount Meru (home of the gods and Olympus of the Hindus). Symbolically, the peak of this sacred mountain is in the sky, its middle portion on the earth and its base in the Subterranean World.

The Scandinavian Eddas also mention this celestial city, which corresponds to the subterranean land of Asar of the peoples of Mesopotamia. It was the Land of Amenti of the sacred *Book of the Dead* of the ancient Egyptians. It was the city of Seven Petals of Vishnu, and the City of the Seven Kings of Edom or Eden of Judaic tradition. In other words, it was the Terrestrial Paradise.

In all Asia Minor, not only in the past but also today, there exists a belief in the existence of a City of Mystery full of marvels, which is known as Shamballah (Shamb-Allah), where is the Temple of the Gods. It is also the Erdamf of the Tibetans and Mongols. The Persians call it Alberdi or Aryana, land of their ancestors. The Hebrews called it Canaan and the Mexicans Tula or Tolan, while the Aztecs called it Maya-Pan.

By the Celts, this holy land was known as "Land of the Mysteries"—Duat or Dananda. A Chinese tradition speaks of Land of Chivin or the City of a Dozen Serpents. It is the Subterranean World, which lies at the roots of heaven. It is the Land of Calcas, Calcis or Kalki. In the Middle Ages, it was referred to as the Isle of Avalon, where the Knights of the Round Table, under the leadership of King Arthur and under the guidance of the Magician Merlin, went in search of the Holy Grail, symbol of obedience, justice and immortality. When King Arthur was seriously wounded in a battle, he requested his companion Belvedere to depart on a boat to the confines of the earth, with the following words: "Farewell, my friend and companion Belvedere, and to the land where it never rains, where there is no sickness and where nobody dies." This is the Land of Immortality or Agharta, the Subterranean World. This land is the Walhalla of the Germans, the Monte Salvat of the Knights of the Holy Grail, the Shangri-la of Tibet and the Agharta of the Buddhist world.[76]

Saint Ephraim transmitted an ancient Jewish tradition according to which Adam would have left the underworld to go up to Eden; only at the point of death would he announce the arrival of a savior by his own place of origin.

Adam's body was embalmed and kept in a secure site until it was taken over by a priest named Melchizedek (Horus), a wise man who would take him to the Earth's core in time for the funeral rites.[77] The Hindus say that Adam was the king of a group of ancients that first penetrated the underground during a great cataclysm and then re-emerged in order to supervise the restoration of life on the Earth's surface. And yet the Jews, who had settled in large numbers in Ethiopia since the eighth century BCE, handed similar ideas down to the Middle Ages as the kings of Ethiopia, called Prester John ("priest with the purple tunic"), had already been converted to Christianity by Frumentius, founder of the Ethiopian Church, in the first half of the fourth century.

In 1165, the king of Ethiopia wrote to Pope Alexander III and Frederick Barbarossa: "Near the desert, among barren mountains, there is an underground world that can be achieved only by chance because only occasionally the earth opens, and the one who wants to enter must do so very quickly, before it closes."[78]

Over three centuries later in the accounts of his trip to America Christopher Columbus brought back stories of the inhabitants of the Caribbean, according to whom there existed huge underground tunnels, extended "beyond all human conjecture." They would be in Martinique, in the ancient kingdom of the virgin warriors—the Amazons, as Columbus called them. The Amazons would have used them as shelters, and they seem to coincide with the underground labyrinths Madame Blavatsky, founder of the Theosophical Society, spoke about, and that the Incas seem to have found on that spot.

A Brahmin manuscript known as the _Code of Manu_[79] speaks of an inland sea in the Taklamakan area, north of the Himalayas, where now there are Central Asian salt lakes and deserts.

Right in the middle was an island inhabited by the "sons of god," keepers of "unlimited control of the elements," revealers of the "word" or "heka" or "magic": they were white men with red or blonde hair and blue eyes, who established there a city.[80]

There were no contacts by sea with the beautiful island, but a number of underground tunnels, known only to the leaders, coming from all directions allow communicating with it. Several majestic ruins of India, Ellora, Elephanta, the Ajunta caves, and a mountain range of Chandor, were connected by these galleries.[81]

These people failed to prevent both their own extinction and the disappearance of the island, Shangri-la, annihilated by some unknown mass destruction.

Archaeology—as we have seen—found the remains of that race, while geology and radar images have confirmed the former presence of the sea: thousands of years ago, the Gobi was an inland sea larger than the Mediterranean (figure 6.5). In the end, it is about the usual legend of Atlantis—land surrounded by the sea, inhabited by white men with blond hair and blue eyes. Simply, the Indians came across the Pelasgians, learned their history, and adapted it to the local geography, such as the Gobi Sea or Lake Titicaca in Peru, from where Viracocha came together with his bearded companions.

The Carthaginian navigator Hanno, in his diary *O Periplus*, gave an account of a journey along the west coast of Africa made around 500 BCE—during the trip he had heard stories of creatures that were hiding

Figure 6.5. Location of the inland Gobi Sea.

underground, with speed and intelligence superior to that of other men. Even Plato spoke of mysterious underground tunnels that cross the continents, and of a great king who would sit at the center of the world. Pliny the Elder in his *Natural History* refers to underground inhabitants that had taken refuge there after the destruction of Atlantis.[82]

Indeed, the *Agrouchada Parikchai* (Book of the Spirits), a manual of Hindu initiation, talks of an underground flowered paradise dating "centuries before our era." Other testimony comes from lawyer and French consul Luis Jacolliot, and from enthusiastic travelers such as the doctor Marquis Saint-Yves d'Alveydre (1842–1909) and philosopher Madame Helena Petrovna Blavatsky (1831–1891). Their sources ranged from the bazaars of Calcutta to the Brahminic temples, where they gathered sacred and popular traditions. We read of an access located in the Himalayas and a network of tunnels stretching from the Ganges, under the great mountain ranges, up to a secret destination.* They speak of "an immense continent destroyed by a geological upheaval" and a "peninsula of Hindustan enlarged by a different displacement of the waters."[83] According to yogis, "There is no cave-temple in the country [India] without its secret corridors that run in all directions, and those endless underground corridors are in turn connected to other caves and corridors."[84] It seems that the underground kingdom of Agharta is governed by twelve members of the "Supreme Initiation" and Manu, the "King of the World,"[85] just like the confederation of twelve independent states that the Sabines called Manzaltu and the Etruscans called Mezlum. Its inhabitants would have created "a secret archive of humanity" to host "the most perfect machines and the specimens of creatures and animals that had disappeared, all in order to safeguard humanity."[86] It even seems that Blavatsky possessed a map of an ancient Peruvian tunnel, given to her by an elder native—the map is now preserved at the headquarters of the Theosophical Society in Madras.[87]

In the 1920s, Russian explorers spotted the "bottomless pit," part of an extensive network of caves in Azerbaijan. Once down inside, the researchers noticed a strange green glow, as well as paintings and prehis-

---

*Interesting comparison can be made here with the legends of "divine" weapons belonging to Manu and those hidden in the Sardinian caves.

toric bones. Sometime later it was discovered that this network of tunnels reached small squares from where a number of ducts extend that joined with the underground galleries of the Gobi desert.

At the end of the nineteenth century explorers Nicholas Roerich and Ossendowsky Ferdinand entered information they received from Tibetan lamas in their travel diaries. According to the lamas the underworld hosted divine creatures, survivors of an ancient civilization governed by the King of the World who had colonized the Earth but after many disasters had taken refuge in its bowels. In Agharta (which literally means "inaccessible") the only source of light and life would be an energy called "Vril," which would favor the growth of plants and contribute to the extension of life span. The mysterious force would dominate over all other human and natural energy.[88]

Definitely, some of these "superstitions" have their origin in the Paleolithic beliefs about the Goddess Mother who inhabited the regions in the middle of the Earth, communicating with the surface through ducts such as caves and chasms. The same "caves" where the sibyls (priestesses) revealed the will of the gods were buildings carved into the rock, referring to the influence of this ancient pre-Pelasgian idea.

We'll talk soon of the Pelasgians' cave building skills—caverns for the sibyls and steep-walled trenches cut into the rock at depths exceeding twenty meters. Their digging exploits gave birth to the idea that their original island was connected to the mainland by tunnels. Etruscans believed it was at Lake Bolsena (a crater lake in central Italy of volcanic origin) and one of its two islands, while the Cimmerians of Cumae favored Lake Averno (a volcanic lake in the Avernus crater in southern Italy). In both cases a white race of civilizers would have come from a specific island connected to the mainland by tunnels.* According to a plausible hypothesis, the myth of tunnels that led to an island city evolved so much that people were able to imagine a kingdom, "Agharta," made entirely of underground tunnels.

---

*Quoting Ephorus's testimony, Strabo says that the Cimmerians had their homes underground. They called them "Agile," and they moved through the caves from one to the other. Homer said that the sun did not cover those people. Viracocha himself appeared in a period of darkness.

The benefit of the doubt remains, however, because the green light that permeates the tunnels has a fantastic interpretation of technological nature that, as it happens, is not the subject of this book.[89]

THE SEA
AT THE CORE OF EVERYTHING

The Pelasgian people, closely linked to the sea, were considered a nation of great sailors and possessed important knowledge of astronomy and mathematics.

Studies conducted thus far have identified them with the Aryans mentioned in the Vedas. Evidence in support of this theory was given by Ralph Griffith, a famous translator of the Vedas, who believed the Aryans had no experience of the oceans and yet he found almost a hundred terms with the unquestionable meaning of "ocean" or "sea."[90] According to Sanskritist David Frawley other more ambiguous references to the sea have been translated incorrectly or treated simply as metaphors. And while admitting that the word "ocean" in the Vedas is sometimes used as a metaphor ("Ocean of Heaven," for example), he argues that "such images do not imply a lack of real contact with the ocean. . . . They show a great intimacy with the sea, not only from the practical point of view, but also as a poetic image born out of life spent in places nearby it."[91]

According to Professor S. P. Gupta of the Indian Archaeological Society:

There are references to the sea, that is *samudra,* and to merchants, or *panis,* engaged in maritime commerce; *navah, samudriah, sata-aritra,* etc are terms that clearly testify this. Piracy is also mentioned. Indeed, it finds clear reference in words like *duserva* and *tamovridha,* which indicate unscrupulous people's attacks on boats laden with goods in order to predate them.[92]

Consider here the hymn to the Maruts, gods of storms, who "removed the rain from the Ocean, and loaded themselves with steam and moisture, to pour in torrents." Such a knowledge of the ocean-evaporation-cloud-precipitation cycle is a cultural element that naturally belongs to a people who lived along the coast, where it sometimes seems that the clouds draw moisture from the sea.[93]

We are a stone's throw from the end of the trip: Osiris has almost arrived at the eastern end of his mission, and must leave a sign . . .

Ten millennia later Alexander the Great built 12 tower-shaped altars to the gods on the left bank of the river Beas, known as the Hyphasis to the ancient Greeks, in order to mark the limit of his conquests: he was imitating his predecessor, in mission and style.

Huge towers were erected by Osiris in the current Angkor, in Cambodia, similar to the Zed tower incorporated by Cheops in his pyramid. Their arrangement traced the Dragon constellation in the northern sky. Time corroded them, making them fall, while the forest absorbed and hid them until 802 CE, when the Khmer king Jayavarman II discovered their existence. An initiate known as "King of the Mountain" had put Jayavarman through an initiation ceremony, after which he was proclaimed "King of the World." He then wandered through the jungle, moving along the kingdom's capital finding one site after the other, and in those places he built his own temples that, now as then, still reproduce the Dragon constellation as it was in the sky of 10,500 BCE!

You have studied physics and, applying its law, you have obtained wonderful results, steam appliances, electricity, etc., for more than twenty thousand years. Instead, we have studied the subtle forces of nature, discovered its laws, and making them act alone or in harmony with matter we obtained even more amazing phenomena than yours.

A BRAHMIN

7

The Connection between Egyptian and Cambodian Monuments

Let them turn, for instance, to such works as those of Vitruvius Pollio of the Augustan age, on architecture, in which all the rules of proportion are those anciently taught at Initiations, if they would acquaint themselves with this truly divine art, and understand the deep esoteric significance hidden in every rule and law of proportion.

HELENA PETROVNA BLAVATSKY

The Cambodians said they were sons of a snake woman, like the Scythians, generated by an inexplicable sexual impulse that Hercules had vented on a reptile woman. Likewise, the Merovingians (between the fifth and seventh centuries rulers of large parts of what are now France and Germany) were a reptile's children, since Merovee's mother, as the mother of Alexander the Great, was fecundated by a sea serpent! And do not forget the amphibian gods of Tiahuanaco and the Akkadian Iohannes. Semigods Kaundinya and Kambu arrived in Cambodia separately, from the sea. When Kaundinya touched the ground, he was attacked by a beautiful snake princess, whom he defeated and then decided to marry. Kambu also married the daughter of a snake king and founded a kingdom in the valley of the river. Its people were called *kambujas* or "sons of Kambu." As time passed, the name changed into Cambodge and then Cambodia.

ANGKOR

The name "Angkor" is probably derived from *nagara*, the Sanskrit word for "city," but curiously assumes a specific meaning in the Egyptian language: "the god Horus lives."*

In this regard, we find that the sites of Giza and Angkor are separated by exactly seventy-two degrees of longitude, a number that is the first and most sacred of processional numerology very often reported in myths.[1]

Angkor as we know it today developed between the ninth and thirteenth centuries CE at the hands of Khmer kings Jayavarman II, Yasovarman I, Suryavarman II, and Jayavarman VII. The inscriptions, styles, and material culture precisely date the beginning of the "modern" restoration: it was started in 802 CE by Jayavarman II after an initiation ceremony that urged him to declare himself "King of the World." The origins of this restoration are obscure, as are his blood ties with the previous dynasty. Some inscriptions describe him as a descendant of "a perfectly pure royal race."[2] Another record states that he arrived by ship from the sea after living for years in a distant place ruled by the "King of the Mountain." He would have arrived in Cambodia in 800 CE, when it was a land in danger, lawless and under an anarchist regime. Jayavarman II established his capital at Indrapura, where he lived under the spiritual protection of Sivakaivalya, a great Brahmin meant to officiate for the

---

*Letter of January 9, 1997, by Dr. R. B. Parkinson, Department of Egyptian Antiquities of the British Museum: "Angkor is a well known First Name, which means 'The god Horus lives.'"

cult of the king-god,[3] very similar to the worship of the pharaoh-god.

During his reign, Jayavarman traveled constantly throughout the Cambodian territory, moving the capital from time to time. He wandered in search of the Pillars of Osiris, the transposition on Earth of the northern sky, centered on the Draco constellation. After leaving Indrapura Jayavarman, Sivakaivalya, and their armies moved to the plains, where the major temples of Angkor are now, to found a city named Hariharalaya. Then he inaugurated a new capital at Amarendrapura (today Angkor Thom), to move on again and found the city of Mahendraparavata (on the hill overlooking the plain of Angkor). Just as we write news is spreading of the discovery of Mahendraparvata by Professor Roland Fletcher, an archaeologist at Sydney University. In April 2012, by using airborne laser scanning technology, or LiDAR, his team revealed the imprint of a vast urban landscape hidden in the jungle and lowlands surrounding Angkor Wat. Fletcher has deduced that the cityscape occupied an area of about 1,000 square kilometers. Here Jayavarman invited a Brahmin more learned than Sivakaivalya, "a scientist very keen on magic who came to establish a ritual . . . under which there could be only one king to lead the country." This Brahmin taught the sacred texts to Sivakaivalya and instructed him in the ritual of the god-king.[4]

Near Angkor there are ruins of many temples built by the Khmer god-kings. There are—not by coincidence—seventy-two main temples surrounded by a thousand secondary temples, with all their fences repeating geometric patterns of mandalas* or yantras.†

Now for the most important and majestic temples: we leave the jungle north of Tonlé Sap Lake, down Phnom Kulen mountains, and reach the vast alluvial plain and its masterpieces, where man and nature have worked in symbiosis.

---

*A design made by the association of different geometric figures and contained in a circular space whose purpose it to provide a detailed symbolism that encodes fragments of cosmic knowledge.

†Sanskrit term for symbolic diagrams and geometric representations used as a visual medium to promote concentration and meditation.

ANGKOR WAT

Angkor Wat, "the temple," is a huge stone building consisting of five rectangular enclosures one inside the other whose short sides are aligned to true north-south, while the long sides are oriented to an axis "rotated three quarters grade south the east and north the west"[5] (plate 20). Three-quarters of a degree, in terms of precession, corresponds to fifty-four years. The number 54 and its double 108 repeatedly return in Angkor's bas-reliefs and architecture.

The outermost fence of Angkor Wat is a ditch that runs for 1,300 meters from north to south and 1,500 meters from east to west.[6] Its walls, 190 meters wide, are made of red sandstone blocks locked to each other with amazing precision. The main entrance of the temple is located on the western side, where a megalithic causeway 373 meters long and more than 9 meters wide[7] leads east across the moat, accessed through a door opened on the walls of the second enclosure, a rectangle of 1,025 by 800 meters.[8] The road continues eastward going up to a cross-shaped embankment that leads to the lowest gallery of the temple, the third fence, with both north and south walls 202.14 meters long. The same precision is found in the fourth rectangle, whose northern and southern walls measure respectively 114.24 and 114.22 meters. Finally, in the fifth fence, the north wall is 47.75 meters and the south wall 47.79 meters.[9]

A detailed study published in *Science* revealed that the causeway was divided into sectors whose length in Khmer *hat** (0.43545 meter) corresponded to the years of Hindu eras:

> These periods begin with the Krita Yuga or human "golden age" and continue through Treta Yuga, Davpara Yuga and Kali Yuga, the latter being the most decadent human era. Their respective duration is 1,728,000 years, 1,296,000 years, 864,000 years and 432,000 years. We believe the passage of time is numerically expressed by the lengths corresponding to yugas along the east-west axis.[10]

---

*A Khmer hat is similar to a cubit, an archaic unit of measurement based on the length of the forearm from the elbow to the tip of the middle finger.

The sections of the causeway indeed measure 1,728 hat, 1,296 hat, 864 hat, and 432 hat (figure 7.1). It seems that Angkor Wat was dedicated to the veneration of the serpent: every corner of the roof is adorned with a seven-headed snakes called Nagas. According to Indian mythology, the Nagas are supernatural creatures, cobra-kings that ruled the Earth and are located among gods.[11] The biggest Naga is the seven-headed serpent Sesha ("remnant"), also called Ananta ("infinite").[12] According to the French Orientalist Alain Daniélou, Sesha represents the cycle of time, and therefore the Naga serpents of Angkor would be tied to the birth and death of Earth periods and the eternal regeneration of time.

The square in the center of Angkor Wat houses a raised platform divided into four square sectors by a "+" of crossed arcades. At the center and corners of the platform are five Gothic-like towers guarding the sacred landscape.

Academics acknowledge that the motif of Angkor Wat is a mandala—not painted on paper or cloth, or on the sand track, but made of water and stone. The mandala is a symbolic diagram used both in the performance of sacred rites and as a tool for meditation.[13] According to Buddhist monks

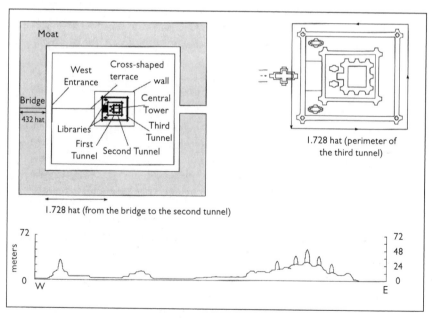

Figure 7.1. Precise measurements in Khmer hat at Angkor Wat.
Courtesy of Graham Hancock and Santha Faiia, Heaven's Mirror.

a mandala consists of a representation of the universe with the purpose of collecting universal forces. Through the "physical" mandala, man can realize the true mandala in his mind and, reaching its center, reach that state of enlightenment that will get to "know the truth."[14]

The main feature of Angkor Wat is its long and massive east-west axis, aligned with the sun at dawn and sunset on the equinoxes. However, there are other key indicators at different times of the year. According to *Science*:

> It is interesting to note that there are two solstitial alignments from the western entrance gate of Angkor Wat. These two alignments (added to the two equinoctial alignments already established) mean that the entire solar year was divided into its four basic sections by the alignments inside Angkor Wat. From this observation point, the sun rises over Phnom Bok (17.4 kilometers northeast) on the day of the summer solstice. . . . The western entrance gate of the temple also has an alignment with the temple of Prast Kuk Bangra, 5.5 km south-east.[15]

A similar interconnection between the sky and Earth is found in Giza. While the Sphinx is facing east at dawn on the equinox, the access roads to the pyramids of Cheops and Chephren (pointing 14 degrees northeast and 14 degrees southeast) are aligned with the position of the sun on the horizon of the solstices.[*]

THE PYRAMID-MOUNTAIN OF PHNOM BAKHENG

The "pyramid-mountain" of Phnom Bakheng, about a mile north of the western entrance of Angkor Wat, is 67 meters high and stands on a natural rock ledge. At the top of the pyramid is a ziggurat-shaped stone temple 13 meters high that develops on four levels until reaching a central sanctuary.

---

[*]To be precise, the northern route is aligned to the rising of the sun exactly one month before and one month after the summer solstice, while the southern route is aligned exactly one month before and one month after the winter solstice.

The sanctuary is surrounded by 108 towers and the staircase on the east side of the pyramid has a slope of about 70 degrees[16]—or even perhaps 72 if accurately measured. 108 and 72 are two of the most important precessional numbers. It could be a coincidence, but Yasovarman II, the builder of Phnom Bakheng, has left us an inscription that clearly states that the temple should symbolize "by its stone the evolution of celestial stars."

ANGKOR THOM

Moving west of Angkor Wat, after crossing the moat and looking north, we see another huge ditch two kilometers away whose southern side measures five kilometers. Inside there is a square island over which a squared perimeter wall, twelve meters high, hovers threateningly. The wall contains five doors, accessible by five causeways, flanked by huge stone figures that pull the body of a huge Naga serpent. This geometric compound is called Angkor Thom ("Angkor the Great") and contains three pyramidal temples: Bayon (Ancestor Yantra Temple) at the geometric center of the fence, Phimeanakas (the Sky Palace) to the northwest, and Baphuon (Bronze Tower) two hundred meters south. These structures served as a symbolic diagram of the universe with the purpose of leading the initiates to an esoteric and cosmic knowledge.[17]

The Phimeanakas, built by Suryavarman I (1002–1050 CE), is a stepped pyramid fifteen meters high with a rectangular base twenty-eight by thirty-five meters, which looks remarkably like a Mayan pyramid (plate 21). According to legend a symbolic sexual intercourse between the god-king and a Naga girl took place in this sanctuary every night.

The short axis of Phimeanakas is perfectly aligned to the north-south axis, an alignment obtained by astronomers observing the northern sky, the Naga constellation we now call the Dragon. The Egyptians would call it "the stretching of the cord." The astronomers metaphorically mated the king (or his pyramid) with the celestial Naga.

The Baphuon, pyramid-mountain of King Udayadityavarman II (1050–1066 CE), stands on a rectangular base 90 by 120 meters, and 50 meters high.[18] The core of the pyramid is an artificial hill of compact ground on top of which rose a temple—now collapsed—as a sanctuary of the Shivalinga. The Baphuon had been hastily constructed on a foundation that was not very solid, but despite the destruction the core of the monument kept the pyramidal shape designed by copying Mount Meru.[19] It was assumed that under the Baphuon there was "an underground area that extended into the ground while the visible part ascended to the sky."[20] The idea that the foundation of these pyramids extends underground is conceivable in both Angkor as well as Giza, and is the same concept as Agharta.

As Graham Hancock points out in *Heaven's Mirror:* "When the star-map of 10,500 BC is transposed to the ground, the perimeter wall of Angkor Thom deliniates a sacred enclosure around the breast or heart of the Naga constellation of Draco. At the exact geometric center of this enclosure, where the diagonals cross the 'heart,' looms the breathtaking edifice known as the Bayon—which is regarded as Jayavarman VII's finest architectural achievement."

In his inscriptions Jayavarman VII stated that his temples formed a scheme to get "the ambrosia of immortality for all those who are struggling in the ocean of existence."[21] The monuments were the tools of this research, carried out for humanity's sake, since they acted as a "mandala of the mind." We can assume that Jayavarman VII wanted to complete the "sacred mandala of the celestial region of the Dragon" inherited from the king-gods, who in turn had received this project from an unknown source. If so, that is to say that Jayavarman VII built the last temples as was designed in the sky-earth diagram inspired by a sort of empathy for the world's sake, it would explain why the program ended abruptly after his death.

The last temple of Angkor Thom, built in the twelfth century CE, is the Bayon, a squat, stepped pyramid placed on top of an existing, and not yet dug, structure. The Bayon is surmounted by a circular sanctuary, surrounded by fifty-four stone towers, each carved with four huge faces of Lokesvara* turned to the cardinal points for a total of 216 faces. According to Jean Boisselier, these faces have the typical expression of

---

*Lokesvara, the main bodhisattva, is a quasi-divine being who is said to delay nirvana to help others attain it.

a Buddhist "in the active state of mind."[22] Those who understood the message expressed by the monuments of Angkor were "high initiates in a system of cosmic wisdom" who came to Bayon in search of the "final mystery."[23] These people knew the "rotation of the sky" due to the Precession of the Equinoxes and discovered that the celestial north pole rotated around the "heart" of the constellation of the Dragon—the ecliptic north pole—in a long cycle of 25,920 years. This point finds its earthly counterpart in the Bayon.

There is a bridge over the ditch leading to the gate of Angkor Thom. One hundred eight titanic statues serve as balustrades in two parallel rows of 54 figures each, engaged in a tug-of-war where the rope is a Naga snake. In ancient times, this bridge served as a "rainbow," a link between the world of the gods and that of men. Those who crossed it could have access to the celestial realms. The same scene of the tug-of-war with the Naga serpent is represented in the reliefs of the southeastern gallery of Angkor Wat.

"THE LAND OF KAMBU LOOKS LIKE THE SKY"

Jayavarman VII wanted to inscribe "The Land of Kambu looks like the sky" in his monuments, alluding to the Osirian practice of building "copies" of specific stars or constellations on the ground. In 1996 a twenty-five-year-old graduate student named John Grigsby discovered that the main monuments of Angkor repeat the sinuous coils of the northern constellation of the Dragon, just as the three Great Pyramids of Giza reproduce the same belt of stars in the southern constellation of Orion.

To demonstrate this correlation Graham Hancock relied on the astronomical software Skyglobe 3.6, calculating the effects of precession over the positions of the stars and simulating the sky visible from Angkor in the past eras. The search starts after 1150 CE, the year of the death of Suryavarman II, the Khmer god-king who wanted to build Angkor Wat for his funeral temple.

The Dragon is a circumpolar constellation, visible looking north, so Hancock needed to look for an era in which men could be south of Angkor and see its temples to the north, with their celestial copies at the horizon.

However, experiments with Skyglobe did not show any correlation between the constellation of the Dragon and the arrangement of the temples of Angkor at sunrise of the vernal equinox of 1150 CE, and indeed, the constellation appeared completely inverted—upside down, rotated 180 degrees. The constellation was in the right position twelve hours later, after sunset, but at that time it was well hidden below the horizon. The experiment was thus extended to the entire period between the ninth and twelfth centuries CE, but not at any time, let alone in the spring equinox, is the entire Dragon above the horizon and in the correct orientation.

At this point it is necessary to make two observations: (1) both Giza and Angkor appear to be intentionally designed as a mandala of the mind; (2) the sky–ground correlations at Giza were perfectly aligned at the dawn of the vernal equinox of 10,500 BCE.[24]

It was therefore decided to simulate the sky over Angkor at dawn of the vernal equinox of 10,500 BCE. Finally, the expected correlation emerged! At that time the constellation of the Dragon was northerly in the middle of the sky, straddling the meridian, well above the horizon with exactly the same pattern replicated on the ground by the main temples of Angkor (figure 7.2).

There is another coincidence that is worth noting: the Great Pyramid has two wells facing north and pointing to the stars Kochab and Thuban. These two stars are represented on the ground by two of the temples of Angkor, belonging to the same model of the sky in the area of the Dragon.

These star patterns were observed for the last time in 10,500 BCE: at that time to the north was the constellation of the Dragon, according to the configuration of Angkor's temples; to the east was the constellation of Leo, combined with the Sphinx; and to the south was Orion's belt as imitated by the pyramids. It almost seems to be in front of a big secret game—a game bequeathed by a lost civilization.[25]

The lives of Osiris and the divine Nagas have come down to us filled with symbols closely related to the cycles of time, creation, and destruction of the epochs of the Earth. The development of these issues involved the knowledge of the precession and a deep interest in issues such as immortality of the soul.

Philosophical questions of this caliber disappeared from the

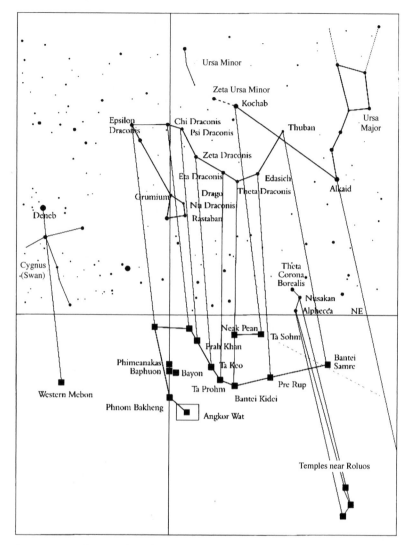

Figure 7.2. The temples of Angkor reflecting the stars of Draco and other nearby constellations at the dawn of the vernal equinox in 10,500 BCE. Courtesy of Graham Hancock and Santha Faiia, Heaven's Mirror.

Mediterranean after 9600 BCE: the second and third floods forced the channeling of all energy toward more practical issues such as finding food and shelter. Yet the same ideas reappeared in Egypt and Mesopotamia 5,000 years ago, perpetuated by groups of sages like the Followers of Horus. At the same time, in the Indus Valley, the Seven Sages had planted the seeds of the Indo-European civilization—the civilization of the Vedas.

Forty-four hundred years ago the latter returned to Europe, disguised as the "Sea Peoples":

> *So, the Pelasgians had given birth to two progenies . . . the first had remained in Europe and still talked their language . . . it created the Basques, the Minoans, and the Etruscans . . . the second was grown in the Indus Valley and was about to go home . . . it generated the Scythians, the Shardana, the Achaeans, the Celts . . . between the two lineages, for a long time, there was no peace.*
>
> DIEGO MARIN, *IL SEGRETO DEGLI ILLUMINATI*
> (THE ILLUMINATI SECRET)

8

A Journey into Language

You can find evidence that all known languages of humanity have a common origin. All derive from an ancestral language spoken from 25,000 to 30,000 years ago.

Vitaly Victorovich Shevoroshkin,
Russian linguist at the University of Michigan

August 20, 2010, San Sebastian, Basque Country. The streets are crowded with people gathered for the feast of La Semana Grande. They are divided between cafés and shops accompanied by the sound of a band and marchers crying for *independencia*. Bilingualism is everywhere, from restaurant menus to tourist signs, but the square, full of traditional dancers, seems to have forgotten Spanish. It comes to naught to try and understand by way of assonance with the Romance languages: there is none, unless you dig really deep.

Their language has survived the Castilians, Arabs, Franks, Goths, and Vandals, virtually constituting the identifying characteristic of Basque people. Many of them ignore the idea of living in a "time capsule" where for nearly 15,000 years the language of the oldest people ever known has been kept alive.

Today, the Basque is reduced to two closed "islands" surrounded by languages that are totally alien in vocabulary, syntax, and grammatical structure. However, it must have previously involved a much more extensive area, as recorded by the ancient Carthaginians and Romans. For this reason, according to distinguished British scholar Michael Harrison, "it is not surprising that Basque has many words in common with members from all over the North African group of languages." In 1821, Wilhelm von Humboldt claimed that Basque was the modern legacy of ancient Iberian: the German philologist claimed that the Iberians had spread from southern France to the British Isles, Sicily, Sardinia, and Corsica.

They were the heirs of the Pelasgians, the Cro-Magnons* of paleontology whose original homeland in the classical tradition would be the legendary Atlantis, submerged under water and trapped in an icy continent. Accordingly, the ice age of Atlantis would begin while the European and North American ice age was ending.

The Pelasgians, forced to flee, would have reached new lands including Europe and the Americas, where the memory of them would have soon become *myth*.

Today the Cro-Magnon physical type is represented by the Berbers and Tuaregs of North Africa, the Basque of northern Spain, and the Aquitanians of Dordogne, Brittany, and the island of Oleron in France.[1] Before their recent extinction, among them there were also the Guanches of the Canary Islands. Displaced in the same manner today as in the high Paleolithic, albeit in a reduced number, many of these peoples call themselves by names ending in the suffix "tan(n)ian" such as Mauritanian or Britannian.[2] Among the "rifianian" Berbers, the lightest-skinned group, 10 percent have light brown or blond hair. The blond tends to be golden or red,[3] according to the stereotype of the Pelasgian civilizer.

---

*Characterized by a facial type different from the other *Homo sapiens* (called "Combe-Capelle"), Cro-Magnons had a round skull, prominent cheekbones, and wide and square orbits. In prehistoric times, in comparison with other men, they were real giants, a factor that can have generated the need to use the term "Giants" to indicate the Pelasgians.

For linguists the absence of changes in the languages of these peoples over extremely long periods of time is a true enigma: Professor Johannes Friedrich, a linguist at the University of Berlin (1957), believed that the Berber language has not changed at all in the past two thousand years.

It is clear that from an unspecified moment in early history the Cro-Magnons had an innate reluctance to interact linguistically, culturally, or sexually with their neighbors. Analyzing their languages we notice that while they are bound to each other, they are separate from other languages spoken in Europe and the Near East.

In previous chapters we have made the effort to find the home of Cro-Magnons, placing it very likely in that part of Antarctica that, according to geology, would have been temperate 15,000 years ago. So, we are going to reconstruct all events such as exodus, battles, and faith from a purely linguistic point of view.

AMAZON EUROPE

During the last ice age, which ended 15,000 years ago, the European and Mediterranean populations were organized into warrior societies dedicated to hunting and were extremely matriarchal, probably unrelated to activities such as agriculture, livestock, and the craft of ceramics. They worshipped a single deity: the great Mother Goddess (Ana or Dana) of whom we have hundreds of paintings, engravings, and sculptures.

As a consequence many people consider the ice age as being the "Age of Amazons and Gorgons," of which the chronicler Diodorus has left a vivid account:

> It was the custom for those women to manage all matters of war . . . after many years so many years spent in their warfare, they accompanied with men, for the preservation of posterity; but the magistracy and all public offices, they kept wholly in their own hands; and the men (as the women do with us) looked to the household affairs, submitting to whatever was thought fit to be done by the wives, and were not upon any terms admitted to intermeddle

in martial affairs, or to command, or be in any public authority, which might any ways encourage them to cast off the yoke of their wives.

As soon as any child was born, they delivered it to the father. . . . If it were a girl, they seared off its paps, lest they should be burthensome when they grew up, for they looked upon them to be great hindrances in fighting.[4]

When, at the end of that era, the Pelasgians finally arrived in Europe, the two realities had to confront:

[The Amazons] executed horrid cruelties upon the conquered: for they put all the men to the sword, and having razed the city [Cernê] to the ground, carried away captive all the women and children . . . the rest of Atlantides (being struck with a panic fear) submitted, and delivered up their cities: whereupon Merina [the queen] received them all into her favor, and made a league with them, and in the room of that which was destroyed, built another city, calling it after her own name.[5]

The episode clearly connects to the flood of the continent Atlantis and the dispersion of its inhabitants, with the following colonization of the Mediterranean and the Americas by the latter.

According to the nomenclature of archaeologist Marija Gimbutas the union of the Atlantean world and Amazon Europe gave birth to the civilization of "Old Europe."

THE IBERIAN WRITING AND THE PROTO-INDO-EUROPEAN

The Pelasgians brought with them a form of writing known as "Iberian writing" or "Pelasgian pre-writing" (figure 8.1). The term "pre-writing" does not indicate any lack of expressive ability, since it is a full-fledged writing; in fact, it is used to distinguish this first phase of its development known as "Pelasgian writing" or "Pelasgian alphabet," which spread in

Italy and the Aegean beginning in the first millennium BCE.* Hundreds of prints in Iberian writing were found on the other side of the ocean, on the Pedra Pintada† in the village of Tarama on the border between Brazil and Venezuela, as well as on a relic found in Cuenca, Ecuador.

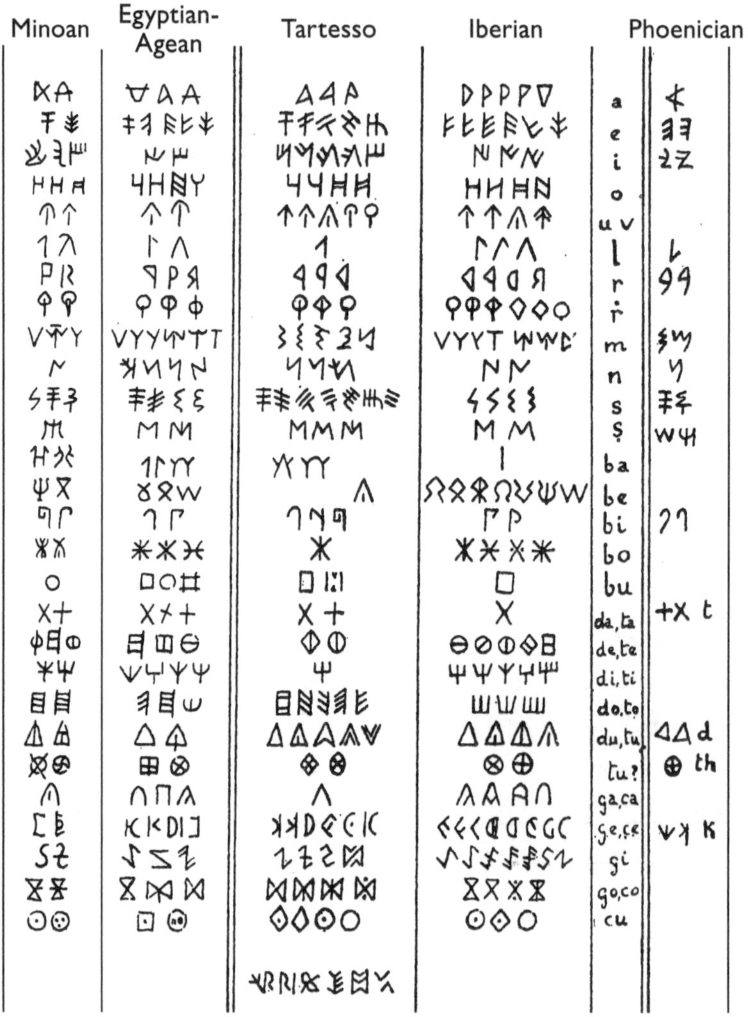

Minoan	Egyptian-Agean	Tartesso	Iberian		Phoenician
				a	
				e	
				i	
				o	
				u v	
				l	
				r	
				r̃	
				m	
				n	
				s	
				ş	
				ba	
				be	
				bi	
				bo	
				bu	
				da, ta	
				de, te	
				di, ti	
				do, to	
				du, tu	
				tu?	
				ga, ca	
				ge, ce	
				gi	
				go, co	
				cu	

Figure 8.1. Iberian writing compared with other writing systems.

---

*One example of this is the Lemnos stele, an inscription found on a funerary stele built into a church wall in Greece.

†The Caverna da Pedra Pintada (Painted Rock Cave) contains the earliest known cave paintings in the Americas.

The language born upon contact with the Amazon people already had some characteristics of the future Indo-European that became the mother tongue of nearly all of the European and Indian languages. However, we are still too far from the Indo-European, and so we use the term "Proto-Indo-European."

One of the facts offering proof of the homogeneity of the language are the words "Iberi" and "Iberian," present from Spain to the Caucasus. Similarly, the name of the river Ebro (Iber), tied with previous ones, finds parallels in Serbia (Ibar) and Bulgaria (Ibar). In a Ptolemy map the name "Iberàn" appears on an island off the southwest coast of Sardinia. Iberia is the Caucasus region between the Black Sea and the Caspian Sea. Also, Professor Barry Fell of Harvard University reminds us that one of the ancient names of Ireland was Ibheriu (derived from Iberiu).

William J. Entwhistle (professor of Spanish language and literature, University of Glasgow, 1925–1932) showed that the Iberian language has connections with Basque and that both are agglutinative languages, in contrast with the inflected languages.* A particular sequence, engraved on a prehistoric bone, has recently been discovered at La Coruna in Galicia, Spain (figure 8.2). Radiocarbon has dated it to before 4000 BCE: it contains the Iberian name of Atlantis (Atl) and the ancient Sardinian city of Tartessos (Tarte).

Indo-European inflected languages have added flexible suffixes to words—"Tarte" has become "Tarte-ssos" and "Atl" has become "Atlantis."

| A | Ta | La | Ta | R | Te |

Figure 8.2. Iberian sequence found
on a prehistoric bone.

---

*In agglutinative languages words are formed with the smallest grammatical unit possible; in inflected languages a word is modified to express tense, mood, gender, or case, and expresses grammatical changes with prefix, suffix, and vowel changes.

Another authority in comparative philology is the German Franz N. Finch, according to whom Basque would be "an undoubted continuation of the ancient Iberian language that, more important than the vocabulary, preserves its structure, which is the most resistant feature to external influences." Professor Henry Fairfield Osborn (1857–1935) declared that the Stone Age Cro-Magnon left two cultural relics: the Berber language of the Guanches of the Canary Islands and the Basque language. In 1974, Michael Harrison wrote, "In support of the theory that Basque, if not an autochthonous language, is at least one of the most primitive languages of Europe, in the sense of its being here before any of the existing others, is the fact that Basque is still a language with no proven congeners."[6] Finch points out that Spanish Basque is connected not only with a Basque spoken in southern France, but also with the language of Auscis, an ancient Aquitaine tribe of central France.

Aquitaine is in fact a language of "linkage" between the old Iberian and Basque.[7] Most of the information relating to it comes from inscriptions in the Latin alphabet, found mostly along the basin of the rivers Garonne and Rhine, in what is now Aquitaine, France. The Roman geographer Strabone[8] stated that the language and the physical appearance of Aquitanians showed a kinship with the ancient Iberians. Hundreds of names of people and numerous names of deities resemble Iberian personal names and are composed in the same way. The meaning of Aquitaine names can be found, instead, by using the Basque vocabulary.[9]

Other languages related to the Iberian language are spoken by Lusitanians, an indigenous tribe west of the Iberian Peninsula, and the languages of the Galician tribes (northern Portugal and Galicia).

Curious is the case of Cymric or Welsh (the language of Wales), composed mainly of Celtic vocabulary, but with a syntax not belonging to the Celtic structure. Professor Morrison Jones said that the Celtic vocabulary is superimposed on the older syntax, resembling Basque. According to his theory, when the conquerors took wives from the people they were forced to learn the Celtic vocabulary but had more difficulty with the syntax. The children, being reared by their mothers, learned a flawed version of the language of the conquerors. Within a few generations, the language spoken by women and children was considered correct, and here appeared the "Welsh." The same thing happened in Scotland when the English language was superimposed onto Gaelic, giving the Scottish dialect its particular musicality. Morrison concluded that syntax more similar to Welsh belonged to the Berber and North African Tamachek languages, both closely related to Basque.

Some physical characteristics (skin, hair, and eye color) of certain natives of western Britain and Ireland seem to be "remnants" of what Thomas Huxley called an "Iberian population."[*] Recent genetic studies suggest that people who now inhabit the British Isles are remnants of a group that left a common heritage between 18,000 and 12,000 years ago. They would have remained isolated from the rest of Europe for at least six thousand years, and then reappeared, fostering the development of a megalithic culture on the European coasts.[10]

Some pockets of this Iberian, or Pelasgian, language have not evolved into the Indo-European and have been acknowledged in our time, like the Etruscan, the Minoan of Crete, the Tartessos, the Basque Caucasus languages, and the Dravidian languages. We could call them "ambiguous languages" for the presence of some (but too few) Indo-European traits.

G. J. K. Campbell-Dunn[†] considered Iberian and Bantu languages as belonging to the same strain, to which the tongue of Dogon also belongs[‡]; close to one hundred Minoan words were recognized as belonging to the Bantu languages.

---

[*]Thomas Henry Huxley (1825–1895) was an English biologist and philosopher, president of the British Royal Society from 1883 to 1885, and convinced supporter of Darwinian evolutionism who fought tirelessly to overcome theological fixity; he was also grandfather of biologist Julian Sorell Huxley, who was considerably influenced by his ideas both scientific and philosophical and of writer and essayist Aldous Leonard Huxley.

[†]G. J. K. Campbell-Dunn taught at the universities of Canterbury and Wellington in New Zealand before he retired in 1991 to focus on research and writing.

[‡]The people of Mali enjoy a tremendous popularity because they knew the existence of the star Sirius B (orbiting Sirius) before it was identified by telescopes. It is in fact invisible to the naked eye. Another oddity is their worship of the plumed/scaled serpent Nommo. They have all it takes to make us suppose contact with the Pelasgians. To learn more about the issue, see Robert Temple's *The Sirius Mystery*.

The real Indo-European evolved within a narrow area from where its inhabitants emigrated to repopulate Europe and India, imposing their evolving language over the Proto-Indo-European. The temporal proximity explains the striking similarities between languages spreading from Spain to India.

PROTO-INDO-EUROPEAN CULTURES

The oldest Proto-Indo-European cultures from which we possess archaeological finds date back to the sixth millennium BCE in the Danube Valley, continental Greece, the Balkans, and the eastern coast of Italy. In the northern part of this area are the cultures of Cucuteni and Lengyel. Further south, we find the cultures of Vinca and Tisza, as well as the "Aegean culture" in the Greek mainland and islands.

Here, the city had no defensive structures (as will be in the Minoan Crete), which is a sign of a peaceful culture. There were no buildings more sumptuous than the communal houses, not even royal or princely monuments. Conversely, we find temples with large deposits of precious objects, the most ancient unearthed in the southeast of Bucharest, near the Danube. For this reason it is supposed to have been a theocratic society, headed by a caste of priests, which then evolved into Indian Brahmins and Roman Flamens.

Moving on to vases used for worship, ritual objects, and figurines of the Vinca culture dating between the sixth and the fourth millennia BCE, we find inscriptions in Iberian writing that were recognized for the first time as such by the linguist Harald Haarmann of the Research Center on Multilingualism of Brussels.

Haarmann showed the identity or close similarity of over fifty signs with the later Linear A writing used by the Minoans in Crete.

In the fourth millennium BCE the writing disappeared from Old Europe and then reappeared soon after in Crete and Egypt. It is likely that the pressure exerted by the Indo-European migration caused some flight toward Crete and the East, with the subsequent movement of writing too.

Linguistic roots prior to these Indo-European movements are found in toponyms or loanwords in the historic Indo-European languages. Related to the concept of "stone" in the toponyms we find the roots kar-, mal-, lap-, and lab-; for example, lap- in Latin *lapis* and in Greek *lepaz* (λεπαζ, pencil), and lab- in Greek *labruz* (λαβρυζ, ax). Sometimes these roots seem to be integrated in a system derived from the Indo-European, highlighting the link between Indo-European and the language of Old Europe (Proto-Indo-European). Concerning this issue, it is advisable to read the work of Francisco Villar, *The Indo-Europeans and the Origins of Europe*.

To give the city a name the root ur- was used, as evidenced by the Basque *uri* and *iri,* and the Sumerian Ur and Uruk. In Basque the word *ur* means "water," and Urumea is the name of the river that runs through San Sebastian. The use of the same root to name the city and the waterways confirms the renowned Proto-Indo-European Pelasgian custom of building cities along rivers. Borrowed from Latin, we find the root ur- in the word *urbs,* "city."

In the civilization of Old Europe the cult of the Mother Goddess merged with the cult of the one God worshipped by the Pelasgians, creating a syncretic deity that showed its male character alternately with its female character. The dead were buried in oval or anthropomorphic graves, evoking the uterus or the body of the goddess. Decorations abound in mazes, vulva, and breasts. The society remained matriarchal but was taking its first steps toward gender equality. The legacy was transmitted through the female line, as well as the name and membership of a family group. However, the equal magnificence of the tombs suggests that men and women shared the same social position.

The women freely chose their husbands, the concept of adultery did not exist, and even virginity had no value. The mother would educate and keep the children, who had no need of knowing their father.

Inheritors of this culture were the Etruscans. According to ancient historians, the Etruscan men had common women, so children did not know who their fathers were. The social position of women was surprisingly high and free, and the system was matrilineal.

In the Aegean in the eighteenth century the islands of Naxos, Kos, and Lesbos had surviving vestiges of matriarchy and inheritance through the maternal line. It was not so long ago that women in Sardinia had the tasks of administering the home and family and managing creditors, debtors, merchants, and banks and were responsible for the care and education of children (they were even in charge of mandating the roles of young men in family feuds). The men were concerned exclusively with the flock, the fields, and public affairs. Finally, in the Cretan frescoes we see women with rich ornaments occupied in games and ceremonies.

The Etruscan language is almost universally considered to be pre-Indo-European, although linguistic scholars such as Paul Kretschmer, Jean Faucounau, and Massimo Pittau notice several similarities with Anatolian Indo-European languages. This was the reason Kretschmer coined the term "Proto-Indo-European" (which we have hitherto used) to indicate an earlier stage of Indo-European when the language was about to develop its characteristic inflectional systems.

Evidently the Etruscan language was resistant to the pressure of Indo-Europeans, at least until the Roman conquest of Etruria in the third century BCE. Until then, the Etruscans were using an evolved form of Iberian writing—the aforementioned Pelasgian alphabet (figure 8.3) from which the Greek and Latin alphabets later developed.

PROTO-INDO-EUROPEAN
IN AMERICA

According to our reconstruction, if the Pelasgians (Cro-Magnons) had arrived at the same time in Europe as the Americas it is natural to expect to find Proto-Indo-European language also on the new continent. Even the presence of Pedra Pintada is a positive clue.

In the Brazilian state of Roraima, bordering Venezuela and Guyana, flows the Urari Coera River, whose name contains the Iberian root ur- (water). Along the river, according to the testimonies of the Maku Indians, is located Manoa, the "stone city."

In the Peruvian region of Madre de Dios, in the area of confluence between Rio Sinkibenia and Rio Palatoa, there is a rock wall thirty meters long and thirty meters high: at its feet are hundreds of Iberian glyphs (known as the Petroglyphs of Pusharo) in the style of Pedra Pintada, up

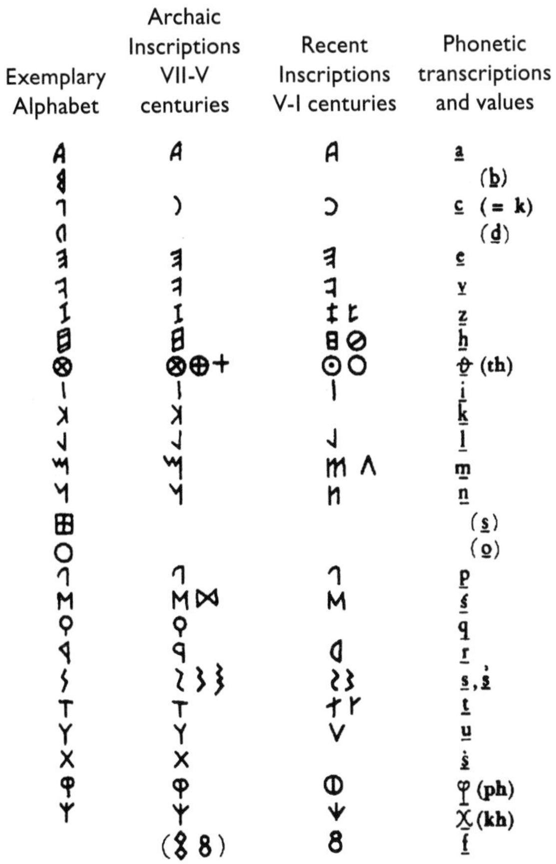

Exemplary Alphabet	Archaic Inscriptions VII–V centuries	Recent Inscriptions V–I centuries	Phonetic transcriptions and values
A	A	A	a
𐌁			(b)
�章	)	Ɔ	c (= k)
ᑯ			(d)
𐌄	𐌄	𐌄	e
𐌅	𐌅	ꓩ	v
𐌆	I	ꭦ ꭤ	z
𐌇	𐌇	𐌇 ⊘	h
⊗	⊗ ⊕ +	⊙ ○	θ (th)
ı	ı	ı	i
Χ	Χ		k
⅃	⅃	⅃	l
ꟽ	ꟽ	ꟿ ∧	m
ꓮ	ꓮ	ꓯ	n
⊞			(ṣ)
○			(ọ)
𐌓	𐌓	𐌓	p
ꟽ	ꟽ ⋈	ꟽ	ś
𐌒	𐌒		q
𐌓	𐌓	ꓒ	r
ꙅ	ꙅ 𐌔 ꙅ	ꙅ 𐌔	s, ṣ
T	T	✝ ꓤ	t
Y	Y	V	u
X	X		ś
Φ	Φ	⊕	φ (ph)
Ψ	Ψ	Ψ	X (kh)
	(ꭤ 8)	8	f

Figure 8.3. The Etruscan language's evolved
form of Iberian writing.

to nearly three meters. Similar writings are on fragments of <u>worked pottery coming from the banks of the Amazon River dated between 6000 and 5000 BCE.</u> The Iberian writing traced there was typically used for Proto-Indo-European languages, but this was not necessarily a fixed rule. For example, there are inscriptions in Greek and Latin (Indo-European languages) made by using the Pelasgian or Etruscan alphabet.

Genetic studies show that nearly 100 percent of Mayans, Incans, and Araucanians of central Chile have blood type O, of which 5 to 20 percent have Rh negative—the original blood type of Cro-Magnons.[11] Those that have this blood type are from the Americas and the Canary Islands, as well as the Berbers, the Basques, the Irish, and the English.

Born in Florence but living in Venezuela since 1948, professor and researcher Natalia de Rosi de Tariffi resolves this question: she pointed out several years ago that the Etruscan language greatly resembles the Quechua and Aymara languages of the Andean civilizations. The professor claims the existence of a unitary language, not only in Europe, but even in Central and South America. Here follows a striking comparison between Etruscan and Quecha-Aymara words, originally taken from her book *América, Cuarta Dimensión.*

Etruscan	Quechua-Aymara*
Anda: cold northern wind	**Anta:** the cold and rushing northern wind that plagues the Andean peaks
Andes: name given to the Gauls, coming from the North. The **Antiati** or **Antiates** were a pre-Latin people, mentioned by many ancient writers, but not identified. The Italian word **Antenati (Antemnati)** was originally used to refer to its members. It means **ancestors** in English.	**Andes:** Cordillera of the Andes
Aulla: ancient Etruscan city	**Aulla:** large, spacious. Possible connections with the Italian **aula** (chamber)
Ayta: infernal deity	**Aytha:** to cry for pain
Calaris (Kalaris): ancient Etruscan city	**Kala:** stone
Canopus: burial jar	**Conopo:** god protectors of the family
Catha: undefined deity	**Qata:** protection, shelter, emergency
Charan: infernal deity (perhaps the Greek Charon)	**Charan:** marshland, swamp, morass, and, by extension, a place of desolation and death
Chiton: short tunic	**Chiti:** short, small
Cuti: god or mythological character	**Cuti:** god of commerce
Cyllene (Celene, Selene, Silene): name of the moon	**Quilla, Killa:** goddess of the moon

Etruscan	Quechua-Aymara*
Haruspex: analyzing entrails of animals	**Aruspichu:** good or bad news
Index: archaic name of the sun god	**Inti:** the sun god
Jupiter: the supreme deity	**Jawa:** the one who is above all
Mercury: god of commerce	**Marqai:** to transport goods
Omen: prophecy	**Omu:** fortune-teller, magician
Orc: hell, god of the underworld	**Orc:** deep, savage, cruel
Pacha: divinity	**Pacha:** god, supreme being
Pileus: cap of leather, felt, or fabric	**Pillu:** head ornament, crown
Semo Sancu: god of good faith	**Simi:** oath, law
Summano: god of the sky	**Sumaya:** to honor, venerate
Uni: goddess	**Unu:** water, unity, the first
Velchan (Velxan, Vulcan): god of fire	**Wilca, Wilka:** the sun god, warmth, passion, fire, flame, light

*Source of table: *Italia, Mistero Cosmico* [Italy, Cosmic Mistery] by Peter Kolosimo.

A larger dictionary was compiled by Tariffi herself to compare Quechua-Aymara words and Italian words (both current and disused) or expressions of the Tuscan dialect. These are probably Etruscan entries, not found in the texts, which were later borrowed by the neo-Latin languages (see the table below).

Italian	Quechua-Aymara*
Acquistare, acquisire: to acquire	**Haquisitha:** to earn working, to find, to conquer
Ala: wing	**Alari:** to fly without flapping the wings
Alpe: alp	**Allpa:** land, soil
Amico: friend	**Amicusitha:** to befriend (in Italian *fare amicizia*)
Ammaccare: to bruise	**Maqai:** to slam/beat

Italian	Quechua-Aymara*
Appartarsi: to go off	**Apartatha:** secluded (as in apartheid)
Arare: to plow	**Haray, harani:** to plow
Bagarino: to tout	**Pacarino:** to hide
Balta: "to tip over, turn over" (archaic)	**Palta:** above
Bautta: archaic meaning of "carnival disguise, hooded cloak, mask"	**Wata, huata:** garment that covers by enveloping
Bazzicare: to haunt	**Wausachay:** ritualized relationship
Bicchiere: glass	**Vicchi** ('vi-kki): cup, mug, drinking jug
Burrasca: storm	**Purayashca:** darkened, troubled by the dark
Canto, cantone: corner (archaic)	**Kantu:** nook, corner, boundary
Cassata: cassata	**Qasa:** ice cream
Cattivo: bad	**Qaqti:** sour, bitter, bad taste
Chiamare: to call	**Kallo:** voice, cry, language
Concimaia: manure	**Conchumayo:** dirty water, septic tank
Cucchiaio: spoon	**Huccharatha:** to sip slowly
Equipaggiamento: equipment	**Quipu:** knot; **paka:** to hide, to pack
Fisciù: triangular scarf worn by women on the chest (archaic)	**Fichu, pichu:** piece of colored cloth used as a shawl
Fusciacca: sash	**Fichuc** ['fi-ʃuk]: colored stripe
Giucco: fool, silly (archaic)	**Chucuc, chucucuc:** idiot
Giunta: to join	**Junta:** full; **juntay:** to fill in/up
Humus: compost	**Huumi:** steam rising from the earth
Lussazione: luxation—joint dislocation	**Lluqsii:** to exit, to take away from where it was, to remove
Magagna: defect, blemish	**Mauka:** worn out, damaged, spoiled
Malattia: illness	**Malatha:** to feel bad/ill
Mannaia: ax, chopper	**Manyai:** to cut; **manyana:** sharp item

Italian	Quechua-Aymara*
Miccino: tiny part of something (archaic)	**Micha:** stingy, miser
Naso: nose	**Nasa:** root
Onore: honor	**Hono:** power, wealth, value
Pacco: pack	**Pakay:** to pack, to hide
Paio: pair	**Paya:** two
Piantare: to plant	**Piantatha:** to introduce, to place in-depth
Pigliare: to take, to catch	**Pillatha:** to seize, to grasp
Piroetta: pirouette	**Pirurur:** to turn, to spin
Pittura: painting	**Pintuy:** to cover, to coat
Poco: a little	**Poque:** a little, the minimum quantity
Posca: water with vinegar, light wine (archaic)	**Posco, pusco:** something acidic
Reddito, rendita: rent, revenue	**Rantii:** to buy or sell, to do an exchange of values
Rio: river	**Rii:** to flow, to go, to move
Ripulsa, ripudio: rejection, repudiation	**Ripuy:** to reject, to push away
Rocca: rock	**Ruqqi:** fortress, rock
Scacciare, cacciare: to chase away, to hound out	**Kacharii:** to detach, remove, let go
Setaccio: sieve	**Sutuy:** pouring a liquid by drops
Stambugio: cubicle	**Tambu:** store, tavern
Succhiare, suggere: suck	**Suksuy:** to suck, to absorb
Tappare: plug up, stop up	**Tappatha:** to close, to patch
Tassa: tax	**Tax:** imposed; **tassatha:** to demand or pay taxes
Tozzo: tubby	**Tuzu:** small, round, like a wool ball

Italian	Quechua-Aymara*
Usatto: high shoes that covered up to the leg (archaic)	**Usuta:** shoes or leather sandals
Vanga: spade	**Vanqa:** lever
Vate/vaticinator: prophet	**Watu, huatu:** omen, hope; **watuc:** prophet, seer

*Source of table: *Italia, Mistero Cosmico* [Italy, Cosmic Mistery] by Peter Kolosimo.

To quote just a few—we could compile an extensive dictionary referring to terms that completely disappeared from the Italian vocabulary and many expressions from the Tuscan dialect that are still used overseas.

AMBIGUOUS LANGUAGES

There was a renowned dividing line between Indo-European Spain and Proto-Indo-European Spain (where migration had not yet penetrated) until the first millennium BCE. To the north and west, onomastics was Indo-European and epigraphs (inscriptions) transmitted Indo-European languages. To the south and east, onomastics and epigraphy are both pre-Indo-European.

The most common evidence is found in coins, sepulchral inscriptions, and seals, mainly realized in Iberian writing except for a group of documents in the Greek alphabet.

The syllabic structure is similar to the one reconstructed by Luis Michelena, eminent Basque linguist,* for the Basque prehistoric phase. In some terms there is the alternation of the elements -r, -n, and Ø that we find in both Basque and Indo-European. In Basque we have *egun* (day), *egur-aldi* (weather), and *egu-berri* (Christmas, literally "new day").

---

*Koldo Mitxelena Elissalt, a.k.a. Luis Michelena, an eminent Basque linguist, taught at the department of philology, University of the Basque Country, and was a member of the Royal Academy of the Basque Language.

Slightly more advanced is the Tartessian language* that appeared in Iberian writing on a number of inscriptions in Algarve (southern Portugal), western Andalusia (southern Spain), Extremadura (western Spain), and Salacia (southwestern Portugal). Swedish linguist Oscar Stig Wikander[†] tracked the use of the Indo-European root kei- ("to lie") with the same suffix of Hittite verbs, and the same distinction between singular and plural. Spanish linguist José Antonio Correa isolated some anthroponyms very close to Indo-European anthroponyms of the peninsula, and noted the use of the suffix -bho for the plural dative, as sometimes happens in the Indo-European area. The Tartessian language is therefore one of the aforementioned ambiguous languages.

To these we add the Luwian language, spoken in Arzawa (Aegean Turkey), which was "Indo-Europeanized" over time by contact with the Hittites (in north-central Anatolia). Used until the first millennium BCE, it employed a slightly modified form of Iberian writing, called, in the same way as the spoken language, just "Luwian."

Luwian inscriptions have been found in Central and South America by the linguist Gabriele D'Annunzio Baraldi, who recognized some on the Pedra do Inga, a huge horizontal boulder twenty-four meters long and three meters high situated in the Brazilian state of Paraiba, eighty kilometers from the Atlantic.

According to Dutch researcher Fred Woudhuizen, the Phaistos Disk[‡] found in Crete contains a variety of languages that the researcher calls "the Cretan branch of Luwian."

---

*The name "tartess" derives from the old belief that the city of Tartessos was in Andalusia, a misunderstanding originating from an incorrect reading of the classics, ignoring that the Pillars of Hercules (at least until the third century BCE) were understood to be on the channel of Sicily and Gibraltar. Thus, the Tartessos of southwest Sardinia, located beyond the Pillars of Hercules, was believed to be in Andalusian Spain.

†Oscar Stig Wikander (Swedish, 1908–1983) was a professor of Sanskrit, an Orientalist, a linguist, an Indologist, an Iranist, and an author of numerous works on history, religion, and Oriental literature. He obtained his doctorate at the University of Uppsala in 1938 with a thesis on the Aryan authorship of the pre-Islamic Iran.

‡A two-sided circular clay tablet that was imprinted on both sides with stamped symbols.

In the Greek vocabulary words with no Greek etymology were identified as belonging to those areas from where the substrate loanwords would usually come from: place names, plants, fruits, animals, material culture (molubdoz/μολυβδοζ = lead; oinoz/οινοζ = wine; qwrhx/θωρηξ = breastplate, etc.). According to the phonetic laws of Indo-European languages these words should not have an etymology—although Bulgarian linguist Vladimir Ivanov Georgiev* became aware that he could build a sensible etymology working with a new set of phonetic changes. Thanks to a new set of rules words that were apparently meaningless assumed clear meanings. The Proto-Indo-European reconstructed by Georgiev was renamed "Pelasgian," and in our opinion, he chose the most appropriate name.

HYDRONYMS

In a large part of Europe there is a relatively homogeneous type of place names that cannot be explained through the different languages historically known in these regions. The names of this class contain Indo-European roots and suffixes but miss other features that characterize Indo-European languages.

German philologist and linguist Hans Krahe† became convinced that such homogeneity of hydronyms was attributable to a specific people with a relatively homogeneous language, which in one way or another, at some point in time, spread almost all over Europe. According to German

---

*Vladimir Ivanov Georgiev was an important Bulgarian linguist, philologist, and education minister. He contributed much to studies on ancient Thrace including a linguistic interpretation of an inscription found at the Kyolmen village of Shoumen, a district in northeastern Bulgaria.

†Hans Krahe (1898–1965) was a German philologist and linguist who spent many decades in the study of the Illyrian languages. Between 1936 and 1946 Krahe taught at the University of Wurzburg, where, in 1942, founded the "Archiv für die Gewässernamen Deutschlands" (Archive for the Names of German Waters). Between 1947 and 1949 he held a professorship at Heidelberg and from 1949 to his death was professor of comparative linguistics, head of Slav studies, and head of Slavs and Indology seminars at the University of Tübingen.

linguist Theo Vennemann* it would be a pre-Indo-European language belonging to a people (the Pelasgians) who colonized Europe from south to north after the last ice age. Holger Pedersen,† linguist at the University of Copenhagen, coined the name Nostratic (from the Latin word *nostras,* meaning "our fellow-countryman"; plural: nostrates), meaning "our language." Thanks to the pioneering work of the Russian comparative linguists V. M. Illic-Svityc and A. B. Dolgopolsky, published in the mid-1960s, we know that after the second flood (9600 BCE) the Afro-Asiatic family‡ (Semitic, ancient Egyptian) had separated from this language. So there is a further indication of the Pelasgian presence in Egypt between the first and second floods.

It's almost certain that from Morocco to the British Isles we are dealing with a single language and a single people. *If the Cro-Magnon was a primitive as many do believe he wouldn't be able to speak even one language. Just look at the many languages of the American Indians, and the thousands of languages in sub-Saharan Africa—each tribe speaks its own language and uses gesture languages to communicate with each other.*

To summarize, before the first Indo-European migrations in Europe,

---

*Theo Vennemann (born in 1937) is a German linguist known for his work on historical linguistics, especially for his controversial hypothesis on the existence of a Vasconic substrate and of an Atlantean superstrate in European languages. He also suggests that the consonantal transition in High German was already complete early in the first century BCE, not in the ninth century CE as many experts believe. He is currently professor emeritus of theoretical and Germanic linguistics at the Ludwig-Maximilian University of Monaco of Bavaria.

†Holger Pedersen (1867–1953) was a linguist at the University of Copenhagen. He made important contributions to Albanian, Celtic, Hittite, and Tocara linguistics. He formulated the Ruki law and Pedersen law on the phonetic changes in Indo-Iranian, Baltic, and Slavic. He also supported the theory of laryngeals at a time when it was "considered an eccentric fantasy of strangers to the subject" (see Szemerényi 1923). Finally, he formulated the glottalic theory and the Nostratic hypothesis.

‡When linguists speak of "distant kinship" between the Indo-European and Afro-Asiatic families it implies the existence of a common ancestor at a time prior to the development of historical grammar systems. The majority of linguists place the date of separation around 10,000 BCE, so we feel entitled to make it coincide with the second flood: it was a traumatic event, capable of breaking long-distance communication between people and their unity of language.

people in the Mediterranean and Middle East already spoke a language that we can call Proto-Indo-European or Nostratic, written in Iberian writing (Pelasgian fore-writing). Where the new Indo-European migrations were not incidental, they continued to employ Iberian until the first millennium BCE, and they later moved to use of the Pelasgian alphabet for writing. But where was the Indo-European born?

THE NEW LANGUAGE

A large group of Pelasgians (Proto-Indo-Europeans) moved eastward around 10,000 BCE. According to myth it was a military campaign promoted by King Osiris, leading a group coming from Hyperborea, the current Po Valley.

A portion of the warriors settled in the East, creating a strain that, for natural evolution and in contact with the aboriginal languages (Dravidian), "transformed" their language into real Indo-European. According to some linguists Dravidian languages would be part of the same substratum of Proto-Indo-European Old Europe. In this case, we can only speak of evolution.

Two global disasters would have favored isolation of the eastern Pelasgians: the second and third floods, generated by the melting ice of the ice age. Cesare Emiliani of the University of Miami, considered father of the study of Earth's past climate and oceans, places the floods in 9600 and 6700 BCE.

Archaeologists say the Vedic civilization—creators of Hinduism's sacred texts, the Vedas—developed in the Indus Valley. It is the oldest of the real Indo-European civilizations known to us, whose gathering centers, like Mehrgarh, arose early in the seventh millennium BCE. Linguists oppose the thesis of its Indo-Europeanism because of the enormous similarity between Sanskrit (India's ancient language) and several European languages.

In fact, if the Indus civilization was Indo-European, then the separation of India from the European strain must be traced to the seventh millennium. According to F. Villar, University of Salamanca, "In particular, any close relation with the Greek could not have survived a period of

5,000 years of separation." Therefore, he believes that the Vedas, whose language descended from Sanskrit, were composed in India and have no link with the Indus Valley civilization.

Nevertheless, archaeological evidence shows that the Vedic civilization coincides with the Indus Valley civilization, as demonstrated by the geographical features reported in the Vedas (the rivers Indus and Sarasvati). Indeed, the criteria contained in these texts for the construction of fire altars and the use of trimeshthin for the construction of the city call for three distinct areas of settlement: the upper town, the middle town, and lower town. Colin Renfrew himself, a pillar of modern archaeology, defends the idea of the Indo-European civilizations belonging to the Indus Valley.

The only possible explanation is that the Indus Valley is the first real home of Indo-European, where the language evolved and from where, only later, between the fifth and the second millennia BCE, there was substantial migration to the West.

It seems that at first the Indo-Europeans preserved the religion of one Pelasgian god, but in fact, historical languages only have in common the proper name of a god. This is *dyeus:* in Sanskrit *dyaus,* in Greek Zeuz (Ζευϲ) and in Latin Iovis (genitive; Diovis in archaic Latin). It is usually accompanied with the word *pater,* in the form of *dyeus pater,* Sanskrit *dyauspita,* Greek Zeuz *pathr* (Ζευϲ πατηρ), Latin Iuppiter (Umbrian Iupater), and Illyrian Deipaturoz (Δειπατυροϲ).

It is difficult to explain the presence of Indo-European peoples in the steppes of southern Russia since the third millennium BCE (Scythians, Cimmerians, and Sarmatians). Logic dictates that it is the barbarian peoples of the arid steppes who aspire to change their living conditions by invading civilized areas, and not vice versa. For this reason, the steppes of southern Russia are now regarded by many as the homeland of the Indo-Europeans. However, as we discuss in the conclusion, such steppes can be found just at the mouth of a route leading from India to Europe along natural waterways.

In the steppes contact with nomads of Altaic origin* would have

---

*The Turkic, Tungusic, and Mongolian language groups.

allowed the introduction of the bit that enabled the riding of horses and the improvement of military technology.

The Indians of the Sanskrit era represent a confirmation of this shift from east to west, considering the fact that their language offers a more conservative phonetic and their military technology is also more backward than neighboring Iran's. Tracking this we find the Iranians in the south of the Caucasus (Medes, Persians) using phonetically more advanced forms of language and using the new bit enabling people to ride horses.

THE SABIANS AND HYKSOS

Since 4000 BCE, for a period of nearly 1,000 years, groups of Indo-Europeans followed a route 3,000 kilometers to the west arriving on the shores of the Azov Sea and the Caspian Sea. After 3000 BCE they moved down to the Black Sea and the Caucasus.

This era brings the formation of the Scythians, according to Herodotus "the circumcised sons of Hercules": they were a confederation of tribes of different social status. At the top are the rulers and the military aristocracy (the "elites") that the Egyptians called the Hyksos ("heads of foreign countries"). Their language is Indo-European or, more precisely, Indo-Iranian. Further down are the common Scythians or Gutei, a nomadic people encountered and subjected along the way.

When in 2600 BCE Scythians came to Mesopotamia from the Zagros Mountains they also brought the Akkadian empire founded by Sargon the Great.*

By the mid-second millennium BCE, an aristocracy of the same strain was governing over the Kassites of Babylon and the Hurrians of

---

*The Akkadian empire was founded by King Sargon thanks to his victory in thirty-five consecutive battles with neighboring kings. The temporal location of Sargon's life and campaign is very uncertain, ranging from 3700 to 2800 BC. Centered in the city of Akkad, the empire comprised the whole Middle East, stretching from the Mediterranean Sea to the Persian Gulf, from Arabia to the Zagros Mountains.

Mitanni, a little further west. The same phenomenon occurred for the royal dynasties of the city-states of Syria and Palestine, whose members were called Sabians (in Proto-Semitic "the circumcised"). They can be recognized by the onomastics of their rulers and titles, as well as from the pantheon of the Vedic deities they worshiped.

Several Indo-Aryan groups were forced to leave Mesopotamia during the revolt of King Utukhegal of Uruk (2400 BCE), who inaugurated the Neo-Sumerian period (Ur III). They reached Greece and Italy, where they imparted the building technique of walls and geometric ceramic style. The arrival of the flamen's role in Italy, which was then introduced into Roman society, is likely to be traced back to this period.

Dated to the eighteenth century BCE are two tablets in cuneiform writing* (I.39, IV.28) that came from the royal archives of the city-state of Mari on the middle Euphrates. They refer to a city of Alatri, re-founded in Lazio under the Sabian influence, of which King Yasmah-Adad writes to his father: "Alatri is strong, it still has the ancient walls and no more have been built."

We have come over 3,000 kilometers from west to east in the wake of Osiris, and another 3,000 kilometers from east to west following the so-called Indo-European migrations. Groups of Pelasgians had left Europe to reach the Indus Valley, where the language of the Cro-Magnon "became" the Indo-European. From the Indus Valley, their descendants repeatedly returned to Europe, through the so-called Indo-European migrations, beginning in the fifth millennium BCE. We are interested in the migration that began a millennium later in 4000 BCE, when there were smaller groups of "selected" wisemen, "elites" who were capable of imposing themselves over people and perpetuating the memory of their origin, generating the so-called Sea Peoples.

In the early days this ancient writing proceeded from right to left and, according to Pausanias, this was a usage already forgotten in 431 BCE.[12]

---

*Cuneiform writing used a wedge-shaped stylus to make impressions in clay, stone, metal, and wax. Most likely invented by the Sumerians, it was later adapted for writing in Akkadian.

The Pelasgian Alphabet

According to Diodorus Siculus, Pelasgian writing was the most antique of humanity. These letters are still used in the alphabets of pre-Roman Italic peoples and were brought to Greece by the Pelasgian Cadmo.*

It is said that Linus, teacher of Hercules, Thamyris, and Orpheus, adapted the Pelasgian letters to the Greek pronunciation, giving them a Greek name and using them to write the story of Bacchus. The same letters were used by Orpheus and many other ancients such as Pronapides, Homer's teacher. Pliny tells us that the forms of these letters were similar to the Latin, as demonstrated by the dedication found on an old Delphic tablet of which he shows the inscription.[†]

The Pelasgian letters were used in Greece even after the introduction of the national writing and were renamed "Attic" because, according to Herodotus, <u>the Athenians (Athens is situated in Attica) had Pelasgian origin.</u> Pausanias preserves the memory of an inscription in Attic letters carved on a monument by Praxiteles.[‡] According to Johann Joachim Winckelmann and Louis Lanzi,[§] another inscription was engraved in Attic letters on the tomb of Herod Atticus, currently shown in the Royal Museum of Portici.[¶]

---

*Agenor, king of Tyre, is Cadmus's father; Europe, Menes's wife, is his sister: this would be sufficient to classify him as Pelasgian. His wife, Harmony, is the daughter of Electra, in turn daughter of Atlas, the third king of Atlantis and therefore Pelasgian himself. The partaking of Cadmus and Agenor to the same strain would seem obvious at this point. In Phoenician memories we find an Agenor who is Cadmus's father who brought from Egypt the first few Pelasgian letters in the country of Sidon, whose people later elected him as king. Apollodorus in his *Library* describes Agenor as the son of Neptune and Libya, daughter of Epaphus, son of Io (Minos's mother), taking us once again to the Pelasgians' genealogies. Pausanias sustains this thesis when he writes that Cadmus and Phoenix, sons of Agenor, were brothers of Electra, whom we have seen as being Pelasgian and mother of the Tuscan Dardanus, founder of Troy.

†Pliny, *Naturalis Historia*, book 8, chapter 58.

‡Pausanias, *Description of Greece*, trans. W. H. S. Jones and H. A. Omerod (Cambridge, Mass.: Harvard University Press, 1918), book 1, chapter 2.

§Johann Joachim Winckelmann (1717–1768), German archaeologist and art historian, was the initiator of archaeology in the modern sense as he carried the study of the ancient art from crude antiquarian scholarship to a more historical concept of it. Louis Lanzi (1732–1810) was a Jesuit, archaeologist, and historian of Italian art.

¶Johann Winckelmann, *History of the Art of Antiquity*, trans. Harry Mallgrave (Los Angeles: Getty Research Institute, 2006), book 12.

Then scholars began to write boustrophedon texts, which alternate direction every line, writing with mirrored letters on the "backward" lines. Finally the practice of writing from left to right prevailed.

If it is true that in ancient times Phoenicians, Greeks, and those who spoke Latin wrote with the same letters, it is clear that the Pelasgians—the first to use them—must have had an influence on their civilization.

It is likely that a study on the elegance of the form had led to a change in the letters compared to the Pelasgic type: the Greeks modeled it, arranging curved, irregular, and tapered lines, while in Latin straight lines, with full and rounded shapes were used. According to Italian scholar and archaeologist Mario Guarnacci,* "By means of the sole and only winding, the Latin writing formed from the Etruscan, and so did the Greek."[13] English scholars, who in the eighteenth century wrote the *Universal History,* report: "We cannot help but believe that the alphabetic characters, which are represented in some Etruscan inscriptions, are at the moment the oldest to be found in this world."[14]

> **Socrates:** *What do we know of the descendants of Atlantis? Can they be said to have disappeared?*
> **Hermocrates:** *Our merchants in Cumae and Pithecoussai report that men fled to Ichnusa, hidden for centuries among the Sabine people of Tuscia. They call themselves "Rasenna" and speak the language of the ancient*

*Mario Guarnacci (1701–1785) was an Italian prelate, scholar, and archaeologist of the Catholic Church renowned for having donated his extensive library to Volterra together with his private museum (the Museum Guarnacci) of Etruscan finds.

Pelasgians. They are very good locksmiths and run the workshops. They have learned the Sabines' techniques, have improved them and are getting rich by trading with Greece. Some call them princes, while the Romans, who call their region "Etruria," call them Etruscans.

The Spartans, instead, say to be brothers of the Semites of Judah and Samaria. They say that on the banks of the Jordan they still practice the ancient cults of Atlantis and worship a single god. But theirs is a second progeny, and beware from defining themselves as brothers with the Tuscias.

9

MISSING

Look at this [holds up a silver pocket watch]. It's worthless. Ten dollars from a vendor in the street. But I take it, I bury it in the sand for a thousand years, it becomes priceless! Like the Ark. Men will kill for it; men like you and me.

RENE BELLOQ, *RAIDERS OF THE LOST ARK*

The sea at night freaks me out a bit . . .
If you just stare at it, you feel like
you'll be swallowed inside
its cold dark waves . . .

GATSU, FROM *BERSERK*
(A GRAPHIC NOVEL BY KENTARO MIURA)

What happened to the Pelasgians after the second flood? After the third? How could the memory of them win over time and arrive in the nineteenth century? In recent years I have had the pleasure of discovering the value of the discipline linguistics, which in almost a mechanical way unhinges words and grammar systems until you can read within them the movements of peoples and the duration of their settlement. The opinions of the greatest modern linguists, partly reported in the previous chapter, inexorably lead to the Indus River Valley, where the Pelasgians' language remained isolated, to later change and evolve into the Indo-European language.

And right here the most ancient civilization recognized by archaeology—the official one—bloomed with the cities of Mehrgarh and Lothal soon after the third flood in 6700 BCE. Who were those "Indians"? They were the writers of the Vedas, mindful of the iced island, of the six months of light and six of darkness, descendants of Manu/Osiris. The expedition of this "god" had led their fathers to the East. They knew it, they were the children of Manu and the Seven Sages, a group of chosen heirs born after the last flood to preserve the seeds of plants and knowledge. They asserted it firmly in front of Alexander the Great!

Some of them have certainly moved again, this time in the opposite direction. Almost all European languages resemble the language of the "children of Manu," so much so that we can consider them to be its dialects. The experts have been keen to find several superimposed linguistic layers corresponding to an older and a younger Indo-European. The first ones who left the Indus to move back to the old European home did it in 5000 BCE, whereas a second group moved in 4000 BCE, stopping for a while in Scythia on the Black Sea.

In those areas they met the nomadic people of Gutei, with whom they merged and created their own tribe. All together they were called Scythians, but the Indo-European tribes represented the "Royal Scythians," those in command, better known as the Hyksos or Sabians. In 2600 BCE they went down to Mesopotamia and wiped out the so-called first empire in the world, the kingdom of Akkad created by Sargon the Great. They stayed there for a couple of centuries before the old nobility pulled out its weapons and forced them elsewhere, but they didn't give in. In fact 200 and 600 years later they went down again, apparently in the vanguard of other tribes, no longer Gutei but Hurrians and then Kassites, but it was them again: the Hyksos.

After 2400 BCE the Hyksos, expelled from Mesopotamia, were scattered around the Mediterranean coast, baptized with new names such as

Achaeans, Shardana, Sabine, Libu, and Teucrians. Today, we call them the Sea Peoples.

GREECE

Now we move to Greece, land of the oracles. It was full of esoteric centers where a god would speak through the voice of a priestess who was drugged—sometimes intoxicated—by poisonous fumes. These oracles were mandatory points of passage before leaving for and at the return of any marine travel, whom one asked and to whom one reported information, keepers of the knowledge of the coasts, shoals, rocks, and submarine benches. They were sources of enrichment for greedy and lascivious priests. The oldest one was at Dodona in northwestern Greece and spoke on behalf of Jupiter. According to Homer it was created by the Pelasgians.[1] The Greek poet Hesiod refers to Dodona as the "seat of Pelasgians"[2] and Greek geographer Strabo confirms it while leaning on Greek historian Ephorus: "the oracle was built by the ancient Pelasgians."[3]

The priests of Egypt and Dodona told Greek historian Herodotus that two oracles were founded in Dodona and the Egyptian oasis Siwa based on the simple fact that a pair of doves—freed from the sanctuary of Amun at Thebes in Egypt—chose to settle on those lands. It is a standard story repeated with small variations in several places, including overseas, with the purpose of classifying the oracles as geodetic indicators or *omphalos* (literally "navels of the world"), which are reference points for travelers well known on the Earth's surface. The release of doves, a gesture the Bible says Noah also made, was a symbol of the measurement of the world after the flood had changed it.

Aeschylus, at the beginning of the *Eumenides*, argued that the oracle of Apollo* at Delphi originally belonged to the Titans or Pelasgians. The

---

*The cult of Apollo was born in Hyperborea, the current Po Valley, but over time the name "Hyperborea" was confused with "Iperea," the name given to plains in southern Sicily. Thus some authors believed that Apollo was Sicilian and a fairy tale was born that the island of Delos originally separated from Sicily and, once arrived in Greece, gave birth to the god.

poet says that when Apollo went to the oracle he did not go there alone but was accompanied by the sons of Vulcan,* the Cyclops/Pelasgians who worked in the forge of Mount Etna and could vouch for him. <u>Since then, 8,000 years have passed.</u>

Around 2400 BCE, the Hyksos were leaving Mesopotamia. In *Il Segreto degli Illuminati* (The Illuminati Secret):

> Utukhegal, king of Uruk, won over the last Gutian king and estab-lished his power in Ur. Probably, the Utukhegal victory pushed the Syrian and Canaanite old nobility to rebel: while the Mesopotamian elites [Hyksos settled in Mesopotamia] retired on Zagros, the Canaanite elites [Hyksos settled in Palestine] fled to the mountains of the West Bank, heading the other nomadic groups: the Shasus.[4]

At this point it is easy to bind the Aryans (Indo-Europeans) to the elite of Zion (the kings of Israel). Indeed, the Jews are a wonderful "three-layered sandwich." The oldest layer—from the lineage of patri-archs Abraham, Isaac, and Jacob—was composed of the indigenous nomad Shasu (Semites who lived in the West Bank plateau and whom the Akkadians called Suti). After the revolt of Utukhegal the Hyksos added to the first layer: they were Aryan to the bone and bearers of monotheism and circumcision. The third layer is the one of the Habiru, a Semitic people of the Canaanite city, indebted citizens, who fled to the mountains or Egypt to avoid debt bondage. Groups of Habirus entered Egypt after the Hyksos/Shasu invasion, when the latter become its rulers; consequently they became slaves, like the Hyksos, when the Egyptians regained control of their own homeland. The children of Habiru were still forced to work in the armies of Ramses II and also fought for the pharaoh's cousin, General Tot-Moses, who returned to

---

*In *Prometheus Unbound* we read that Vulcan was on Mt. Etna, in Sicily. Later writers put him in Lemnos, where the first stele in the Pelasgian alphabet was found. Accord-ing to Homer the inventor of the arts was Vulcan and it was thanks to him that people who had previously lived wildly on the mountains and in the forests were able to obtain a stable and peaceful life. According to Pliny, the Cyclops were the first in Vulcania (an Aeolian island) to learn how to make use of iron.

Akhenaten's monotheism* and was condemned for heresy. Tot-Moses and the Habiru fled to Palestine and came back to the others, Shasu/Hyksos/Habiru, who had remained in the Near East, amalgamating with them and, after several centuries, becoming the people of Israel.

Let's go back to the era of Utukhegal: To aggravate the situation there was an alarming famine. Those Hyksos who had not returned to the mountains took the sea and some of them arrived in Greece. In chapter 3 of *Greek History* by Marco Bettalli, the basic text in Italian universities, we read:

> Destruction and downsizing characterized these years in much of the central and southern Greece . . . and generalized destructions overwhelmed Mesopotamia in the same period. Such a similarity in such a wide area justifies the idea of invasion. An Indo-European population with predominant warrior features would have approached the Aegean and replaced the "old" Neolithic population devoted mainly to agriculture.

Poets will call them <u>Achaeans,</u> the bearers of new customs, like circumcision, and new knowledge, especially in architecture—they built tombs and tholoi (beehive-shaped stone tombs),† cist tombs, palaces, and Cyclopean walls with massive, irregularly sized stones. The Achaeans restructured the oracles and set them up again. Similar groups occupied Troy on the Dardanelles, the strait in northwestern Turkey that connects the Sea of Marmara with the Aegean—they were the Teucrians (including the Trojans); some, like the Lukka, moved to Lycia (Anatolia) on the southern coast of Turkey, while the Shardanas went to Sardinia, the Sabines arrived in Italy, and the Libus settled on the Tunisian-Algerian coast.

The Egyptians and the Hittites called them <u>the Sea Peoples, the last heirs of the Pelasgians.</u> Initially they were builders who moved coast to coast creating beautiful tholoi from Hattusa to the Canary Islands,

---

*Akhenaten was of Hyksos blood by his mother and became pharaoh in 1359 BCE.
†The Tomb of Atreus in Mycenae, a tholos tomb whose lintel stone above the doorway weighs 120 tons (the largest in the world), is one of the most impressive monuments of Mycenaean Greece.

and then they slowly took control of the local people, becoming the elite power. They were similar to the workers of the freemasons who were moved throughout Europe by the Benedictine monks to raise majestic cathedrals, first Romanesque and later Gothic. And we all know what the Benedictine lodges became in time: steeped in Hermetic, Neo-Platonic and Rosicrucian culture, they have become the modern Freemasonry that, according to some, should be protecting the dynasty of the Merovingian kings of France. This might be only speculation if recent studies had not adduced the Merovingians as the direct heirs of the Sea Peoples, who mingled with the Franks only in the third century CE.[5]

The Egyptians claimed that the Sea Peoples had clear skin and hair and blue eyes, a sign perhaps of their genetic link with the Pelasgian Cro-Magnon race. In *Life of Romulus* Plutarch argued that the Sabines' navigation to Italy represented only a return of the Pelasgians to their homeland, while also asserting that the name of Rome had been imposed by "Romo who had chased the Tyrrhenians/Pelasgians come from Thessaly to Lydia and from Lydia to Italy."

The Achaeans organized the city-state population under the guidance of their elites, dwelling in palaces. In the latter's stores they used to gather the agricultural production of the countryside around the city and distribute it to all the population, as well as to the farmers, artisans, and employees.

In the fourteenth century BCE the Achaeans reached their peak and founded colonies on the opposite shore of the Aegean, approaching the city of Troy. But a century later another famine (related to climatic change taking place since the second half of the thirteenth century), more serious than the previous one, hit the entire Mediterranean and overtook the unprepared Middle East, whose economy was based mainly on the palatial redistributive system. After a long period of moderate warm and rainy weather (the glaciers in the Scandinavian peninsula had completely melted and even here they cultivated the vine) there were convulsions and natural disasters—earthquakes, tsunamis, volcanic eruptions, and hurricanes—followed by a decrease in temperature that was accompanied by drought. Marco Bettalli, professor of Greek history at the University of Siena (Italy), writes in his *Greek History:*

If we accept the idea that the palatial system was based on an elaborate control mechanism, one of the reasons for the collapse can be
found in these forms of excessive centralization and exploitation,
which ultimately would make the system weaker, that means easy to
be destroyed: once achieved their maximum territorial expansion,
the city-states would no longer be able to support the economic
weight of their organizational apparatus, up to the collapse.

In central Turkey things went differently, because there flourished
the Hittite empire, characterized by a different resource management,
capable of exploiting the weakness of opponents to enlarge its borders.
The Hurrian empire* and the lands of Arzawa in western Turkey (with
the exception of Troy) fell into the network of Hattusa, the empire's
capital. In Greece, the failure of Achaean elites unleashed a revolt of the
people and led to the election of new leaders of indigenous blood, the
kings of the *Iliad*—essentially shepherd kings who lived in sumptuous
abandoned palaces. Then and for several centuries the Aegean writing,
complex architecture, crafts, and technique of parietal fresco disappeared
almost completely and trade in luxury goods ceased. Looking for new
resources to meet the famine, these kings organized the invasion of Troy,
last scapegoat for Teucer-Achaean faults. After the fall of the city, however, the unexpected happened: the few city-states remaining under the
control of elites in Arzawa called to their aid the Shardanas, the Sabines,
the Lukka, and the Libus, who were expecting the occurrence to cope
with the famine by taking in new lands.

They brought down the Hittite empire, including Ugarit's city-state
and commercial crossroads, Carchemish, and they razed the Greek cities of
the "new" kings, while Egypt resisted by a miracle. At Babylon, the revolt
broke out and the Kassite elites were overthrown. In his inscriptions on a
wall at Karnak, Merenptah mentions a victory over the Sea Peoples during

---

*This empire is better known as Mitanni. The head of the Hurrian displayed an elite
ethnicity distinguished from that of the common people, having the first light hair and
light eyes, evidence of how the palatial system should be credited to the Sea Peoples. See
Birgit Brandau and Hartmut Schickert, *Hethiter. Die unbekannte Weltmacht* (Munich:
Piper Verlag GmbH, 2001).

a first invasion in 1225 BCE. An inscription in the temple of Medinet Habu, Thebes, tells of Pharaoh Ramesses III having to face them again forty years later (1180 BCE). In Arzawa, the Teucer kingdom of Mira was reconstituted and the Greek conquerors were driven from Troy; the Greek city-states were burned and the so-called dark age began, ending in 800 BCE with the rise of the poleis, the Greek city-states. The case of Athens is interesting: it was the only major Greek city not destroyed by the invasion of the Sea Peoples, who instead only took the women. According to Herodotus, the native Athenians descended from the Pelasgians, and perhaps the city was spared in the name of their common origin.

ARZAWA:
TURKEY ON THE AEGEAN SEA

Substantially independent until the arrival of Cyrus the Great and Persians in 550 BCE, the people of the lands of Arzawa, corresponding to the current Aegean Turkey, coexisted with the people on their eastern borders: the Hittites, the Assyrians, and the Medes. Greek colonies already flourished in the fourteenth century BCE in the Achaean or Mycenaean period, including the famous Millawanda or Miletus. From the sixteenth century BCE Arzawan lands appear in the Hittite chronicles and Egyptian correspondence found in the archive of El-Amarna in Middle Egypt, dating to the reign of Amenhotep III in 1386 BCE. The three most famous cities of Arzawa were Troy, Imbros, and Lemnos, occupied or founded by the Teucrians around 2400 BCE.

As we have seen, the foundation of Troy is due to the Pelasgian Dardanus. Herodotus, dealing with Imbros and Lemnos, describes a Pelasgian population who had been recently subjugated by the Athenians (500 BCE), and in the same context he remembers the old raids of such Pelasgians in Attica and their temporary settlement on the Pelasgian Hellespont. According to Herodotus's *Histories* these events would occur at a time when "the Athenians began, first, to call themselves Greeks." Apparently, the Pelasgian Tyrrhenus and Sardan, mythical monikers of Sabine and Shardana, had arrived from Arzawa. Historians refer to Pelasgian colonies in western Turkey, as well as in Thessaly, until the archaic period (800 BCE). The Tirreni (the companions of Tyrrhenus) are described as close to the Pelasgians or as Pelasgians themselves, while in the *Iliad* we read that the Lydians (peoples of central Arzawa) and the Pelasgians were fighting for Priam. In the *Odyssey,* Homer described the Cretan population as a mixture of peoples: "The Achaeans, the Natives, the Cidons, three generations of Dorians, and the Pelasgians." It seems that the link between the Sea Peoples and the Pelasgians in Greece was so obvious as to identify them as one single people.

Greek literature does not distinguish between the movements of Teucrians and Pelasgians, referring to them in the same way: the classics seem to ignore the 8,000 years between the arrival of Danaus—and the Pelasgians—in Turkey, and the flight of the Teucrians/Hyksos from Mesopotamia. They belonged to the same strain, so for the Greeks they were all Pelasgians!

The Telchines*

The ancient Teucrians dated the first Arzawa civilization back to the Pelasgian era when some amphibian creatures, half marine, half terrestrial, and endowed with great intelligence, emerged from the waters: the Telchines.

The lower part of their body was like the tail of a fish or snake, and their feet could be palmate. Evidently, the Telchines are the Teucrian version of the Mesopotamian Iohannes, bearer of art and culture, the body covered with scales and a fish tail. They belong to the pantheon of amphibious and reptilian deities that includes the Nommo of the Dogon, the Mayan Quetzalcòatl, and the fish-tailed gods of Lake Titicaca: Chullua and Umantha. These "demons" were children of Pontus and Talassa (or Gaia) and lived on the island of Rhodes, where together they brought up Poseidon. A little before the second flood they had a premonition of the disaster and left Rhodes to disperse throughout the world. One of them, Licos, gave name to the Lycian region and built the temple of Apollo Licio on a riverbank.

The Telchines are credited with the invention of a number of arts, particularly the carving of the gods' statues. It is said that they were magicians with power over falling rain, snow, and hail—reminiscent of the traditions of Easter Island, according to which in the past the "big magicians" were able to move the statues with "the words of their mouth." Here the magicians used a round stone called Te Pito Kura to "concentrate the power of their *mana* and then order the statues to walk." In ancient Egypt and ancient Mexico it was said that large statues were built by magicians who carved and moved them with their music, or their voice. Tiahuanaco in Peru is said to have risen in a single night with its stones miraculously raised from the ground and transported through the air to the sound of a trumpet. Likewise, the achievement of the Promised Land is said to have taken place by destruction of the walls of Jericho to the cry of seven trumpets played by priests. A similar legend is told about the bishop of Ravenna, St. John Vincent, who shortly before the year 1000 CE used the sound of a trumpet to carry over the mountain Pirchiriano (near Turin) the stones that would serve the construction of the Abbey (called "Sacra") of Saint Michael the Archangel.

*See www.theoi.com/Pontios/Telkhines.html.

Many traditions refer to a Pelasgian or Atlantean foundation of some cities in Asia Minor such as Troy, the cities of the Mysians to the north, and all the Ionian cities to the south.[6] Herodotus in *Euterpe* explains that the Cabiri gods, the gods of mystery cults of Samothrace, an island that faces the Straits of the Dardanelles, were in fact simple men of Pelasgic race. Diodorus adds that Electra, the Pelasgian daughter of Atlas, founded the republic in Samothrace and ordered the mysteries to be taught in the cults, which thereafter became famous throughout Greece. The geographer Strabo claimed that the Cilicians were ever since known as Pelasgians and that the Pelasgians built Larissa and Cumae* on the Ionian coast. This suggests a link with the Cumae in Campania (southern Italy), and it was not by chance that the inhabitants of both places were called

---

Cumae is derived from the homonymous area of Campania as well as that of its inhabitants, Cimmerians, thus making clear the origins of the founders.

"Cimmerian." Strabo also refers to the testimony of Menecrates the Elaite, who, in his book *Dell'Edificazione delle Città* (On the Building of Cities), states the Ionian coast, and nearby islands such as Mycale, were inhabited by the Pelasgians. Diodorus also confirms that the first inhabitants of these areas were the "Aborigines" ("inhabitants of the hills"), a name already used by the author to indicate the Pelasgians. From here, according to Herodotus, the Pelasgians founded Athens first and then moved to Thessaly (called Pelasgic Argos), Arcadia, and Macedonia.[7] In Athens, according to Myrsilus, they built a wall creating a fortress around Athens.*

The latter, in polygonal style, does not differ in size and shape from the Sabine fortresses in Italy or the Achaean fortresses in Greece. So, the presented evidence must, at least in part, have to refer to the Teucrians, leaving two possible explanations: either the Sea Peoples were recognized as descendants of the Pelasgians and called by the same name, or these are all stories "made up" by the Sea Peoples in order to underline their common origin with the ancient Pelasgians.

Of course, some passages bring us very close to the time of flight of Danaus/Seth, 8,000 years ago. Orpheus the Ancient in his hymns *On the Salii* reveals the origin of the "eternal genius or spirits" that were adored in Samothrace: he calls them "Salii, Indigeti, Mamotracii," referring with the first name to a sacred institution revered from time immemorial similar to the Followers of Horus or the Seven Sages. The Pelasgian civilization, implanted in the colony of Electra in Samothrace, would be taken along the coasts of Asia Minor by her son Dardanus, the founder of Troy. The Egyptians themselves, proclaimed the oldest civilization ever since, confessed to Herodotus to have been preceded by the Phrygians[†] in Asia Minor.

At the time of Virgil an ancient and confused tradition was widespread according to which the Pelasgian Dardanus would have come from Tuscany or elsewhere in Italy to relocate in Samothrace and then on the beaches of Asia Minor, emphasizing the western origins of the Pelasgians:

---

*According to Homer, as reported by Diodorus, the first colony in Crete was Pelasgian, but probably referred to the times of Minos and the conquest of the eastern Mediterranean.

†Frigya was a kingdom of Anatolia in what is now Turkey.

The Latin king haranguing the suppliant Trojan said: "And in truth I remember, though time has dimmed the tale, that the Auruncan [people neighboring the Etruscans] elders told how that in this land sprang Dardanus, and hence passed to the towns of Phrygian Ida and Thracian Samos, that men now call Samothrace. 'Twas hence, from the Tuscan home of Corythus, he came, and now the golden palace of the starry sky admits him to a throne, and with his altars he increases the number of gods."[8]

A confirmation to Plutarch (see above) comes from an obscure warning from Apollo, who advised Aeneas, fleeing from Troy, to seek the original land of his ancestors: "Long-suffering sons of Dardanus, the land which bore you first from your parent stock shall welcome you back to her fruitful bosom. Seek out your ancient mother."[9]

As we know Aeneas came to Italy and his descendants founded Rome. It is very interesting to note this circularity since it allows recognition in the Roman empire of the rebirth of the Pelasgian empire, which ten thousand years ago flourished along the Mediterranean coast.

Finally, there are the people of Lesbos, who considered themselves subjects of Pileus (Marcus Pilius), called "King of the Pelasgians": "The Chians also say that the Pelasgians from Thessaly were their founders."[10]

Lastly Homer—who identified Cumae, on the Asian coast, as the seat of the Pelasgians who rushed to the aid of Priam at Larissa: "The Misii believed their country was sacred for the Cabiri Gods, and boasted of their Pelasgic origin."[11]

LIBYA

In North Africa still lives a white-skinned people with Cro-Magnon features regarded as indigenous: the Berbers. They include the Gaetuli, Moors, and the Sea Peoples' immigrants, the Libu. The alphabet used in their language is the Tifinagh, which is a derivation that evolved from the Iberian writing, like Cretan Linear A. The Berber language shows strong affinities with the language of the Minoans—which was written in Linear A.

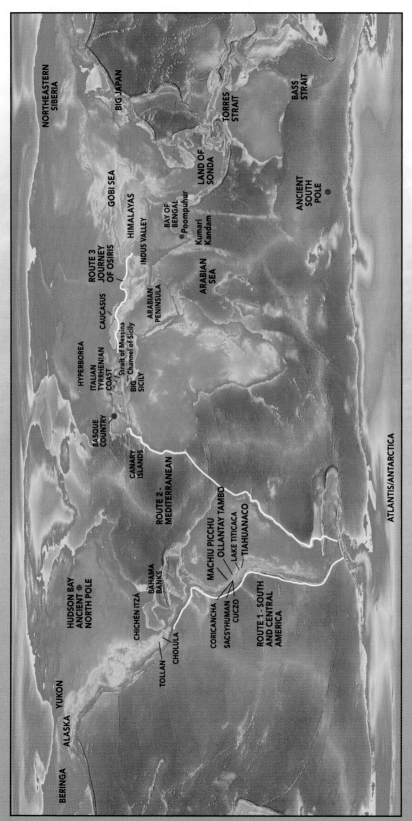

Plate 1. Map of the world containing many important Pelasgian sites. White lines represent the three routes the Pelasgians took after leaving Atlantis.

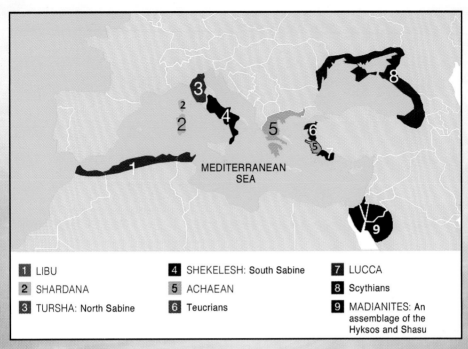

1 LIBU	**4** SHEKELESH: South Sabine	**7** LUCCA
2 SHARDANA	**5** ACHAEAN	**8** Scythians
3 TURSHA: North Sabine	**6** Teucrians	**9** MADIANITES: An assemblage of the Hyksos and Shasu

Plate 2. Locations of the Sea People.

Plate 3 (below). The Intihuatana at Machu Picchu.

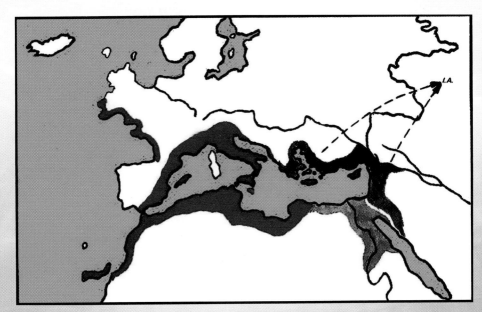

Plate 4. The red area represents territories on the Mediterranean colonized by the Pelasgians from 13,000 BCE to the death of King Baal (around 10,500 BCE), who left the empire to his sons Danaus and Menes (Osiris). The green area represents the territories then annexed by Menes, while the dark gray territories are Danaus's (Titan's) conquests.

Plate 5. The Pedra Pintada near the village of Tarame (Amazon forest, Brazil).

Plate 6. Tablet depicting an Egyptian-style pyramid with Iberian inscription, found at Cuenca in Ecuador.

Plate 7. The twelve-angled stone at Cuzco.

Plate 8 (below). Sacsayhuaman fortress; in the highlighted box is the 361-ton block.

Plate 9. Wall of trapezoidal blocks with niches in Ollantaytambo. Close-up of two niches.

Plate 10 (below). The six megamonoliths weighing from 100 to 200 tons on top of Ollantaytambo.

Plate 11. Semi-subterranean temple of Tiahuanaco. In the background you can see the east door of Kalasasaya.

Plate 12. Sun rising at the east door of Kalasasaya. At top you see the sun at the equinoctial dawn (at any epoch); in the center you see the sun at the solstitial dawn in 10,500 BCE; at the bottom the sun is depicted at the solstitial dawn in 2010.

Plate 13. Viracocha's statue, called El Fraile, in the middle of Kalasasaya in Tiahuanaco.

Plate 14. Representation of Iohannes in a rocky bas-relief inside an Assyrian temple.

Plate 15. The pyramid of Kukulkan at Chichén Itzá. In the box you see the image of the serpent-shaped shadow of the western steps, during equinoctial setting.

Plate 16. The twenty-first tarot: The World. Here you see the constellations that were holding the world in 10,500 BCE—Aquarius-Angel, Scorpio-Eagle, Leo, and Taurus.

Plate 17. The Grand Gallery in the Cheops (Khufu) Pyramid.

Plate 18. The Osirion at Abydos.

Plate 19. The image on the left depicts a Tocharian Cro-Magnoid monk with long ears with a Chinese Buddhist monk to his right; this image is from the Caves of the Thousand Buddhas at Tunhwang. Note the similarity in the shape of the ears and hairstyle with the *moai* of Easter Island (right).

Plate 20. Temple of Angkor Wat. Easily distinguishable is the axis of the lifted road.

Plate 21. The Phimeanakas, the stepped pyramid built by Suryavarman I (1002–1050 CE).

Plate 22. Iberian writing on a cave painting in Tadrart Acacus (Libya).

Plate 23. Pictures of the Alatri fortress: the niches (above) and the major door (below).

Plate 24. Clockwise starting from top left: Large pin found inside the Tomb of Littore at Vetulonia, now displayed in the National Archaeological Museum of Florence; breastplate found in the Bernardini Tomb at Palestrina (Rome), now displayed in the National Etruscan Museum of Villa Giulia; earring found in a necropolis on Poggio del Sole (Hill of the Sun), now displayed in the Archeological Museum of Arezzo; bracelet found in Regolini-Galassi Tomb at Cerveteri, now displayed in the Gregorian-Etruscan Museum at the Vatican.

Plate 25 (below). Circeii's fortess from four viewpoints. Photos on right by Daniele Baldassare, Center for the Study of Polygonal Walls.

Plate 26. Sybil's Cave upstream of Cuma.

Plate 27. Vie Cave in the necropolis of Sovana, Tuscany.

Plate 28. Commemorative incision of the battle of Kadesh in the temple of Ramses II at Abu Simbel. The drawing underneath (made by Rossellini) depicts four Shardana warriors, on the left, beside two Egyptian warriors (the picture has been kindly provided by L. Melis).

Plate 29. Entrance to the Nuragic well of Paulilatino (Oristano, Sardinia).

Plate 30. The ziggurat of Mount d'Accoddi, discovered in 1954 near Sassari in Sardinia.

Plate 31. On the left, a Carthaginian stele showing the caduceus found in Marsala. On the right, a picture of a Shardana boat on a Phoenician stele found in Carthage.

Plate 32. The three small phalluses on the architrave of the minor door of Alatri (top) and an auspicious phallus on the sacred way of Colli Albani (bottom). Source: Mario Pincherle, *La Nuova Etruscologia,* Labris, 1999.

Plate 33 (below). The Baalbek trilith. In the middle are two men, scarcely visible.

Plate 34. The "stone of the pregnant woman" in Baalbek.

Plate 35. Known as the Burney Relief or the Queen of the Night (its nickname from a 2003 exhibition) relief, this Paleo-Babylonian clay bas-relief represents Lilith as a succubus.

Plate 36. Sculpture of the astral Mithras in the act of killing his material part in order to ascend to the divine state. The material part is represented by a bull with a spike in place of its tail, which symbolizes death as a rebirth. Close-up of scorpion attached to bull's genitals.

Plate 37. Theseus and the Minotaur

The Berbers traced their origins to a land called Atarantes, or according to more ancient traditions Atala or "White Island," a name that obviously leads to Atlantis. Herodotus himself spoke of the Ataranti people who lived in Africa at the foot of Atlas.

It all started with the Amazons, whose sign remains in Berber society. Among the Amazons judiciary and public affairs were managed by women, who were devoted to war while men were devoted to taking care of the home. They used to burn their daughters' breasts so that they could not grow at puberty because otherwise they could represent a disadvantage during military operations.

The Amazons lived in the Isle of Espera (Tirrenide). They subdued the cities of the island except for Mene, which was considered sacred and contained large deposits of precious stones that the Greeks called "carbuncles," "sardones," and emeralds. Led by Myrina the Amazons faced the Pelasgians in North Africa and seized the city of Cerne. The cruelties inflicted on the Cernei convinced the Pelasgians to deliver the cities and find agreements of friendship. It was Heracles who freed the Pelasgians and exterminated the Amazons, "feeling that it would ill accord with his resolve to be the benefactor of the whole race of mankind if he should suffer any nations to be under the rule of women." According to Diodorus, shortly after, while Horus/Deucalion was king of Egypt—no coincidence, since Horus was Hercules—Tirrenide disappeared due to earthquakes "when those parts of it which lay towards the Ocean were torn asunder."[12]

Diodorus provides a genealogy of the Pelasgian kings and explains how they, by their magnificence, were honored as gods after their death. He begins with Uranus, who is followed by his daughter Basileia (the name by which the Egyptians identified Sardinia), "who reared all her brothers showing them collectively a mother's kindness; consequently she was given the appellation of Great Mother"—an aspect that she shares with Isis. Basileia married her brother Hyperion, just as Isis married her brother Osiris. And just like Osiris, Hyperion was killed by his own brothers, and their son was thrown into the Eridanus River, just where Osiris's son (Horus or Phaethon) is said to have fallen. Basileia was succeeded by Atlas.[13]

Thus we see North Africa was inhabited by both Pelasgians and

Amazons. Relying on the books of King Jemsale and on African folk traditions, Salustio talks about the African origins of three Berber peoples:
the Gaetuli, Libyan (not Libu), and Mauri or Moors, connecting them to
Hercules the Uranide—which is synonymous with Pelasgian. He writes:

> The first inhabitants of Africa were Getulli and Libyans, rude and
> uneducated. After the death of the Uranid Hercules in Spain, his
> army consisting of various countries was scattered, and part of it was
> transported to Africa, mixing with the Libyans. Most of it, however,
> moved to the ocean and mingled with the Getulli, becoming the
> Numidians. Over time, these also mingled with the Libyans, and
> moved to the Mediterranean, with the name of Mauri [or Moors].[14]

Now that we have clarified the relationship between the modern
Berbers and the Pelasgians, let's delve deeper into the Amazons.

Southwest of Libya in the area of the Fezzan mountains petroglyphs
have been found that show a female figure wearing a Phrygian cap like
the soft conical hats worn by the Amazons. Other figures are holding
a bow. Curiously, the representations of the Mother Goddess, be it Isis
or Cybele, always come equipped with the same headgear. Therefore it is
reasonable to suppose that the cult of the Mother Goddess, already widespread in the Paleolithic before the arrival of the Pelasgians in Europe, is
related to the matriarchal culture of the Amazons. Even today, the Berber
people call themselves "Amazigh" and women still enjoy an important
position in their society. Indeed, only women were able to read and write
Tifinagh, thus acquiring a certain political influence. A Berber tradition
says that at the time of the first Islamic invasion of the territory in 700
CE a woman named Kahina fiercely resisted the Arab conquerors, emu-
lating the Amazon queen Penthesilea. The Tuaregs of Hoggar claim to
be an Amazon progeny: among them, it was the women who inherited
the family fortune and had the prerogative of art, including the composition of beautiful poems. They had queens (the Tamenokalt) who were
ready to take up the sword against enemies. In Hoggar's ancient capital of
Abalessa is the tomb of the most famous of these queens, Tin Hinan, who
arrived in this region from Tafilalet in southern Morocco accompanied by

her servant Takamat. She became the first Tamenokalt and is still called the "Mother of All." Her tomb became a place of pilgrimage, and when archaeologists opened it they found the skeleton of Tin Hinan on a bed of carved wood covered by her jewelry, including seven silver bracelets on her right arm and seven gold bracelets on her left.

Between the nineteenth and twentieth centuries there existed in Dahomey a "Black Sparta" where women were trained from childhood to fight like men, organized into female battalions. In 1850 this army had six thousand warriors, and in 1892 it faced the French legionnaires who were amazed to be in front of women killers wishing to make trophies of their heads. The last of these Amazons died in 1970.

Greek and Latin historians remind us that the Amazons formed an alliance with Osiris during the campaign in the East and later settled in Scythia in the area of the Caucasus and the Black Sea. In this migration they founded Magnesia (on the banks of the river Sipylus), Ephesus, Chersonese, and Mytilene. Millennia later, the queen Penthesilea would fight in the Trojan War alongside the Teucrians.

Twenty-two sarcophagi containing the bodies of warrior queens were found on the bottom of Simenit Lake in northern Anatolia among the remains of a sunken city. Archaeologists have identified that city as Themiskyra, the capital of the Scythian Amazons. Indeed, according to tradition, it was situated on the estuary of the river Thermodon, the current Terme, fifty kilometers east of the city of Samsun.

Therefore, we conclude that the Berber people of North Africa still bear a dual heritage, both Pelasgian and Amazon.

Professor Fabrizio Mori tracked down two vertical lists of Iberian writing on a rock painting of Tadrart Acacus, initially thinking it was in the Tifinagh alphabet, which was derived from Iberian (see plate 22 and figure 9.1).[15] In 2007 French researcher Thèodore Monod published six epigraphic bodies in Iberian writing found in Libya and then classified as an unknown language (figure 9.2).[16]

The first inscription was found in Sidi Khrebish in Cyrenaica Benghazi (figure 9.3), the second and third in the resort of Er Roui in Madama, Niger (figures 9.4 and 9.5). The latter is the most interesting because it features a cartouche enclosing a name translated as "Sovereign

Figure 9.1. An example of an inscription in the Tifinagh alphabet.

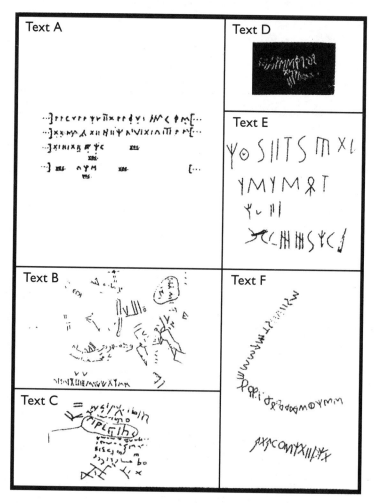

Figure 9.2. An example of Libyan pre-writing (some inscriptions are neither Arabic nor from the Tifinagh alphabet) by Theodore Monod, a keepsake of the Society of Natural Sciences and the Natural Science Museum in Milan, volume 26, fasc. 2, 1993. (For a closer view of each text see pages 279–81.)

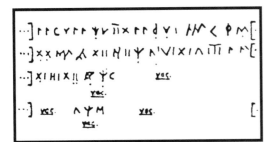

Figure 9.3. Text A.

Figures 9.4. Two views
of text B, one with the
different inscriptions
numbered.

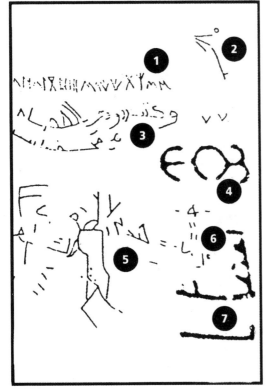

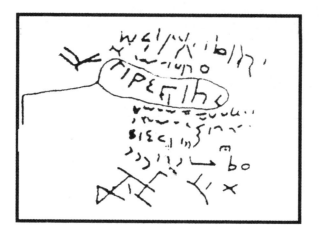

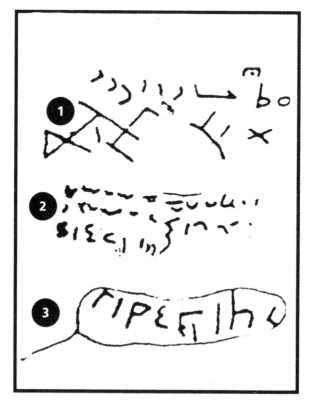

Figures 9.5. Two views of text C,
one with the different inscriptions numbered.

Figures 9.6. Two views of text D.

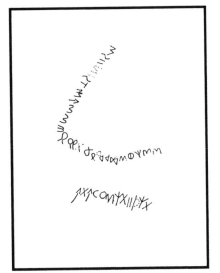

Figures 9.7. Two views
of text F, one with the
different inscriptions
numbered.

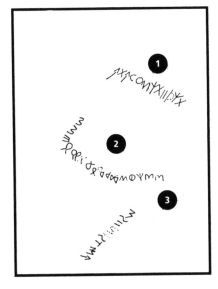

of the Sea," anticipating the cartouches of royal names during the Pharaonic Egypt. More relics with Iberian writing have also been found in Egypt at Hierakonpolis and in the Wadi el-Hol (carvings on the stone sides of a road that linked Thebes and Abydos).[17] Inscription number four was found at the Maknusa Pass in Wadi al-Ajal (today Wadi al-Hayat) toward Murzuk (figure 9.6). The fifth was at Bu Niem, in the north of the Tripolitan region and the last in Id el Koumas, Fezzan, currently southwestern Libya (figure 9.7).

THE RUINS OF LIXUS

The archaeological site of Lixus, situated far to the west of Libu territories, owes its existence to the Libu of the Sea Peoples and so has little to do with the Amazons or early Pelasgians. It is a town in Morocco largely neglected by archaeologists: they have conducted excavations on only about 20 percent of the ruins. Located between Rabat and Tangiers, perched atop a hill overlooking the Atlantic Ocean in the vicinity of the Loukkos River, it was once a prehistoric seaport. The Carthaginians occupied this port in about 800 BCE, constructing buildings on top of existing walls and megalithic foundations. It would be appropriate to also date the more ancient ruins already existing. According to Dr. Gerald S. Hawkins of the Smithsonian Astronomical Observatory, the inferior megalithic walls are accurately aligned with the sun—not coincidentally, the former name of the city was Maqom Shemesh, "City of the Sun."

The Norwegian explorer Thor Heyerdahl noticed a marked similarity between the polygonal style of masonry of Lixus and that of Peruvian and Bolivian structures. The same style is also found in Andalusia in southern Spain and in the underwater ruins along both Atlantic coastlines. Blending polygonal stone blocks of various shapes with more regular stones forms one of the most efficient techniques used by ancient masonry to offer protection from earthquakes. Apparently locking together stones like a puzzle scatters the effect of seismic waves coming from below (depending on size, each stone is liable only to its own resonance frequency), with the result that these walls are virtually earthquake-proof.

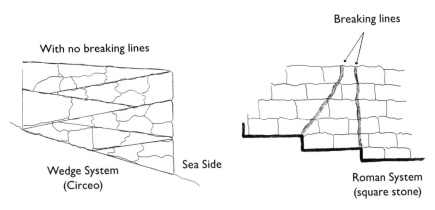

*Figure 9.8. Earthquake-proof versus
non-earthquake-proof walls.*

The rocks are positioned so as to create a continuous system of slip planes that support each other in a succession of overlapping wedges, one against the other (figure 9.8).

The alternate contrast of wedges creates a static internal equilibrium that takes advantage of the large resistance of the material of construction when it is subject to compression. This construction skill shows that the megalithic walls, as well as playing a very good defensive function, were built with such criteria as to be intact still today, unlike the square walls built by the Romans.

The same type of wall is found in Italy, with its epicenter in Ciociaria—imported from the Sabines, of course—as well as at the far eastern end of Libu territory, which is Dougga,* a short distance from Teboursouk, Tunisia.

Important and worthy of note is the opinion of Dr. R. Cedric Leonard,

---

*The polygonal wall of Dougga is similar to the best examples in central Italy and Greece. Nearby are extensive megalithic necropolises (with dolmens and cromlechs) of the pre-or proto-historic period; the dating is very uncertain. The stratigraphy and construction techniques show that these are at least pre-Punic (Carthaginian) structures and the construction is generally attributed to the eighth century BCE, but the proximity of extensive prehistoric burial sites and the style of the megalithic works suggest a more ancient dating. Throughout the region (Maktar, Eltes), there is a trace of fine megalithic culture whose forms and manifestations are similar to the megalithic Maltese and central Mediterranean.

who, during the 1975 expedition called the Morocco Exploration, funded by the Europa House of the University of Illinois, detected the existence of three different levels of construction representing three totally different cultures. The recent upper layer is Roman, while the one below is Carthagean. However, what attracted his interest was a deeper layer composed of stone masonry structures that represent a completely different culture, Libu, as it incorporates massive blocks of stone and reflects the classic polygonal style similar to the Italian type.

SABINES

Greek-Latin tradition insists on the persistence in Italy of a group of Pelasgians or Sicels who survived both the second and the third floods. This persistence explains the name Ombroi (Greek for "survivors," reminiscent of the city of Imbros in Arzawa), who could not accept the arrival of the Sea Peoples, those Sabines who were used to ruling over natives in any region they had been. The Ombroi fought until they were finally relegated to the current Umbria or obliged to flee to Sicily.

All authors speaking of ancient inhabitants of Italy refer to a common strain of "Aboriginal" or "Survivors." Dionysius of Halicarnassus considered it the same strain of Tyrrhenian. Popular belief of ancient Italians was that their ancestors were civilized and educated by Saturn and Janus (Baal and Osiris), who dedicated the first cities ever built with the name of Saturnia and Janiculum, of which, at the time of Troy, only the ruins were left (*Aeneid*, book 8). The Ionian Sea derived the name Jon, Jan, Jano, or Janus (equated with Osiris), a king of ancient Italy ("Appendix: The History of the Etruscans," from *An Universal History: From the Earliest Accounts to the Present Time*, vol. 18, sec. 3). Homer reported that the oldest navigations ever known were the ones of Bacchus, or Janus, adding that these occurred in the Tuscan seaside. Diodorus Siculus in his lost books (from 5–11) described a succession of peoples who dominated the sea. Of these, Eusebius retained a summary in the *Chronicle*, with no mention of the Tyrrhenians, although the same Diodorus mentions them several times in his work. The only logical explanation: they were including the denomination of Pelasgians, which in fact appears in the text above, confirming membership in that strain. The Greek writers said Janus was the first to coin money; in Aristotle we find evidence that the Italians anticipated or were at least contemporaries with the Egyptians.*

*See Aristotle, *Politics*, book 7, chapter 10.

The Sabines had consulted the oracle of Dodona, obtaining an accurate response:

> *Fare forth the Sicels' Saturnian land to seek,*
> *Aborigines' Cotylê, too, where floats an isle;*
> *With these men mingling, to Phoebus send a*
> *   tithe,*
> *And heads to Cronus' son, and send to the sire a*
> *   man[18]*

After a long wandering they arrived in Lazio and discovered an island in the Lake of Cutilia—a huge patch of dried-up marshland with dense brush and trees growing wildly, moving constantly as they were pushed by the waves. When they saw this wonder, they realized it was the Earth predicted by the oracle. They drove away the Sicels/Ombroi and occupied the region. The Sicels arrived in Trinacria, which then took the name of Sicily. In *Il Segreto degli Illuminati* (The Illuminati Secret) we read:

Near the towns of Arpino and Atina [in the province of Frosinone] is Posta Fibreno Lake [figure 9.9]. Its characteristic feature (perhaps unique in Europe) was already mentioned by Pliny in his work *Naturalis Historia*: in the lake there is a floating island formed by rhizomes, peat, and roots, able to move in the water by a light breath of wind or by increasing the flow of the springs that abound along the shores of the lake. Perhaps for the chemical composition of that island, the trees that are on its surface do not develop as their peers that have roots on the mainland, but become little more than mere shrubs. The "Rota," as the floating island is locally called, which has a diameter of about thirty meters and a conical shape with the tip pointing down, was almost certainly originated from an exceptional undercurrent that made the bottom of the peat lift.

The Sabines, who were driven from their homelands in the East and would then come to Lazio, would have seen the island of Posta Fibreno, and would have driven away the Sicels.

In lists of the Sea Peoples there are the Sicels or Shekelesh (allies of the Shardana), the Achaeans, and the Sabines. . . . It seems rather strange that those Sicels driven out by the Indo-Europeans ultimately allied with them. The reason is right under our noses and Snorri tells us in his *Edda* (*Gylfaggynning*, 53): "So the Aesirs narrated that, to distort the history of human facts, after each change were given to the winner men the same identical names by which the vanquished had been named before. This they did so that,

Figure 9.9. Posta Fibreno Lake with its floating island.

once many centuries were past, posterity believed that the peoples to which they were given the same names were the same peoples as before."

So it is likely that the Sabines of southern Lazio (Ciociaria) took the name of Sicels from the people they had beaten and driven away in Trinacria. Moreover, on the lists of the Sea Peoples, the Sabines do not appear as a united nation, but we find the Tursha, the Sabines of Tuscia or Tuscany.* It is also likely that the Sabines of southern Lazio also partook in the invasion of 1200 BCE, veiled by the name of Shekelesh. In this regard, it must be remembered that Professor Alberto Mazzoldi, in his book *Italic Origins*, had shown how the term "Sicels" was sometimes used in classical Greece as a synonym for "Pelasgians."

At the time of these events, fortresses and stone circles appeared in the peninsula and surrounding areas of Corsica and Tunisia, almost in imitation of the works built during the Pelasgian golden age (about 10,500 BCE). Though they are not comparable in size and sophistication to constructions such as Baalbek (in the Beqaa Valley of Lebanon), Sacsayhuaman, and Osirion, we have to consider that the latter date back to the first Pelasgian period in the Mediterranean, between 13,000 BCE and 9600 BCE, when ideas and techniques were brought from the original Atlantis, while Greek or Italic constructions are the result of a revival that took place thousands of years later, when the means and the memory had weakened.

The best-preserved fortress, with walls more than 16 meters high, is located in Alatri, in the province of Frosinone, in the Lazio region of Italy (plate 23).

The name "Alatri" appears on two clay tablets (ARM I.39, ARM IV.28) found in the archives of the royal palace of Mari on the middle course of the Euphrates: these date back to the eighteenth century BCE

---

*In *Il Gello* the sixteenth-century Florentine writer Giambullari Pier Francesco wonders about the countless coincidences he found between the Tuscan language and the Syriac or Phoenician language, which he called Aramaean. Indeed, most Sabines came from Mesopotamia and Syria, so his is a simple confirmation.

when the city was under the Assyrians. The Assyrian emperor, Shamshi-Adad I, sent his son Yasmah-Adad, king of Mari, to the conquest of Alatri. In a letter to his father, Yasmah-Adad says: "Alatri is strong, its walls are still the ancient ones and no others have been built. It is built on a hill and its ramparts are huge." Is there a link with the majestic Acropolis of Alatri, built in those years by the Sabines in southern Lazio? After all, they had Mesopotamian origins. In Alatri, a Middle East–style necklace was found, which archaeologist P. Cesare Antonio de Cara speaks of in the magazine *The Catholic Civilization:*

> What is certain is that a necklace of archaic Eastern style, which others would recognize as Mycenaean or likewise, is preserved in the museum of Campidoglio and comes from Alatri.[19]

THE POLYGONAL WALLS

It is commonly agreed that polygonal walls preceded the birth of Rome in about 750 BCE. The oldest evidence of the existence of such walls is provided by Livy,[20] according to whom the last king of Rome sent some settlers to the Cyclopean cities of Circeii and Signia, which evidently existed before 510 BCE.

This building style has stones that are cut not at right angles but with seemingly random forms, building walls like an interlocking puzzle. Under a careful analysis it turns out the "pieces" often engage in a game of arches, alternating their convexity upward and downward, drawing a serpentine along the walls. The system releases the boulders' weight to the ground to avoid pressures on the edges. Furthermore, the different shapes and sizes create a structure that is hyperstatic (if we remove some blocks the others do not fall) and earthquake-proof, with each block subject to a different vibrational frequency. This is a building style used by the Pelasgians and resumed—in scale—by the Sea Peoples: the Sabines in Italy, the Achaeans in Greece, and the Libu in Morocco.

A Controversial Idea

French researcher and author Zacharie Mayani found connections between the Etruscan and Iberian languages and the modern Albanian language. However, most scholars believe Mayani's theories are extremely fragile.

The Albanian researcher Nermin Vlora Falaschi (writer, poet, tireless scholar, and activist) has translated several Etruscan and Pelasgian inscriptions such as the Stele of Lemnos using the modern Albanian language. The same method has been shown to apply to the names of Greek gods because the Greeks said without mincing words that their gods were first holy men of the Pelasgian people.

Using the Albanian language we can interpret De-Mithras (Dhe = Earth, Mithras = uterus, i.e., the Mother Goddess Earth), and Aphrodite, Afer-Dita (Afer = close, Dita = Day, later called Venus by the Romans). And the territory west of the Balkan peninsula, the Roman Illyria? Easy! Liri (Lir = free), namely: the country of the free people.

How can we explain these correspondences? First of all, we observe that they are phonetic and etymological matches, not grammatical, so we can exclude a bond of descent between Albanians and Pelasgians.

However, as in the Welsh case observed in the previous chapter, it is possible that the conquerors (or fugitives) speaking the Pelasgian (Iberian) language occupied Illyria and took wives from the people. These wives were forced to learn new words that were then grafted onto the local grammar system. The mixed language, with the old grammatical system and the new vocabulary, was conveyed to the children and so remained. The recent discovery of engravings in Iberian writing on a monolith in the underground tunnels of Visoko, in Illyrian territory, seems to confirm this. Who could they be, these fugitives who arrived in Illyria without wives? Most probably they were the Ombroi who had fled from the Sabines and were the self-proclaimed "Free People"!

It seems that in the sixteenth century BCE civilization spread in Italy not as a result of a slow evolution and secular culture but as a sudden explosion (similar to what happened in Egypt) with the knowledge of metal alloys, the development of new settlements, and a more complex stratification of social classes. The culture of the Hyksos/Sabines "exploded" on the peninsula a little later than in Sardinia, almost simultaneously with the Achaeans' golden age. This does not mean that they didn't arrive earlier.

The Sabines were Hyksos, and therefore Indo-European, but only if we talk about the commander caste. The Gutei collected in Scythia (who formed the Sabines' lower classes too) were largely Semitic, which cost the Sabines a partial cancellation from the history books during the Nazi-Fascist propaganda.

Gaius Julius Igino[21] bluntly wrote that the Sabines came from Mesopotamia, and Mario Pincherle,[22] who spoke extensively about the Sea Peoples in several works, responded as follows to those who objected to a lack of Mesopotamian finds in the Sabine sites:

Do you know, dear friends, the reason why around the polygonal walls there is a vacuum? Antonielli had reason to repeat: "Walls and nothing but walls . . ." Where have the Sabines'* wonderful "things" got to? Those objects of gold, silver, precious stones, and ivory, have they dematerialized? Certainly, they did not. The Etruscans have taken these treasures as a legacy. Their women have used them to pretty up. Grandmothers have left them to their grandchildren. The Etruscans have had almost half a millennium to dig, rummage, despoil, and comb through the old silent walls that they had "discovered" amidst the hills protruding out from the jungle of the Italian peninsula. Those typically Mesopotamic† pieces, those ivories, those objects of granulated gold [plate 24] they have collected with infinite respect. And then, when they had learnt how to do it, they started copying, tracing, and reproducing them. . . . They were

---

*Here Pincherle used the term "Pelasgians" but clearly specified that, in this context, he was referring to Sabines.

†Pincherle used the term "Akkadian" because he was persuaded that the Sabines had been part of the great empire of Sargon.

anchored to, crystalized in a civilization that was "not theirs," like flies in a transparent "inclusit." The last testimonies of those things still exist. . . . They peep from museums' windows. Archaeologists get off with saying "Orientalizing Period."*

The Etruscans coexisted with the Sabines of Tuscany for over 450 years before overpowering them and stealing their gold. In *Il Segreto degli Illuminati* (The Illuminati Secret) we read, "The Etruscans may be those Sardinians preceding the arrival of Shardanas and forced by the latter to flee beyond sea."

Pincer-closed by Etruscans and Romans, the Sabines disappeared from history in the first century BCE, but did we miss something? How many Sabines had merged with the Roman nobility and the people? Were not enough of the first kings of Rome Sabine to believe Rome a Sabine city? It is interesting to remember here how the legend of Sargon became the legend of Romulus and Remus in Rome.

A second connection is found in the Hyksos-Jewish myth of Jacob and Esau, where Esau (as Remus) was exiled from the city founded by the second-born Jacob (as was Romulus) and died in the attempt to conquer it.[23]

The legend of the "Rape of the Sabine Women" is a tale of Hyksos origin. It tells of how Romulus, to solve the problem of the lack of women among the Roman people, invited their Sabine neighbors to a party in honor of the Sabine god Consus. During the feast he gave his warriors the order to kidnap the women of their guests, who had been left alone in that moment.

The Hyksos version is transcribed in the Bible, specifically in the book of Judges. The Benjamites injured the city of Gibeah when they killed the wife of the high priest of Shiloh (at the time the most important sanctuary in Israel), causing all Israelites to vow: "Not one of us will give his daughter in marriage to a Benjamite." Soon afterward, however, they repented of the oath: "The Benjamite survivors must have heirs, so that a tribe of Israel will not be wiped out. We can't give them our daughters as wives, since we Israelites have taken this oath." So, they said to

---

*Referring to the period covering the late eighth and seventh centuries BCE, when the Etruscans were in contact with the first Greek colonies in Italy and partially absorbed their culture.

Benjamites: "Look, there is the annual festival of the Lord in Shiloh.
. . . Go and hide in the vineyards and watch. When the young women
of Shiloh come out to join in the dancing, rush from the vineyards and
each of you seize one of them to be your wife. Then return to the land of
Benjamin."[24] Many ancient writers agree in identifying the Sabines with
the progenitors of most Italic peoples thanks to the mechanism of the
ver sacrum.* This fact is confirmed by the Italic peoples themselves, who,
during the social war in 90 BCE, minted coins bearing the inscription
Sabin, using the common origin of Italic peoples to remind Rome of the
sacrilegious nature of their behavior and to motivate their allies toward
their joint goal (figure 9.10). (Fought in 90 BCE, this war saw the people
of Italy, already under Roman rule, united in acquiring the full rights of
citizenship.) The ancient poets also called the Sabines Ausoni (this is not
to be confused with the modern meaning of Ausoni as a reference to a
particular people who lived in southern Lazio) or Curetani, from Latin
curtius = "circumcised." Not by chance in Coptic and proto-Semitic the
term sabé means circumcision!

The Sabines were practicing a mystery religion that fits very well with
the teachings of the Hermetic and Gnostic texts. Mario Pincherle quoted
an important passage from their traditional texts: "the peoples of the first
civilizations of Egypt, those of Menes [Osiris], practiced our religion."[25]
In the Mu'jam Al-buldan, an eleventh-century gazetteer of the Arab geographer Yaqut al-Hamawi, it is written, "after having indicated the measures of the two main pyramids of Giza, the Sabines made pilgrimages to
both."[26]

The Sabines did not pray to delegate to God the efforts assigned to
men, convinced that if necessary God would have helped them immediately, without the need to be asked.[27] Therefore, they just praised him.
They also believed in reincarnation (a belief that has remained in India),
were vegetarians, and did not make sacrifices.[28] It is amazing how much
this corresponds with what Plato said of the Pelasgians: "It is a people

---

*An ancient Italic tradition where people, when faced with a difficult situation, voted
for the removal of a generation from the territory as soon as the youth became adult.
The expelled people founded a new community by hunting or subjecting the previous
inhabitants.

*Figure 9.10. Coins minted in 90 BCE by Italic peoples
in order to prove their common origin from the Sabines.*

that does not kill animals . . . does not make blood sacrifices to the gods, does not pray and does not make offerings. They do not have gods but only one god and worship the infinite and the invisible."[29]

The Sabines took a large number of liturgies and rites of initiation used by the Egyptians during the domination of their country between 1780 and 1570 BCE. When the Theban kings regained control of their country the Sabines were forced into slavery, and the same fate befell the Shasus and Habirus who had enjoyed their protection. Three hundred and fifty years later they fled with the help of Moses (Tot-Moses) and Shardana mercenaries, bringing their liturgies to Palestine, where they formed the sect of the Essenes in the nascent Jewish state. Between 68 and 70 CE the war against Rome forced the Essenes, largely Christianized, to return to Egypt, where they contributed to the birth of Gnostic-therapeutic Christianity.

In the fifth century a Gnostic community of Christians fled from Egypt, persecuted by the Catholic archbishops of Alexandria, and took refuge in Harran, Turkey. Here, in the area of Edessa (current Urfa), on the borders with Syria, they took up the name of "Sabines."

The Arabs called them Al Saba'ia, namely the people of Saba', which in both ancient Egyptian and Aramaic means "star," so the "people of the stars." How did it come to be that the people of the circumcision became the people of the stars? It is due to a phonetic similarity, of course, but this is not all. The Egyptians believed that the dead pharaohs became stars, as well as that Osiris had become a star after his death. Isis was impregnated by the deceased Osiris, that is to say, by the stars of Orion. The channel to the King's Chamber pointing to Orion allows the fertilization of Isis, or her representative, by the stars. So the stars become phallus and *sabé* becomes *saba'*. It is therefore likely that the peoples of the Near East were using phonetically similar words to indicate "circumcision" as well as "star."

The sacred text of the communities of Harran, the *Asclepius*,* speaks of a plan to build an entire city "toward the setting sun" with monuments, statues, temples, and buildings carefully designed in the "image of the stars." The same text calls for a future generation of "wise men" to participate in the "reestablishment and full restitution to the world of the true religion." The *Picatrix*, an Arabic manuscript that draws inspiration from the ideologies of the Sabians of Harran, says that a city built in the image of the sky already existed in Egypt, designed by Thoth-Hermes, east of the country: its name was Adocentyn and many authors identify it with Giza. It was located in a place with "abundant waters," with statues of a lion, an eagle, a bull, and a dog placed at four gates oriented toward the cardinal points. These were the constellations on whose background stood the sun at the equinoxes and solstices in the First Time (10,500 BCE), with the eagle, which is the ancient name of the scorpion, and the dog probably acting as an Aquarius, although this association is yet to be confirmed. With the lion (Sphinx) facing the east, the dog-Aquarius will look to the west, the direction of the sunset and the lower world. This takes on greater significance

---

*The *Asclepius* was part of the sacred texts of the Gnostic Christians and was supposedly written by the same Hermes, considered the greatest of the prophets and sometimes identified with Moses.

considering that ever since mythology has depicted the soul of the deceased in the company of a dog or a canine figure.

The link of the Sabians/Sabines with Giza and the desire to build another city in the image of the sky is a point in favor of their bond with the Cyclopean fortresses of Alatri and Circeii (Ciociaria), where, as at Giza, a part of the sky is copied on Earth. Indeed, in San Felice Circeo (plate 25) the acropolis follows the profile of the constellation of Taurus and the center follows the outline of the constellation of Perseus (figure 9.11).

Similarly, as historian Don Giuseppe Capone had already pointed out in 1982, the perimeter of Alatri's acropolis reproduces the constellation of Gemini (figure 9.12). The French abbot Louis Francois Petit-Radel (1740–1818) listed over 120 Sabine strongholds, most of which are still waiting to recover their outstanding value through proper archaeological excavations. Historian Luigi Zanzi said that French architect Petit-Radel, when traveling from Rome to Naples in 1792, was struck by the walls of the town of Fondi a few miles from Sperlonga, Terracina, and Circeo. Petit-Radel "observed the remarkable difference which ran between the

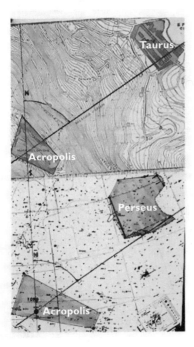

Figure 9.11. The San Felice Circeo acropolis follows the profile of the constellation of Taurus (top) and the outline of the constellation of Perseus (bottom).

Figure 9.12. The perimeter of Alatri's acropolis reproduces the constellation Gemini.

masonry of small stones and mortar that make the top, which according to the inscription there written, is from the Roman colony at the time of Augustus, and the immense stones, cut into irregular polygons, that make up the bottom." He had the thought that the building was from two different and distant eras and that "the wall, restored eighteen centuries ago by the Romans, had been firstly built of those big rocks that now form only its basis."

Intrigued by such research the abbot consulted *Memorie dell'Academia Francese d'Iscrizioni e Belle Lettere* (Memories of the French Academy of Inscriptions and Fine Arts), where he found interesting notes written in 1729 by Fourmount about the megalithic structures of other ancient civilizations. He soon realized "that kind of wall had been kept in very remote antiquity, both in Greece and Italy; and this was what Euripides, Strabo, and Pausanias attribute to the Cyclops, when speaking of the walls of the aforementioned cities." Following his predecessor's example he began to call the ruins he observed "Cyclopean walls" and judged they had been made by the Sea Peoples that also built the walls of Argos, Mycenae, and Tirintus.[30]

I am not going to use too many words trying to describe their beauty because you can still visit them all: walls hundreds of meters long, boulders weighing from twenty to thirty tons, cut into polygonal shape, adherent to each other to form a giant 3-D jigsaw. In Norma and Alatri (that the Greeks believed to be built by Daedalus and Orion) you can see walls whose height exceeds sixteen meters! Ask to enter the "underground Alatri"! In Segni there are long tracts of wall climbing the slope of the hill for over a hundred meters from the Saracen door to the Pianillo; at Circeii there still is the perimeter wall, which needs to be visited soon before bulldozers demolish it or the woods reclaim it.* Ferentino is famous for its underground tunnels, and Arpino holds the first pointed arch of Italy. Other Italian sites with Sabine fortresses that were built with polygonal megalithic blocks include Alba Fucens, Amelia, Arce, Cori, Fondi, Osteria Nuova, Pescorocchiano, Roccasecca, Santa Severa, Saturnia, Sezze, Trevi, Veroli, and Vicovaro—see the astronomical alignments of St. Erasmus of Cesi. And go to Buccino (old Volcei), which tradition says was founded by the "Oenotrian Pelasgians" who came from Mycenaean Greece.

In the eighth century BCE Rome was born in Italy, while in Greece were born the poleis of Athens, Sparta, Thebes, and Corinth. The Greeks, however, made no controversy when major explorers like nineteenth-century Heinrich Schliemann shed light on the Mycenaean civilization that flourished well over nine hundred years before the poleis. Some scholars have tried to show the existence of a civilization—the Sabine—linked to it, on Italian soil, but clearly did not have as much luck due to an incontrovertible unwritten law: *before Rome there is and must be nothing!* Like the poleis, which have their roots in the Mycenaean Greeks, Rome has its roots in the Sabines.

This does not mean that all polygonal walls are not Roman: in fact, Romans were good architects and builders and knew how to copy the styles of their predecessors, as evidenced by the temple orders imported from classical Greece. Many polygonal works are certainly Roman and were used as substructures in the streets—like the Appian Way (Via Appia)—in the

---

*Many funds were allocated in 1988 for recovery of archaeological and artistic sites in anticipation of tourism related to the 1990 World Cup, but the local authority did hasty studies with poor or nonexistent planning, entrusting the work to companies that lacked competence in archaeological and geological restoration. Most of the Circeo walls were demolished by bulldozers, shovels, and jackhammers, damaging the monument much more than World War II bombs had.

terraces, and even in some defensive structures such as the Sezze towers. A careful examination of the context and history of places and findings is necessary from time to time, without lapsing into trivial generalizations.

ITALIAN NON-SABINE MEGALITHISM

Several traces of megalithic construction that, for stylistic differences or lack of evidence, we cannot estimate to be Sabines are present in various parts of Italy: in Valle d'Aosta in the area of Saint Martin de Corleans there are several tombs and dolmens and on San Bernardino a stone circle with a diameter of seventy-one meters has been found. Another circle of standing stones has been unearthed at Cavaglià in Piedmont. Other prominent megaliths are located on Mount Musiné in Piedmont and at Apicella in Liguria. Also, apparently belonging to the same culture, a double circular enclosure of stones with a diameter of about seventy meters has recently been found on the outskirts of Como in Lombardy. Li Muri has the oldest megalithic monument of Sardinia, dating back to before 2500 BCE, consisting of five intersecting circles around a rocky outcrop. According to studies made by the architect and painter Giulio Romano (1499–1546), many Neolithic astronomical stations would be found in South Tyrol and Veneto. In Apulia there are megalithic walls at Altamura in Bari province and Manduria in Taranto province. In Sicily there are polygonal walls in Erice and other places as well. There were numerous prehistoric huge statues discovered in Corsica by the French scholar Roger Grosjean in 1956.

GALLERIES AND THE *VIE CAVE*

In Italy many hypogeal sites have emerged: in the cities of Artena, Alatri, Norba, Circeii, and Segni were found wells, beginnings of underground tunnels, caves, and grottoes that lead us to assume the existence of some underground past life. Some of these structures were considered by independent researchers to predate both the Romans and the Sabines, who would only have reused them for cultural or funerary purposes, or as quarries. Alessandro Marcon, writer for the magazine *Mystero,* is among those who refer to the "first" Pelasgians and, in order to support this hypothesis, has conducted research on the type of works found in the considered sites. One of these sites is described below:

The tunnels and underground passages in question have a section that is, for the most part, ogival or semicircular, with scratch-processed walls. This process is uniform and constant throughout the course of the tunnels. According to official archaeology the excavations were made using a pick and finished by hand with chisel and mallet, but the process is similar to the excavation of galleries by means of mechanical drilling rigs.[31] In some areas of the Lazio region and other parts of the world there are underground sites consisting of tunnels and chambers often linked to the surface through narrow wells. The type of process used and the regularity of the excavation, together with the precision of the sections and the direction of the scratches, represent unequivocal evidence of the intervention of a technology similar to that used in modern times. Official archaeology dates the construction of such tunnels and underground passages back to the Etruscans, who would have made these excavations in order to take refuge during war. If so, however, it would make no sense to build small, easily accessible galleries as a defense where they could soon find themselves trapped in case of siege, and then there would be no reason to dig a shelter with such precision and regularity. In conclusion, all evidence points to exclude a type of handwork done by historical populations, while reinforcing the hypothesis of a technology owned by a civilization that disappeared during the last ice age.

At Lake Averno and Cumae in the Campania region of southern Italy there are ancient recesses dug in the ground that were once inhabited by a Sibyl who placed her oracles there since time immemorial. The priestess, inspired by the divinity, wrote down her predictions in hexameters on palm leaves, which, at the end of the prediction, were mixed by the winds coming from the hundreds of openings in the cave, making the oracles "sibilant" (from which the name "Sybil" derives).

In 1932 during his research in the "Roman Crypt," an Augustan gallery running through the entire mount of Cuma, archaeologist Amedeo Maiuri discovered an environment with a trapezoidal section identified as the Sibyl's Cave (plate 26) that can be compared with the Great Gallery in the Pyramid of Cheops. Walking along the first coverless section you enter a long corridor (131.2 meters) excavated in the tuff, porous rock, with a perfect rectilinear course. In ancient times it received air and light from some wells, still partially visible. From the western wall (on the right) at almost regular intervals nine branches open—six communicate with the outside and three are blind. At about the middle of the path, on the left, is a branch divided into three rectangular rooms that are arranged in a cross. Used in Roman times as tanks that were supplied by an external channel, their traces are still visible along the left wall of the gallery. At the bottom of the tanks masonry boxes and burial ditches indicate that this part of the gallery played the same role as catacombs in the Christian age. With reference to the same period there is also an arcosolium (an arch carved into the tuff and adorned with paintings surmounted by niches) visible a little further along the corridor. Finally we come to a rectangular room where there is a vestibule on the left, once closed by a gate (as shown by the holes of the door jambs on the outdoor benches), leading to a small room that is further divided into three smaller cells arranged in a cross. This room has been interpreted as the oracle room (*oikos endotatos*) where the Sibyl seated on a throne would pronounce her prophecies. However, the vaulted ceiling caused the room to be dated to the late imperial period. A month after its discovery the cave, freed from all the debris, appeared very similar to a *dromos,* the long corridor leading to the entrance of the Achaean tholos tombs. After its discovery Maiuri could claim:

> The long trapezoidal corridor, high and solemn as the nave of a temple, and the vaulted and niche-shaped cave, make a single unit. It was the cave of the Sibyl, the cave of the oracle as appeared to us from Virgil's poetic vision and from the prosaic and not less moving description of the Anonymous Christian writer of the fourth century.

Plutarch in *On the Failure of Oracles* and Pausanias in *Phocis* inform us that the Sibyls had Titanic-Pelasgic origins. Eustathius also supports this and in Homeric scholia says how the Pelasgian Dardanus was the father of the Phrygian Sibyl. This is no wonder, indeed, since already the oracles of Greece originated with the Pelasgians!

The recesses of the Sibyls, as well as Maltese hypogea, are a demonstration of Pelasgian ability in digging tunnels, but the most sublime evidence of this artistry is found in the Etruscan Vie Cave.

The Vie Cave (known in Italian also as Cavoni) are an impressive road network linking several Etruscan settlements and a necropolis in the area between Sovana, Sorano, and Pitigliano, consisting mainly of trenches excavated in the tuff as nearly vertical cliffs, sometimes over twenty feet high (plate 27). In Roman times the Vie Cave became part of a road system that branched off from Cassia Road in Lazio and was connected to the main trunk of the Via Clodia, an ancient road linking Rome to Saturnia by passing through the city of Tuscania. All Vie Cave converge at Lake Bolsena, which, like Lake Averno, has a legend that an island in the middle of the lake was connected to the mainland by tunnels: the first civilization would have arrived here through these tunnels. Doesn't it recall Atlantis, the island in the middle of the ocean?

THE SHARDANAS

The Shardanas, or "princes of Dan" (if we accept the derivation from Akkadian *sher* = prince), were the people who led the invasions of the Sea Peoples in the east beginning in 1400 BCE. In 2400 BCE they left Mesopotamia scorched by riots and famine and reached what the Greeks called the "Island of the Blessed," where Saturn was entrapped, closed in one of the tens of thousands of Nuragic towers (or nuraghes, towers that are enclosed by several rings of holy enclosures). They had learned the route from the Akkadians themselves, who with Sargon had conquered Anatolia, its piers, and its ways to the West.[32]

Thus during the Bronze Age from the second half of the third millennium BCE the Shardanas lived in Corsica and Sardinia, entertaining a flourishing trade with Greece, Asia Minor, and Egypt. Here in particular their presence as mercenaries is attested and detectable, for example, through the reliefs of the mortuary temple of Ramesses II in Memphis* (plate 28).

---

*The Poem of Pentaur reports 520 Shardana mercenaries in the Battle of Kadesh against the Hittite king Muwatalli II. In National Geographic's *Historic* magazine (issue no. 12, February 2010) professor of Egyptology Fernando Estrada Laza said: "In the second year of his reign Ramses II rejected an assault of the 'sea peoples' on the Mediterranean, Shardana pirates, and incorporated them into his army."

During the kingdom of Ramesses II (1298–1232 BCE) we find happening both the biblical Exodus and the betrayal of the Shardanas that, in the name of the common Hyksos origins, formed the tribe of Dan and helped the Habiru/Hyksos fleeing from Egypt. We will discuss this in detail in chapter 10.

The excavations carried out in Tharros, Sardinia, brought out more than four thousand Egyptian scarabs* (figure 9.13), some related to the pharaohs Tuthmosis III (1505–1450 BCE), Tuthmosis IV (1450–1400 BCE), Amenhotep III (1400–1365 BCE), Seti I (1318–1298 BCE), and Ramesses II (1298–1232 BCE). On a beetle's surface we can read "Menes" enclosed in a cartouche, but we already know that that name was a simple epithet, and certainly does not apply, in this case, to the first pharaoh of Egypt. Aristotle reports that the Shardanas provided Egypt with salted fish (in Italian *sard-ine*) in large quantities. Herodotus adds *colchicum lingulatum* to their products. They called the Shardanas the "Kings of the West Islands," this being the position of Sardinia compared with Egypt, and more: those who "come from the islands and the mainland located on the great circle of water" or who "come from Basilea, a high island with red, white, and black rocks and rich in copper."†

After the betrayal and the alliance with the Habiru, Shardana relations with Egypt cracked, so that Ramesses III defeated them in a battle on the Nile Delta in 1180 BCE.

Their main legend includes Hercules, the hero of the royal house of Mycenae, son of Alcmene and Amphitryon. Or rather, it is said that Zeus took the form of Amphitryon when the latter was already dead, and that he had slipped into Alcmene's room pretending to be her husband.[33] It is a story already heard, isn't it? It is the story of King Arthur, son of Uther Pendragon, who took the form of the deceased duke of Cornwall and got into his wife Igraine's bed, conceiving Arthur. It is no coincidence because those Celts who spoke of Arthur have their origins

---

*Stone or earthenware ornamental beetles.

†Egyptian sources include the writings of Wilbour, the Poem of Pentaur, the stele of Merenptah, the reliefs of Medinet Habu, the Harris Papyrus, and the bas-reliefs of Luxor and Karnak.

*Figure 9.13. Sardinian-Egyptian scarabs; in the center are
the ankh and the Zed.*

in the Hyksos/Black Sea Scythians, like the Shardanas! It was the same
legend (an alteration, as we shall see) of the older life of Isis, Osiris,
and Horus, subject to variations due to the long journeys that took the
Pelasgians to the Indus and brought their children (the Sea Peoples)
back to Europe only millennia later. Strabo introduces Hercules as an

amphibian hero,[34] like the Mesopotamian Iohannes or the fish-tailed gods of Tiahuanaco.

When Hercules was still in the womb his mother was forced into exile in Arzawa* after the death of King Electryon and the rise of Sthenelus. Zeus had sworn that the firstborn of the royal house (of Electryon) would become his legitimate heir, but his jealous wife Hera hastened the birth of King Sthenelus's son, Eurystheus. Not being able to retract the oath, Zeus persuaded Hera to confer immortality upon Hercules if he accomplished twelve labors imposed on him by Eurystheus. When he was eighteen years old, Hercules offered to hunt a lion that was raging among the cattle of the neighboring King Danaus.[†] As a reward, Danaus gave him permission to lie with his fifty daughters, who begat fifty-one children, the Heraclanians, among whom Sardan stood out. Hercules then led a personal campaign against the people of the Mini, which threatened the reign of Danaus, and ousted them, earning the king's trust. It is said that Hera, jealous of his victories, drove him mad and caused him to kill six of his sons and two sons of his brother. After remaining locked in a dark room for a few days, he agreed to go to the oracle of Delphi. Here the priestess (Pythia) advised him to serve Eurystheus to obtain immortality by going through the twelve labors, in which his cousin Jola also participated as a charioteer and squire. It was during the eleventh labor that Hercules arrived for the first time in Sardinia. He had to seize the cattle of King Geryon, kept on an island near the river Ocean (Tyrrhenian Sea) ruled by King Forcus. We are sure this happened in Sardinia since the island is mentioned explicitly in reference to Norace, the grandson of Geryon, who led a group of settlers (probably in an attempt to recover the herd) and founded the town of Nora (exactly in Sardinia). In the twelfth labor, Hercules returned there to steal the apples in the garden of the Hesperides from the tree that Mother Earth gave as a gift to Hera, which was protected by the serpent, or dragon, Ladon.

---

*Herodotus said: "The Tyrrhenian lived in Arzawa ruled by the Eraclicis, descendants of the god Baal/Belo, father of Danaus and Menes."

†In the myth of Hercules Danaus is often referred to as Thespius, which explains why the descendants of Hercules are also called Thespians.

Who are the Hesperides? They are nymphs, daughters of Ocean, born from the Tyrrhenian Sea in a time of turmoil. Each one protects an island or a muddy shoal—they are guardians of the pieces torn from Tirrenide during the cataclysms of 9600 BCE. In the myth, Tirrenide, or Espera, was in the middle of Tritonian Lake (the Tyrrhenian Sea) but the earthquakes melted the edges of the big island and scattered it in the water, turning it into a swamp, the Tritonian marsh. So it seems that the nymphs guard the shallow seabeds—a mixture of sand and mud—of the Syrtes and the Strait of Sicily, and also the golden apple trees within the Sardinian garden of Espera

In his *Theogony*, Hesiod describes the Hesperides as daughters of the night, beyond the Ocean (the Tyrrhenian Sea) and in front of Atlas (the Alps). In those days, the Greeks marked Italy with the extreme edge of the habitable earth at Hesperus (namely, west) and called it "the border of the night" because there opened the gate to the underworld kingdom of darkness. The intrepid Ulysses descended to Hades at Lake Averno near Cumae, Campania.

A Roman legend explicitly draws our attention to Sardinia, telling of Forcus, king of Corsica and Sardinia, and father of the Gorgons of Espera and of the "snake" Ladon, guardian of the golden apples of the Hesperides!

For those who like quotations, see some quotes and hints about the Hesperides and the Tritonian, taken from Sergio Frau's book, *Le Colonne d'Ercole: Un'inchiesta* (The Pillars of Hercules: An Inquiry) in the table on pages 306–7.

During the umpteenth attack of madness, Hercules punched the sons of Eurystheus to death during a banquet just because he was given a serving of meat inferior to that of other guests. It was the opportunity Eurystheus was waiting for. Increasingly concerned about the throne after the successes of the army of the Heraclanians in Africa and Asia, he began to persecute them and forced the Heraclanians, led by Sardan (son of Hercules), to flee to Sardinia, where they would be buried under the Nuraghe (ancient edifice symbolic of Sardinia) built, according to Diodorus, by the same Daedalus who had created the labyrinth of Knossos.

Quotes from *Le Colonne D'Ercole* (The Pillars of Hercules)	Period
Strabo (book 4, 1.7, quoting Aeschylus): "You'll come among the warlike Ligurians . . . and from here you will embark for the Hesperides." (p. 210)	Fifth century BCE
Stesichorus (fragment of the Oxyrhynchus Papyrus): "Facing the famous Erythia, at the headwaters of the river Tartessos. Across the waves of the deep sea, they came to the island. Here the Hesperides have houses entirely made of gold." (p. 196)	Sixth century BCE
Apollodorus (*Library* book 2, 5): "Erythia was an island located near the Ocean and now its name is Gadeira. From here Hercules sailed across the Ocean and up to Tartessos." (p. 193)	Third to Second centuries BCE
Diodorus (*The Historical Library,* book 2, 53–55): "While Horus was the king in Egypt . . . the Tritonian swamp disappeared, because there had been earthquakes, when the banks of the Ocean broke." (p. 391)	First century BCE
Apollodorus (*Library,* book 2, 5): "Eurystheus ordered Heracles an eleventh labor: he had to bring him the golden apples of the Hesperides Gardens. These apples were not in Libya, but near Atlas in the country of the Hyperboreans." We understand here how those Greeks who sought a single location for the Hesperides fell into confusion. The more so that the poor Apollodorus, who had seen Eratosthenes moving the Pillars westward, along with all the myths that were nearby, including the Hesperides. (p. 209)	Third to Second centuries BCE
Pliny (book 5, 31): "The Cyrenaica (region of the 5 cities: Bernice, Arsine, Ptolemais, Apollonia, Cyrene). Bernice is at the end of the horn of Sirte; once it was called the city of the Hesperides, we mentioned above (about Lixius), being the Greek tales nomadic." (p. 212)	First century CE
Sergio Ribichini (Lixius Conference): "Hesiod, Euripides, Pherecydes located the Garden of the Hesperides in front of Atlas. Hesiod in his Theogony: 'Beyond the illustrious Ocean'; Euripides, in his Hippolytus 'there where the murky sea cease giving a way to sea men.'" (p. 212)	Fifth century BCE
Sergio Ribichini (Lixius Conference): "Virgil and Ovid, place a temple and the country of these Nymphs (Hesperides) in the region of the giant Atlas, beyond the Pillars of Hercules." (p. 212)	First century BCE

Quotes from *Le Colonne D'Ercole* (The Pillars of Hercules)	Period
Apollonius of Rhodes: "The Peloponnese was just beginning to show. Then a storm of Boreas captured them and took them to the sea of Libya, for nine days and nine nights, until they came right into the Sirte, inside, where there is no return for ships forced to enter. [The pilot Anceus despaired] 'for as much as I look at the sea from everywhere, I see but mud and here only flows non-navigable water that just covers the land.' [The group loaded the ship on their shoulders and marched for a long time.] The Argonauts went happily in the waters of Triton Lake. [Soon after] they came to the sacred plain where, since the day before, the earth-born dragon, Ladon, was watching the golden apples in the kingdom of Atlas, and the nymphs Hesperides carried out their office, singing a lovely song. Triton stretched out his hand and showed them the passage between the shoals in exchange for the bronze tripod. When one of the descendants of the Argonauts had carried off the tripod, then it would necessarily have happened that one hundred Greek cities were founded around the Tritonian swamp." The wind direction and the prophecy about the foundation of Cyrene lead to identify the place with the Great Sirte. (pp. 241, 242, 245)	Third century BCE
Herodotus (book 4, 180ff.): "The Mahli and the Ausei have the Tritonian Lake as a boundary between them. Here ends the flat and sandy Libya, and begin the wooded mountains. These are the nomadic Libyans who live along the coast; beyond them, towards the interior, there is the Libya of fairs, and above the fairs, stretches a ridge of sand that runs from Thebes (of Egypt) to the Pillars of Hercules. At a ten days' journey there is another hill of salt, water and people living around the hill. They are called Atlases (Atlanteans). It is said that they do not feed on any living creature and that they do not have dreams [do not pray?]." This passage seems to refer to the Little Sirte. (p. 157)	Fifth century BCE
Hyginus Astronomer: "Near Mount Atlas, Hercules killed a giant snake [Ladone, E.N.], son of Typhon, who guarded the golden apples of the Hesperides." (p. 208)	Second to Third centuries CE

It is a legend, but it shows how strong the Shardana link was with the epoch of Danaus, Sardan, and Hercules (who is none other than Horus himself). In Sardinia there are many names of places referring to the son of Alcmene: Arcuentum (Erculentum), Herculis Insula (current Asinara), and Portus Herculis. "Saint" characters as Sardan appeared in the inscriptions of "twinning" with other peoples, for example with the Teucrians, whose "saint" was Asclepius/Iolaus. In the inscription found in the 1950s in San Nicolò Gerrei (Cagliari-Pauli Xrexèi in the southern Sardinian language) are the names of both "saints" in the writing "Sardan-Asclepius."

Diodorus Siculus brings us back to the days of Horus/Hercules and tells of the violent occupation of Sardinia by the first Pelasgians, not Shardanas. To lose land—and life—were the warrior women:

> At length both they [the Gorgons] and the Amazons were utterly extirpated by Hercules, at the time when he travelled into the western parts, and erected the pillar in Africa. For it was a thing intolerable to him, who made it his business to be renowned all the world over, to suffer any nation to be governed any longer by women. It is reported, likewise, that by an earthquake the tract towards the ocean opened its mouth, and swallowed up the whole morass Tritonis.[35]

In 2400 BCE Sardinia was occupied by the Hyksos/Shardana who came from Mesopotamia to drive out the Ichnusitani, mixed-blood descendants of Pelasgians and Amazons. The best expression of Shardana's architecture—which the myth traces to Daedalus—is found in the holy wells, temple structures for the worship of the waters. The most important part of the temple consists of a circular room with a tholos (circular) vault with a hole at the top. The structure is underground, and one of its functions was to collect the water that gushed from a sacred spring. A monumental staircase connects this space to the atrium of the temple, located at ground level (figure 9.14).

Outside of the structure, huddled along the walls, are stone benches on which offerings and cult objects were placed. In some sites sacrificial altars have been found, and it has been ascertained that all the architec-

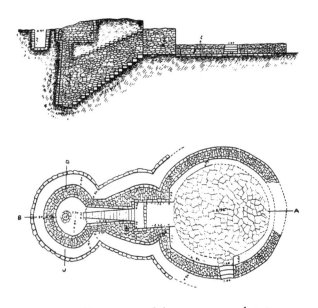

Figure 9.14. Two views of the monumental staircase connecting the vault to the atrium.

tural details were designed to celebrate the mysterious cult rites of the sacred water. In the opinion of some scholars holy wells were constructed following a specific astronomical orientation. According to this attractive hypothesis the moon in its maximum declination (every eighteen and a half years) is mirrored exactly into the well through the hole in the tholos. Even the sun is reflected through the steps of access to the source, in some wells at the equinoxes and in others at the solstices.

The finest holy well is situated in Paulilatino (plate 29). The archaeological site covers about one hectare and is characterized by a magnificent sacred well in basalt that is the most beautiful example of Nuragic architecture. Like other sacred wells, it is composed of three parts: entrance hall, staircase, and tholos room. Outside, the entrance is surrounded by a semicircle joined by parallel walls, which in turn are contained by an elliptic stone twenty meters by twenty-six meters. These external groups are the traces of a stone cover that has been lost. The rest of the underground facilities, however, are in perfect condition. The staircase, perhaps the largest known, is composed of twenty-five steps and a trapezoidal section. The chamber has a circular diameter of two and a half meters and is seven meters high; the floor was paved in rock and in the center is a circular basin.

Archaeologist Dimitrina Mitova-Dzonova, author of *Origin and Nature of the Sacred Proto Sardinian Wells,* has recently discovered a holy well in Garla, a hamlet of Breznik, a town not far from Sofia, Bulgaria:

> [It was] built on top of a hill, oriented with a longitudinal axis in the direction of the hill length, so that its southern parts sink completely into the ground. The northern one is raised and covered with earth. The well-shaped temple includes a dromos—entrance hallway—occupied by a stone staircase, and a tholos with a deep well in the center. The access is eastward, with a half-covered 7-meter long dromos, entirely occupied by 13 stone steps that descend for 2.60 meters and lead to a small room in front of the tholos entrance. On each wall there is a small niche. The tholos—4.15 meters in diameter, and 2.34 meters high—featured an opening (opaium) in the center of the hemispherical roof. The well in the middle goes down for further 5.50 meters with a diameter of 1.33 meters. From an architectural point of view, parallel structures can be found at Perseus (Mycenae tank) and in the underground tanks of Palestine. Perfect analogies are found in the Sardinian well of Funtana Cuberta in Ballao and in the so-called *asklepieion* of the Chersoneses: even *in size there are only differences of a few centimeters.* The number of steps, the size of the tholos, and the depth of the well are almost identical.

In the remains of Garla some horns are recognizable and the horn is the fundamental attribute of Shardana anthropomorphic plastic. This attribute is a symbol of the islanders by assimilation with the Shardanas of the Sea Peoples depicted at Medinet Habu. The only Shardana style helmet was found in Bulgaria, about 200 km east of Garla, nearby Sardika, in a Thracian tomb of the sixth to fifth centuries.

Sardika (or Serdika) is the ancient name of the Bulgarian capital, founded by the Scytho-Celtic tribe of Serdi. Celts, Achaeans, or Shardana, it doesn't really matter. At first they were all Scythians (or Hyksos), all located on the Black Sea, partway to Mesopotamia, then crossing the sea, returning to central Europe by sailing up the Danube. The ethnic name Sherdànu already existed when the Hyksos were living in Mesopotamia,[36] and it was written in cuneiform writing! Other than to Sardinia, the same name was brought northwest along the river. The asklepieion, the well of Ballao, and the well of Garla are testimonies of a culture that involved the whole Mediterranean coast. When the Achaeans extended their boundaries on the Cyclades (at the expense of the Minoans-Ichnusians), they built the well of Burana, the Shardanas' type.

THE STRANGE CASE OF
THE FLORENTINE PHILOLOGIST

Two hundred years was the length of time the Hyksos stayed in Mesopotamia before spreading along the Mediterranean and becoming the "Sea Peoples." That period, eight to ten generations, came at a high price to the memory of their people. In *Il Segreto degli Illuminati* (The Illuminati Secret) we read:

In 2600 BCE [Hyksos/Gutei] arrived in the Middle East and led to the collapse of the Akkadian empire, which then extended over the whole of Mesopotamia. As it did for the Romans against the Greeks, the Hyksos conquered Akkad but were inured to its culture: thus the Hyksos became a hybrid culture, later spread to Greece and our country [Italy]. This is the reason why several independent researchers actually believe that the Akkadians did colonize Italy.

Among these researchers Mario Pincherle was impressed by the frequency with which the Akkadian version of the labrys (double ax) appeared in Sardinian, Italian, and Greek engravings. The same text continues, a few pages later:

The holy enclosure or témenos, which is located around the Temple of Santa Vittoria is oval-shaped such as those of Khafaji (western Asia, 2600–2400 BCE) and the platform of the temple of Tell Ubaid

(2000 BCE). Very important is that, in the pre-sacred area in front of the esplanade, we find the peripheral sanctuary called "hut of the double ax," another element derived from Halaf. The cult of this weapon, born in Halaf-Arpashyah [Sumerian center located in northeastern Syria], spread in the Aegean and the Mediterranean along with other elements of the same area. For example, the mother goddesses found therein were considered by Sabatino Moscati very similar to the Sardinians'. Inside the "cottage" on the pavement of the floor in an eccentric position, at the bottom, to the left of the entrance, there are a limestone stele and a small altar for sacrifices. In the stele was a bronze double ax, also found in the Sardinian tombs of the same period.

In Mesopotamia the sacred well was considered the seat of the meeting between Dumuzi (whose symbol is the labrys) and Inanna, during the spring cults. If the Hyksos had come to Canaan and, from there, spread to Sardinia, it is natural that during their two-hundred-year stay in Canaan they had absorbed the symbolism of the Sargonide's empire (along with an extensive Sumerian-Akkadian vocabulary). In Sardinia we find place names like Kara-Mitta, which in Sumerian means "the room of the weapon of gods" and Mar-Midda, meaning "the chariot of weapon of gods," now Italianized in Marmilla.

In addition to the wells and the double ax in Sardinia there were the ziggurats, as those of Monte d'Accoddi (plate 30) and Pozzomajore. The biggest uncertainty, however, seemed the language: there were thousands of Sumerian and Akkadian words that resembled or were identical to Sardinian, Italian, French, or English words. And here John Semerano, the Florentine philologist, plays his role. His Moorish-sounding name, inspiring Islamic wisdom, well befits his ability to "unhinge" words and understand their origin. *The Origins of European Culture* is his main work, published between 1984 and 1994 in four independent volumes. The first two volumes, *Dictionary of Latin and Modern Entries* and *Dictionary of the Greek Language*, can help in our study and consist of etymological dictionaries in which the philologist examines 7,300 words from Greek, Latin, German, and English dictionaries, tracking correspondence in the lexicon of ancient Semitic languages.

The author affirms from this comparison that a semantic affinity (about meaning) and phonetic affinity (about sound) emerge between the vocabulary of European and Mesopotamian languages, especially Akkadian, bearing traces of Sumerian substratum. The conclusion? Sargon, the great king of Akkad, unifier of Mesopotamia, expanded his empire far beyond what we have imagined so far, distributing the Akkadian language as far as Spain, Britain, and—on the other side—Indochina. There were even printed maps showing the immense, although nonexistent, Akkadian super-empire, like the one shown in figure 9.15.

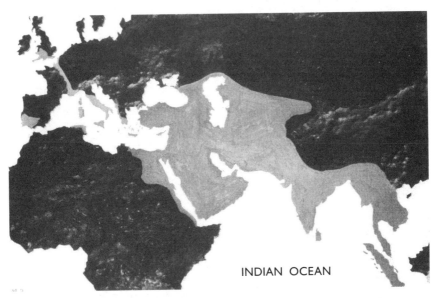

INDIAN OCEAN

Figure 9.15. A map of the Akkadian empire (shown in gray).
From Mario Pincherle's La Civiltà Minoica in Italia
(Minoan Civilizations in Italy)

Then, the scholars of Indo-European language arrived to spoil the games. Again, in *Il Segreto degli Illuminati* (The Illuminati Secret):

It is important to emphasize that the above linguistic coincidences cannot in any way be ascribed to a close linguistic kindred (same ancestor as 1500–2500 years ago) or a medium linguistic kindred (same ancestor as 6000–6500 years ago) between European and

Sumerian-Akkadian languages. These kindreds would be justifiable only in the presence of coincidences in grammatical systems, but such coincidences, in the words of F. Villar, are virtually nonexistent. The only explanation is that of a not too long settlement of the Hyksos in the Middle and Near East before their immigration to Europe. So, 200 years, about 8–10 generations, would have been more than enough.

So, just a flash in the pan, but let's go deeper into the figure of Sargon:

On the cylinder of the foundations registered by Nabonidus, King of Babylon won by Cyrus, annotations of the first are found, in which he spoke of the discovery of the foundation stone belonged to the original temple built by Naram-Sin, son [or grandson] of Sargon of Accadia, the conqueror of Babylon that, according to Nabonidus, lived 3200 years before himself.[37]

The first Semitic empire, according to all, was that of Sargon of Akkad, who founded a great library, protected literature, and extended his findings over the sea up to Cyprus. Now we know that he reigned as early as 3750 BCE. The Akkadian monuments found by the French in Tel-loh must be even older, dating back to around 4000 BCE.[38]

Today the official recalibrated chronology places Sargon at the beginning of the third millennium (we do not understand why), but there are still many diehards who do not want to restore to him almost eight hundred years.* Pincherle believes Sargon was born in 3761 BCE, at the same time as the Jewish calendar. Absurdity? I would not say so; the Hyksos who lived in Mesopotamia absorbed much of the Akkadian culture, calendar included probably. The Jews have a Hyksos component, so it was natural to adopt the same calendar!

Melis confirms that the first calendar was born in Nippur, Mesopotamia, beginning on October 6, 3761 BCE, and later brought

---

*This chronology is supported by archaeologist James Mellaart, among others, and confirmed by the team of Professor Herbert Haas who in 1987 collected and analyzed different organic samples from Egypt and Mesopotamia using carbon-14 dating.

to Dendera by a certain Ab.Ram (Sumerian for "son of the father") or Ab.raham (Sumerian for "head of nations"), who had fought for Sargon against a coalition of eastern kings.[39]

Sargon's father was an unknown god, and his mother was a priestess of the temple. Forced to get rid of the baby, she put it in an ark or chest smeared with tar and gave him into the river current. He was taken and brought up by a water carrier of the city of Kish, whose name was Akka.* Akka behaves just like the Roman she-wolf who suckled Romulus and Remus, who were abandoned by their mother, Rhea Silvia, a vestal who despite taking the vow of chastity could not resist the god Mars. Abandoned in a basket on the Tevere, he was collected by the shepherd Faustulus and the she-wolf (or prostitute—in Italian the word for she-wolf, *lupa,* also means prostitute) Akka Larentia. Both Sargon and Romulus became king after a forced flight and private warfare, which ended with the killing of the usurper, Amulius on one hand and Lugalzaggesi on the other.†

The legend arrived in Mesopotamia and was brought to Italy by those Sabines of the Sea Peoples who ruled Rome at the beginning of its history. The first three kings of Rome after the mythical Romulus—Numa Pompilius, Tullo Ostilio, and Anco Marzio—had Sabine origins and ruled from 715 to 616 BCE.

Back to Sargon . . . the king of Uruk, Lugalzaggesi, was gathering under his power the cities of Uruk, Ur, and Lagash in southern Mesopotamia and was destroying the neighboring cities. Sargon was able to get into the good graces of the king of Kish and became one of his most effective ministers. When Lugalzaggesi attacked Kish, he fled with a few faithful friends to the city of Agade (Akkad) on the Persian

---

*According to another version Akka found him in a "stone coffin" at the first light of the day when "the morning stars sang together." In the book of Job [38, 4ff.] we read the same memory: "Where were you when I laid the earth's foundation? Who laid its cornerstone—while the morning stars sang together and all the angels shouted for joy?"

†This comparison from L. Melis's *Shardana—I Principi di Dan* makes it easy to recognize the ancient motif of Horus killing his uncle Seth. Similarly, Uncle Amulius commissioned the murder of Romulus in the waters of the Tevere and Arthur ordered the murder of Mordred in the sea. In both cases, the vengeance of the "saved from the waters" falls onto the avenger.

Gulf. From there he summoned up groups of soldiers and soon was at the head of a strong army that practiced a kind of quick war: a light infantry attacked the battle from afar with a rain of arrows and then pursued the enemy until they engaged in hand-to-hand combat, where they used the ax and the short spear.[40] The Hyksos learned the quick-attack technique and use of warlike weapons, such as the short spear (*sardesca*) and ax, directly from the Akkadians. Lugalzaggesi was beaten, dragged in chains to Nippur, and exposed in a cage at the door of the temple of the god Enlil. Emboldened by success, Sargon went on to win thirty-four great battles that allowed him to put the whole Middle East under his power—from the Mediterranean to the Persian Gulf, from Arabia to the Zagros Mountains. There must have been some relationship between Sargon or his descendants and the earliest dynasties of Egypt because they imported the Egyptian unit of measurement, the sacred cubit,[41] used to make religious buildings according to its integer multiples.

Sargon was called Sarrukin or Melkisedek, which means "righteous king." Sargon's story shows through in the Epic of Gilgamesh—"the return (*gilg*) of the messiah (*mesh*)." It says:

> *Still in heaven*
> *all the stars sang in chorus.*
> *The child was born.*
> *It seemed he had three years already*
> *and protruded from the manger*
> *of a beautiful pink granite*
> *lapped by the waters of the Euphrates.*

Reminiscent of the granite manger where Osiris was killed, it's as if he was reborn in Sargon. The memory of this monarch must have been greatly admired by the Hyksos, although upon their arrival at the time of King Su-Turul his empire appeared weak.

In southern Iraq the Gnostic Christian sect of the Mandaeans survives, heir to those Essenes who chose to flee to the east rather than to Egypt after 70 CE. The latter Mandaean origins date back to the Hyksos, as confirmed by the statements of archaeologist and anthropologist Ethel

Drower, who lived among the Mandaeans for forty years, until 1912, and stayed in touch until 1937. In her study, *The Mandaeans of Iraq and Iran,* she tells that each of them:

> must, at the time of death, wear the ceremony gown, the sacred *Rasta,* the long and white robe that comes down to cover the feet and on whose right side is sewn a small disc of *granulated gold* onto which Sargon's face (Malka) is depicted.[42]

Drower also reports that the story of the discovery of Sargon in a pink granite sarcophagus along the banks of the sacred river is still part of the liturgy of the Mandaeans.[43] The archaeologist asserts the existence of a link with the ancient Italic people of the Sabines and highlights some linguistic similarities.[44] Giuseppe Flavio noted that in the Essene culture there already existed the belief that pious souls dwelled beyond the ocean (Tyrrhenian Sea), in a region with no storms of rain or snow, nor oppressed by the heat, but refreshed by the gentle breeze that always blows from the sea.[45] The Mandaeans believed that the inhabitants of this remote land (Sardinia) were the guardians of such purity that it made them invisible to the mortal eye, and argued that the place was marked by the point where there was a star called "Merica," namely the planet Venus or "aster of the morning."[46] When they began to call the mass of water between Europe and the West Indies "ocean," the latter were believed to be under the star Merica, or better, A-Merica. Over the years, such a memory has faded to the point that we have referred to an Italian navigator named Amerigo Vespucci to justify that name.

It is believed that a sect of the Mandaeans were the Nazarenes, a term with which the Jews identified a vow of abstinence including the prohibition of the cutting of hair, which was considered the "bearer" of strength: this was the vow of Samson, part Jewish and part Sardinian, of the tribe of Dan! The Nazirites arrived in Europe with the Sea Peoples, also reaching the Merovingians and the Spartans.[47] Nazarenes, who were members of the most conservative class of the Essenes, practiced the same vow.

OTHER SACRED GROVES

Previously we encountered the sacred grove dedicated to Poseidon in the city of Atlantis. Well, the Hyksos dedicated some sacred groves to the "feminine" side of divinity and hung strips of colored fabric on their trees according to a Jewish tradition.[48] When no tree was available they used some poles carried in procession and then planted these close to a temple.[49] Round the mid-eighth century some important evidence came from inscriptions found in Kuntillet Ajrud, a stronghold well into the Sinai desert. Inscriptions on plaster walls include invocations such as "I bless you to Yahweh of Samaria and his Asherah [the wife or female part]." Also, in the tomb at Khirbet el-Qom near Hebron, there is a text containing the invocation "Uriyahu be blessed by Yahweh and his Asherah, He saved him from his enemies." It is clear that there was a cult of Yahweh and his associated goddess, Asherah.[50]

Then the Hyksos became Shardana, and the tradition of sacred groves still survives today in Sardinia. In celebration of the Assumption (which assumes the role of Asherah) huge poles several meters high, adorned with ribbons and topped with a cross of wheat, are carried on the shoulders of dozens of believers.[51]

PHOENICIANS

It is said that one day Hercules was in Phoenicia together with the nymph Tyre. She was fascinated by the color of the blood of a mollusk with which her dog had been stained, and asked the hero for a suit of that color. Thus Hercules gave chase to the mollusk and invented purple. Why is it that a Phoenician invention, such as the color purple, was involved with Hercules, the Shardana hero? In the Bible we read that the Shardana (Danita) Aholiab, son of Achisamach, was a brilliant craftsman who was attributed the technique of "weaving the blue purple with scarlet red and embroidering on linen"[52] three or four centuries ahead of the Phoenicians. Along with Bezaleel of Judah, he built the Ark of the Covenant and was called by Moses "the project's developer."[53]

The story cites the Phoenicians' maritime power starting in 1000 BCE, when they came to prominence with the best-equipped naval fleets and a surprising store of routes and knowledge. Not many years had passed since the raids of the Sea Peoples in the East and we know that after such invasions centuries are needed before a civilization resumes its glory. An example is the fall of the Roman empire, which took the civilized world to a state of barbarism for nearly half a millennium. It is impossible that the Phoenician cities had remained untouched by a disaster that wiped out the Hittite empire and severely destabilized Egypt (so much so that in 945 BCE the pharaohs were Hyksos/Libus).

In fact Byblos, Tyre, Ugarit, Sidon, and other cities were razed to the ground and the inhabitants put to the sword.[54]

Shardana ships were not inferior to Phoenician ships: we have faithful reproductions in the Sardinian bronzes, decorated with figures of animals from distant countries such as the sable antelope, the cobo (antelope of water), the bongo, and then deer, gazelle, and others. Their fleet provided silver to the entire Mediterranean for over a thousand years before the Phoenicians made their appearance in history.

We invite you to compare the image of the small bronze of a Shardana ship with the relief of the Phoenician stele of Carthage: in both we see a tree installed at the bow, out of the center of gravity and supporting a ring topped with a crescent, called a caduceus (plate 31). Another Carthaginian stele—found in Marsala and depicting the caduceus together with the symbol of Tanit—was identical to a mosaic unearthed in the ancient Karalis (Cagliari). The Shardanas and their allies had settled in the Phoenician territories and had simply continued their trade on preexisting routes that had been used in the past to trade bronze and fish. So the Phoenicians were Shardana: it is no coincidence that in ancient Greek the word *foinikeos* means "purple, scarlet red," while *sardux* means "live red."* Erodorus and all the learned Persians, Greeks, and Egyptians said they were from the Red Sea. But Herodotus himself—as we said in chapter 1—clearly stated that the Tyrrhenian Sea and the Red Sea were the same sea! So, it was certainly not the current Red Sea but the Tyrrhenian Sea inhabited by the Sardinians, the "Reds."

It is interesting to note that in part of the book of Judges known as the "Song of Deborah,"[55] the tribe of the Shardanas of Dan did not

---

*In the Suda Lexicon it is read "Bàmma Sardianica," meaning "Sardinian scarlet dye."

participate in the fighting between Israel and the Canaanite city-states because they were engaged in the Phoenician fleet.*

It seems safe to assume that Phoenicians and Shardanas were actually the same people. A little further south—as certified by official archaeology—other Sea Peoples had settled in the Gaza Strip, during the great invasion of 1200 BCE. They were the Philistines or Pheleset.

DOMUS DE JANAS

The popular name literally means "house of the fairies" (baby-women, beautiful and half-naked, no larger than a bird). The Domus are rock-cut tombs often linked together to form a vast necropolis, sometimes very elaborate and accompanied by an anteroom, often with niches carved into the walls and a separate room with numerous small cells looking over it where the dead were placed. More than two thousand such tombs have been found scattered all over Sardinia (more or less one per square kilometer), but many are yet to be excavated. Some tombs are decorated with carved reliefs or engravings, which often represent spiral patterns and horns that are a symbol of divinity. According to a variant of popular legends, hidden within them would be the deadliest weapon of an ancient people who died thousands of years ago. Given the similarity of their name with Janus/Osiris, we are certainly allowed to use our imagination.

INTERVIEW WITH LEONARDO

With reference to the extinction of the Shardana people we interviewed Professor Leonardo Melis, a leading expert on the subject, about the events that caused the end of the most well-known Etruscan history, closely linked to the history of the Shardana. Here follows a list of such events, each followed by Professor Melis's comments.

Event: The Greek Phocaeans, from Asia Minor, founded Marseille between the seventh and sixth centuries BCE, at the mouth of the

---

*The conflict can be placed at the end of the eleventh century BCE. See Mario Liverani, *Oltre la Bibbio—Storia antica di Israele.*

Rhone. From here they expanded along the west coast up to Spain and, reinforced by a wave of refugees who left their homeland conquered by the Persians, they settled in Corsica, founding Alaliē (Aleria) on its eastern side. In 540 BCE, the Etruscan Caere, allied to the Carthaginians, fought the "battle of the Sardinian sea." The Phocaeans were forced to leave Corsica to the Etruscans, which, in turn, left full scope to the Carthaginians in Sardinia.

Melis's Response: The Shardana cities remained neutral in the battle of Allalia (Aleria) in the Sardorum Sea. Involved in this battle were two allied peoples (Carthaginians and Etruscans) and one people (the Phocaeans) with which there was an economic treaty that will be consecrated in the temple of Apollo at Delphi later on. The same year, Carthage decreed the invasion of Sicily (540 BCE). The general Malko (Mlk = Re) conquered much of the Sicilian land and, emboldened, thought it well to invade the sister island: Sardinia. He landed with an army of eighty thousand men and drew up in the Plain of Campidano. Anyway, he was soundly defeated by a confederate army from the Shardana cities. Returning to his homeland he was prevented from returning into the city and was exiled for daring to attack an allied nation. Malko, with the rest of the mighty army defeated by the Shardana, laid siege to Carthage and took it.

Event: At the end of the sixth century was the expulsion of the Etruscan kings from Rome, the Tarquins. This event marks the insulation from the territories of Campania. Attempts to maintain open contacts were opposed by Aristodemus, lord of Cumae in 504 BCE, and Hiero of Syracuse in 474 BCE, which have a common influence on the Romans. With the increasing power of Rome, the Etruscan city-states are divided between those who seek an alliance and those who want war. After a long siege in 396 BCE the city of Veii, ignored by its allies, is plundered and destroyed, its territory incorporated into that of Rome. Between 311 and 309 BCE Etruscan armies are repeatedly defeated by the Romans. The northern cities negotiate with the victors, who assume the right to interfere in their internal affairs. Tarquinia, where the campaigns of war against Rome were carried out, is forced to recognize the supremacy of the enemy and to renew a truce. In 283 BCE the Roman victory over the army of the central and southern Etruscan cities at Vadimone Lake, near Orte, decrees the final Etruscan defeat and the cities take on the legal status of "allies." This implies a renouncement of war and autonomous international politics, as well as the commitment of mutual help in case of danger. The northern cities renew the peace treaties. In 265 BCE Rome conquers and destroys Volsini, capital of the Etruscan League, deporting the population to a new home at Lake Bolsena. The federal sanctuary of Fanum Voltumnae is violated and looted, irreversibly marking Roman hegemony.

Melis's Response: By expelling the Etruscan kings from Rome, the Shardana were also ousted from "Terramanna." The kings of Rome were in fact Etruscan and the Etruscan kings were appointed by Shardana thalassocracy*: *Reges soliiti sunt esse Etruscorum qui Sardi appellantur* ("those who call themselves Sardinians, are used to be kings of the Etruscans," Festus) and again: *Quia Etrusca Gens horta est Sardibus* ("therefore the Etruscan people was originated by Sardinians,"† Ludi Capitoline). Please note that, contrary to what many professors have affirmed, "Horta est Sardibus" does not indicate Sardinian origins; in fact Sardibus is plural. Unfortunately, Shardana thalassocracy also began to be less present due to the loss of the bronze monopoly and the naval power of a fleet fitted out for trips over Gibraltar in search of tin, now useless for the increasingly widespread use of iron.

Event: After the First Punic War (264–241 BCE) Corsica also passed under Roman rule.

Melis's Response: In the same years Rome also took the Sardinian

---

*Domination of the sea.

†A close relationship between the Shardana and the old Etruscans is obvious if we think that the latter are an emanation of the Sabines. Sabines and Shardanas, who were in fact the same people, arrived in Sardinia and Italy from the Akkadian empire.

coast . . . but could never completely conquer Sardinia, which will endure indefinitely even after the fall of the empire and the barbarian invasions. The Vandals, in fact, did not dominate Sardinia, but asked for asylum and hospitality for the fleet stopover in the Gulf of Cagliari, which served as the basis for the supply of wood in Corsica and a starting point for the attacks on the Italian coasts and subsequent invasion of Rome. . . . In the fleet that sailed up the Tiber to enter the Urbis (city) and plunder, militated also some Shardana soldiers. One of the most important tribes of the Vandal people was the Sardones. . . . A noteworthy episode is the war of Ampsi.Korra (Apsikora), the largest center of purple production. Judike of Korra (Kornus) and his son Josto will resist the armies of Rome with several ups and downs, until the death of both. After their death, the Shardana cities will choose to join the inland tribes (Gens Barbaricina) and with them will start an endless resistance to the Romans, who will never defeat them completely.

Event: So, ultimately, when would you ascribe the end of the Shardana people?

Melis's Response: The great invasion of 1200 BCE takes the Shardana and other peoples *again* to the East. Here they give birth to other peoples we do know: Philistines (Pheleset), Spartans, and Phoenicians. The Jews felt themselves brothers with the Spartans, as descendants from the same lineage. In 1 Maccabeus 12.21 we read: "It is found in writing, that the Lacedemonians [Spartans] and Jews are brethren, and that they are of the stock of Abraham" and again in 2 Maccabeus 5.9, "Thus he that had driven many out of their country perished in a strange land [Jason bribed the priest of Jerusalem] retiring to the Lacedemonians, and thinking there to find succor by reason of his kindred."

Some Shardana will stay in Egypt forever to preside over the eastern delta. Others will mingle with the tribes of the northern Israel as Dan, Asher, Zebulun, and Issachar. Among the eponyms of Zebulun we find Sered [Genesis 46:14 and Numbers 26:26], which can be interpreted as "Sardinian."

The western coastal cities will be repopulated by some *return-ing* groups: Shardana/Sardinians, *Carthaginians* . . . in other words those people who *mistakenly* have been confused with Phoenicians in the ninth through eighth centuries BCE. During this period the Shardana no longer have the monopoly of bronze and their military/naval power has decreased.

The discovery of iron on Elba Island frees the Etruscans from the Shardana hegemony. In 540 BCE and for half a century yet, the military force of Shardana shows in the battles won against Carthage. The complete disappearance of Shardana occurs after the fall of Ampsis. Korra at the hands of the Romans in 216 BCE. The Sardinians remain independent (only within the island), but we hear nothing more from the Shardana . . .

Sparta was built in the eighth century BCE from the union of a few villages scattered on the plains that form the river Eurotas in Laconia, the southernmost region of the Peloponnese (Marco Bettalli, *Greek History*). Its inhabitants were the remnants of invader peoples, the Dorians. In *Histories* I:56 Herodotus wrote: "Croesus, king of the Lydians, gave thought to inquire which people of the Hellenes he should esteem the most powerful and gain over to himself as friends. And inquiring he found that the Lacedemonians and the Athenians had the pre-eminence, the first of the Dorian, and the others of the Ionian race. For these were the most eminent races in ancient time, the second being a Pelasgian and the first a Hellenic race: and the one never migrated from its place in any direction, while the other was very exceedingly given to wanderings; for in the reign of Deucalion this race dwelt in Pthiotis, and in the time of Doros the son of Hellen in the land lying below Ossa and Olympos, which is called Histiaiotis; and when it was driven from Histiaiotis by the sons of Cadmos, it dwelt in Pindos and was called Makednian; and thence it moved afterward to Dryopis, and from Dryopis it came finally to Peloponnesus, and began to be called Dorian." According to the testimony of Herodotus and Thucydides the Dorians were those descendants of Heracles who, around 1200 BCE, after a 50-year exile from Greece, would have pushed into the Peloponnese, Laconia, and Messenia. This so-called Dorian invasion can only indicate the invasions of the Sea Peoples and fifty years had elapsed since the ousting of the Pelasgian—or rather Achaean—elites, upon their return, under the guidance of the Shardanas. These Dorians gave birth to Sparta. Irad Malkin, professor of Greek history at Tel Aviv, writes, "We find references about Heraclanians in Athens [Iolaus asks for help for the common origin] in Hellanicus, Herodotus, Thucydides, and others. The Heraclanians always appear in Thucydides as the leaders of the Dorians: 'Also, 80 years after the Trojan War, the Dorians occupied the Peloponnese in the same times of Heraclanians. One group considers this a return while another sees in it an invasion.'"

Event: We need further clarification. We have seen how the latest news on the Shardana goes back to the battle of Ampsis.Korra in 216 BCE, but you add that they guaranteed their military support to the Vandals who invaded Rome. Now, the Vandals of King Genseric entered the city in 455 CE upon invitation of the Empress Eudoxia. Widowed by the death of Valentinian, she was forced to marry the sixty-year-old senator Petronius Maximus and so turned to the barbarians (then settled in Morocco, Algeria, and Tunisia) to seek justice. How can these two statements tally?

Melis's Response: All that refers to the inhabitants of Sardinia after 216 BCE regards indeed the *Sardinians*, direct descendants of *the Shardana* that mingled with the tribes living inland on the island. They are the ones who will come out of anonymity during the *Judikale* period between 700 and 1400 CE, the period of Leonara of Arborea and Judici/Templar kings of Torres and Arborea. Gunnar/Gonario of Torres was friend of Bernard of Clairvaux (French abbot and theologian who inspired the Templar Order). . . . Therefore, *Sardinians*, not Shardanas, or better, not *precisely* Shardana, but their descendants . . .

In 730 BC, among the peoples of the sea, the Greek Heraclides got over the imposing Mount Taygetos, between Laconia and Messenia. The region Messenia was subjected, its inhabitants enslaved, forced to cultivate the land of their owners, whose only job became going to war. In 710 BC they sent their settlers to found Taranto, and in 668 BC the first and last revolt of the slaves was crushed. Their city was Sparta, secured by the mount. It was the last manifestation of the capacity of the few to impose over the many, typical of the Indo-European "elites"...

Spartans do not ask how many are the enemies, but where they are.

AGIS II, KING OF SPARTA, FIFTH CENTURY BC

THE LEGENDARY CITY OF RAMA: THE DRUIDS AND THE GRAIL

The ancient chronicles of the Susa Valley in the Piedmont region of northern Italy reported the existence in ancient times of the mammoth city of Rama: point of origin of the druidic tradition, the descriptions of which make it similar to the megalithic fortresses of Peru and Oceania (figure 9.16).

During the golden age the valley belonged to Hyperborea, in the days when Osiris visited the districts to gather his armies. Where today stands Turin Osiris erected a temple to Isis, whose remains—they say—would be under the neoclassical temple of the Great Mother. The ancient legend is connected to the myth of the fall of her son, Phaethon or Rama. It tells of a god descended from heaven accompanied by two attendants of gilded metal. His appearance was that of a wise dragon made of flame that by dancing created glades in the grass.

Rama would come into a circle of stones built by his assistants and there would teach men sciences, agriculture, and the secrets of metal casting, and would have transmitted the understanding of Shan* through the

---

*Shan in the archaic culture of the native Europeans represents the immateriality of existence, the ancient name of the Grail, the Aboriginal Australian "dream time."

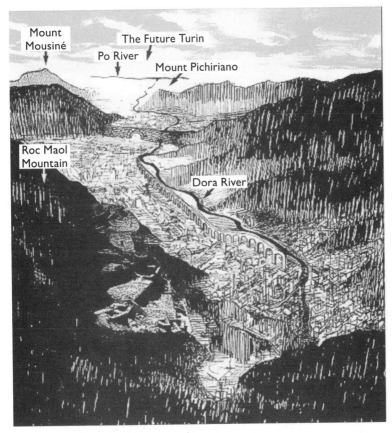

*Figure 9.16. A reconstruction of the city of Rama in its
maximum extension area.*

art of alchemy. Later he melted a large golden wheel with a hole in the
center, derived from the metal of the divine chariot, where the gift of
knowledge he was leaving to humanity would be kept.

When God returned to heaven, he left on Earth one of his golden
aides to assist those who had collected his teachings: the creature of gilded
metal could take different forms at will.

A medieval legend takes us to a great cavern inside Monte Musinè
where this "shape-shifting" creature lived: a huge golden dragon who had
emerged from the primordial vacuum, carrying out the will of the cosmic forces, protecting a bright green gem (or an emerald), and endowed
with immense powers. The first reports on the Grail described it as
a cornucopia looking like a stone or a gem. Only later did it acquire a

romantic touch, becoming the cup of Christ. For this reason, in the Middle Ages, the city of Rama was held as the hideout of the Grail, with the figure of St. Eldrado—a monk in the abbey of Novalesa—echoing Merlin the wizard.

The dragon taught the knights of the period to fight and dance in the wind and introduced them to the mystical knowledge of Shan, kept in the large circle of stones. Men from all over the world came to see the great stone circle to learn its secret (figure 9.17).

The relics of Rama and the great wheel of gold were collected by the Ard-Rì, his students, to be kept in the Fire Temple, a cave at the foot of the Sacred Mountain around which the city was built. On several occasions the legendary heroes expanded it and extended its power over all the known lands. His greatness came from the ancient knowledge kept there—Shan, archaic name of the Grail, a light that radiated throughout the Earth that was the basis of the knowledge of the Druids.

The myth of the city has survived the centuries through oral traditions of local druidism, and thanks to the researchers of this early century who collected firsthand data documenting confirmation of its existence.

The polygonal walls visible today may date back to over 1,100 years before Christ. The Scythians of the Black Sea were then those of the Sea Peoples—the returning Pelasgians—who preferred avoiding the descent to Mesopotamia. Their companions had meanwhile enjoyed a brief settlement between the Tigris and the Euphrates before being driven to the west. In 1200 BCE famine and popular revolts in Greece led groups of Achaeans to return to their home on the Black Sea. From here, the Scythians and Achaeans sailed up the Danube to central Europe and northern Italy.* Their mingling with the local "Culture of the Urns Fields" gave birth to the Celts and, among their tribes, to Sigambri or Merovingians, guardians of the Grail and ancestors of the future kings of France.

The megalithic city of Rama stood at the foot of the mountain

---

*A vessel from the Black Sea was found in the megalithic site of Chiomonte, near the city of Rama. It is kept in the Archaeological Museum of Chiomonte in "La Maddalena" (figure 9.18).

Figure 9.17. The stone of the "sun wheels"
of Balme in Valli di Lanzo.

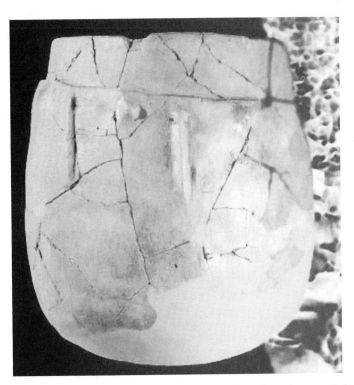

Figure 9.18. A vase from the Black Sea was found in the megalithic
site in Chiomonte, near the city of Rama. It is preserved in
the Archaeological Museum of Chiomonte.

of the Roc Maol, the ancient name of Rocciamelone, whose peak had hosted several ancient cults, the last of which worshipped Jupiter. Its mammoth walls stretched for nearly twenty-seven kilometers and its huge stone arches developed for the entire length of the valley on the line along the cities of Bruzolo, Chianocco, and Forestoon on the banks of the Dora River.

Rama was not the only large stone building but was part of a huge agglomeration of smaller buildings that stretched from the city of Susa to the gates of Turin. Rama, the only fledged city at that time, was the peaceful and intellectual seat of a mysterious people.

When the water took away the mother civilization, Rama was the only witness to the ancient power of the dragon. Millennia wiped it out but the knowledge it kept is still alive in traditions all over the Earth. Even today it is said that the stone circle exists but appears visible only on the night of Samain, and only to those who have eyes to see it. On that night all locals, human and not, visible and not, meet within the eternal majestic stones and celebrate the return to the ancestral land.

10

PELASGIAN RELIGION AND CULTS

This is it. This is all there is left. This ocean and this place here.
We are stuck in a bloody snow globe!
There's no outside world! There's no escape!

DESMOND DAVID HUME, *LOST* (SEASON 2)

There is no world, there are only islands.

JACQUES DERRIDA, *SÉMINAIRE LA BÊTE ET LE SOUVERAIN.*

It was not a godless people that approached our beaches—the Mediterranean—15,000 years ago.

I imagine building the time machine I used to dream of as a child: at that age I only cared about dinosaurs, but, following the instruction of Dr. Emmett "Doc" Brown, inventor of the machine in the movie *Back to the Future,* it is sufficient to change the date on the display, turn the knob to some degree, load the plutonium, turn on the flux capacitor to 1.21 gigawatts, and shoot the DeLorean to 88 mph.

In the film the first to experience time travel was Doc's dog Einstein, but this time we'll wear the helmet of a fearless rabbi of Jerusalem, taking him straight to 10,500 BCE, when the Pelasgians steadily ruled over Mediterranean countries. We expect the travel account to provide a complete description of the religion of the period—the one that had the most followers. Maybe we will discover that the rabbi was at ease among the faithful of that time, who were circumcised, monotheistic, and devoted to a god whose image could not be carved or painted.

THE RELIGION OF THE PELASGIANS

Originally the Pelasgians worshipped a deity without giving him a name, shape, or corporeal image—much like the beliefs of the Jewish people. This closeness was essential to Tot-Moses in the Exodus from Egypt when groups of Sea Peoples—who had fought as mercenaries in Egypt for generations—allied with the Habirus, organizing themselves into the tribe of Dan. Herodotus gives us only a few clues about the cult of the Atlanteans: "The Pelasgian offered sacrifices of all kinds, and prayed to the gods, but had no distinct names or appellation for them, since they had never heard of any. They called them gods (*Theoi* = disposers) because they disposed and arranged all things in such a beautiful order."[1]

Herodotus speaks of gods and not of God because he was influenced by polytheistic conceptions. The existence of many anonymous gods would have generated some difficulties when choosing whom to pray to—what god would have heard the call of the faithful if they called them all equally? What god would have turned his head? Maybe, then, they worshipped one god and therefore had no special name indicating him.

The aforementioned *Suidas* supports the existence of one god worshipped by Pelasgians,[2] and Seneca in the first century CE spoke of the Tyrrenhid's religion, evidencing that "they have a belief in one God, indicated by the names of Fate, Providence, and Nature."[3]

The worship of one god prevailed among the Assyrians and the Hyksos of Canaan* early in their history, though curiously claiming it was

---

*Canaan was a territory in current Syria, Lebanon, and Israel considered to be the "Promised Land" and sought by the Jewish people during the Exodus.

imported from Egypt.[4] In the Indian Mahābhārata, with reference to the inhabitants of Atala, it turns out that "the men that inhabit that island have complexions as white as the rays of the Moon and that are devoted to Narayana. . . . Indeed, the denizens of White Island believe and worship only one God."[5]

Some ancient writers mention altars and temples in Greece dedicated to the "Unknown God," well described by Pausanias.* The altar of the Unknown God still existed in Athens in the days of the apostle Paul when he exclaimed in his Areopagus sermon:

Men of Athens, I have seen for myself how extremely scrupulous you are in all religious matters, because, as I strolled round looking at your sacred monuments, I noticed among other things an altar inscribed: To An Unkown God. In fact, the unkown God you revere is the one I proclaim to you. Since the God who made the world and everything in it is himself Lord of heaven and earth, he does not make his home in shrines made by human hands.[6]

After the diaspora the Pelasgians' religion was contaminated with the cults of the civilized peoples so that the phallus became the symbol of the Pelasgian people, and around the phallus they drew a mystery cult. The same symbol was handed down by the Sea Peoples, and in Italy we find it on the walls of Buccino (Volcei), on the lintel of the minor gateway of Alatri, and on the holy road of the Colli Albani (plate 32).

When the Pelasgian religious ideas were introduced to the Mediterranean peoples the attributes of divinity were divided among many heroes, kings, legislators, and benefactors who in the eyes of the natives appeared above the human condition. Over time, they were assigned a cult and an image.

From the few remaining memories available we know that the first deity was symbolically identified with the sun, "the image of the perpetual cause of all incomprehensible things." Macrobius in the fifth century

---

*The Unknown God of the Pelasgians and the God to whom this altar was sacred are in fact the same, as the learned Ciampi demonstrates in a note to his translation of the first book of Pausanias.

CE declared that the names of the gods were nothing but synonyms of a single one, namely the Sun.[7]

In his *Preparation for the Gospel* Eusebius reports the stories of Sanconiatone, esteemed man of the twelfth century BCE. Sanconiatone argued that in his country religion was initially addressed to one God by revering his image in the sun, moon, stars, and elements. Then some men were worshipped for their inventions as benefactors and patrons; statues and temples were erected in their honor, creating mortal and immortal gods. The latter, namely the sun and the moon, took the names of Beelsamen and Astarte (or Astharteth, depicted alike the Egyptian Isis).

Eusebius's work begins with a transcription of the Tagetic books dictated by Tages, prophet and founder of the Etruscan religion. The cosmological portion describes creation, chaos, darkness, spirit of life, origin of light, and animals, followed by Protogenus (or Prometheus), and with him the Giants (to whom the use of fire, worked iron, ship sailing, fishing, hunting, and the invention of the first houses and porticos or atriums are due). From these Giants was born Terreno, whose name means "indigenous," also called Sky (Uranus). From him and the Earth came Saturn, Proserpina, Minerva, Atlas, Ascarte or Astarte, Jupiter, Hercules, Aesculapius, and all appelled Titanìds. We already identified Prometheus with Manes-Atis; therefore the presence of a descendant of Prometheus named Terreno fits perfectly with the presence of Tyrrhenus (Tirreno), son of Atis.

So in the beginning the Pelasgians worshipped a kind of "unknown God," while later they gave a face to this divine essence by mixing his traits with those of the Mother Goddess, worshipped in Europe before their arrival. They committed themselves to the regularization of their worship, building temples for the natives and refining their representational art with the purpose of obtaining control over the civilized peoples. Inevitably, Pelasgian religious ideas merged with the historical traditions of these peoples. The contact with primitive peoples caused the worshipping of the great Pelasgian men, who were gradually assigned attributes that originally belonged to the one God.

Following a sort of code, described in *Hamlet's Mill* by the historians Giorgio de Santillana and Hertha von Dechend, the Pelasgians inserted their astronomical knowledge into the myths and cults of the natives so they could be perpetuated without clear and direct understanding. Over time the characteristics of the first deities were split, as happened for example in Egypt, where Hathor became the goddess of motherhood, absorbing some of Isis's traits; from primordial god, Osiris passed to be the great-grandson of Amon, and the latter had the role of creator.

In the following section we will describe how Pelasgian religion and cults spread and evolved within civilized peoples.

THE REPRESENTATIONS OF THE DEITY

During the Paleolithic period in Africa and Eurasia an entity was adored that embodied procreative power and whose emanations were the sun and the moon, the two stars whose cycles are connected to life on Earth. This entity was depicted in different ways in sculptures and cave art: as a rounded woman with broad hips, better known as the Mother Goddess, in the form of a bull, or, most stylized, as a *menhir,* a huge stone embedded vertically in the ground.* In some cases the Mother Goddess was horned or had a bull's head, with horns resembling the crescent moon, often with a solar disk between them. Even when in its taurine shape there appeared at times the solar disk above the neck. The one God of the Pelasgians inevitably merged with the Mother Goddess, whose cult is easily attributable to the presence in Libya and Sardinia of the Amazon matriarchal people (see chapter 9).

---

*Menhirs are monolithic megaliths that reach twenty meters or higher, such as the Broken Menhir of Locmariaquer in Morbihan, Brittany. Erected individually or in groups with varying dimensions, their shape is generally (but not always) square, sometimes tapering toward the top. Distributed in Europe, Africa, and Asia, although more numerous in western Europe, particularly the British Isles, menhirs appear in both genders: male as a phallic symbol with a pillar section and female with a plano-convex or concave-convex section.

In the Egypt of the Pelasgians the gods ended up mixing their features with those of real "great men" and over the millennia evolved into the figures of Isis and Osiris, often depicted with a horned headdress with a sun disk between the horns or with a taurine head/whole body. While connotation of the Mother Goddess was confined to Isis, bulls were evident in paintings in Cretan palaces, and a sacred bull was the cause of discord between Poseidon and Minos, which gave birth to the Minotaur, a half bull.

In a temple of Memphis a sacred bull called Apis represented Osiris, in whose honor great parties were celebrated. At the death of this bull, priests would search all over the country for a new Apis with specific characteristics; it was imperative that it be black with some white markings, which included a triangle on the front (according to Herodotus a square), a crescent moon-shaped mark on the side, and an eagle-shaped mark on the back. These signs were the most popular, but in all there were twenty-nine. Its analogue in Heliopolis was known as Mnevis.

In some cases the menhirs of the goddess were carved on meteoric stones, as if to bring together the creative power of the deity with its destructive power that would materialize as asteroids, and certainly had a strong ability to charm the Paleolithic peoples.

In the temple of Heliopolis there was a square-section menhir topped by a capstone of meteorite iron called Benben. In the beginning it was venerated as a simulacrum of Osiris, but later it passed to Amon.

The Teucrians of western Anatolia worshipped an image of the mother goddess Cybele* (to the Greeks, Demeter, and Isis to the Egyptians) in a black conical-shaped meteor stone. In 204 BCE the statue, called for by the Roman Senate to King Attalus I of Pergamum, was solemnly brought

---

*In the myth Cybele was wife of Atis-Manes, king of Arzawa, father of Atis II and grandfather of Tyrrhenus, mythical ancestor of the Etruscans. They say Atis died by castrating himself after Cybele drove him crazy in revenge for betraying her with another woman; tradition says Atis is then resurrected. The comparison with Osiris, who was torn to pieces by his brother Seth and his companions, is immediate: Isis reassembled all his parts, yet was unable to find his phallus. Considering that Osiris also resurrects we note the strong similarities that confirm the relationship between Cybele and the Pelasgians.

to Rome, where, with the official title of "Great Mother of the Gods," a temple* on Palatine Hill was dedicated to her on the *Ludi Megalenses,* an annual festival in April.

In India to this day images of Shiva, called Shivalinga, are perfectly cylindrical menhirs visible in every temple of the deity, and from time immemorial cows have been sacred animals.

With time the cult of meteoric stones detached from the phallic symbol. At Mecca they worship the sacred black meteoric stone known as Ka'ba, a name that translated through ancient Egyptian means "strength of the soul." The hieroglyph for the word *ka* (strength) is once again a bull.

Graham Hancock in *The Secret of the Holy Grail* states that since ancient times the Semitic tribes like the Israelites worshipped the stones that fell from the sky. He states that a direct line of cultural transmission linked the tables of the Ten Commandments to the pairs of sacred meteoric stones called *betyls*† that pre-Islamic Arab tribes brought with them in their travels.[8]

Often meteoric stones called omphalos served as geodetic indicators marking the points of known coordinates, the so-called navels of the world.

The bull and the Mother Goddess are recurring motifs in both Maltese temples and Shardana art. The burial of sacred cows is found in pre-dynastic Egypt near Lake Nabta Playa at the edge of the Sahara. The bull's horns still appear in some representations of Acheru, the "double" lion that indicated the duality between Heaven and Earth, between the Sphinx and the constellation of Leo (figure 10.1). There is an interesting similarity between this representation and the giant horns outside the palace of Knossos (figure 10.2).

---

*This building is right next to the Augustan temple of Apollo, renowned for the porch of the Danaides (the fifty daughters of Danaus). The order for the recovery of the simulacrum was driven from the Sibylline books composed by the Sibyl of Cumae, the oldest oracle and of Pelasgian foundation.

†In her essay "The Book of the Covenant" (*Hebrew Union College Annual*), Julia Morgenstern writes: "The most natural assumption is that the Ark contained a *betyl.* . . . This view was, of course, common among the primitive Semites, and there is evidence that it was common also in ancient Israel."

Figure 10.1. The double lion, the duality between Heaven and Earth.

Figure 10.2. Giant horns outside the Knossos palace in Crete.

We must therefore observe the Mesopotamian deities represented with horned headdresses similar to those of the Shardana bronzes. Finally, throughout Eurasia and Africa, we find sculptures and representations of bulls and mother goddesses both in pre-Pelasgian Paleolithic crude styles and in the refined versions of the Pelasgians and their descendant populations (such as the colorful representations of bulls inside the Minoan palaces).

THE ISLAND OF PANCHAEA

The Greek historian Evemerus from Messina (330–250 BCE), recorded by Diodorus Siculus (book 5, 41–46 and book 6, 1) and by several fragments of the translation of Ennius titled *Euhemerus,* told of his exploration in Panchaea, an island of an Ethiopian archipelago.* Here, in addition to the indigenous people—including the Oceanites—he would have met Indians, Scythians, and Cretans, all peoples with great wisdom. Most of them lived in the capital Panara, provided with its own laws and governed by three judges who, along with the priests, administered ordinary justice. On a plain ten kilometers from Panara they had erected the temple of Zeus Trifilio, whose name connects it to the three original tribes of the island: the Panchaeans, Oceanites (Pelasgians), and Dois. The area of the temple was very rich in flora and fauna, as remarkable as the temple itself, 60 meters long with a driveway 720 meters long and 30 meters wide. The plain, dominated by Mount Olympus Trifilio, was home to the first islanders and many natural astronomical observatories. Evemerus briefly described the worship paid to the gods by Panchaeans and the internal structure of the temple, where there was a gold stele bearing inscriptions

*Ennius writes "India," which, at the time, indicated both India and Ethiopia. According to Virgil, and the Florentine fourteenth-century traveler Simone Sigoli, the Nile was born in India. The Byzantine theologian Rufinus in the fourth century, speaking of Christianity in Ethiopia, calls the latter India. Even Marco Polo in the thirteenth century was referring to Ethiopia "as the middle or second India." Finally, Father Francisco Alvarez, Portuguese chronicler in Ethiopia in the sixteenth century, wrote a work titled "Truthful Information about the Countries of Prester John from the Indies," but Prester John was the title of Ethiopian kings.

in Egyptian hieroglyphs about the deeds of the gods that priests sang in their hymns and divine rites.

According to the priestly caste, the gods were born in Crete and were conducted to Panchaea by the great king Zeus, whose genealogy and deeds are narrated by Evemerus. He begins by describing the patterns of power that helped Uranus become the first king of the inhabited world, honored for his knowledge of astronomy as a god of the sky. Evemerus also reports that Chronos (Saturn), Uranus's youngest son, overthrew the legitimate heir, his brother Titan, and married his sister Rhea (Ops in Ennius), giving birth to Zeus, Hera, and Poseidon. We see here a more direct analogy between the Titanomachy (War of the Titans) and the vicissitudes of Menes, usurper of the legitimate king Danaus, his brother.

The last great king was Zeus, son of Chronos, who freed brothers and uncles from the confinement Chronos had forced them into and through several marriages guaranteed a large progeny. Once allied with Belus, king of Babylon, Zeus conquered Syria and Cilicia (south coastal region of Asia Minor) and then Egypt,* where he received the honorary title of Ammon. By this name he was honored in the guise of a ram, since during the battle he had worn a helmet adorned with golden ram's horns.

After traveling the Earth five times spreading the seeds of civilization and religion, Zeus in the years before his death led his descendants to Panchaea, where he left them specific tasks of government. His brother Poseidon ruled over the seas and maritime routes, Hades took charge of funeral rites, and Hermes presided over the spread of literacy and culture. Zeus ordered that his deeds, and those of his ancestors, should be engraved on a gold stele. After his death they erected the temple of Zeus Trifilio for him. Hermes engraved a stele with the deeds of his descendants, who were all—including Hermes—honored as gods.

Of particular interest is that on this stele the Uranids (descendants of Uranus, another name used to indicate the Pelasgians) Zeus, Artemis, Apollo, and Hermes (presumably with their Egyptian names) are shown not as gods but as kings, captains, pilots, wisemen, and craftsmen, devoid of any divine nature. This supports the idea that polytheism was born

---

*Note the similarities with the conquests of Menes/Osiris.

"late" among the civilized Pelasgian peoples, as a result of the deification of those "great men."

THE JEWS AND THE TRIBE OF DAN

When describing Abraham as belonging to the "Order of Melchizedek," the sacred scriptures seem to refer to an institution similar to the Followers of Horus. Melchizedek (a name taken by Sargon the Great) was the nephew of Noah, son of his brother, Nir. The story of Noah's flood could connect Noah to Da-Nao and Melchizedek to Horus, son of Menes/Nir/Osiris. Like Horus, Melchizedek came into the world despite the death of one of his parents, the mother in this case. In the transition from the myth of Horus to that of Melchizedek, it is possible to trace a process of "evolution" of the myth, which transforms an act of necrophilia (the union with the dead body of Osiris) into an immaculate conception:

> Sofonim [the mother] is old now, and while approaching the day of her death, she conceives a child in her womb. Nir, the priest, has not joined her since the Lord had appointed him as his priest in front of people. Sofonim, noticing the pregnancy, is ashamed and feels humiliated. And until the end of pregnancy she hides. [Nir realizes this and cries to have shame thrown upon him, and all Sofonim's apologies are worthless. Nir turns her out, but his wife falls at his feet and dies. Then, Nir and his brother Noah go to dig the grave in secret, but when they come to take the corpse . . .]. So, the baby of the dead Sofonim is born without aid. His body has developed as one of three years. He already speaks and blesses the Lord. The priestly seal appears on his chest. His appearance is glorious! [They give him the name of Melchizedek].[9]

At the end of this chapter we will discuss in detail this process of evolution.

The one God of the ancient Pelasgian tradition, later taken up by the Hyksos and the Sea Peoples, was called Yah'co (Giacco, then Bacchus or Janus), from which may derive both Yahweh and Yah'cobb (Jacob); for

Shasu-Edomite nomads of Sinai he was the "god of the storms living on Mount Horeb," to whom they devoted the circumcision.

Although Osiris/Giacco/Menes/Yah'co had been exalted as the greatest benefactor, in fact he had usurped the throne of his older brother Seth/Danaus. If Jacob can be identified with Giacco, then in his history we can expect to find the story of such a theft against his older brother Esau. In Genesis 25 we read:

> Once, when Jacob was cooking stew, Esau returned from the countryside exhausted. Esau said to Jacob, 'Give me a mouthful of that red stuff there; I am exhausted'—hence the name given to him, Edom. Jacob said, "First sell me your birthright." Esau said, "Behold, I am dying: Why do I need then the birthright?" Then Jacob said, "First give me your oath"; he gave him his oath and sold his birthright to Jacob. Then Jacob gave him some bread and lentil stew; he ate, drank, got up and went away. That was all Esau cared about his birthright.[10]

Later his father Isaac, blind on his deathbed, asked Esau to procure and cook him some game before receiving the blessing. In his absence, his mother Rebecca convinced his brother Jacob to take his place and cooked for him two kid goats to take to Isaac in place of the game. To avoid recognition, Jacob wore his brother's clothes impregnated with his smell, and he covered his smooth arms with gloves made from the goats' hairy skins. Falling into the trap, Isaac invoked blessings on him:

> May God give you dew from heaven, and the richness of the earth, abundance of grain and wine! Let peoples serve you and nations bow low in front of you! Be master of your brothers; let your mother's other sons bow low in front of you! Accursed be whoever curses you and blessed be whoever blesses you![11]

Returning from the hunting, Esau discovered the deception and begged his father to bless him in turn:

> Father, bless me too! [. . .] His name should be Jacob right enough,

for he has now supplanted me twice. First he took my birthright, and look, now he has gone and taken my blessing![12]

All petitions were vain and Isaac stated:

I have already made him your master; I have given him all his brothers as servants. . . . Far from the richness of the earth and the dew of heaven above, your home will be. By your sword you will live, and your brother will you serve.[13]

So far the stories of Osiris and Jacob look the same. At this point, though, there is a reversal of parts: it is not Jacob/Osiris who threatened Esau/Danaus with death and forced him to flee, but vice versa. Eventually, however, the heirs of Jacob/Osiris will carry on the legacy of his people.

In 1750 BCE the Hyksos/Shasus invaded and conquered Lower Egypt and founded their capital Avaris on the Nile delta. For two centuries they provided Egypt with foreign pharaohs, hosting in their court the family of Joseph (Jacob's son), who was a Shasu capable of interpreting dreams. Then the Egyptians regained control over the country and drove the Hyksos and Habirus into slavery, which would last for over three hundred years.

In 1359 BCE Akhenaten, of Hyksos blood by his mother, became pharaoh and was married to a Hyksos-Kassite woman (Nefertiti) and a Trojan woman, among others. The slaves took advantage of the situation and with the support of his wife and his mother revealed the common Pelasgian origin of Egyptians, Hyksos, and Teucrians in the hope of gaining freedom. Such revelation resulted in the reintroduction of the ancient religion of the one God, which Akhenaten made the "state cult for the god Aton." The opposition of the Theban clergy and the resentment of the people were such as to condemn him to the *damnatio memoriae* (condemnation of memory), which, after his death in 1342 BCE, led to the destruction of all monuments and documents relating to him.

Meanwhile in Sardinia the Hyksos flowered in the Nuragic, or Shardana, culture, the cradle of skilled navigators, merchants, and mercenaries recruited by the pharaohs and kings of Ugarit and Carchemish. The Nuragics also urged the return to the religion of the one God: in

The evidence of a common origin for Jews and Egyptians was sought in the seventeenth century by the Venetian Titus Livy Burattini, and found by Sir Isaac Newton in the nineteenth century.

His results, published by Father Kircher, established that the Great Pyramid was built with two separate units: the heart of granite (the Zed) was achieved by choosing multiple measures of a unit equal to fifty-three centimeters. The rest of the pyramid, made in limestone, used instead the "standard" cubit of forty-four centimeters.

The only peoples known in history for using the unit of fifty-three centimeters were the Akkadians and Hebrews, who indicated it as the "sacred cubit." This measure is mentioned several times in the Bible when a prophet receives from God the order to build sacred objects or buildings.*

Indeed, it is not a real proof, because both the Egyptians and the Hyksos (and from these, the Jews) had learned from contact with the Akkadians and not by their common descent from the Pelasgians.

We must remember that Abraham had fought with Sargon against a coalition of "East Kings" and when his nephew Naram-Sin (or Narmer) conquered Egypt Abraham received a land for his descendants, the land claimed by the Shasu in 1750 BCE.†

---

*See God's instruction for constructing the Ark of Noah, Ark of the Covenant, or Solomon's Temple in Genesis 7:15; Exodus 36:9 and 37:1; I Kings 7:2, 6, 10, 15, 16, and 23–39.

†See the first page of chapter 5, "Megaliths and Gods among Men in the Time of Osiris," and chapter 5, "Hyksos Become Scythians," in II Segreto degli Illuminati (The Illluminati Secret).

1355 BCE, Akhenaten and Nefertiti welcomed a Shardana delegation exhorting them to return to the worship of the Great God.[14]

The Shardanas, both for fellowship in light of their common origin and because of corruption, helped the Shasus and Habirus escape from Egypt.

In the thirteenth century BCE the Shardana, located in the region of Jessen on the Nile delta, rebelled against Ramesses II, careless of the honor the pharaoh had conceded by enrolling them in his personal guard. According to the annals of Seti I, Moses (Tot-Moses), the cousin of Ramesses II, general of the Shardana troops, returned to Akhenaten's monotheism and was therefore banished from the kingdom.

The historian Manetho tells us that Moses would have corrupted the Shardana, promising them the restitution of their capital, Avaris.

The Shardana organized themselves into the "tribe of Dan." During the Exodus, while the "Jewish" people camped in the Sinai, Moses (Tot-Moses) settled the tribe of Dan (established by the Shardana) to the north. When the men resumed the march, "Dan served as rearguard."[15] Such organization was in response to the danger of a possible attack by the Egyptians: they could do it only coming from the north by land, as the Sinai peninsula was surrounded by the Red Sea on three sides. Most of the people were not convinced of wandering in the desert and some also tried to go back (see the biblical story of Dathan and Core). In Numbers 10:25 it is said that the tribe of Dan had the task to collect. To collect what, precisely? Probably the deserters.[16]

Once in the Promised Land, half of the tribe of Dan went away. In Judges 5:17 we read that "Dan did stay in ships." The other half "went up and fought with Leshem and captured it. Then they struck it with the edge of the sword and possessed it and settled in it; and they called it Leshem Dan."[17] It is clear here that there is a differentiation of the tribe of Dan from the other Israelite tribes. In Revelation (7:3–4) we read, "Do not harm the earth or the sea or the trees until we have sealed the bond-servants of our God on their foreheads. And I heard the number of those who were sealed, one hundred and forty-four thousand sealed from every tribe of the sons of Israel." It goes on to list twelve thousand slaves for each of the twelve tribes, replacing the tribe of Joseph with two tribes named after his two sons, Manasseh and Ephraim, but no mention of Dan. Why?

Again in Kings (11:29–32; 11:35–36): "And Ahijah caught the new garment that was on him, and rent it in 12 pieces: And he said to Jeroboam, Take thee ten pieces: for thus saith the LORD, the God of Israel, Behold, I will rend the kingdom out of the hand of Solomon, and will give 10 tribes to thee: but he shall have 1 tribe for my servant David's sake." The tribe left to Solomon was that of Judah (son of David). Again, why are there named only eleven tribes? Where is the missing one?

Still, in the book of Chronicles there is a list of the genealogies of "Judah, Reuben, Gad, Manasseh, Levi, Issachar, Benjamin, Naphtali, Manasseh, Ephraim, and Asher." In all, they are twelve, but Manasseh is mentioned twice, and there is no sign of Dan. The reason is simple: they were not Hebrews (Habirus) but Shardanas, men who loved the art of war and were accused of idolatry by the Jews. Just read, for example, Judges 18 with reference to the worship of idols, or 2 Kings 18:4 for the cult of Nehustan (a bronze snake or caduceus).

In Exodus we read that Moses, getting out of Egypt, made a detour toward the south, "fearing that watching the fights, the people could get frightened and try to return to Egypt."[18] Who was fighting, then, if not the Shardanas? The book of Exodus 12:38 confirms the presence of other groups within the people of Israel and says (Exodus 13:18) that they came out armed from Egypt. This is important because:

> Now no blacksmith could be found in all the land of Israel, for the Philistines said, "Otherwise the Hebrews will make swords or spears." So all Israel went down to the Philistines, each to sharpen his plowshare, his mattock, his axe, and his hoe. . . . Neither sword nor spear was found in the hands of any of the people who *were* with Saul and Jonathan, but only Saul and his son Jonathan had them. (I Samuel, 13:19)

A people could not fight without swords. Finally, we note the work of Aholiab of the tribe of Dan who used the Shamir* and engraved the Ephod, the breastplate of Aaron.[19] The breastplate included twelve stones, one for each tribe—for the tribe of Dan the stones were the Sardio or Sardonyx. The exact same breastplate, later used by the high priest of the temple, is depicted in some Shardana bronzes (figure 10.3).

---

*The Shamir, a tool capable of cutting stone without any contact to the surface, was kept in a box of lead, its secret safe for years within the hollow columns of Boaz and Jachin in the temple of King Solomon.

Archaeologist Dimitrina Mitov Dzonova has gathered 170 Sardinian bronzes, discovering 82 iconographic subjects sacred to Judaism.

> In Sardinia in the tenth to eighth centuries BC there is a sacred modeled bible, which precedes by about a millennium the first transcript of the Jewish legends. Found in some sacred wells, the bronzes show a close relationship with Judaism, and allow relating the Shardana sacred wells to the wells sacred to Judaism, frequently crafted since the most ancient period, since the time of the patriarchs and Moses, and so widely known from the architectural point of view in Palestine.*

*Quoted from S. Frau, *Le Colonne d'Ercole* (The Pillars of Hercules).

Figure 10.3. A Shardana bronzetto, or small bronze figure (left), and the high priest's breastplate with the twelve stones of the twelve tribes of Israel (right).

Among the graffiti left by the Israelites in the Sinai desert, depicting for example the seven-branched candlestick and the Star of David, is the Shardana caduceus (figure 10.4).

In the Bible, the tribe of Dan is often accused of idolatry for

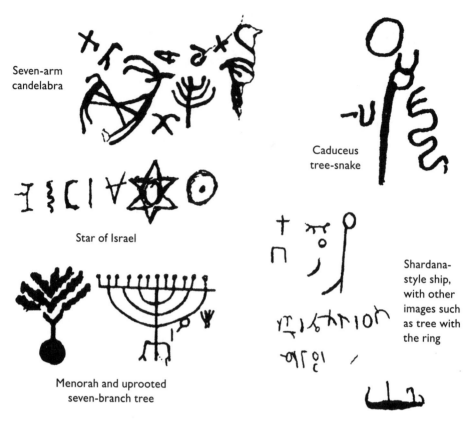

Seven-arm candelabra

Caduceus tree-snake

Star of Israel

Shardana-style ship, with other images such as tree with the ring

Menorah and uprooted seven-branch tree

Figure 10.4. These represent graffiti found in Har Karkom in the Negev Desert, Sinai. The discoveries in this zone of temples, caves, geo-glyphs, graffiti, and paintings have convinced many researchers, including Professor Anati, of the presence of the people of the Exodus in these places. (Labels point out which image can be found in each example.) Source: L. Melis, Shardana—I popoli del Mare (Shardana—The People of the Sea).

worshipping the serpent, a cult which at the time of writing had been extirpated from Judaism thanks to the reforms of the kings Hezekiah (716–687 BCE) and Josiah (648–609 BCE). Therefore such accusations have been posthumously added to tradition: the Nehustan, Moses's sacred serpent, is still visible in the church of Sant'Ambrogio in Milan, though it might be a copy.

Cultural symbolism of the Pelasgians also contains references to the snake as a dragon. In ancient times it was not always associated with evil: the Sabians-Canaanites themselves worshipped the serpent or dragon for a period, and even Moses erected one in the desert. The idolatry of the serpent is abandoned as it came symbolically close to Satan: examples are the defeat of the dragon by St. George, in the Christian version, or by the hands of Manes-Atis, in the tradition of Herodotus, so that after the second flood the Lydians gained freedom. In the Greek legend of the Argonauts Jason defeats the dragon while Hercules, grandson of Janus and faithful to the worship of the serpent, leaves the company indignantly. Apollo defeats the serpent-dragon of the oracle of Delphi, and takes its place; San Pietro in Sardinia defeats the Scultone, the dragon of the Shardana cult.

After Josiah, the Jews despised the worshippers of the serpent, including the Sea Peoples and the priests of Dodona. Indeed, the snake was associated with evil, and they coined the terms Cainites, that is, sons of Cain, or Vampires, to identify Pelasgian progeny. Actually, the Vampires are remembered uniquely for being white-skinned, and their synonym Cainites indicated the children of Cain who lived before the flood. In the book of Judges, chapter 18, we read:

> Now in those days the tribe of Dan was in search of a territory to live in, for until then no territory had fallen to them among the tribes of Israel. From their clan the Danites sent five brave men . . . to reconnoiter the country and explore it. The five men came to the highlands of Ephraim, as far as Micah's house, and spent the night there. When they were near Micah's house, they recognized the voice of the young Levite and, going nearer, said to him, "Who brought you here?" . . . He replied, "Micah has made certain arrangements with me. He pays me a wage and I act as his priest." They replied, "Then consult God, so that we may know whether the journey we are on will lead to success."

The priest replied, "Go in peace; Yahweh is watching over your journey." The five men then left and, arriving at Laish, saw that the people living there had an untroubled existence . . . there was no lack or shortage of any sort in the territory. . . . They then went back to their brothers at Zorah and Eshtaol and, when the latter asked them, "What have you to report" they said, "Up, we must go against them." . . . From these places, consequently, from the clan of Danites at Zorah and Eshtaol, six hundred men set out equipped for war. They went up and camped at Kiriath-Jearim in Juda; and for this reason the place is still called the Camp of Dan today. . . . From there they entered the highland of Ephraim and came to Micah's house . . . took the carved statue, the ephod, the domestic images and the idol cast in metal. The priest, however, said, "What are you doing?" . . . "Come with us, and become our father and priest. Are you better off as domestic priest to one man, or as priest to a tribe and clan in Israel?" The priest was delighted . . . and went off among the people. . . . They had gone some distance from Micah's house, when the people living in the houses near Micah's house raised the alarm and set off in pursuit of the Danites. . . . The Danites said, "Let us hear no more from you, or quick-tempered men may set about you, and this might cost you your life and the lives of your family!" So the Danites . . . marched on Laish. . . . They put it to the sword and they burned down the town. . . . They rebuilt the town and settled in it and called it Dan, from the name of Dan their ancestor who had been born to Israel. . . . Johnathan son of Gershom, son of Moses, and his sons after him were priests for the tribe of Dan.[20]

BAALBEK, THE CITY OF CAIN

One of the most important archaeological sites of the Near East is Baalbek in Lebanon, declared a World Heritage Site by UNESCO in 1984. Located about sixty miles east of Beirut, it is part of an area inhabited by Shasu shepherds during the Bronze Age and by Phoenicians during the Iron Age.

The name of the main Phoenician settlement is Tyrus in Greek, Zar in Hebrew (we find the same root in the Nuragic god Sid, also known as Sardus Pater), Sarra in archaic Latin, and Tharros in Sardinian, where the "z" or "ç" from any origin is rendered with the Greek *theta*, "th." The root "tyr" is connected to Tyrrenid-Pelasgians, while Homer mentions Tyre as a daughter-in-law of Aeolus and daughter of Salmoncus the Pelasgian.[21]

Tyre of Phoenicia owes its birth to another Tyre in Sardinia who "kidnapped" Europe, goddess of the sunset: the same as saying that Tyre was located to the west of the Greek world. This Tyre was in turn founded by the Sidonians, those of the Sardinian Sidon that Homer's Menelaus meets traveling throughout the west, beyond Egypt, before the Erembis, also known as Erebanti, which Ptolemy places between Sardinia and Corsica. Strabo (book 1, 2.31) confirms that they are not the Sidonians of Phoenicia. Even Homer, in his *Iliad*, made them arrive in Greece "navigating a vast and misty sea" or put them far away in the *Odyssey*. In Euripides' *Phoenicians* the choir begins with:

> We have left behind the Phoenician island, washed by the Tyrian sea, to come here as the finest prize to Apollo, to serve in his temple, his home, beneath the snow-covered peaks of Parnassus. We have sliced the Ionian waters with our oars, aided by the blasts of Zephyros [the wind that comes from the west] that sang sweet songs in the skies above the unharvested briny fields along the shores of Sicily. Our city chose us as the fairest in beauty to be a gift for Loxias Apollo and so we have been sent here, to Cadmus's land, to Thebes' towers.... Friends share the pains of friends and Phoenicia will share the pains of this city of seven gates. . . . The race and the children are from the same mother . . .

He is speaking of Sardinia because the Phoenicians and Shardanas are the same people! Quintus Curtius informs us that, in the first century CE, Thebes was a colony of Tyre, abandoned because "the number of earthquakes had weakened the indigenous [Sardinians] who were, therefore, forced to seek home elsewhere than the homeland."

Not only was the island of the Phoenicians in the west, but Homer also places in the west a "Syria," homeland of the swineherd Eumaeus. Near the Sardinian Tyre there is Mount Sirai, but Syros, Tyros, Tire, Tiryns, and Siris are in the Mediterranean. Tira is a river that flows into the Black Sea near a city named Olbia, another Sardinian name (there's a famous city in Sardinia called Olbia too). Near the Siris of Basilicata two coins have emerged with the inscription "Serdaios," along with one of the most beautiful Nuragic ships. Finally the Tyrii (inhabitants of Tyre) of Sardinia appear in the treaties between Rome and Carthage reported by Polybius.*

*See S. Frau's Le Colonne d'Ercole (The Pillars of Hercules), chapter 42.

So we now move eastward, toward the new Phoenicia. A tsunami has changed Sardinia's appearance, filled Campidano with mud, and stocked the area with wetlands: famine is spread all over the Mediterranean. Beyond the sea they are all called Phoenicians.

Phoenicians worshipped a certain Adonis or Adosiris as carrier of corn and made festivals in honor of his son Horus/Hercules, who, according to the traditions of the Numidian king Jemsale, enlisted an army in their country. According to the myth Hercules, patron of sailors, instructed the men to reach a pair of floating islands and on one of these he showed them an olive tree that housed an eagle and a snake in the middle of a fire that burned without consuming. Once the eagle had been sacrificed, one of the islands was rooted to the bottom of the sea and on its surface the new Tyre was built: this is the reason why in Tyre and Thasos there are temples dedicated to Hercules.

According to Plutarch, Adosiris must be identified with the Egyptian Osiris and the Greek Bacchus/Dionysus. This possibility leads directly to the Jewish prayer of Shema where the faithful turn to Yahweh by using the name of Adonis: "Hear, O Israel, Adonai our God, Adonai is one." Already in chapter 9 we have assumed a possible identification between Yahweh and Bacchus, and this seems to be the ultimate evidence.

When the Shardanas attacked the Middle East, the Canaanites

still celebrated the Cabiri's mysteries introduced in Samothrace by the Pelasgian Electra, and the Shardanas/Phoenicians did so keep them.* Thanks to their efforts, the city of Baalbek maintained its sanctity.

Today Baalbek is a town in the valley of Beqa, the capital of a homonymous district in Lebanon. Located east of the headwaters of the Litani River, 1,170 meters above sea level, it is famous for its monumental ruins of Roman temples of the second and third centuries CE, when Baalbek was Heliopolis of the Roman province of Syria and hosted an important sanctuary dedicated to Heliopolitan Jupiter. The city, though located in a convenient location near the sources of the rivers Orontes and Litani, did not play a major strategic or commercial role initially.

The first oracle and shrine date back to the Bronze Age and are dedicated to Baal and Anat.† The courtyard of the sanctuary was changed by builders in the Ptolemaic period; at its west end they began the construction of a Greek-style temple, exploiting a huge preexisting platform (88 by 48 meters). The southeast wall of the terrace contains a row of nine blocks, each measuring approximately 10 by 4.2 by 3 meters, with a weight of *over three hundred tons each.* On the same level, but on the southwest adjacent wall, are six blocks of three hundred tons on which three enormous megalithic blocks are based, known as the trilith or "the wonder of the

---

*In ancient records we find an Agenor, father of Cadmus, who brings the first Pelasgian characters from Egypt into the land of Sidon, where he was elected king by popular vote. Apollodorus, in his *Bibliotheca,* describes him as the son of Neptune and Libya, daughter of Epaphus, son of Io, conducting us to the genealogies of the Pelasgians. Pausanias made that same point when he wrote that Cadmus and Phoenix, sons of Agenor, were brothers of Electra, who, as we have already seen, was the Pelasgian mother of the Tuscan Dardanus, founder of Troy.

†Baal (= Belo) is the Canaanite god of the sun, storm, and fertility, also accompanied in iconography by a bull; Anat (= Cybele) is his wife. Both are related to Tammuz (= Adonis = Atis-Manes) that also sometimes appears in Greek mythology as the son, or sometimes the husband, of Cybele. In myth Cybele was wife of Atis-Manes, king of Arzawa, Atis II's father and grandfather of Tyrrhenus. In other places she is the wife of Adonis, who was killed by a boar but is allowed to return to Earth for four months a year to see his bride. The story thus becomes a symbol of resurrection and rebirth, in connection with the cycle of seasons, as happened in Egypt with Osiris. Both Atis-Manes and Adonis are undoubtedly identified with the latter, so Cybele is one step closer to the figure of Isis.

three stones" (plate 33). These blocks of granite, surprisingly measuring 19.5 by 4.5 by 3.6 meters, with a weight of *eight hundred tons each*, are the sixth visible layer of the wall. Michel Alouf, the former superintendent to the ruins, observes that "in spite of their immense size [the trilith stones] are so accurately put in position and so carefully joined that it would be almost impossible to put a needle between them. It would be impossible to describe the first impression which a spectator has on seeing these huge architectural masses."

The immense size of the trilith can be better assessed thanks to a slightly larger block, the "stone of the pregnant woman," lying in a quarry nearby. It measures 21 by 4.8 by 4 meters and weighs *twelve hundred tons* (plate 34). When we compare the platform of Baalbek with buildings such as the Osirion of Abydos, the Kalasasaya, or the Ollantaytambo, the Pelasgian style is evident. Thus, we could link the construction of Baalbek with the campaign of conquest of the east wanted by Osiris.

After the Roman conquest in 64 BCE at the hands of Pompeius, the city of Baalbek-Heliopolis was included in the tetrarch's domain of Palestine. The Roman emperors undertook long journeys to reach this place to bring offerings to the gods in order to receive oracles on the destiny of the empire. The deity of the sanctuary was identified with Jupiter, which retained some characters of the ancient indigenous god and assumed the form and the name of Jupiter Heliopolitanus. The god was depicted with a flared hat with lightning in his hands, framed by two bulls (the bull typically accompanied the god Baal-Saturn). The other gods associated with the sanctuary were identified with Venus and Bacchus. The worship of the Heliopolitan triad took on a mystical and perhaps mysteric character and spread to other regions such as the Balkan provinces of the empire, Gaul, Britain, and the Hispanic provinces.

In 15 BCE the sanctuary became part of the territory of the colony Julia Augusta Felix Beritus, the current Beirut. The temple of Jupiter was built on a platform and was constructed in stages: the temple itself was completed in 60 CE under Nero, and at the same time he built the tower-shaped altar in front of the temple. Only six pillars of the temple survived earthquakes that followed in later years, but these pillars are still an imposing vision with their twenty meters of height. Under Trajan (98–

117 CE) the large courtyard began to be rearranged. Under Antoninus Pius (138–161 CE) the temple of Bacchus was erected. These works, including those concerning the temple of Venus, were completed during the dynasty of Severi, especially under Caracalla (211–217 CE). The hexagonal courtyard of the shrine was finally built under Philip the Arab (244–249 CE), Roman emperor born in nearby Damascus. During this age, Heliopolis was elevated by Septimius Severus (193–211 CE) to the rank of colony under Italian law with the name of Colonia Iulia Augusta Felix Heliopolis, and it became the main center of the province of Syria-Phoenicia, established in 194 CE with Tyre as the capital.

The Arabs believed that Baalbek belonged to Nimrod/Narmer/Naram Sin. According to an Arabic manuscript, Nimrod sent giants to rebuild it, because the flood had destroyed it. Another legend says that Nimrod rebelled against his God and built the tower of Babel at Baalbek. Other legends associate Baalbek with the biblical Cain, son of Adam, and argue that it was he who built it as a refuge after Yahweh had cursed him. According to Estfan Doweihi, the Maronite Patriarch of Lebanon:

> Tradition tells us that the fortress of Baalbek is the oldest building in the world. Cain, the son of Adam, built it in the year of creation 133, during a crisis of fierce dementia. He gave it the name of his son Enoch and peopled it with giants who had been punished by the flood for their iniquity. Even the Muslim inhabitants of those places believed that the transport of the enormous stones of Baalbek went far beyond human capabilities. But instead of attributing that work to the giants, they said the builders were demons or djinns.

Connection between the Cainites, or Vampires, with the Giants, or Pelasgians, is also apparent here. The fall of man from Eden is ascribable to the flood in 13,000 BCE. The same Genesis informs us that during Noah's flood the Giants disappeared forever. It therefore seems that the tradition leads us back to that period between 13,000 BCE and 9600 BCE, when we have already placed the construction of the other megalithic sites and Osiris's eastern campaign.

In the book of Enoch the Pelasgians are described as angels who descended on Earth to get wives, bringing to men the gifts of civilization, in the same way as the Pelasgian Prometheus brought fire to the people in the Greek myth:

> And Azâzêl taught men to make swords, and knives, and shields, and breastplates, and made known to them the metals and the art of working them and using them to create bracelets and ornaments, and the use of antimony, and the beautifying of the eyelids, and all kinds of gemstones, and all colouring tinctures. And there arose much godlessness, and they committed fornication, and they were led astray, and became corrupt in all their ways. Semjâzâ taught enchantments, and root-cuttings, Armârôs the resolving of enchantments, Bârâqîjâl astrology, Kôkabêl the constellations, Ezêqêêl the knowledge of the clouds, Araqiêl the signs of the earth, Shamsiêl the signs of the sun, and Sariêl the course of the moon.[22]

As Prometheus was tied to the mountains of the Caucasus, the fallen angels were punished and received the same response that the Greek myth addresses to the Titans: "From this time forward, never shall you ascend into heaven; He has said, that on the earth He will bind you, as long as the world endures."[23] To the ends of the Earth will also be bound those women who had generated children with the angels who "will become sirens."[24] It is curious that again in Greek myth mermaids are found on the Tyrrhenian coast of Italy, believed to be the end of the world, and the place where the Titans had been chained. According to Enoch the sons of the fallen angels and the sirens were the previously mentioned Giants! In the *Jewish Sagas of the Origins* (found in Erich Von Daniken's *Il Giorno del Giudizio è Già Cominciato*) we can read a different version of the episode of the original sin: "The chieftain angel Samael tempted Eve, then seduced and impregnated her. . . . After the seduction of Eve two different lineages had been formed, that of Cain, son of Samael, and that of Abel."

The biblical figure of Lilith, referred to as the Assyrian demon Lilitu, was a *succubus* demon, the female version of the *incubus*, demons who cause bad dreams. It is the feminization of the figure of Samael and appears as the first and evil wife of Adam. In the Jewish tradition Lilith is considered the mother of all Vampires: like all succubae, she is greedy for human semen, and for this reason she slips into men's beds at night to drain all their vital strength.*

So, whether Cain is the son of Adam and Eve or of Lilith and Samael, the figure of the Cainite or Vampire is inevitably linked to the figures of the Pelasgians, or Titans, for both the names match ("Giants" for example), as do the events, such as the confinement to the edge of the world. The Burney Relief, a Paleo-Babylonian clay, depicts Lilith in a context reported in the Sumerian Epic of Gilgamesh:

> *Then a serpent who could not be charmed*
> *Made its nest in the roots of the huluppu-tree.*
> *The Anzu-bird set his young in the branches of the tree.*
> *And the dark maid Lilith built her home in the trunk.*

In the bas-relief the succubus grabs with her claws the double feline or Acheru, a symbol belonging to the Egyptian tradition as well as to the Maya and Inca (plate 35).

A further clue about the similarity between the fallen angels and the Pelasgians comes from the Tibetan tradition: referring to Manu, the king of Atlantis calls him "King of the World," one of the epithets that Judeo-Christians assign to the fallen angel Satan or Sataniel. In particular use of the title "King of the World" for Manu refers to his manifestation as king of the underworld, getting even closer to the role of Satan as lord of the netherworld.

HISTORIES OF THE ASSYRIANS

During the military campaign to the east the Pelasgians crossed Assyria on the northerly path of the Tigris. Their transit through the region was

---

*Lilin, who sucks the blood of children, is also derived from Lilith. According to tradition if a child smiles in his sleep during the night of the Jewish Sabbath, it is said that he is playing with Lilith: to rescue him, his nose is rubbed three times and the auspicious sentence "Adam, Eve, Lilith out!" is said. Slips with this same auspicious sentence are hung in the room and house of a pregnant woman.

described in the *Histories* by Ctesias of Cnidus,* Greek historian of the the fifth century BCE.

The Assyrians claimed that their God and their main oracle were of Egyptian derivation when such worship in Egypt was not yet corrupted.[25] These are the years immediately following the Pelasgian colonization of Egypt under Menes-Osiris. This deity, unique and incomprehensible, was known as Diu, or Dia, which recalls the Pelasgian one God (Latin: *Deus, Deo*).

Some traditions bring us back to an Assyrian empire that preceded the historical one beginning with the Amorite Shamshi-Adad I in 1813 BCE, which, according to *Epitome* by Justinus, would have preceded all the empires of the world. Castor wrote in *Istorie degli Assiri* (Assyrian Histories) that Belus, father of Menes, was one of the Titans, as were Hercules and Bacchus, and added that Ogygi (hence the name of the island Ogygia) was king of these Titans. According to him after Belo comes the Pelasgian Nino, which begins the history of the Assyrian kings. Also from Nino and Queen Semiramis begins the genealogy of the Assyrian kings Cefalione Gergizio, Abidenus, Herodotus, Ctesias Cnidus, Diodorus Siculus, and Syncellus. Alexander Polyhistor, narrating events that were chronologically close to each other, used to quote verses of the Sibyl and wrote of how "men, wanting to rise to heaven, were punished for their audacity: they, who spoke the same language in the beginning, suddenly spoke different languages and dispersed throughout the earth at the time of Prometheus and Titan."

Abidenus repeated the same stories, correctly setting them to the time of the Titans' war. Dorotheus of Sidon stated that Babylon was founded by Belo Tyrrhenus. The first Assyrian empire would expand under the guidance of Semiramis, Pul, and his son Sardanapalus (Shardan-Pul

---

*Physician to the Persian court, Ctesias cared for a wound suffered by King Artaxerxes II in the battle of Cunassa, gained his trust, and provided diplomatic functions between the Persians and the Greeks in 399–398 BCE. Ctesias of Cnidus tells of expeditions to Assyria by Perseus, Bacchus, and Hercules (identified with each other), to which Apollodorus adds credibility by saying that royal Assyrians descend from the Pelasgians, putting Cinyras, first king of the country, as a son of Sandoco Astinoo, son of Phaethon (= Horus). Greek tradition affirms the entry of Bacchus in India by Assyria and confirms the theogony of the Pelasgians—scattered in these countries with all its moral and cosmological beliefs—and the Pelasgian genealogy implanted there.

equals Sardan, son of Pul). Shardan was the son of Hercules, the "saint" of the Shardanas, so Pul is Hercules and Semiramis is the biblical Dinah, daughter of Danaus, later masculinized in Dan. This Shardan must not be confused with the historical Sardanapalus, who was defeated by the Medes and let his people be subjugated.

The existence of two Sardanapaluses is confirmed by the prophet Amos, who lived ten or twenty years after a certain King Pul, who would speak to Israel, predicting how God "would provoke the Assyrian people for its ruin." If he were referring to Pul as the father of the historical Shardan-Pul, his prophecy would be senseless because, twenty years after the historical Pul, the Assyrian empire had already submitted to the Medes.

ZOROASTER AND MITHRA

In Herodotus we read that King Xerxes argued the common origin of Argives (Argo is notoriously considered a Pelasgian foundation by Greek tradition) and Persians by tracing back to a Pelasgian man named Perses,[26] whom Aeschylus[27] also appoints as ancestor of the Persians.

Their neighbor Armenia was said to be a colony run by a friend of Jason of Thessaly, who had originated among the Albans of Italy, passing by the Asiatic coasts at the time of Hercules and therefore during the campaign of Osiris.[28] All of these kingdoms or empires, Assyrian, Persian, Mede, Bactrian, and Parthian, were influenced by the doctrines of Zoroaster, who was called Chaldean, Assyrian, Medean, Persian, Indian, or Bactrian by reason of his travels through these countries. Such doctrines were based on the ancient Pelasgian doctrine of the one God, infinite and incomprehensible. Here we read:

> God is the first of what is imperishable, everlasting, non-generated; similar to him alone, the giver of all goods. He does not expect gifts and offerings, and he is great; very prudent; father of reason, and a doctor of himself; perfect in nature; wise; a unique factor of sacred nature.

These doctrines also added that even the wise men received a cult, since they are, after God, the most worthy of veneration.[29]

Volney asserted that Zoroaster established the religious system of most ancient Egyptians among the Medes and Bactrians. Among the Persians we find recollection of how they should worship fire, keeping the *eternal fire* as the Sabines did, followed by the Romans who kept the *fire of Vesta.*

One of the major deities of Zoroastrianism is Mithra, whom the ancient texts identify with Orion.* In the iconography we commonly find the image or sculpture of the astral Mithras in the act of killing his material part in order to ascend to the divine. His material part is represented by a heavenly bull whose tail is replaced by a spike, which symbolizes that his death is actually a rebirth (plate 36). Osiris was also represented by a bull, and one of his symbols was the spike. Osiris was dismembered by Seth (often symbolized by a scorpion) and then ascended into the region of Orion. In the scene of Mithras, a scorpion is hooked to the bull's genitals. The very word "scorpion" derives from the Greek *skorpizo* = "to disperse, to dismember." The same motif recurs in the Jewish Kabbalah, where the soul of the first man, Adam Kadmon, is dismembered in the souls of all men. At the foot of Mithras is the celestial dog, or the constellation of Canis Major, whose main star is Sirius. It is important to compare the image of Mithras with Theseus and the Minotaur, son of Osiris/Minos (plate 37).

When Emperor Aurelian made the cult of Mithras the state religion of the Roman empire in 275 CE many followers, disillusioned by the loss of elitism, merged with Gnostic Christianity (and perhaps with those Sabines of Harran we mentioned). Certainly some elements of Christianity were imported from Mithraism: Mithras was connected to the sun with his birth, venerated with the feast of the Sol Invictus on December 25, when the days begin to lengthen (in fact, at the time the solstice fell on the twenty-fifth, not twenty-first), and he was known as "lord of the caves," taking us back again to Christianity, with Christ born in a cave.

---

*A connection was suggested between Mithra and Melchizedek by author Jason Cooper in *Mithras* (York Beach, Maine: Red Wheel/Weiser, 1996).

THE MYSTERY RELIGION

Religions bore the mark of a hidden knowledge that could be delivered only to those who had proved worthy by passing tests. This knowledge, known by the terms *mysteries, Heka,* or *magic,* was concerned with the origin of man and nature, his relationship with extra-sensory worlds, and the laws of the physical world. Accompanied by balanced and right conduct (the Maat), it was the essential prerogative to come to eternal life. At its beginning the mystery religion brought the worship of one God, free from all dogma. It believed architecture was a means to join the gods, so architects of the past such as Thoth in the mists of time, Imhotep during the third, and Senmut during the eighteenth Egyptian dynasties were worshipped as gods themselves.

Current Christianity contemplates the Maat, the right behavior, disregarding the Heka, the "magic," but it was not always so. The Christian community of Alexandria was born after the arrival of Mark the Evangelist in 64 CE, absorbing and converting groups of Essenes who fled to Egypt after the destruction of Qumran by the Roman general Titus (68 CE). These Christians, later condemned as "heretical Gnostics," taught the mysteries and were opposed to the institutions of the official church. In one of their codes, known as the Apocalypse of Peter, we read: "And there are others also outside of us who call themselves bishops and also deacons, as if they had received this charge from God. These people are dry canals. They make profit in my name. They praise the men who spread the lie." The Gnostics were already being defamed by Orthodox Christians at the end of the second century CE, when at the same time in Alexandria they enjoyed a fairly quiet existence. With the edict of Theodosius and the closure of pagan temples (391 BCE), the Orthodox archbishops, at the height of their power, burned countless Gnostic books under the eyes of judges.

The same process of divination was adopted by the prophet of the mystery religion, Osiris of the Egyptians or Dionysus of the Greeks. The figure of the prophet is fused with the figure of his son in a cycle that can be summarized as follows: (1) death of the prophet and his ascension as a star; (2) conception of the son, new incarnation of the prophet by a copulation with the cadaver; (3) the son is in fact the prophet resurrected and after his death he resumes his original appearance to start a new cycle. This concept was transferred to Egypt in the person of the pharaoh, who was identified with Horus, the son, in life, and with Osiris, the father, after his death.

In time, various cultures took distance from this act of "divine necrophilia," transforming it into an immaculate conception away from any idea of physical contact. The deceased parent disappeared from history while the other was conceived by magical or divine intervention. Thus, the mother became a virgin, all the more by virtue of a singular astronomical coincidence: "Three wise men appeared in the East and for the first time it was seen behind them the morning star: it shone on the Leo [of David]. The light left the Virgin and moved to the Leo, heralding a new era."

This story, which is certainly very familiar, narrates the birth of Horus. The brackets containing "of David" were added by us purposely, to underline the link with the Gospel story. We are in 10,500 BCE, a few minutes before the equinoctial dawn, and the three stars of Orion's belt have just risen to the east: they are the "three wise men" as was meant in European folklore until the Middle Ages.[30] In 10,500 BCE Sirius, the "morning star," so called because its rising behind Orion announced the dawn, became visible *for the first time*. The sun, which for two thousand years had risen in the equinox of Virgo, had moved and now bridged the Virgin and the Lion, marking the beginning of the new Zodiac era.

Over centuries the ritual moment of observation passed from sunrise to sunset and the same scenario was visible from Alexandria, Egypt, just after that moment on December 25 around the year zero. Not by chance, here in Alexandria between 40 and 80 CE the Gospel of Matthew was written, the only telling of the story of Jesus that speaks of the Magi, of a star in the East, and of the escape of the holy family into Egypt.[31]

The proof of transformation of the act of necrophilia into the immaculate conception emerges from the story of King Arthur[32] (Ambrosius Aurelianus, nephew of Constantine III). Although it recounts the English events of the fifth century when Britain, abandoned by Rome, had to face alone the invasions of Saxons, Angles, and Jutes, it contains all the events related to the "great civilizer."

Like Osiris, Arthur sleeps with his sister, Morgause, conceiving Mordred, namely "Horus the avenger." As was the case in the birth of Moses or Jesus, the birth of Mordred is predicted by Merlin as an untoward event: "you have sinned with your sister, creating a son who will destroy you and all the knights of your realm." As with the pharaoh and King Herod, a death edict was issued by King Arthur against neonates. The babies were sent on a ship and delivered to the fury of the sea. The boat was pushed violently against some rocks and sank, and all the children died except Mordred, who was dragged by the waves to the beach. Like Moses, Osiris, or Sargon, he was rescued from the water and picked up by a good man who reared him like a son. Mordred joined the Knights of the Round Table but, like Judas, betrayed Arthur, accomplishing his vengeance.* At his death, the body of Arthur was brought to the island of Avalon, or Atalon, where the Celts thought the axis of the world passed. (In Breton Avalon means "apple orchard." Curious that in Basque, the heir language of the Pelasgian, the word "pelatch" means apple.) According to the legend King Arthur will return—like Osiris, Quetzalcòatl, and Christ—on the day of the apocalypse.

Like Horus, Hercules, and Melchizedek, King Arthur was also conceived when one of the parents (the duke of Cornwall) was already dead. Merlin intervened, giving the appearance of the duke to the son of Constantine III, Uther Pendragon. While the duke is dead Uther deceives Igraine, the mother of Arthur, and lies with her, conceiving the child. Curiously, there is a second version of the story in which Igraine

---

*It's curious that here the traitor is also the son-avenger. Unlike the Egyptian myth, the revenge strikes on the father and not on the uncle. In many versions of the story, like the Icelandic *Amlodi,* the uncle becomes the adoptive father. This is an intermediate step between revenge against uncle and revenge against father, while the last step is the required insertion of the betrayal.

conceives Arthur by immaculate conception magically induced by Merlin. So the transition from the act of necrophilia to immaculate conception is evident.

The Book of the Dead describes Osiris as a great "initiator" of ancient humanity who gave men writing and the wheel and taught them how to regulate water flow through sluice gates, to transplant the vine, to weed the wheat, to understand the motion of celestial bodies. In return for all this, the great benefactor was torn to pieces. His pieces were found and collected and sprouted wheat plants and vines. These seedlings were planted and took root. Eating that bread and drinking that wine the followers of Osiris accomplished a ritual of communion *ante litteram* (ahead of their time). In the Book of the Dead we read, "I have made for you three consecrated breads from white grain, and wine from red grapes. This is the bread and this is the wine of your communion. Taking communion with such heavenly food, you can get eternal life."[33]

In another part, it refers to the rite of baptism: "I, too, was baptized in the same waters in which Osiris, in ancient times, had purified."[34] Moreover, it is commonly accepted that the Jews took the sacrament of baptism from the Egyptian tradition. Like Jesus, before his death Osiris promised he would return to the Earth:

When the tower will be erected again [the Cheops Pyramid shafts aligned to the stars] and the earth, finally purified, will be covered of flowers and spring fruits, then I will reappear. Master of Life, and great will be my glory at the core of the wonderful harmony on this day of rebirth.[35]

The granite structure incorporated into the great Pyramid of Cheops and known as Zed is a tower, or a portion thereof, which includes at least the King's Chamber and the above discharge rooms. From the King's Chamber two square shafts twenty centimeters per side come out horizontally. The covering of the tower by means of the limestone pyramid was carried out in the twenty-fifth century BCE, carefully extending the two shafts with an inclined path, achieving the perfect alignment with the pole star Alpha Draconis (King's Chamber, north wall) and Al Nitak of Orion (King's Chamber, south wall): Osiris was reborn!

Mario Pincherle believed that Osiris and Sargon were the same person—a hypothesis we do not endorse—and pointed out the strong similarity between their lives. Osiris as Sargon was rescued from the waters: he was urged by deception to lie in a stone coffin, where he was cloistered and thrown into the river, but the coffin floated. Isis sailed on a "boat of rushes sealed with bitumen" and found him. In chapter 3 of *La Grande Piramide e Lo Zed* (The Great Pyramid and the Zed), Pincherle writes:

> In ancient invocations, God Osiris is also called Onnophris: "O God Onnophris, o eternally good, return to your house." Sargon also was invoked with the words "On Sarrukin!" Both characters were good kings beloved by their subjects, both bestowed great benefits to their subjects in the form of creations, inventions and discoveries. Both died of a violent death. In both their stories, great importance acquires an empty coffer, a "cenotaph." In the symbolism of the two kings, corn and vine spilled out of this tomb. Both have been blown to pieces. Both are represented as king of the two powers, and this double power is symbolized by the scepter or shepherds' rod and by the peasants' scourge or whip. Another symbol they have in common is two wings on either side of their heads. These wings represent truth and wisdom. They are the symbol of the Hebrew cherub, the Akkadian karabu, and the Christian cherub, spirit of wisdom and truth.

Clearly the Akkadians, as did the Celts with Arthur 4,000 years later, associated their king with a stereotyped story whose sole purpose was to ennoble and deify him.

A biblical character whose adventures are connected to Sargon is certainly Moses, saved by the waters on a basket of reeds and bitumen. The Pharisee historian Josephus Flavius (first century CE) claimed that the birth of Moses had been predicted by an Egyptian "sacred scribe," a person "with a remarkable ability to accurately predict the future," who had informed the pharaoh that among the Israelites was about to arrive:

a man who, when he became an adult, would overshadow the sovereignty of Egyptians and who would surpass all men in virtue, by acquiring the eternal fame. Alarmed, the king, on the advice of the sages, ordered that all the male children of the Israelites were thrown into the river and left to die.

On hearing this edict a certain Amram (the future father of Moses) fell into a "painful perplexity," because "his wife was then expecting a child." But, as Josephus continues, God appeared to him in a dream and comforted him with the news that:

> this child, whose birth has filled the Egyptians of such fear as to urge them to condemn to death all the Israelite progeny, will escape from those who try to kill him and, provided with prodigious wisdom, will acquit the Jewish race from slavery in Egypt, and will be remembered for the duration of the universe, not only by Jews but also by other nations.

History repeated 1,300 years later when King Herod feared the prophecy of the prophet Micah on the advent of a leader for Israel:

> But you, Bethlehem Ephrathah, though you are small among the clans of Judah, out of you will come for me one who will be ruler over Israel, whose origins are from of old, from ancient times.[36]

Then Herod issued a decree ordering that all children aged two years and younger in the area of Bethlehem were to be killed; Joseph the carpenter was warned in a dream by an angel and fled to Egypt with Mary and Jesus. Moses was brought into the royal family and educated, according to the Bible, "in all the wisdom of the Egyptians" and, as successor to the throne, was initiated into the mysteries.

The mystery religion in Egypt experienced a collapse at the end of the ancient kingdom, the age of the pyramids, to reappear almost a thousand years later, re-imported by the Hyksos in 1750 BCE. The Sea Peoples had spread around the Mediterranean with their workers of freemasons, blacksmiths, and potters, expert in the so-called Mycenaean style. In the previous one thousand years Egypt had worshipped multitudes of deities and architecture but had not produced any appreciable monument. During the four hundred years when the Hyksos and the Habirus were slaves in Egypt, things get reversed: as a result there appeared great architects such as Senmut, and even Moses was compared to Thoth (Artapanos), the "first" between architects. Works like the obelisks of Thutmose I (1504–1492 BCE) and of Hatshepsut (1473–1458 BCE) at Karnak appeared, as well as the colossal statue of Ramesses II (1278–1213 BCE) at the mortuary temple in the Theban region, respectively weighing 143, 320, and 1,000 tons. They say that the Hyksos/Shasu possessed an instrument capable of cutting the stone without direct contact, without abrasion: the Shamir.* Kept in a box of lead, its secret was kept for years inside the hollow columns of Boaz and Jachin in the temple of King Solomon.

When the Habirus came together with the Hyksos and Shasu in the country of the pharaohs they settled in a land that was given to Abraham by Pharaoh Narmer centuries earlier during his visit to Egypt, as reported in many traditions as well as in Genesis.

Moses, just like Sargon and Osiris, was saved from the waters in a basket made of "reeds and bitumen" and rescued by the daughter of the pharaoh. From childhood he was initiated into the Heka, and the Bible itself tells us "he can speak well," although several passages emphasize his stammer. The Heka never disappeared from Judaism and found its highest expression in the Kabbalistic schools, Christianized by Pico della Mirandola and transplanted in modern Freemasonry. There are rumors of an officially sanctioned collaboration between the Freemasons and the Universal Israelite Alliance at the Congress of Lausanne in 1875. The Knights Templar embedded themselves in the same Masonic tree when their order was suppressed by Philip the Fair and Pope Clement V in 1307: the arrest warrant was not implemented in Scotland, where the pre-Masonic Benedictine Lodge of Kilwinning accepted the escaped knights with the consent of King Robert the Bruce.

---

*Similarities may be found in the Jewish Mishnah, the first major written version of Jewish oral traditions, called the "Oral Torah," and in the Masonic Old Ritual, which had no written record.

In 1460 the ruler of Florence, Cosimo de Medici, received from a monk a nearly complete collection of Hermetic texts (which are considered sacred books written by Thoth himself). They were written in Greek and found in Macedonia. Cosimo ordered the Florentine scholar Marsilio Ficino to set aside the translation of the Platonic texts (which had been accepted by scholars from all over Europe for 700 years) to devote himself to the Hermetic texts.

The first of these was translated: its title is *Poimandres*. Here Thoth-Hermes has an ecstatic vision of light that fills the space. Part of this space is transformed into a spiraling abyss of darkness that in turn transforms itself into a watery substance, with fire and smoke, from which "an indescribable echo of wailing" is heard. Finally, from the light comes "a sacred Word that places itself on the liquid substance and it seems to be the voice of light." A voice proclaims, "I am that light, the mind, the first God who existed before the watery substance that emerges from the darkness; and the Word which comes from the light is the Son of God" (as seen in *Poimandres*, 6).

Moses, who wrote Genesis, like Thoth had seen "a darkness at the mouth of the abyss and the spirit of God in meditation on the waters." He also claimed that creation was thanks to the powerful Word of God. Ficino noted other similarities with Genesis: for example, man is made in the image of God. Thoth, like Moses, is the one that "gives the laws," and, in the Libellus I, the author uses almost the same words as Moses when he describes a commandment given by God to humanity: the need to multiply.

In an essay by Rene Guenon, *The Reign of Quantity and the Signs of the Times* (1945), she discusses a possible control of the Templars over the pressing of coins:

The ancient coins are literally covered with traditional symbols, often chosen from among those that carry some particularly profound meaning; thus for instance it has been observed that among the Celts the symbols figured on the coins can only be explained if they are related to the doctrinal knowledge that belonged to the Druids alone, which implies a direct intervention of the Druids in the monetary domain. There is not the least doubt that the truth in this matter is the same for the other peoples of antiquity as for the Celts, of course after taking account of the modalities peculiar to their respective traditional organizations. . . . The control of money by the spiritual authority . . . is by no means exclusively confined to antiquity, for . . . there is much to indicate that it must have been perpetuated until toward the end of the Middle Ages, that is, for as long as the Western world had a traditional civilization. It is impossible to explain in any other way the fact that certain sovereigns were accused at this time of having "altered coins"; since their contemporaries regarded this as a crime on their part, it must be concluded that the sovereigns did not have the free disposal of the imprint of the coinage, and that, in changing it on their own initiative, they overstepped the recognized rights of the temporal power.

    . . . The case of Philip the Fair is specially referred to, suggest[ing] that there may be a fairly close connection between the destruction of the Order of Templars and the alteration of the coinage, something easily understood if it is recognized as at least very plausible that this Order then had the function, among others, of exercising spiritual control in this field; the matter need not be pursued further here, but it may be recalled that the beginning of the modern deviation properly so called has been assigned precisely to this moment. . . . An element of another order must therefore have been involved, and it must have been of a superior order, for unless that had been the case the alteration could not have assumed a character so exceptionally serious as to end in compromising the very stability of the royal power; but the royal power by acting in this way usurped the prerogatives of the spiritual authority, which is without any doubt the one authentic source of all legitimacy.

Those with malice claim control of paper money is today one of the goals achieved by the Universal Israelite Alliance that, through its members, controls the U.S. Federal Reserve, the European Central Bank, and the Bank for International Settlements in Basel.

References to the mystery tradition traceable in both the sacred scriptures and the life of Jesus (Holy Communion, promise of a second coming, immaculate conception, and walking on water*) connect to the existence of a coven of wisemen: the conservatives of the Heka, which the Indians call Seven Sages. The Jewish community called them the Order of Melchizedek, and St. Paul talked about it in relation to Jesus in Hebrews 5:8–10:

> Son though he was, he learnt obedience, Son though he was, through his sufferings; when he had been perfected, he became for all who obey him the source of eternal salvation and was acclaimed by God with the title of high priest of the order of Melchizedek.

Jesus at the Last Supper broke bread and poured wine "in the manner of Melchizedek" (Genesis 14:18). In Matthew 22:41–45, Jesus quoted Psalm 109, one of the very few Old Testament passages that speak of Melchizedek, and gives its interpretation of the fundamental qualities that the Messiah should have.

Some have suggested a link between the Order of Melchizedek and the sect of the Nazarene Essenes (whose name is based in N-Asar, literally "follower of the Asar"), and equated the moon god Asar with Melchizedek, so Jesus would be a Nazarene, with no connection to a certain Nazareth that in his period probably did not even exist. Among the ceremonies of initiation of the Nazarenes it is worth highlighting the transformation of water (the common man) into wine (the member of the sect). The same

---

*It is told that when Viracocha/Osiris came to Cacha he reached the nearest coast and, clutching his cloak, went out in the middle of the waves without leaving any trace. And yet "Viracocha, when he reached the District of Puerto Veii, was joined by his followers who then took to the sea with the same ease with which they walked on the Earth. . . . Everywhere he went, he healed the sick and gave back sight to the blind" (Juan de Batanzos, "Suma y narracion de los Incas," in *South American Mythology,* by Harold Osborne (London: Paul Hamlyn, 1968).

ritual was performed by Jesus at the wedding of Canaan and is known in the Christian tradition as the first miracle. The common people were also indicated by the Nazarenes with the unfortunate term of "dead," to distinguish them from their brothers, the "alive," so that the ritual became a kind of resurrection, like that of Lazarus.[37] St. Clement of Alexandria refers to a second gospel by Mark, addressed to the followers of the mysteries:

> Mark came over to Alexandria, bringing both his own notes and those of Peter, from which he transferred to his former books (the canonical Gospel) the things suitable to whatever makes for progress toward knowledge (divine knowledge). Thus he composed a more spiritual Gospel for the use of those who were being perfected. . . . He left his composition to the church in Alexandria, where it even yet is most carefully guarded, being read only to those who are being initiated into the great mysteries.[38]

In *The Essene Origins of Christianity* Professor Edmond Bordeaux notes, "The Hebrew form for Nazareth is NZRT, which is recent and it was written as Nazrat or Nazeret. . . . The Greek form 'Iesous' or 'Nazoraios' derives from the aramaic Nazorai." In *Manuel d'Histoire Ancienne du Christianisme* Charles Guignebert, professor of the history of Christianity at the Sorbonne University in Paris, notes, "The small town Nazareth, where gullible pilgrims can visit the workshop of Joseph, was identified as the city of Christ only in the Middle Ages." In *Breve storia delle religioni* [Short History of Religions] Ambrogio Donini, academician of Harvard University, specializing in Hebrew and Syriac, notes, "In the Gospels we don't read the phrase 'Jesus of Nazareth,' but only 'Jesus the Nazarite,' sometimes written also 'Nazoreno' or 'Nazarene.' . . . Even striving to find its etymology, 'Nazareth' is derived from these appellations and not vice versa." In the Gospel of Philip (Gnostic text from the second century CE) it is written, "The apostles who were before us have called him so: Jesus Nazarene said the Christ . . . 'Nazara' is the 'Truth.' Therefore, 'Nazarene' is 'The one of the truth.'"

Morton Smith, professor of history at Columbia University, discovered fragments of the text of the second gospel in 1958 in the Great Lavra of St. Sabbas the Sanctified, a Greek monastery about twelve miles from Jerusalem. The main fragment, which Smith would place in the middle of the passage of the canonical Gospel of Mark (10:46), reads as follows:

And they come into Bethany. And a certain woman whose brother had died was there. And, coming, she prostrated herself before Jesus and says to him, "Son of David, have mercy on me." But the disciples rebuked her. And Jesus, being angered, went off with her into the garden where the tomb was and immediately heard a loud cry coming from the grave. As he approached, Jesus rolled away the stone from the entrance of the tomb. Straightway entering in where the youth was, he stretched forth his hand and raised him, seizing his hand. But the youth, looking upon him, loved him and began to beseech him that he might be with him. And going out of the tomb they came into the house of the youth, for he was rich. And after six days Jesus told him what to do and in the evening the youth comes to him, wearing a linen cloth over his naked body. And he remained with him that night, for Jesus taught him the mystery of the Kingdom of God.

According to the Masonic initiation during the ceremony of the Third Degree the candidate wearing a linen cloth has to stand up after his symbolic death. Originally the coat of the Knights Templar, which underwent a similar ritual, also was of white linen. In the Canonical gospels there are possible references to rituals of initiation into the mysteries. In the garden of Gethsemane, where Jesus is about to be arrested by the Roman soldiers, we observe the same scene:

A young man followed him with nothing on but a linen cloth. They caught hold of him, but he left the cloth in their hands and ran away naked.[39]

ALEXANDER AND THE OTHERS

Olympia of Epirus was the mother of Alexander the Great, initiated into the mysteries in the temple of Zeus at Dodona. In the works of Plutarch we read about the dream of the princess's wedding night with Philip II of Macedonia: in the dream world the lightning of Zeus penetrated her, conceiving Alexander. Other legends tell of Philip not in her bed, fearful of the snakes with which Olympia used to sleep. Instead, it was Zeus who took advantage of the situation, turning into a snake and crawling under the covers to fertilize the queen.

Olympia descended from Achilles and, thinking about her, I seem to hear the words of Thetis, mother of the hero, who, taking leave for the Trojan War, is told: "If you stay in Larissa, you will find peace. You will find a wonderful woman, and you will have sons and daughters who will have children. And they'll all love you and remember your name. But when your children are dead, and their children after them, your name will be forgotten. . . . If you go to Troy, glory will be yours. They will write stories about your victories in thousands of years! And the world will remember your name. But if you go to Troy, you will never come back . . . for your glory walks hand-in-hand with your doom. And I shall never see you again."[40] These words are likely to be the same said to Alexander by Olympia in the spring of 334 BCE, while his gaze was lost in the void beyond the strait of the Dardanelles. His name would live forever, but the death of the body would have reached him in a few years.

Alexander offered sacrifices on the tomb of Achilles at Troy and fought and won at Granicus, Miletus, and Halicarnassus, at Issus, Tyre, and Gaza. At the end of 332 BCE he entered Egypt, where the satrap of Memphis spontaneously gave him the region and the priests received him as a liberator. At the beginning of 331 BCE the Macedonian king, become pharaoh, founded Alexandria near the fishing village of Rhakotis. With a group of friends he traveled six hundred kilometers of desert toward Siwa, the oracle linked to Dodona by the myth of the doves. At the foot of the mountain where the temple stood the chief priests and hierophants greeted Alexander with cries of "son of God, son of God." For centuries after his death, his body, mummified and wrapped in a gold coffin, was revered in the city of Alexandria. During the early days of Christianity, the body was transferred to a glass coffin and crowds of admirers filed past the tomb during the celebrations of his birth (September) and death (June), to celebrate the resurrection of the god in the form of Dionysus.[41] The Koran calls him Iskander Dul El Qarnein, "The Two-Horned One," like Ammon the ram god.

In a campaign that lasted ten years (from 334 to 324 BCE), Alexander conquered the East, beyond the Indus up to the Beas River. He spent the last months of his life in Babylon, where he received the homage of the Greek world, as well as the Italics (Bruzians, Lucanians, Etruscans), Iberians, Romans, and Carthaginians.[42] A red thread connects these ancient conquerors—Alexander, Osiris, and Sargon—who aimed to gather the entire planet under their own monarchy, and the same thread connects them to all "spiritual" conquerors like Moses and Jesus. As Alexander began preparations for a second campaign to the west, at his command was the Greek explorer Pytheas, who had sailed from Marseille around 330 BCE to explore the western regions, ending up in Great Britain, perhaps following once again the route of Sargon. In *I Mandei* Mario Pincherle says:

> Once united this vast territory [Mesopotamia], the ancient chronicles report that he [Sargon] began a series of extraordinary expeditions by land and sea, bringing with him the seeds of the first great civilization of the earth and spreading them through a very wide area that stretched from Syria to Lebanon, from Turkey to the Black Sea and to the Caspian Sea and, within the Mediterranean, from Cyprus to Crete, from Palestine to Egypt, at the mouth of the Nile, and then along the course of the fourth largest river, the Indus, coming to the peninsula of Malacca and the islands of Moluccas. Perhaps the most famous of his many trips mentioned in the chronicles is the one Sargon made throughout the Mediterranean with the flagship of its fleet beyond Gibraltar and coming to England. With such expeditions that seem almost incredible for an age so distant from our time, Sargon of Acadia joined in a single territory, ruled by him, the Persian Gulf to the Mediterranean, along an axis of two thousand kilome-

ters. Therefore it is no wonder if, towards the end of his fifty-six years of happy reign, he was defined by the singers of his glory: "the sea serpent that has traveled the four regions of the world," which has moved up "to the four corners of the earth," "the king winding on the ocean, pushed by the mainstream."

The imagination of the poets has been stimulated by the grandeur of his exploits and the immensity of his conquests. When, a few centuries later, the famous Epic of Gilgamesh was written, the hero in this figure was overshadowed by the image of Sargon.* Even Homer, in narrating the adventures of Ulysses, must have received and passed on the millenary echoes, not yet entirely disappeared, of the legend of the Akkadian king.[43]

The voyage of Pytheas, as he described in the book *On the Ocean*, may be summarized as follows: Leaving Marseilles, he skirted France and Spain and passed through the Straits of Gibraltar, avoiding the watchful eye of Carthage. He advanced to the Atlantic, and once he arrived in Great Britain, he circumnavigated it, gathering information on the mysterious island of Thule. The great misunderstanding that has risen from the voyage of Pytheas is the correlation of the island of Thule with Hyperborea because of the Nordic features that Pliny assigned to this land in his *Naturalis Historia*.

Placed somewhere in northern Europe, Thule has been the subject of much debate. Until some time ago, it was believed the island in question was one and the same as Iceland or Greenland, but more recently it was thought to be the archipelago of Orkney or Shetland. We believe it is the legendary Hy-Brasil, which, as some Gaelic legends tell, emerges every seven years west of Ireland. It appears in a number of portolan charts from the fourteenth and fifteenth centuries and it is almost certain that it is part of the recently submerged Porcupine Bank, which corresponds with the size and position.

---

*Just like Sargon, Gilgamesh is a king and the son of a priestess, Ninsun.

Pytheas was the first person of the classical era to describe the midnight sun, the aurora borealis, and polar ice. But Alexander did not have time to carry out his project since he died at only thirty-three years (the same age as Jesus) in 324 BCE, struck by malaria.

An attempt to revive the feats of Osiris was made at the other end of the world. Jayavarman II in 802 CE began the restoration of the temples of Angkor: his relationship with the former ruling dynasty through the female line is still doubtful, while the inscriptions have him as "a descendant of a perfectly pure race,"[44] an epithet that in Egypt was assigned to the Followers of Horus. As Osiris in Egypt he would become king to "save his people."[45] He gathered around him an oligarchy of Brahmins who, according to the archaeologist Bernard Groslier, were "initiates who were descended from the Indian settlers or who had studied in India."[46] These initiates:

> kept possession of the sacred books, which they alone were competent to interpret, composed the inscriptions and guaranteed the accuracy of the astronomical calculations. Indeed it sometimes happened that political power passed from the hands of a too weak or youthful monarch to this veritable priestly oligarchy which acquired an almost feudal power. . . . Until its extinction the dynasty of Angkor surrounded itself with these Brahmins.[47]

The astronomer-priests of Heliopolis in Egypt held the same power: they initiated monarchs, held secular power when appropriate, composed inscriptions, and watched the stars. As in Heliopolis, where the symbol of royalty was the phallic simulacrum of Benben, in Angkor there was the phallic lingam, received by Jayavarman II at the hands of a Brahmin on a sacred mountain.[48] This episode was meant to revive the original reception of the pillar on the part of Shiva, made possible thanks to the aid of a Brahmin. We have already seen the link between the Jewish Tables of the Law and the Benben, a connection that here is reinforced by the presence of a sacred mountain, Sinai for Moses and the heights of Kulen for the Khmer monarch.

So it is time to turn the DeLorean flux capacitor to the present, leaving the good rabbi to take home his records. He found out that the salient features of his religion and monotheism are ancient, much older than he could ever imagine. If his God was already loved indeed in his essential features 15,000 years ago, then his faith strengthens: if Yahweh belongs to the dawn of time, then he is really the only true God. But this is just the thought of a rabbi.

Meanwhile, we have discovered that a fundamental feature of our culture has traveled a long way, from Atlantis to the third millennium.

Saint Yves D'Alveydre said the white race originated on the lost continent. Perhaps they were the Cro-Magnon, with light hair and blue eyes . . . were the others, the Combe-Capelle in the Europe of the Amazons, dark-skinned indigenous?

THE END OF
THE DIALOGUE

Men are haunted by the vastness of eternity. And so we ask ourselves: will our actions echo across the centuries? Will strangers hear our names long after we are gone, and wonder who we were, how bravely we fought, how fiercely we loved?

ODYSSEUS (FROM THE 2004 MOVIE *TROY*)

Among thousands of comrades and tens of thousands of enemies, only one, only you, and you alone, obscured the vision of my dream.

GRIFFITH, *BERSERK* (GRAPHIC NOVEL BY KENTARO MIURA)

Those who cannot remember the past are condemned to repeat it.

GEORGE SANTAYANA

We have now reached the point where it is time to say good-bye, unpack the luggage, and get back to our ordinary lives. But we are now richer than before with all we have gained along this journey—memories, myriad photos, and notes to leaf through.

It's been five years since we started our research, and while today it still seems far from complete we have done our best to compress the knowledge we acquired into this book. The story of Atlantis and its inhabitants may appear surreal, or pure fantasy, but it is based on material evidence and written documents whose authenticity has been proven.

Academic society has difficulty accepting our conclusions, but not because they desire to cover up the information. It is due instead to their being convinced, as so many teachers are, that their *students* cannot possibly teach them anything new. These scholars' minds are closed, and they feel the need to convince their sponsors that no one but the elite members of their group has the right to explore new ideas. The "outsiders" are then accused of being meddlers, mythomans, or incompetents, with any suggestion they make being marked as ridiculous. Any scholar who would dare to give credit to an outsider will receive taunts from his colleagues and eventually find that his publishing will be blocked.

THE END OF ATLANTIS

Is it really so unthinkable that a modern-type society could have emerged and flourished in ancient times, but disappeared abruptly in the middle of nowhere? However indirectly, a mathematical theorem does prove this possibility. It is called the "zero-resetting of complex systems": the more that a system is complex and advanced (civilizations included), the less strong it becomes, turning it into a candidate for "zero-resetting," or a return to its primitive state, if even only one of its components is missing.

Imagine what could happen to Western civilization if oil disappeared suddenly. Trucks, ships, trains, tractors, power plants—everything would be instantly paralyzed. All of a sudden a terrible famine would hit industrialized populations; with hungry and desperate crowds forced to go plundering, society would disintegrate, and in a short amount of time the population would be decimated by starvation and epidemics.

Probably the present civilization would not be totally destroyed, and after a long "Middle Ages" period it would eventually start again from where it was 50 or 100 years before. This would be possible only because in our society there are people who still remember our grandparents' way of living, how they used to yoke up their oxen and horses, cultivate fields, illuminate their houses, bake bread, and so on.

But we should rather ask ourselves what would happen if all sources of energy were to disappear in a hundred years, when our grandchildren have become overly dependent on technology, and no one can recall our grandfathers' way of life. It will almost certainly be a total collapse, with civilization forced to painstakingly start over again.

So the power paralysis would be enough to wipe out civilization, but the results are irrelevant when compared to a global catastrophe like the one that hit our planet 15,000 years ago. If such an event were to happen again today, it would extinguish most of the population, cities, and industries. Even Einstein was worried about a possible zero-reset of civilization when he stated, "I know not with what weapons World War III will be fought, but World War IV will be fought with sticks and stones."

The population of Atlantis suffered an almost total annihilation and its territory was buried by ice in a short time. The destiny of the White Island was transcribed in detail in myths ranging from those of the Fueguian people of Tierra del Fuego in southern Argentina to those of the Indian Mahābhārata, the Toba Indians of the Gran Chaco, the Norse Edda, and the Persian Avesta, telling of an earthly paradise suddenly covered by ice where the stars neither rose nor set, but drew circles in the sky. The few survivors found themselves isolated, lacking any technological potential on devastated continents inhabited by cavemen. Even though they came from an advanced civilization, within a few generations they would have inevitably lost any knowledge in science and technology.

Admiral Flavio Barbiero was the first to consider this possibility, demonstrating the scientific value and its link with climate change and mass extinctions of 13,000 BCE. Unfortunately he had to be content with the publication for general readers,[1] insofar as the majority of scholars have completely ignored him.

THE BUILDER GODS

The exiles of Atlantis must have appeared as gods in the eyes of indigenous people, who were amazed by their knowledge of the stars, building skills, agricultural and farming techniques, and all that they showed of what can be accomplished with the natural elements.

The cultural luggage of the new arrivals becomes evident in the structure of their monuments, built with the intention of lasting an eternity in order to witness the great catastrophe. Our engineers look at them speechless, amazed, and full of questions. At Sacsayhuaman the stone blocks weigh almost 360 tons; the building blocks of the Temple of the Great Sphinx at Giza and the Osirion at Abydos weigh between 200 and 300 tons; the stone blocks of the Baalbek acropolis weigh over 800 tons. How were they able to cut, dig, carry, raise, and lower these huge blocks of stone? How could they align them with the cardinal points with an average error of only around three minutes of arc?

We are talking about something that weighs as much as 800 cars, with a length of 20 meters.

Orthodox archaeology continues to insist on their having been built in recent times by decades of work by many slaves and laborers. Today it is possible to find a sufficient number of men and ropes strong enough to move the blocks, but in any case we would not be able to lift and align them so precisely, and in such a narrow space as the inside of a temple.

Unfortunately stone cannot be accurately dated, but lava, like that which erupted from the Ajusco volcano covering the pyramid of Cuicuilco from Mexico City, can be. According to geologic reports the eruption took place around 5000 BCE, so the pyramid had to be even older. Although this finding came from a qualified institution—the National Geographic Society—it was completely ignored by academic archaeologists.

AS AT THE BEGINNING OF THE CREATION

Modern man is accustomed to accepting routine with the belief that everything remains the same always and everywhere. People are often unable to imagine what extraordinary action or act of rebellion could make their lives better. And the situation is expected to worsen drastically if we ask them to imagine an event that was dated 15,000 years ago.

The apostle Peter spoke with extreme foresight about this close-mindedness as we read in his second letter:

This is now, beloved, the second epistle that I write unto you; and in both of them I stir up your sincere mind by putting you in remembrance; that ye should remember the words which were spoken before by the holy prophets, and the commandments of the Lord and Saviour through your apostles: knowing this first, that in the last days mockers shall come with mockery, walking after their own lusts, and saying: "Where is the promise of his coming? For, from the day that the fathers fell asleep, all things continue as they were from the beginning of the creation." For this they willfully forget, that there were heavens from of old, and an earth compacted out of water and amidst water, by the word of God; by which means the world that then was, being overflowed with water, perished: but the heavens that now are, and the earth, by the same word have been stored up for fire, being reserved against the day of judgment and destruction of ungodly men.[2]

Our imagination has been sedated by television and we are unable to consider any type of event that could disrupt or block the advancement of progress. On the other hand, there is no difficulty accepting the cataclysm that extinguished the dinosaurs simply because it does not concern human history. But it is the same planet we are talking about.

We know that 30,000 years ago there was a global language spoken on all continents, which would have been totally absurd with a population composed only of cavemen. In fact, it is quite obvious that a global language could not survive without continuous contact over long distances.

Language wasn't the Pelasgians' only distinguishing trait strong enough to reach our times. They also had the cult of the serpent, an animal sometimes representing the civilizers themselves. When it comes to Pelasgian ancestors it is not unusual to come across humanoid figures with the appearance of snakes, fish, or dragons. In many cultures the dragon has the appearance of a snake—its name comes from the Proto-Semitic *dagan* or *dag* (fish) + *an* (sky), "the fish of the sky." Thus, we find a connection between the fish and the snake.

According to myth Scythes, the first king of the Scythians, was a child of Hercules and Echidna, half woman, half snake goddess;

the "gods of the lake" from Tiahuanaco, Chullua, and Umantha were amphibious beings with bodies covered in scales; the same for Iohannes (Oannes), the ancient Akkadian fish-god, and for the Nommos worshipped by the Dogon. The semi-gods Kaundinya and Kambu, ancestors of the Cambodian people, conceived their children with two naga (the Khmer divine serpent) princesses. The Jewish Genesis reveals something similar in 3:13, where Eva turns to God with the words "the serpent deceived me," where the Hebrew *hshiany* (seduce, deceive) can be translated as *fructify*.[3]

Amongst the Jewish folktales collected by Mikhah Yosef Bin-Gorion in *Die Sagen der Juden,* (The Legends of the Jews) we learn that even Cain was conceived by Eva with a fallen angel, a demon-serpent named Semael. The same myth eventually appears again at a later time for Alexander the Great and Merovee (the founder of the Frankish Merovingian dynasty), whose mothers were said to have been impregnated by serpents.

The myths of the peoples mentioned here mark the beginning of the current age of the world by the appearance of the "primordial" egg, fertilized by a snake, from which hatched the whole of creation.

The cult of the serpent was also represented by the Benben and the lingam, the phallic stone columns that are still sanctified today by the Hindu religion. Egg, seed, and phallus symbolized a rebirth triggered by the fall of a celestial body, probably referring to the meteorite, a fireball of 200 billion tons that crashed off the coast of what today is Florida, which caused displacement of the geographic poles.

The snake played a key role in the ancestral religion practiced by the Pelasgians, a monotheism inherited by the Hyksos, and through the Hyksos it passed to Pharaoh Akhenaten and the Jewish people, for whom the serpent was sacred—during the Exodus Moses, instructed by God, made a serpent of bronze and put it upon a pole (similar to the rod of Asclepius, the ancient Greek symbol of medicine that still survives today). Whenever a serpent bit someone, that person would look at the serpent of bronze and live. The bronze serpent, who came to be called Nehushtan, was worshipped by the Hebrew people until the reign of King Hezekiah. In the name of the iconoclastic reform he instituted, Hezekiah destroyed the symbol, breaking the bronze serpent that Moses had made into pieces.

THE ARCHITECTS OF THE SEA

In addition to reptiles we find the same symbols and the same succession of events in the mythology of ancient civilizations. Although enriched with elements of fantasy, the background story remains the same: Berbers, Greeks, and Egyptians describe the arrival of the Pelasgians from the west and their subsequent conquest of the Mediterranean Sea, leading their dynasties up to Baal-Saturn and offering space for the dynastic struggle between Osiris-Menes and Danaus-Seth.

Moving along to the military campaign of Osiris, from Egypt to the East, many soldiers were recruited in the region of Hyperborea, a territory north of Greece, but not as far north as was supposed. The expedition reached India and the arrival of the god Osiris was recorded in the traditional Indian texts. We find the same news in the testimonies of the historians of Alexander the Great, collected from the Nisaeans of Turkmenistan, the Malloi (or Malla), and the Hydrakes (or Oxydrakai) of India. The same facts are also confirmed in the reports of the Roman ambassadors to the Mauryan court.

On the border between India and Pakistan the followers of Osiris founded the new civilization of the Indus and Sarasvati rivers, the oldest officially recognized. That was 12,000 years ago, when the Sarasvati, now lost, ran uninterrupted from the Himalayas to the Indian Ocean.

The immigrants brought with them (or developed locally) a hieroglyphic writing consisting of about four hundred signs called graphemes. A similar style exists in only one other place in the world that is exactly opposite: Easter Island (see figure C.1).

The Sea Peoples, descendents of the Pelasgians, came from the Indus Valley; they destroyed the Middle East empires and provoked the Trojan War in 1200 BCE. They were the Shardana, the Libu, the Sabines, the Teucris, and the Achaenans, founders of an architectural rebirth all over the Mediterranean, creating monuments like those built in the Egyptian Old Kingdom. Imposing megalithic temples were built in Greece, Italy, and Sardinia; in Egypt were raised the obelisks of Tuthmosis I (1504–1492 BCE) and Hatshepsut (1473–1458 BCE) at Karnak, and the colossal statue of Ramesses II (1278–1213 BCE) in Luxor, weighing respectively

*Figure C.1. Indus Valley hieroglyphs compared to
Easter Island hieroglyphs.*

143,320 and 1,000 tons. All this had been done by very skilled archi-tects who were traveling the length and breadth of Mediterranean coasts, like the Benedictine monks during the Middle Ages who through their missionary travels all around Europe established monasteries and built abbeys, churches, and cathedrals.

WHEN THE SKY COLLAPSED

The Pelasgians used astronomy in their architecture, copying the sky on Earth, mapping constellations on the ground through the monuments they built by placing them in the same position as the stars. This great cosmic scheme was based on the belief that the world is only the reflec-tion (or shadow) of the perfect reality of the celestial realms. The imita-tion of the sky brought to Earth a bit of heavenly perfection, spreading upon the inhabitants the beneficial influences of the stars. For this rea-son on the Giza plain they copied the Orion constellation through the Zed towers, replaced later by the great pyramids of the Fourth Dynasty. The position of the temples of Angkor in Cambodia is likely the mirror of the constellation of Draco, and the Acropolis of Alatri and Circeo mirror the Gemini, Taurus, and Perseus constellations.

The whole zodiac is represented in the Mayan city of Uxmal and similar connections are emerging in the Mayan sites of Chichén Itzá, Palenque, and Yaxchilan.

■ ■ ■

At this point the information we have gained we consider to be a clearer and wider overview of the symbols that lead us to acknowledge the presence of the Atlantean heritage in both ancient and modern culture. All this should not be a mere intellectual exercise, but rather must urge us to learn from the past so as to be prepared for the future. Although undesirable, the fall of another meteorite could happen, especially considering that such a catastrophic event occurs on average every 10,000 years.

In the meantime we should find out what might be recovered from the golden age of Atlantis—technological knowledge, medical therapies, comprehension of the universe, and human history. There are indications about the existence of two secret "halls of records" where tangible artifacts and tablets may have been hidden by priests of Atlantis—Atlan, Iltar, and Hept-supht. The search is still in progress at the pyramid complex of Giza and also at Piedras Negras, in Guatemala.

Antarctica may also hold surprises, particularly at coordinates 66° 36' 12.89" S and 99° 43' 14.00" E, 66° 33' 14.97" S and 99° 50' 19.51" E, and 66° 28' 44.32" S and 99° 58' 22.84" E, where there is something very similar to artificial tunnels.

The already quoted Admiral Byrd reported that he had seen the remains of a city while flying over Antarctica, but his statement was considered the result of an incredible hallucination.

A promising area of research is undoubtedly the exploration of the sea beds. During the ice age the number of perennial glaciers was more than double that of the current one; in fact the sea level was actually 120 meters lower than it is today. The reason is very simple: the pole shift and displacement of the Earth's crust had also tilted the Earth's axis, which before then was probably nearly perpendicular to the plane of the ecliptic. This means that the temperature range between winter and summer must have been much reduced, so that ice and snow amassed in large quantities at high altitudes and high latitudes, to the detriment of the sea level. When the ice melted only half of the resulting water would freeze again at the new poles, and an inhabited area of twenty-five million square kilometers would become permanently flooded by the remaining water.

Civilization was wiped out by the merciless waves of the Great Flood, an event deeply rooted in the myths and religious consciousness of all peoples of the Earth. The submerged structures found off the coast of Yonaguni in Japan, or Dwarka and Poompuhur in India, are just a small sample of what awaits us beneath the waves.

The shifting of weight from the glaciers to the oceans must have produced violent shockwaves, enough so that the entire planet began to shake and the great part of the extinct volcanoes returned to an active state, spreading a thick fog of ash and dust across the sky, obscuring the sun and lowering temperatures. In the words of the Kojiki,* "So thereupon the Heaven-Shining-Great-August-Deity, terrified at the sight, closed [behind her] the door of the Heavenly Rock-Dwelling, made it fast, and retired. Then the whole Plain of High Heaven was obscured and all the Central Land of Reed-Plains darkened."

What could the inhabitants of the Earth have felt? It is difficult to find something stronger than the word "terror," with earthquakes that are strong enough to create waves of rock as tall as a four-story building. All this should remind us that the Earth—nothing but a ball of mud drifting through space—is at the mercy of events.

Thinking that our civilization is untouchable is pure arrogance. Glossy magazines, rating agencies, cable TV, skyscrapers, luxury cars— everything can disappear in a flash.

THE LIGHT OF GÖBEKLI TEPE

As we write, a real archaeological revolution is happening in the town of Göbekli Tepe in Turkey, just north of the Syrian border near the cities of Sanliurfa and Harran.

This is an enchanted place, which during the Bronze Age hosted meetings of the Brotherhood of the Serpent[4] (also known as the Brotherhood Sarmoung or All-Seeing Eye Cult), later becoming the Gnostic center of Sabians and Messalians. Papyrus scrolls found in excavations in 1888 in

---

*The Kojiki, "Record of Ancient Matters," is the oldest chronicle in Japan, dating from 711–712 CE).

the Libyan desert describe secret meetings of similar groups in 2000 BCE.

The official version of academic archaeology maintains the occupation of the site as being from 11,500 to 8000 BCE! Excavations have initially uncovered a megalithic monumental sanctuary surrounded by dry walls of rough stone. There were then found four circular fences, bound by huge limestone pillars heavier than ten tons each. Klaus Schmidt, director of the excavations from the Archaeological Germanicus Institute, observing these stones that were placed upright and arranged in a circle, suggested they symbolize assemblies of men.*

Eventually about forty pieces of T-shaped pillars up to three meters high came to light. Most of them are decorated with carved reliefs of different animals (lions, bulls, boars, foxes, gazelles, donkeys, snakes and other reptiles, insects, arachnids, and birds), while others have incisions of dots and geometric patterns. Geomagnetic surveys indicate the presence of another 250 stones still buried in the ground.

Some of the pillars depict long, thin human arms clasping hands around their narrow sides. The T-shaped pillars have a link to the *moai* (humanoid statues on Easter Island) because their arms and hands are depicted in the same formation and position. On the back some of the moai, recently unearthed, are several reliefs very similar to the ones found on the Göbekli pillars.

In the near future, new discoveries will shed light on the origin of civilization and we must be ready to consider them without too many prejudices, with eyes and mind wide open. Our main belief is that any effort made to better understand human life is fully justified, regardless of the consequences.

Socrates: *We have then followed the vessels from the White Island to the land where the Merica sets, the morning star you call Sirius. It seems that things beyond the large*

---

*While we speak of this, near Rome in the town of Palestrina (formerly Preneste, a Sabine city), a group suspected of seeking to facilitate the birth of a new world religion—by moving the interest of Christianity from Jesus to the Holy Spirit—is building its first temple precisely in the likeness of Göbekli Tepe (see www.spiritosanto.org/info/english/work.html).

expanse of water, never explored by the Greeks, are like those on this side.

Hermocrates: *There are sacred mountains, carved by man and even more majestic than the ones Solon saw in Egypt. The people over there love the sun and worship its manifestation in Dionysus, whom they call Viracocha. They calculate the motion of the stars and foresee the periodic dimming of both the celestial vault and the moon circle.*

Critias: *Therefore, 12,000 years before Solon, the Earth would have unhinged its rings, staggering in search of new hubs. Earthquakes and floods would have caused the extinction of the human race. The golden age was over.*

Socrates: *What about the glorious Age of Silver?*

Timaeus: *You say right, because silver became the most wanted precious metal for all Mediterranean peoples, when the children of Atlantis passed the last strait, where Libya is close to Cadiz. The Amazon warriors guarded the brightest and purest strands, mixed with the orichalcum in the Island of Espera, the current Tartessos.*

Critias: *These women were alien to shame. They did not feel ashamed in outraging the men they used only to procreate. They kept them in reserve, throwing the excess male children from the rocks.*

Hermocrates: *Let's not believe too literally the stories of our fathers: they are fables, told to discredit a world that was incomprehensible to them. Perhaps you forget the value of the Amazon Myrina?*

Socrates: *Myrina fell into a trap at the hands of Dionysus, but did not break into tears, nor did she cry under torture, and, finally, she moved our Lord. She proved so proud as to earn his trust and his covenant. Upon the death of Dionysus's father, Baal, he held her at his side, to oust his brother Danaus and conquer the East.*

Hermocrates: *They say it was she who took the name of Isis.*

Critias: *You are talking nonsense! A noble and learned God would have never taken a woman devoid of all grace in his bed. Rather a milkmaid.*

Hermocrates: *Your mind is closed, and your soul is perverse, Critias. A dame, a milkmaid, or a woman-soldier, the heart of a god knows how to look beyond your schemes and the appearance of weapons and jewelry.*

Timaeus: *Who knows what happened in the endless expanses of India?*

Hermocrates: *Certainly, they fought with valor and gained large territories. Right from there came the great master builders of Mycenae, Argos, and Tiryns. If we listen to the words etched in stone, they were the sons of Dionysus, returned to Greece after 8,000 years.*

Socrates: *Did we say everything?*

Hermocrates: *All that we know and which is unknown to the most. It does not suit us to replicate such widespread knowledge.*

Critias: *You forget the prophecy of the return!*

Timaeus: *The people beyond the large expanse of water were awaiting the return of Viracocha, and the people of Siwa Oasis lit candles every day in his honor. He will walk on water and build a town west of the Nile . . .*

Hermocrates: *Do you really believe in Alexander the Great? Is it not natural to the human species, at the mercy of events, to wish for a savior full of certainties?*

Critias: *Now your mind is blinded by progress. You deny what you cannot understand. The oracles are safe, they all agree: Dionysus will return on Earth and put the East in the hands of Greece . . .*

Socrates: *Shall he see the towers he himself has built, beyond the Indus, beyond the Hindu Kush mountains in the land of Kambu?*

Critias: *Dodona and Delphi are silent.*

Socrates: *It is bedtime; we should turn off the lamps. One*

last thought before leaving: Hermocrates voluntarily forgets
that everything that has been, must come back, because
time is a wheel. Dionysus will return and so the ice; and
then it will dissolve again, the Earth will tremble and
there will be another great flood. The day will come when
the towers give back what they have been entrusted, the
pyramids jump like rams, and the sad Iron Age comes to
an end . . .

History is much more complex than is usually accepted, marked by slaughters more than by progress. The history of the Pelasgians tells only of some of these massacres, but it gives an idea of how much has been, intentionally or not, omitted. Sooner or later the Earth's crust will slide and tremble another time, and the human race will risk extinction once again. Maybe it is a system of self-defense that our planet is ready to take on to save itself from the cancer called "progress" that is killing it.

Our meeting has come to an end, this long monologue on disasters and migrations in a world whose borders keep on changing. Now it is up to you to develop an interest and formulate new questions; perhaps this historical report can be your starting point.

Buona vita.

APPENDIX A

THE SUMERIAN HOAX

To fight, brave, and overcome any limit!
These are precisely the hilt, the blade, and the tip of
*   the only sword of whom faces death!*
Never forget!

EMPEROR GAISSELICK, FROM *BERSERK*
(A GRAPHIC NOVEL BY KENTARO MIURA)

If we open a book of ancient history, any of those recommended textbooks at university, we will find that most of the information is free from source: there is no indication showing where that information was derived from. So it takes a little effort, several visits to the old library, in search of the first texts where the information appeared for the first time as the result of fresh theories and recent excavations.

Here one realizes how much work was done by German archaeologists in Mesopotamia between the end of 1800 and the first half of 1900. Almost a century of excavations were interpreted according to pan-Germanism and, worse, anti-Semitism. A nation was created out of nothing and its story has fossilized into an indisputable dogma: no one remembers how it was discovered, no one bothers to check and see if those people had really ever existed: the Sumerians. Only Mario Pincherle, a few decades ago, had the courage to lodge a complaint.

In 1893 the Institute of Germanic Archaeology began to get seriously worried by the news that came from distant Mesopotamia. Their most influential man, Theodor Mommsen, reported:

> We grew up believing that human civilization, writing, art, were originated in ancient Greece, which is considered the "pearl" of the Indo-Germanic peoples. Unfortunately, we are now witnessing a sad spectacle. The people are wanting to believe that the splendor of the Greek civilization drew its vitality from some Semitic tribes: the Jews, the Phoenicians, the Cretans, and the Babylonians. The news of recent discoveries made in Mesopotamia is coming to our institute. They speak of a nation that traces its roots back to ancient times and of an empire that could be defined "the first empire of the world." The founder of this koinè [union of populations] would be Sargon of Acadia and that empire would be the "empire of Akkad." Many artifacts have been unearthed in recent years to dispel our reasonable doubts: the existence of these events is supported by many documents of their art and culture. One thing is certain: Sargon of Akkad is an ancestor of the Jews. The inhabitants of the center of his empire are certainly Semites and it seems that these semi-barbarous people developed such an advanced and perfect civilization as to be not attributable to their rough primitive minds. But where this culture was born remains a big question. Who does not agree today that barbaric minds cannot be creators of a great civilization?

Today, there is a lot of confusion about the history and archaeology of the fourth millennium BC in Mesopotamia. What we'll know about this period will be the result of several factors: the interpretation of the excavated texts, archaeologists' agreed conclusions, and late cuneiform writings relating to those early days. On this fourth pre-Christian millennium still lingers the twilight of prehistory. Testimonials of this thesis will be the ceramics' scalar series, the more or less primitive forms of clay idols depicting the bull and the Mother Goddess, a multitude of primordial and primitive little temples come to light from the lower layers of Eridu. The starting point for future research will be this incontrovertible fact: until the fourth millennium BCE, all the inhabitants of both North and South Mesopotamia were Semites. The country was called Akkad and the inhabitants were called Akkadians, that is Semites, that is Jews. An Indo-Germanic people only appears at the end of this millennium, and this event gives rise to the truly great urban civilization of the ancient East. These great and mysterious Indo-Germanic people are the author of a civilization that cannot be born overnight. Cosidering that these Indo-Germanic–speaking people are not from this country, light needs to be shed on these people the writers do not speak of. Also Herodotus, who traveled two thousand five hundred years ago in Mesopotamia, did not mention this people. Indeed, he speaks only of the Babylonians and therefore Semites. Nobody speaks of the coming of the great Aryan people. Their name is alien even to the Bible. Three centuries ago the first cuneiform tablets arrived in Europe from Mesopotamia. In 1626, the traveler Pietro della Valle brought them to Rome after a long stay in the Near East. Two hundred years were to pass for those tablets to be deciphered by Georg Friedrich Grotefend and the Englishman Henry Rawlinson.

When it was finally possible to read those writings, Jules Oppert, an expert in cuneiform writing, found himself in front of an enigma, a big question: "What is the source of such perfection?" Jules Oppert shares the ideas of Germanic science and is an authority on excavations in Mesopotamia.

In these years, what is happening in Mesopotamia is what happened half a century ago regarding the problem of artifacts that came to light in Italy, in Tuscany and Lazio. Objects that shone with so much perfection but could not come from the East. They understood then that an Indo-European people, more precisely, Indo-Germanic, coming from the North, had brought a great civilization to the Italian peninsula: the Etruscans. The Etruscans and not the legendary eastern Semitic peoples were the authors of those perfect products. The semi-barbarous people of the Sabines were deprived of a merit they did not have, indeed. Thanks to the work of another archaeologist, the Frenchman Dumezil,[1] the Etruscan idea was formed, which is now firmly confirmed.[2]

Today we know that the Etruscans certainly did *not* come from the north and were *not* Indo-European; yet the story has not been rewritten. The same applies to the Sumerians, a mysterious people who would bring civilization to Mesopotamia, of which nothing was known except that their existence was required: it was Assyriologist Jules Oppert who baptized them the "people of Sumer." The Sumerians would have settled in southern Mesopotamia three thousand years before Christ, pushing the Akkadians northward. Then, it seemed inconsistent that just the Akkadian port of Agadé (Akkad), founded by Sargon of Acadia and located in the Persian Gulf, was placed in Sumer, southern Mesopotamia. It was just then that Oppert declared to the world of science:

> As resulting from the translation of some clay tablets, the capital of Akkad, namely the great port city of Agadé, was connected by Sargon to the Lower Sea, the current Persian Gulf, through an efficient system of canals.
>
> In these texts we read of vessels arriving at the port of Agadé from the countries of Magan, Dilmun, and Meluhha (all three referred to as important trading centers in Sumerian writings) through some channels.
>
> So it's not unreasonable to suppose that the port of Akkad was situated right in the land of Akkad, namely northern Mesopotamia, near the current Baghdad, and then at the point where the rivers Tigris and Euphrates are closest to each other and linked to the Lower Sea by a long channel.[3]

It is amazing that Oppert seriously spoke of a port four hundred kilometers from the sea. If you look up "Akkad" on Wikipedia you will discover that the site has not yet been discovered, although it has been sought for a long time in northern Mesopotamia: can a capital city disappear into thin air? It is clear we are looking in the wrong place!

Some young German philologists sought to prove the real existence of the Sumerians by relying on linguistic analysis, but their results were inconclusive.[4] There is currently no single finding among those classified as "Sumerian" that is distinguishable from an Akkadian equivalent. The arguments in favor of the existence of the Sumerians came from some texts and compositions found in the palace of the Assyrian king Ashurbanipal (the last great king of the Neo-Assyrian empire) in Nineveh. A considerable number of tablets of the royal library were engraved with a series of cuneiform compositions, but not in the Semitic language of the Assyrians, Babylonians, and Akkadians. The scribes had added to many of these compositions the translation into Akkadian, while other tablets reported lists of words together with their translation. Oppert attributed this new language to the Sumerians despite opposition of the famous Orientalist archaeologist Joseph Halévy, who believed that these compositions showed a kabbalistic method of writing invented and developed by Akkadian priests. In his opinion those texts were Semitic compositions, written according to a secret system or code comprehensible only to priests. According to Halévy the fact that this "language" kept exactly the same phonetic values of the Akkadian symbols was in itself evidence. Halévy won several supporters, including Professor Delitzsch and a considerable number of young German schools of criticism.[5]

More recent studies have distorted the nature of the debate, strictly excluding the idea that Sumerian could belong to the Indo-European languages. In fact, even today it is not possible to place the Sumerian language in any of the known strains, making plausible the hypothesis of an artificial language built for ritual purposes. In this light the comparison with the Haida language made in chapter 1 acquires a wider meaning, and the Sumerians might have never existed.

CHAPTER-BY-CHAPTER COMPARISON TO THE FINDINGS OF EDGAR CAYCE

Edgar Cayce was born in Kentucky in 1877 and for most of his life earned his living as a photographer. Nevertheless, he has gone down in history for an unusual ability to read the "soul" of people, a talent discovered by accident and never exploited for his own profits.

While a young man, working as a clerk in a bookstore, Cayce lost his voice. None of the local doctors knew how to help him; feeling helpless, he sought the help of a hypnotist. Through hypnosis he reached a state of trance during which he described his condition and proposed a remedy. The treatment was successful and he could soon speak normally.

The doctor attending his healing encouraged him to try the same technique on other people. Despite an initial fear of proposing the wrong diagnosis and harming the health of his patients, Cayce instead proved to be extremely accurate, accumulating a long list of healings including the saving of his son Hugh Lynn's sight following the explosion of a can of powder used for photographic flash.

People came from all over the United States to receive a reading and diagnosis, and the total number of recorded readings eventually exceeded fourteen thousand.

In 1923 a wealthy man who was passionate about metaphysics came to Cayce for a reading, during which he asked for and obtained a description of his past lives. Upon awakening, Cayce was shocked by his work. Then he spent over a year in philosophical discussions with his strange "patient," Arthur Lammers, who tried to convince him of the strong influence that past lives can have on the present.

Although skeptical and unable to reconcile his Christianity with reincarnation, Cayce agreed to grant the same service to others when requested, convinced that in no case could it be harmful.

After Lammers 2,500 other people received a reading of their previous lives: 700 of these readings contained references to lives intertwined with the history of Atlantis.

In this book we did not want to talk about anything that did not emerge from the ground or from ancient chroniclers, but too many coincidences have convinced us to dedicate a special section to the link between Atlantis and Edgar Cayce. He knew nothing about ancient history, geology, or mythology. Nevertheless, his readings have allowed collaborators writing the history of the world to go back in time more than archaeologists have been able to. Certainly it is a controversial approach, but as we became aware of Cayce's work at the end of our research we were surprised to find that the majority of dates and events he has described coincide with our studies.

The Association for Research and Enlightenment (ARE), a nonprofit organization with the purpose of verifying the readings of Edgar Cayce, was founded in 1931. Against all odds the association has received considerable credibility over time, even obtaining permission to perform drilling and seismographic analysis on the Giza plateau by the Egyptian authorities. We were able to contact the association and meet its representative in Italy and were provided with the yet-unpublished material that appears in the following pages.

Those wishing to know more about Edgar Cayce can refer to www .edgarcayce.org.

COMPARISONS WITH THE FINDINGS OF EDGAR CAYCE—CHAPTERS 1, 2, 3, AND 8

Edgar Cayce spoke of three major destructions that befell Atlantis that were connected to the mass extinctions of large animals. The dates he gave do not coincide with ours (13,000, 9600, and 6700 BCE), but they are important dates such as 10,600 BCE (a date close to the construction of the Sphinx and zed towers in Egypt) and 50,700 BCE (the date of a previous slide of the crust). We do not know if Edgar Cayce spoke in metaphor, or if he intentionally encrypted some information. He told of the abuse of technology in Atlantis in a period when people had become cynical, arrogant, and selfish. In his pantheistic view everything is part of the Creator, including humans and planet Earth—and he believed the Creator was also the creation.

So when Cayce tells of how the Atlanteans used a technology that he called "prismatic tuning" in order to extinguish large animals, perhaps he skips a step that for him was implicit. According to a reasonable interpretation the misuse of this technology by the Atlanteans would have upset the balance of the Creator-creation, awakening the Earth, triggering earthquakes and eruptions, and changing the climate. *It was this chain of events, which Cayce deliberately skips, that ultimately killed the animals. In his vision the people of Atlantis, with their weapons and will, would have killed the animals directly.*

Cayce makes no distinction between the first Atlantis (in Antarctica) and its rebirth in the Mediterranean or Central and South America. Nevertheless he explicitly mentions the migration of the Pelasgians (the red race, a.k.a. Cro-Magnons) to Peru and the Yucatán, as well as to Morocco (Berbers), the Pyrenees (Basque), and Egypt. Cayce devotes a space to matriarchy that in his opinion ruled the world before the deluge, as we have found in our research.

The following texts were supplied by ARE–Italy.

The First Disruption: 50,700 BCE

In Atlantis existed two powerful groups: the Children of the Law of One and the Sons of Belial. Over time the latter had the upper hand. Under Belial's suggestion the level of electric energy was raised in the "prismatic tuning" so the rays of death had sufficient penetrating power to enter into the Earth's bowels, where Belial was convinced some of the most menacing monsters could still hide. Not only were animals huddled in caves eliminated, *the whole continent was overwhelmed by seismic activity and destructive fire.* Volcanic upheavals rained death and destruction over much of Atlantis and fragmented the vast continent into a new scenario consisting of five separate islands.

Second Disruption: 28,000 BCE

A reading of Cayce's on that sad and defeatist era reveals that a sense of spiritual malaise had descended over the entire nation, allowing lawless elements to achieve dominance over the forces of the One.

Then, *the earth shook and trembled once more from end to end.* When the perturbation ended, many thought that what had happened was at the admonishing hands of God. Only three out of the five islands of Atlantis remained: Og*, Aryan, and Poseidia.[1]

Third Disruption: 10,600 BCE to 9600 BCE

The final sinking of Atlantis took place in several phases over a period of several centuries. The last island to be submerged was Poseidia, which, according to the readings, is now in the Sargasso Sea: "The Sargasso Sea—that into which the caldrons of the earth were turned with the destructive forces in the Poseidian land in its last activity" (reading 1159–1). Some Pelasgians fled to the Pyrenees, others toward the current Yucatán, Peru, Morocco, and Egypt.

The Testimonies of Atlantis

One of the places chosen by the exiles was the Giza plateau in Egypt, under which was buried the Atlantean record, later enriched by Egyptian

---

*For the Jews there was Og, king of Bashan and the last of Refa'im. In Nazorean tradition the Refa'im are the "spirits of the dead," a name that we find in Egyptian references to the Followers of Horus. According to Jewish belief Refa'im were localized, especially in Bashan, the land dotted with megalithic tombs. In Rabbat 'Ammon was the legendary "iron bed" by Og, perhaps a basalt slab covering a dolmen. It is likely at this point that Refa'im is yet another synonym for the Pelasgians.

vestiges and documentation, with a view to future discovery. Another collection of records was taken to the Yucatán by a Pelasgian named Iltar and placed in a pyramid, not yet discovered, that would be lying under the most recent Mayan ruins, maybe at Piedras Negras. Finally, in the pyramid of records submerged near Bimini (buried under the mud of the Sargasso Sea in a sunken part of Poseida) we would find the original collection along with numerous artifacts sealed on the spot by the great Atlantean sage Hept-supht (readings 378–16, 3976–15, 958–3, and 440–5).

The Story of Atlantis from the Readings of Edgar Cayce, Series 364

According to Cayce the land mass of Atlantis was enormous; part of it would be placed "between the Gulf of Mexico on one side and the Mediterranean on the other." (Here Cayce is referring to a colony, as we shall see soon. Indeed the same prophet said that this area was a refuge for the priest Atlan, exiled from Atlantis after the first flood.)

It was in these lectures that he described the current Sargasso Sea as an important part of Atlantis, the place where Poseidia—"the Eden of the World"—one of the five major regions of Atlantis, sank into the sea (reading 1159–1). Cayce said that today it would still be possible to see some "protrusions" that "one or another time must have been part of this great continent: British West Indies or the Bahamas. If we did a geological survey in some of these, especially in Bimini and the Gulf Stream, the lands of Poseidia could be detected even now."

Cayce said that on one hand "evidence of this lost civilization are found in the Pyrenees and Morocco," on the other in the "British Honduras, Yucatán, and America."

Cayce referred to the North American "royal Iroquois" (reading 1219–1): "The *entity* [the person who has asked for a reading] then was among the people, the Indians, of the Iroquois; those of noble birth, those that were of the pure descendants of the Atlanteans, those that held to the ritualistic influences from nature itself." The royal Iroquois were made up of the Mohawk, Oneida, Onondaga, Cayuga, and Seneca tribes. The Iroquois were matriarchal, and according to Cayce's belief before the legendary Great Flood the feminine was dominant throughout the ancient world. "It was natural," he said. After the destruction in those ancient times the male would become dominant.

Cayce explained that in the beginning the Atlanteans were "thought forms, or able to push out of themselves, much in the way and manner as the amoeba would in the waters of a stagnant bay, or lake, in the present. As these took form . . . of the existent human body of the day, with that color as partook of their surroundings much in the manner as the chameleon in the present. Hence coming into that form as the red, or the mixture people—or colors; known later as the red race" (reading 364–3).

According to the Edgar Cayce readings, the glorious period for Atlantis was from 210,000 BCE up to about 50,722 BCE, when the first destruction took place. Cayce affirmed that the Atlanteans were originally a peaceful people whose development in physical shape and strength grew rapidly.

Their evolution was rapid because "they recognized themselves as part of the surrounding environment. So with regard to what was needed to sustain physical life as it is known today, namely some clothing or bodily needs, such things were provided by natural elements." Thanks to their union with the Natural Forces the Atlanteans quickly developed skills that "would be termed the aerial age, or the *electrical age*, and supplying then the modes and manners of transposition by that ability lying within each to be transposed in thought as in body." They could travel with the mind as well as with the body. Surprisingly, this did not happen only within the earthly kingdoms! Cayce said that they were able to "physically move from one part of the universe to another."

In addition to their ability to "move," Cayce also spoke of the crystal of Atlantis, the famous source of their power. Actually there must have been several crystals or stones similar to crystals that were used for a variety of purposes throughout the history of Atlantis. Still, Cayce indicated that originally there was a crystal tuned with the universal cosmic forces that provide life. This tuning was used to regenerate their physical bodies, promote longevity, and connect their minds to the cosmos and the Creative Forces. A reading of Cayce (reading 440–3) indicates that the

Atlanteans had a "crystal set" that channeled rays coming from the distant Arcturus star, giving them the "power to transmit etheronic energy" in order to get a "heating source."

Finally, there was the Tuao stone. In reading 2072–10 Cayce said that this stone was originally "the means and the source or the manner by which the existing powers focused to make the children of men and the children of God aware of the forces or powers that guided them." Doesn't this recall the Te Pito Kura stone used by the magicians of Easter Island to concentrate their *mana* and order the statues to walk?

Around 106,000 BCE the Atlanteans created a new physical body to help souls incarnating into this difficult world. Actually there were two bodies, one male and one female. Cayce called it the "body of the third original race." In Mayan legends this body was called the Blue Labyrinth, emphasizing its perfection in all respects.

According to Cayce at that moment in history the two souls we know as Jesus and Mary would come to Atlantis embodied in Aemilius and Lilith. Their arrival was used to help souls get over the needs typical of the incarnation in this dimension. Initially Aemilius and Lilith were united in a single super-soul, the Logos or Christ (Edgar Cayce said "there never was a time when there was no Christ"). Aemilius and Lilith eventually became aware of how the duality of this dimension separated the twin aspects of the soul into its two parts, yin and yang, and according to Cayce it took seventy-eight years to completely divide Aemilius and Lilith into two independent bodies, separating male and female aspects of the same soul. After they split most of the other souls did too, resulting in more friendship in this world of separation and duality.

In the Bible the episode is masked by the action of God, who observes the solitude of Adam, unable to find a suitable mate among all creatures. Then God sent down a deep sleep upon Adam and took from him his feminine side, separating it from the male side so they could be friends and companions for each other.

According to Cayce, Aemilius continued to create and improve conditions and physical forms so that souls could incarnate with a greater presence of their higher consciousness, using it in their physicality. They built temples to preserve and teach the importance of union with the cosmos, with the Creative Forces, and with other creatures. These were glorious times for Atlantis.

Tragically many embodied souls Cayce called Sons of Belial increasingly sought to pursue their own interests and selfish gratification with less concern for the integrity and cooperation necessary to be one with Life and its creations. Moral decay, madness for power, lack of respect for nature, ignorance of being one with the cosmic forces, and a growing sense of hierarchy and superiority over others threw Atlantis into turmoil. As much as the Children of the Law tried to draw attention to these things, the influence of the Sons of Belial reduced Atlantis to an era of destructive thoughts and activities. The leadership of Aemilius was replaced with that of Esai. The no longer peaceful vibrations attracted a large number of dangerous animals that came to the continent for the first time (saber-toothed tigers, mastodons, mammoths, etc.). The need arose to create new weapons to protect people.

Cayce marked the reign of Esai as a turning point in the history of Atlantis. "With this reign, with these destructive forces, we find the first turning of the altar fires into that of sacrifice of those that were taken in various ways, and human sacrifice began. With this also came the first egress of peoples to that of the Pyrenees first, [then] into Og or those peoples that later became the beginning of the Inca [and to] those of the mound dwellers."

Cayce explained that such evil activities "made in nature form the first of the eruptions that awoke from the depth of the slow cooling Earth, and that portion now near what would be termed the Sargasso Sea first went into the depths." With melancholy Cayce pointed out that the destruction not only took the lives of many negative souls, but carried with them "*all* those forms of Amilius that he gained through. . . . Hence, we find in those various portions of the world even in the present day, some form of that as *was* presented by those peoples in *that* great *development* in this, the Eden of the world" (reading 364–4). These violent eruptions broke the great continent into five islands. The first, Eden, as Cayce called it, no longer existed.

Despite the violent reaction of the planet the Sons of Belial continued to fight and they took control of the Children of the Law of

One. The problem was complex: if the Children of the Law of One had stayed they would have had to fight against the Sons of Belial, producing attitudes and energies they did not want to develop. Many chose to migrate to other lands and to continue their union with the Creative Forces, teaching those who would listen. Cayce stated that those who remained in Atlantis struggled against the darkness of Belial, Baal, Baalila, and even Beelzebub! At the end, the ruling council of Atlantis was under the total control of the negative energies and desires. The Cayce readings describe how some priests and priestesses, well intentioned and in great harmony, had tried to connect with the Sons of Belial in the belief that cooperation would have brought them back to the truth. Unfortunately, they found themselves corrupted by Baal and finally sank into darkness and despair.

Three priests of Atlantis—Atlan, Iltar, and Hept-supht—determined that the era of Atlantis was over. They retained the story of Atlantis by carving it on tablets of stone. Each of them took a number of these documents with the intention of storing them for a future in which humanity would once again seek to know the truth. Iltar sailed with ten companions to the coast of Yucatán. Hept-supht sailed for Egypt. Atlan hid his tablets all at once at his temple to Poseidia, near the current Bimini.

Between 28,000 and 22,000 BCE there was a second destruction. (Although the dates do not coincide, Edgar Cayce also thinks that the second flood happened only after the migration wave to America and the Mediterranean.) This flood left only three islands above the water surface, with only parts of them habitable, whereas the temple of Atlan was destroyed, sinking it into the abyss. It also destroyed the temple of Iltar, but he recovered the tablets and moved them inland, perhaps in the current Piedras Negras, Guatemala. (Here we are no longer talking about the original Atlantis, but of its re-foundation, in this case in Central America.) Hept-supht's tablets were on the Giza plateau, to later be hidden in an underground chamber beneath the right front paw of the Sphinx. (Egyptian texts such as the Book of What Is in the Duat, or the Book of Aker, make explicit references to secret chambers under the Sphinx and show pictures of a room under its front legs. The image of the room is sometimes replaced by the god Sokar, the "god of the secret chamber." The tablets left by pilgrims at the temple of the Sphinx would often show his figure on a high pedestal with a door at the base.) Cayce stated that under the Earth some "connecting rooms from the right paw of the Sphinx" led to the testimonies. The "dream stele" that stands between the front legs of the monument shows the drawing of an underground chamber with a door.

After Hept-supht was gone, migration became critical. Those who understood the value of truth and the purpose of life created ways to preserve their wisdom and initiatory knowledge, at the same time saving the physical body. For the following ten or twenty thousand years, souls emigrated from Atlantis and established temples in new lands. The final destruction occurred in 10,040 BCE (according to our research in 6700 BCE) when the remaining lands of Atlantis sank into the sea.

In this series of readings Cayce predicted "Atlantis would have re-emerged near Bimini in 1969." The ARE, working on research with the help of Global Underwater Explorers, released four underwater missions in 2010 identifying architectural structures, definitely not natural, like mounds of sand in the shapes of a shark and cat, and especially the "Bimini Road," with the ruins of an ancient port.

The ARE is also pursuing research for the recovery of the "Hall of Records" identified by Cayce in the Yucatán in Piedras Negras, Guatemala, working with great difficulty because the site is located in a jungle devoid of access roads.

Peru, Mexico, and the Basque

The first exodus of Atlanteans to other lands took place after the first upheaval (13,000 BCE according to our research, 50,700 BCE according to Cayce). Initially they founded some colonies in the current Peru, at the time called Og by the Atlantean colonists (some of these colonists must have come from the Atlantean island carrying the same name).

Most of the Atlantean priests, together with other men who were faithful to the teachings of the sacred Law of One, chose to evacuate well before the final catastrophe. It was a large-scale diaspora that led to the extinction of the Atlanteans as a race and power, or united world influence. Specifically mentioned among their various points of dispersion were Egypt, Morocco, the Pyrenees, the peninsula of Yucatán, and Peru, along with various parts of North America not covered by glaciers.

The original pyramid that bears the traces of Atlantis, built by Iltar in the Yucatán, was alternately called the Sun Temple or the Temple of Light. Like the Great Pyramid in Egypt and the Pyramid of Records sunk and left at Poseidia, the original pyramid was also built, they say, by means of "the lifting forces of those gases that are being used, gradually in the present civilization" and thanks to the spiritual activities of those who knew "the source from which all power comes" (reading 5750–1).

In other readings Cayce spoke of raids by the fleeing Atlanteans during the final upheavals in the region of the Pyrenees, but few seem to have stayed for very long—that isolated Atlantean outpost seems to have been regarded primarily as a transition point to Egypt and other safe lands (readings 1998–1, 315–4, and 1681–1).

The Shift of the Poles

According to the Cayce readings the entry into a new era will be accompanied by a shift of the poles that would have started around 2000 or 2001, and which was actually measured. This is one of the readings:

> (Q) What great change is to take place in the earth in the year
>   2000 to 2001 AD?
> (A) When there is a shifting of the poles. Or a new cycle begins.
>   (reading 826–8)

When he was asked to explain how the new age would be Cayce replied (reading 1602–3): "In the Piscean Age, in the center of same, we had the entrance of Emmanuel or God among men, see? What did that mean? The same will be meant by the full consciousness of the ability to communicate with or to be aware of the relationships to the Creative Forces and the uses of same in material environs. This awareness during the era or age in the age of Atlantis and Lemuria or Mu brought what? Destruction to man, and the beginning of his needs in the journey up through that of selfishness. Then, as to what will these be, *only* those

who accept same will even become aware of what's going on about them!
. . . And yet ye ask what will the Aquarian age bring in mind, in body, in experience?"

Cayce expressed excitement for this new era when he gave a reading for one who had caught the "vision of the new age," the "new understanding, the new seeking for the relationships of a Creative Force to the sons of men" (reading 1436–1).

(Q) What can I do to help bring about the New Age?
(A) You will have to practice it in your own life. (reading 5154–1)

Cayce said it would be necessary for us to achieve "the full consciousness of the ability to communicate with the Creative Forces or to be aware of the relationship with them, and how to apply these things to the material environment." This capability used to be ours in the days of Mu and Atlantis, but we abused it.

In relation to this troubled period of violent Earth changes Cayce spoke of "safety lands," referring to protected parts of the tired world, from which "the fifth root race will appear" (reading 5748–6)

COMPARISONS WITH THE FINDINGS OF EDGAR CAYCE—CHAPTER 5

The ARE began a series of archaeological investigations with the twenty-seven-year-old Rhonda James in 1957 to verify the veracity of Cayce's readings on ancient Egypt. The first drillings, carried out at the base of the Sphinx in 1978, began an extensive search for cavities using high-frequency seismic detectors, resistivity measurements, and aerial prospecting.

ARE also took part in the mapping project of the Sphinx in 1982, followed by the exclusive funding of a project that used carbon-14 dating. Samples were taken from the Sphinx and the outer surface of the pyramids through fragments of straw and wood inserted into the mortar used to join the blocks. They resulted in dates between 3809 and 2869 BCE. Between 1991 and 1993 ARE participated in geological dating of the Sphinx and its enclosure with a project directed by John West and geologist Robert Schoch from Boston University that dated the Sphinx back at least 2000 years. It was on this occasion that the seismologist Thomas Dobecki spotted a cavity nine by twelve meters and five meters deep under the right paw of the Sphinx, confirming the results obtained in the 1970s. Other seismographic surveys followed from 1995 to 1997 that extended to the so-called tomb of Osiris under the causeway between the Sphinx and the second pyramid. On this occasion Dobecki reconfirmed with new and more powerful means the existence of the room under the front leg. He also identified another room under the hind limbs, and a tunnel leading from this room to the Second Pyramid, passing beneath the tomb of Osiris.

In 2009 ARE became a member of the American Research Center in Egypt (ARCE, formerly EAO), thus collaborating with prestigious American universities working in the Egyptian territory.

Cayce's views on the Great Pyramid rely on the Anglo-Israelites, an order of 1,800 founded by the Richard brothers in the 1940s with the belief that the Anglo-Saxons are direct biological descendants of the ancient Israelites, and thus God's chosen people. One of their branches, Pyramidology, argues that the Great Pyramid is a prophetic monument and that the size of its system of corridors corresponds to the dates of attainment of the biblical prophecies about the Second Coming of Christ.

Pyramidologists Aldersmith and Davidson, authors of *The Great Pyramid: Its Divine Message*, claimed that the passage of time—from an ancient beginning until a specific moment in a near future—was engraved in the stone corridors of the Great Pyramid.

We do not share the Pyramidologists' views, but, for completeness and gratitude to those who gave us credit, we consider it necessary to give space to the views of Cayce in this area. A further point of disagreement is in the establishment of the age of the biblical Exodus: about 1250 BCE according to our studies, in 1486 BCE according to Cayce. Everyone will decide for themselves, since none of us has the arrogance to believe we own the truth. By the way, many of Cayce's indications, discredited from the start, have been confirmed by satellite research, as will be verified when we talk about the Sahara and the Nile.

The Great Pyramid and
the Prophecies Therein Contained

The Egyptologist Sir Gaston Maspero wrote: "The Pyramid and The Book of the Dead reproduce the same original text, the one in stone, the other in words."

While in trance Edgar Cayce was asked whether the inferences and conclusions of Pyramidologists Davidson and Aldersmith were correct, to which he replied: "Many of these deductions are correct. Many are far overdrawn. Only an initiate may understand" (reading 5748–5). Moreover, his readings extend the chronological period from 2001 to 2033, indicating that the timeline continues upward through a structure resembling the shape of a Japanese pagoda, placed above the King's Chamber. Although the readings argue that the timeline is so specific as to indicate year, day, hour, and place of the various events, we have not yet learned how to read these signs.

In Cayce's reading on the prophecy of the Great Pyramid (reading 5748–5), he actually said: "There are periods when even the hour, day, year, place, country, nation, town, and individuals are pointed out. That's how correct many of these prophecies are as made."

How could the ancient Egyptians see the fate of all from such a far period? Can all that we are living be predicted in the stones of this enduring building? It shakes our sense of free will and free choice, reminding us of Jesus's comments: "the very hairs on your head are all numbered" (Luke 12:7).

Cayce also said: "All changes that came in religious thought in the world are shown there in the variations in which the passage through same is reached, from the base to the top—or to the open tomb *and* the top."

According to Cayce the chronological period covered by the Great Pyramid began with the "Journey to the Pyrenees"—a reference to the end of the old land of Atlantis, Mu/Lemuria, Oz, Og, Zu, and others by means of heavy floods, earthquakes, meteorites, and volcanic eruptions (an era that the ancient Maya called the "Age of the Burning Rain"). These terrible Earth changes urged a residue of ancient peoples to migrate to a new more elevated land. One of those migrations traveled from

Atlantis to the Pyrenees, between Spain and France. Cayce said that after this migration the timeline moves to Egypt with the creation of that great culture. Afterward it continues from the era of Giza to the time of Jesus, which Cayce described as the "death of the Son of Man as a man"; this represents a major shift in consciousness and human potential. The chronograph will then progress "until 1998," the date that Cayce sets as the beginning of the changes toward a new period, a new era.

Cayce's readings state that the top of the King's Chamber in the pyramid marks the shift to both a new era and a new kind of body he called the "fifth root race," indicating that there had been four previous ages and physical types (in accordance with Maya mythology). For some time the body change had taken place through evolution, but perhaps through induced mutation there will be new bodies—more suitable for a deep consciousness. Today, we can be satisfied with our bodies, but let's imagine being reincarnated into a model developed to allow greater cosmic consciousness. It sounds like a very good thing, especially if this coincides with a new era in which "Satan is tied up," with no evil distractions and no temptations testing the new souls living on Earth.

The chronograph of Aldersmith and Davidson uses a pyramid inch that corresponds to one month. Cayce said that the open areas between the stones represent periods of expansion, while the stone's volumes represent times of consolidation. Eventually, we will reach the summit, and a new era will begin and a new body will develop. There's little time to go.

The Great Pyramid of Giza

The only remaining wonder of the ancient world, the Great Pyramid of Giza, was designed to be more than just a tomb for a pharaoh—the Great Pyramid was built as a permanent timetable of human history.

According to Cayce's readings, the construction of the Great Pyramid began in 10,490 BCE and lasted 100 years. His readings also say it was designed by the Atlanteans, whose chief architect, Hermes, was helped by a high priest named Ra Ta.

The readings assert that the Great Pyramid was built to provide a lasting testimony to the experience of the current "root race." It was meant to be a place of initiation in which the seekers of truth could learn the ancient wisdom and knowledge there engraved. The readings say that both John the Baptist and Jesus of Nazareth received teachings in the Great Pyramid before beginning their ministry. The Mandaeans of Iraq, current descendants of the Essene community of which Jesus and John the Baptist were both members, still consider as sacred the pilgrimage to the Great Pyramid. "In this same pyramid did the Great Initiate, the Master, take those last of the Brotherhood degrees with John, the forerunner of Him, at that place" (reading 5748–5). The readings add that the construction of the pyramid was designed to reflect events in human history "as related to the religious or the spiritual experiences of man" (reading 5748–6). In addition, "The rise and fall of nations were to be depicted in this same temple" (reading 294–151).

The outer surface of the Great Pyramid was composed of 144,000 casing stones, all well polished. The number 144,000 is a sacred number in Christianity—Cayce's readings suggest that the third group of souls, led (on Earth) by Aemilius, consisted of 144,000 souls.

The Great Pyramid, along with two sister pyramids of the Giza Plateau, the two pyramids of Dashour, and the tower of Letopolis, copied perfectly on the ground the positions of the stars in Orion in 10,500 BCE. Cayce gave this *same date* for construction of the pyramid, well before the match with the stars was discovered.

A Journey through the Great Pyramid

The following descriptive journey through the rooms of the Great Pyramid has been interpreted through the readings and confirmed by the research of Davidson and Aldersmith. Cayce corrected the original dates provided by Davidson for the period covered by the King's Chamber and the gallery in the House of Chaos from 1936–1953 to 1938–1958, the dates indicated below.

The Descending Passage

Entering the Great Pyramid you are in the descending passage, one of two main routes through the building. Near the entrance a line is engraved that represents the date of 2141 BCE. During the vernal equinox of that year the North Star (at that time Thuban in the constellation of the Dragon) aligned for the last time with the entrance of the pyramid and its light went into the passage. By measuring back from the line to the beginning of the passage we calculate the date of 2623 BCE, the year of the death of Pharaoh Khufu (Cheops). This date marks the moment of the "re-discovery" of the original teachings of the Great Pyramid by the Egyptian clergy. It was not until the reign of Khufu that the Great Pyramid was again used as a center of teaching and initiation to the great mysteries.

Continuing down you reach an intersection where the first passage joins a second with an ascending angle that is identical to the first. The date corresponding to this intersection would be 1486 BCE, the period of the Exodus when Moses led Israel out of captivity. The descending passage continues down past the level of the soil and finally ends in the House of Chaos.

The House of Chaos

The House of Chaos, or subterranean canal, is little more than an underground hole with a rocky floor and a low ceiling. It can confuse a visitor so much that finding the way to go uphill would be impossible. On the far side of the room there is a small gallery, so low that you can cross it only by walking on all fours. People who have not been initiated think this gallery is the way out, but after fifty feet they find there is no way out. The beginning and the end of this gallery correspond to the dates 1938 and 1958.

The Descending Passage and the House of Chaos represent the downward spiral of human development, the devolution of the spirit in the material world and the journey from light to darkness. If we had followed this path, instead of turning up at the intersection mentioned above, we would have been on a downward spiral, ending finally in a blind alley of chaos and destruction. The dates of the gallery, 1938–1958, certainly represent a low point in human history, as evidenced by the Nazis, the Holocaust, World War II, the atomic bomb, and the arms race. Since the tunnel ends in 1958 it was thought this path would lead to the destruction of the world in that year, probably due to nuclear annihilation.

Fortunately humanity made the right choice at the intersection of

Exodus and began to move upward along the Ascending Passage. If we imagine extending the ramp of the ascending passage downward, from the point of intersection to the outside of the pyramid, the end point of this line is 4000 BCE. According to biblical genealogy this date corresponds to the creation of Adam and Eve.

The Ascending Passage

Entering the Ascending Passage for the first time modern archaeologists had to dig around a cap of twenty-nine feet of granite that was blocking the entrance. Without doubt this cap was put in place to protect the pyramid tombs from marauders. The presence of this cap, still intact, would certainly have prevented looting at the hands of treasure hunters and makes it unlikely that a mummy was introduced into the pyramid once works were completed. The first section of the ascending passage is called the "Hall of Truth in Darkness" or "Israel under the Yoke of the Law." It represents the period in which the human race considered submission to the law a means of finding salvation. The block of red granite mentioned above is connected to 1486 BCE, the year of the Jewish Exodus. It symbolizes the liberation of mankind from the captivity of the material world as they were beginning to choose spiritual freedom at the expense of material comforts: the long journey to the Promised Land. The Hall of Truth in the Darkness ends in 4 BCE, according to Cayce the birth of Jesus of Nazareth. At this point the ascending passage opens into the Great Gallery and, at the same time, connects to a secondary horizontal passage leading to the Queen's Chamber.

The Queen's Chamber

The Queen's Chamber is also called the "Chamber of the Second or New Birth." A step heading downward from the horizontal passage represents the symbolic death of the self and the rebirth in an afterlife. This was the place of judgment, where the heart of the deceased or the initiate was compared with the Feather of Truth on the balance of judgment. The Queen's Chamber ends in the year 1918, a date that marked the signing of the armistice at the end of World War I and the beginning of the League of Nations. Although this political body failed, the principles for which it arose were focused on spiritual truth, and its simple appearance marked a high point in human history. The readings indicate that even the spirit of Christ was present at the peace table with Woodrow Wilson, who was fighting against serious disparities in order to establish this visionary organization: "In the manner as He (Christ Consciousness) sat at the peace conference in Geneva, in the heart and soul of a man not reckoned by many as even an unusually Godly man; yet raised for a purpose, and he chose rather to be a channel of His thought for the world" (reading 364–8).

The return from the Queen's Chamber in the Ascending Passage is called the "Path of the Presentation of the Regenerated Soul" and symbolizes the soul's spiritual rebirth.

The Great Gallery

The section of the Ascending Passage increases in height and width after the intersection with a horizontal passage, where the entrance of the Great Gallery, or "Hall of Truth in Light," is. The starting point of this gallery corresponds to Jesus's year of birth so the increase in width symbolizes the expansion of consciousness determined by his teachings. The Big Brother, the One who Shows the Way, had gone past the limits of the flesh and, overcoming death itself, had demonstrated the reality of our spiritual being. So, the law was respected and humanity could walk in "Truth in Light," understanding that salvation was achieved not by submitting to the law but by overcoming it. A change in the surface of the stone on one of the sides of the tunnel marks the year 30 CE, the date of the crucifixion and resurrection. Moreover, another change in the surface of the stone, on the opposite side of the gallery, corresponds to 1776, the year of the American Revolution, when the colonists made a written covenant with God guaranteeing to all "life, liberty, and the pursuit of happiness." The gallery ends on the date 1909, just before the First World War. At its end is the Big Step, a thirty-five-inch step that must be passed by straddling or climbing.

The Big Step

The Big Step covers the dates from 1909 to 1914, just before the First World War. It is also the point at which the timeline's length changes:

indeed, the scale of the pyramid inch now represents one month instead of one year. It feels like the Great Pyramid is now telling us that time has been accelerated. This step very likely represents the beginning of those "times and half-a-time" mentioned in the Bible when God would accelerate the speed of time so humanity can survive the forthcoming horrors. This idea was supported by a reading made in 1933 stating that the time of times and half-a-time "has been and is being fulfilled in this day" (reading 262–49).

The Big Step leads to the first low passage of the Antechamber.

The Antechamber

The first low passage of the antechamber is so low that you have to crawl to cross it. It marks the dates from 1914 to 1918, a low point in human history identified with the First World War. The Antechamber itself represents a period of ten years, 1918–1928, when the signing of the armistice of World War I and the beginning of the Great Depression occurred. It is also called the "Chamber of the Triple Veil" for the threefold section division of its granite walls. A second low passage leads outside the Antechamber and covers the years 1928–1938, a period characterized by a loss of spiritual values. This passage ends at the entrance of the King's Chamber.

In the Antechamber there is a large slab of stone known as Granite Foil whose center marks the culmination point of an imaginary extension of the ascending passage corresponding to September 17, 2001.

The King's Chamber

The entrance to the King's Chamber, or "The Chamber of the Open Tomb," corresponds to 1938, while the opposite wall bears the date of 1958. These dates coincide with dates in the gallery of the House of Chaos, reflecting the principle of "as above, so below."

When the King's Chamber was opened archaeologists found an empty sarcophagus of red granite. According to the readings the purpose of the empty sarcophagus was to clarify the interpretation of death: even if the physical body dies, the soul is eternal. This room was the site of the final initiation, where the initiates came to understand this truth. It is said that the initiate had to spend three days in the sarcophagus in deep meditation, during which the soul left the body to travel through spiritual realms. Upon return the initiate understood that the soul is the true self, and could understand it thoroughly, reminding the powers of his divine history.

While Davidson made the timeline finish at the end of the room, the readings assert that in fact the timeline continues up through the structure of the five "rooms of discharge" situated over the chamber that resembles a Japanese pagoda and consists of five rooms of red granite with intervening spaces. Two stones of gray limestone are arranged at an angle to form a pointed top. Following upward from the date of 1958 at ground level the timeline extends to the top of the pagoda, marking the year 2033.

The Green Sahara

Cayce revealed that, in ancient times, the poles of the Earth were overturned and the Nile flowed into the Atlantic (reading 276–2), a fact that we have discovered only recently thanks to satellite images that show traces of the ancient course of the Nile toward the ocean. "What is now the Sahara was a fertile land," said Edgar Cayce in 1932 (reading 5748–6). Yet when asked about the climate in ancient Egypt he replied: "More fertile than even in the present with the overflow as occurs, for only about a third of the present Sahara was there, though it was sandy loam with silt, in the use of the agricultural portions" (reading 275–38).

Here Cayce referred to seasonal flooding that would cover the land with mud that was rich in nutrients. Today the Nile has two dams and uses controlled irrigation, and although this has provided Egypt with three growing seasons while the natural rhythms of the Nile flood used to allow only two, the lack of rich river silt has created a need for agricultural fertilizers.

It is fascinating that science has confirmed the psychic vision of the *green* Sahara and that these dates match up with those of Edgar Cayce. On August 15, 2008, *Science Daily* reported the discovery of the largest Stone Age graveyard, found in the Sahara desert in Gober, Nigeria, south of Libya, southwest of Egypt. The Stone Age covers a wide span of time from about 3 million years until about 6000 BCE. It is estimated that this tomb dates back some 10,000 years, according to Cayce shortly after the advent of the protagonists of ancient Egypt: Ra Ta, Hermes, Axtel, and the tribe of Ararat. The article argues that this tomb provides "an unmatched testimony of life when the region was green."

Paul Sereno, professor at the University of Chicago, described the place as "ancient, apparently never visited." The Saharan winds had removed the sand from the bodies, all of which were in good condition with no signs of wounds. The skeletons of many animals that were unfit for the desert, along with corpses in more than 200 graves, made Sereno conclude, "We were in the green Sahara."

Two groups were buried in this place. The oldest people were sometimes over six feet tall, and their ceramics had wavy zigzag lines. There is some evidence that these men used to catch big perch with harpoons and lived in the Sahara during the most humid period between 10,000 and 8,000 years ago.

The second group, who lived there approximately 7,000 to 4,500 years ago, was composed of shorter persons, with lighter bodies, which had been buried with precious stones. Their ceramics were designed with Pointillist patterns (very close dots to create diversity of visual density and patterns of energy). One of these tombs was described as "a magnificent triple burial containing a woman and two children in a poignant embrace."

The article in *Science Daily* explained: "Although the Sahara has long been the world's largest desert, a slight oscillation of the Earth's orbit and other factors occurring some 12,000 years ago caused the North African seasonal monsoon to move slightly northward, bringing new rains to the Sahara. From Egypt in the east to Mauritania in the west, lakes with shorelines rich in vegetation dotted the landscape previously parched, drawing animals, fish and eventually people. To separate these two populations was an arid interval of perhaps a millennium that began about 8,000 years ago when the lakes disappeared and the site was abandoned."

Cayce's Egyptian period began 12,000 years ago and includes the arrival of a group from the sunken Atlantis led by Axtel (reading 615–1). Cayce said: "Nature, God, changed the poles" (reading 5249–1) and this also changed the weather patterns.

The Hall of Records under the Sphinx

In the readings of 1933 we find many references to the Hall of Records, a room that was hidden by Ra Ta, Hermes, and Ararat, underneath and near the right front paw of the Sphinx.

"With the storehouse, or record house (where the records are yet to be uncovered), there is a chamber or passage from the right forepaw to this entrance of the record chamber, or record tomb" (reading 5748–6).

According to Cayce the room contains ancient documents on the history of the human race, confirming that Atlantis was a real place, where we all, in other bodies, have lived and worked together.

According to the readings the Hall of Records is a secret chamber—a sealed room—where the documents of the "true teaching" as the priests of Atlantis had set forth were hidden by Ra Ta and his companions.

> *(Q) Give in detail what the sealed room contains.*
>
> *(A) A record of Atlantis from the beginnings of those periods when the Spirit took form or began the encasements in that land, and the developments of the peoples throughout their sojourn, with the record of the first destruction and the changes that took place in the land . . . and the buildings of the pyramid of initiation, with who, what, where, would come the opening of the records that are as copies from the sunken Atlantis; for with the change it must rise (the temple) again. (reading 378–16)*

According to various readings given to different people, in addition to the documents the hall also contains various objects such as musical instruments, linen textiles, and plates with seals.

Through these documents the world would find intimate roots in the One, the presence of "I AM," unity with God. Many people are earnestly looking for the documents that Cayce spoke of, but so far none have been found. Many of Cayce's readings refer to the period of Ra Ta and the documents of Atlantis: this epoch played a vital role in preparing for the Messiah and understanding it would have a part in the Second Coming. The readings stress that the Hall of Records will be found *in our times.*

For, these were to be kept as had been given by the priests in Atlantis or Poseidia (Temple), when these records of the race, of the developments, of the laws pertaining to one were put in their chambers and to be opened only when there was the returning of those into materiality, or to Earth's experience, when the change was imminent in the Earth; which change, we see, begins in '58 and ends with the changes wrought in the upheavals and the shifting of the poles, as begins then the reign in '98. (reading 378–16)

Analyzing the "Akashic Records"* Cayce said (60 years before Robert Bauval) that the plateau of Giza reflects the arrangement of the stars in the sky, and its monuments were designed to last thousands of years as a fascinating puzzle for humanity.

The testimonies coming from Atlantis tell of the beginning times when "the Spirit took shape" and started entering bodies, describing the development of these bodies and these people in the olden days of the legendary Lemuria and Atlantis and the subsequent migration of the new peoples moving to new lands, including the then young Egypt. The testimonies also describe the final destruction of Atlantis (the definitive end of the Pelasgic empire in the Mediterranean, according to our research) and the reconstruction in Egypt (which we believe was with the black pharaohs and the migrations of the Semitic peoples from Akkad). According to Cayce they would contain the "who, what, where, and when" of these ancient times and their rediscovery should take place in our time (reading 378–16). He pointed to the presence of thirty-two tablets or slabs of stone written in a form of pre-Atlantean hieroglyphic writing, perhaps Iberian, which will need to be translated (reading 2329–3).

Cayce explained how the ancient peoples "rebuilt" some (already old) monuments onto the "plans" of Giza and raised some new ones. Among the projects of reconstruction was the Sphinx, which according to Cayce is older than the Great Pyramid. Our attention then turns to the buildings that are connected with the Sphinx (the Temple of the Sphinx and

---

*The Akashic Records are a kind of spiritual archive containing all of the actions and thoughts of humanity that is accessible to those with an elevated consciousness.

the Valley Temple), well restored by the pharaohs, or to the pyramids of the plain built in the place where the Zeds were.

A temple of Isis would have been lost in the ancient flood "centuries before" the existence of the Sphinx. Cayce attributed this great flood to 22,006 BCE, consistently anticipating any archaeological dating of early Egypt. Cayce's pre-dynastic period begins with the constructors, the conquerors of Egypt, metaphorically called "the tribe of Mount Ararat"* to link them to Noah's flood. These conquerors were the demigods of the legends of ancient Egypt and those who sculpted the amazing Sphinx (around 10,700 BCE) before building the Great Pyramid (reading 195–14) in 10,500 BCE (reading 5748–5). (According to our research 10,500 BCE was the era of construction of the towers that are now situated inside the pyramids, whose covers have been correctly dated to around 2500 BCE.)

Around this period (10,500 BCE) a second group of survivors from Atlantis, with precious prehistoric testimonies in tow, arrived on the shores of Egypt. In front of the Sphinx, the Atlanteans and the Egyptians agreed to build what Cayce called the Pyramid of Records (reading 239–7), the Hall of Records (reading 519–1), and the Tomb of Records (reading 2329–2).

When asked where this secret storehouse was Cayce said it was between the Sphinx and the Nile (readings 378–16 and 5748–5). He also said that the "storehouse" is "facing same" (reading 5748–5) and is in "a pyramid of its own" (reading 2329–3). We believe this opens the possibility that the tunnel Dobecki discovered beneath the Sphinx is connected with the alleged room of the Great Pyramid behind the door of Gantenbrink or the door discovered by the Pyramid Rover.

The complex of the Sphinx is designed with two temples, and the pyramid of the testimonies can be found under the Temple of the Sphinx near the right front paw.

Recently, the Egyptian head of the Department of Antiquities, Dr. Zahi Hawass, announced the existence of an opening in the bedrock beneath the Sphinx, as Cayce had predicted. Hawass's group performed some drillings

---

*Mount Ararat is the mountain mentioned in the Bible that collapsed on the Ark of Noah.

in this opening and found it filled with groundwater. Hawass and his team are also exploring the vast system of caves, passages, and tunnels at about ninety-eight meters below the pyramids of Giza, described by Andrew Collins in his new book, *Beneath the Pyramids*, in collaboration with the Archeological Research Fund of the Edgar Cayce Center in Virginia Beach.

The Second Colonization of Egypt

According to our reconstruction, around 3600 BCE the Akkadian king Nimrod/Narmer/Naram Sin, grandson of Sargon the Great, extended his domain to Egypt. The Followers of Horus, groups of Nubian initiates, black-skinned but nevertheless descendants of the first Atlantean settlers, proclaimed Nimrod "first pharaoh." After his death the empire was divided into Pharaonic Egypt on one side and the Akkadian empire on the other with the appointment of a second indigenous black pharaoh. He, or his immediate successor, would have re-sculpted the head of the Sphinx according to his somatic features.

According to Cayce the events look more or less the same, with a victorious dynasty coming from the east to Egypt, where it was met by Nubians who shared the ancient treasures saved from Atlantis[2] millennia before.

COMPARISONS WITH THE FINDINGS OF EDGAR CAYCE—CHAPTER 6

Around 10,000 BCE a massive migration of Cro-Magnon headed from Europe to the Far East, leaving the mark of its passage in Mongolia in the areas of the Gobi Sea and the Indus Valley. The Cro-Magnon race remained isolated here after the earthquakes and inundations associated with the second flood (9600 BCE). Its language and physical traits evolved over millennia to be "transformed" into the race currently known as Indo-European, also known as the Aryan race.

Cayce and the Arî

Readings trace the ethnicity of the Arî, or Aryans, from the name of one of Atlantis's islands and its inhabitants:

(Q) What were the principal islands called at the time of the
final destruction?
(A) Poseidia and Aryan, and Og. (reading 364–6)

For this reason, following the flight of its inhabitants to various "safe" lands, the people coming from the Aryan island, called Arî or Aryans, settled in various parts of the world. The historical period is between 50,000 and 10,000 BCE approximately. Geographically closer to their homeland was the Yucatán, where some groups fled and settled:

. . . and another in the Aryan or Yucatan land. (reading 2012–1)

Both . . . in the Atlantean or Yucatan or Aryan. (reading 1895–1)

. . . the Aryans in the American land. (reading 1947–1)

We find some isolated references to ancient Persia as an "Aryan land" in the early post-Atlantean period, indicating that settlers from that island of Atlantis settled there, bringing that name:

. . . the Persian or Aryan land. (reading 1472–10)

. . . of that ruler in the Arian land [here a synonym of Persia]. (reading 204–1)

. . . the entity was among those who set about the unifying of the teachings of the Atlanteans, the Egyptians, the Indian, the Indo-Chinese, the Mongoloid, and the Aryan peoples. (reading 1681–1)

The effect of the entity's study of astrological effects . . . Study those that have been written from the ancient Chaldean, Egyptian, of those of the Achaic, also of the Aryan, also those of the Mongoloid. (reading 256–2)

Generally, the readings would talk about a vast region that today includes the Carpathians (from the Czech Republic to Ukraine), Iran (Persia), and Iraq (Chaldeans). Most likely, the Arî, who moved eastward with Osiris toward Mongolia, inhabited this area, which was included in the Mediterranean Pelasgian empire.

Elsewhere, Aryan is synonymous with Chaldean:

. . . then afterward known as those of the Aryans, and of the Chaldeans. (reading 4505–1)

. . . a period which will be between that which is called the modernistic and the Egyptian, Aryan, or Chaldean. (reading 345–4)

There also exists a reference to our recent history:

. . . the theme of the Nazis (the Aryan). (reading 416–7)

The Land of the Gobi

While in his hypnotic state Edgar Cayce would refer to a sunken continent between the Pacific and the Indian Ocean (now reduced only to the Philippines, Indonesia, and Singapore) alternately with the name "Lemuria" and "Mu." The latter name identified for a certain period the northwest end of the continent. In its later days, when the son of Mu, Muzuen, became king, most of the original continent had already disappeared into the sea, long before the definitive end of Atlantis. What remained was its western end, also called the land of the Gobi. Its population dispersed from current Indochina to the north, bringing that name up to the current Gobi desert, which was then a fertile land. Perhaps this race met the red race of Osiris in Mongolia and mingled with it, contributing to its evolution toward the Indo-European type. "Land of the Gobi" was also the name given to a few isolated colonies of descendants of Mu on the other side of the ocean in the Andean mountain ranges and, surprisingly, in the plateau region of the American Southwest. Both areas apparently represent the ends of Lemuria in the past. Cayce explained that the poles were then reversed (actually, geology tells us that they "only" moved), thus changing the orientation of the compass (reading 364–14).

Muzuen founded a city in the "Land of the Sun" (as Cayce called it):

the Gobi. Cayce said that in ancient times the Gobi was not a desert but a paradise. Here Muzuen's son built what Cayce called the "City of Gold" with a "Temple of Gold" (reading 877–12). According to Cayce both will be rediscovered, and when that happens people will know that despite evolution not all ancient things were primitive because there was involution of the Spirit before ascending evolution through matter. Although Muzuen and his son were males, Cayce claimed that in those ancient times females ruled (reading 2067–4).

COMPARISONS WITH THE FINDINGS OF EDGAR CAYCE—CHAPTER 10

According to Cayce connections we have identified between characters of different ages (like Thoth, Sargon, and Jesus) actually represent their reincarnations. The following material about connections between Christ and other figures of the past was provided by ARE–Italy.

The readings tell us that the "Savior" of the Bible, both in physical manifestation and as a Christic impulse that drives others in tune with the Cosmic Consciousness, has influenced *all* forms of philosophy or religious thought that through history have taught that there is one God (reading 364–9).

This entity was created as the first Son of the Creator, as a thought form with the name of Aemilius who shouldered the carnal experience for Himself. Aemilius projected Lilith, creating her "from out of self" as "the first of that that was made" in order to be husband and wife (reading 364–7). Therefore, Lilith was Aemilius's soul mate.

By mentioning the most important incarnations of Christ throughout world history Cayce confirmed the apocryphal tradition long established by listing:

- Adam: The earthly Adam was projected in the three-dimensional world from its own "universal soul." Aemilius, provided at the beginning with an androgynous body in carnal form, originated from the Universal Soul itself. He came as Adam in a part of Atlantis known since ancient times as Eden, a sacred city in Poseidia (reading 390–2). In that fateful incarnation he represented the red race (Cro-Magnon).

- Enoch-Thoth: Cayce places the birth of Enoch twenty-two years after the death of Adam. The people knew Enoch by a different name: Thoth-Hermes. Cayce says that, in the guise of Thoth-Hermes or Hermes Trismegistus,* he designed the Great Pyramid (reading 294–151).
- Melchizedek-Sargon: From Ur, which Cayce identifies as "a land, a place, a city," Melchizedek was able to command or guide the "thoughts" of that time or experience (reading 364–9).
- Zend: Father of Zoroaster (readings 364–7, 288–6, and 288–48).
- Joseph (son of Jacob), Joshua (spokesman for Moses and his successor), Asaph (musician and confidant of King David), Jeshua (readings 364–7, 5023-2, 362–1, and 5749–14), and Jesus: Of the thirty earthly lives attributed to Christ it is interesting to note that, of the most important nine lives just given, all but one (Zend) can be traced to the Bible, while the last five—including Jesus—follow the lineage of Abraham.

In all his incarnations, from the "first Adam" to the "last Adam," Jesus was a personification of the Universal Christ Consciousness that brought the Word of God to man. But with Melchizedek ("Without father, without mother, without genealogy, having neither beginning of days nor end of life, but made like the Son of God," Hebrews 7:3) there was the first *improvement* of the lower self absorbed by the superior self and become one with it. Undoubtedly for this reason Cayce referred to "Melchizedek, in the perfection" (reading 5749–14). Evaluating according to logic there was no apparent need for Him to pass through additional embodiments in his own interest; it was in the interest of all humanity that He continued to return.

Gnosticism in Cayce's Readings

The word "Gnosticism" appears in a single reading of Cayce:

---

*Hermes Trismegistus is the professed author of the *Corpus Hermeticum,* a series of sacred texts.

> *(Q) The eleventh problem concerns a parallel with Christianity. Is Gnosticism the closest type of Christianity to that which is given through this source [the Akashic Records]?*
>
> *(A) This is a [good] parallel, and was the commonly accepted one until there began to be set rules in which there were the attempts to take shortcuts. And there are none in Christianity!*
>
> *(Q) What action of the early church, or council, can be mentioned as that which ruled reincarnation from Christian theology?*
>
> *(A) Just as indicated, the attempts of individuals to accept or take advantage of, because of this knowledge, see? (reading 5749–14)*

Even without mentioning it one can describe Cayce's attitude toward Christian Gnosticism: in terms of intention and often of teaching in many ways a deep understanding of the nature of faith and Christian life emerges that certainly suggests a Christianity without shortcuts or ideas of "cheap grace." The Christian gospel declares the full opening of God's love for humanity, heightened by the very compassionate advent of Christ for our redemption—a liberation that goes absolutely beyond anyone's merits. The proper response of man includes not just one but many conversions or bonds of faith and obedience. This implies that every day is the "moment" of an ever-evolving salvation not as an eternal recurrence but as an ascending path that involves active commitment. Every day has its graces and its renewal, opportunities for growth in the service of God and mankind, all in the context of the grand cosmic plan of the God who in Christ has allowed our daily appropriation and application of these opportunities—a fair God and a universe with no limits.

Bimini

In June 1940, four years before his death, Edgar Cayce stated that an island in the Bahamas, Bimini, "will be among the first parts of Atlantis that will rise, expected between 1968 and 1969, in not much time."[3]

Twelve thousand years ago, the submerged plateau of the Bahamas, or

Bahama Banks, was above sea level. The wide area contained inlets and inland waterways that are now evident on depth maps and represent parts of the deep ocean that penetrate the Bahama Banks and surround them. Before the lifting of water at the end of the last ice age this ground area formed one large island or several islands. Since 1968 there has been a certain lifting of the bottom of the Great Bahama Bank, revealing traces of formations in places where previous aerial photos had distinguished none. Later, confirming Cayce's prediction, underwater discoveries were made, especially in the vicinity of Bimini, of what appears to be massive masonry on the current seabed: huge blocks of stone placed one beside the other, perhaps to form roads, platforms, harbor works, or collapsed walls. Partially fossilized mangrove roots, grown over the stones, have been C-14 dated back to 12,000 BCE.*

The most famous finding was that of the Street or Wall of Bimini, first discovered in 1968 by Dr. J. Manson Valentine with divers Jacques Mayol, Harold Climo, and Robert Angove. Here are the words of Valentine:

> [The structure is] like a large paving made of rectangular or polygonal stones, of variable measure and thickness, evidently adapted and carefully aligned, so as to form a layout that convincingly suggested intervention of man.[4]

The larger pieces, at least three to four and a half meters long, cover the entire length in four straight and parallel lines, while the smaller stones form mosaic-type floors. The longest road is a double row of regular boulders interrupted by two enlargements that contain very large, flat stones supported by vertical elements at the corners (similar to the ancient dolmens of western Europe); to the southeast the end of this great street ends in a beautifully curved corner. The three shorter streets have uniform widths and end with cornerstones. It seems that the giant construc-

---

*In one reading Cayce claimed that in an area around the Bahamas, now belonging to the then unknown Bermuda Triangle, there were energy sources belonging to the lost civilization and that area has now sunk into the "Tongue of the Ocean," a deep trench 1.8 kilometers deep and 160 kilometers long, off the island of Andros.

tion draws a turning point and reappears in other parts of the ocean floor. Further observations in deeper water have pointed out the existence, at least in one area, of a multilayered construction. Exploratory flights carried out since 1968 have revealed extraordinary formations, evidently artificial, on both the Bahama Banks and the seabed from Cuba, Haiti, and Santo Domingo. Some seem to be huge pyramids or dome-shaped creations—one of these in Bimini measures forty-two by fifty-five meters and could be the top of a truncated pyramid. A wall nine meters high and one hundred sixty kilometers long extends into the ocean off the coast of Venezuela near the mouth of the Orinoco. In the sea there are said to be other large pyramids or platforms of temples, and it seems that in Cuban waters there is a whole complex of submerged ruins waiting to be explored.

This was what was known in 1974, when Charles Berlitz wrote the best-seller *The Bermuda Triangle*. Since then we had no other information about this area of the Bahamas until 2001, when Reuters reported that a group of scientists from Advanced Digital Communications had identified a "sunken city" off the coast of Cuba and identified what appeared to roads, ruins of buildings, and even a pyramid. But after the initial excitement, the story fell into oblivion. In his book *The Doors of Atlantis* (2000) Andrew Collins advanced the thesis that Cuba had been the center of a vast pre-Columbian civilization like Atlantis. Ivor Zapp and George Erikson, in their book *The Road of Atlantis* (2002), put Costa Rica in charge of a very advanced maritime empire. The adventurer F. A. Mitchell-Hedges suggested that the remains of the lost civilization were in Honduras. All this adds clues to the presence of Pelasgians in the New World.

On December 17, 2009, correspondent Alessandra Farkas released the following article in the *Corriere della Sera*:

New York—A group of archaeologists has discovered the ruins of a great ancient city on the seabed of the Caribbean Sea whose location remains secret but according to rumors would be older than the pyramids of Giza, Egypt. It could even be Atlantis, the disappeared legendary island mentioned for the first time by Plato. The news, published exclusively in English from the Paris newspaper *Herald de Paris*, was quickly echoed by American websites. Satellite images of the city show something completely different from the submerged city discovered in 2001 off the coast of Cuba by joint Russian-Canadian researchers. In an interview from Washington with the *Herald* the project leader—who asked to remain anonymous—was careful not to reveal the coordinates of the place, presumably to avoid crowds of divers hunting for treasure during the festive season.

"We found a structure resembling a pyramid, tall and slender," said the head of the expedition, "and even a structure with parallel standing pillars and beams among the rubble of what looks like a ruined building. But you cannot find pillars and beams without human intervention."

At this point everyone can believe or not believe, but what is important to us is that the ARE will continue to unearth, year after year, all the pieces of the puzzle that is our forgotten history.

NOTES

INTRODUCTION:
BEYOND THE MIRROR

1. Louis Charpentier, *Le Mystère Basque* [The Basque Mystery] (Paris: Robert Laffont, 1975).

I. THE SLIDING
OF EARTH'S CRUST

1. Albert Einstein, "Letter to Charles Hutchins Hapgood (August 5, 1953)," in Charles Hapgood, *The Path of the Pole* (Kempton, Ill.: Adventures Unlimited Press, 1999).
2. Plato, *Laws*, trans. Trevor J. Saunders (London: Penguin, 1970), book 3.
3. Alphonse de Candolle, *Origin of Cultivated Plants* (New York: Hafner Publishing Co., 1959).
4. Nikolaï Ivanovich Vavilov, "The Origin, Variation, Immunity and Breeding of Cultivated Plants: Selected Writings," *Chronica Botanica* 13, no. 1–6 (1951).
5. Hubert Howe Bancroft, *The Native Races of the Pacific States of North America*, vol. 3 (Whitefish, Mo.: Kessinger Publishing, Inc., 2005).
6. Penelope Farmer, *Beginnings: Creation Myths of the World* (London: Chatto & Windus, 1978), 127.
7. William Tyler Olcott, *Sun Lore of All Ages* (New York: G. P. Putnam's Sons, 1914).
8. Rand Flem-Ath and Rose Flem-Ath, *Atlantis Beneath the Ice: The Fate of the Lost Continent* (Rochester, Vt.: Bear & Company, 2012), 43–44.

9. Rand Flem-Ath and Rose Flem-Ath, *When the Sky Fell: In Search of Atlantis* (Toronto: Stoddart, 1995), 28.

10. Hiram Bingham, "The Story of Machu Picchu," *National Geographic,* February 1995.

11. See Zecharia Sitchin, *The Lost Realms* (New York: Avon Books, 1990).

12. Hiram Bingham, *The Lost City of the Incas* (New York: Duell, Sloan and Pearce, 1948).

13. Georges Cuvier, in Robert Silverberg, *Mammoths, Mastodons and Man* (Columbus, Ohio: McGraw-Hill Companies Ltd., 1970).

14. Georges Cuvier, *Revolutions and Catastrophes in the History of the Earth,* in *A Source Book in Geology* (curated by K. Mather, Hafner Publishing Company, 1964), reprinted in facsimile from a 1939 edition by Harvard University Press.

15. Ibid.

16. Louis Agassiz, in Edward Lurie, *Louis Agassiz: A Life in Science* (Baltimore: Johns Hopkins University Press, 1988).

17. Louis Agassiz, *Geological Sketches* (Boston: Ticknor & Fields, 1866).

18. Flem-Ath and Flem-Ath, *When the Sky Fell,* 45 and 166.

19. James Hay, John Imbrie, and Nicholas Shackleton, "Variations in the Earth's Orbit: Pacemaker of the Ice Ages," *Science* 194 (1976): 1121–32.

20. Albert Einstein, in Charles Hapgood, preface to *The Earth's Shifting Crust* (New York: Pantheon Books, 1958).

21. Flem-Ath and Flem-Ath, *When the Sky Fell: In Search of Atlantis* (Toronto: Stoddart, 1995).

22. Ibid., 153–54.

23. Flem-Ath and Flem-Ath, *Atlantis Beneath the Ice,* 154–55.

24. Flavio Barbiero, *Una Civiltà sotto Ghiaccio* (Milan: Editore Nord, 2000).

25. Flem-Ath and Flem-Ath, *When the Sky Fell,* 77–78; Flem-Ath and Flem-Ath, *Atlantis Beneath the Ice,* 140.

26. Donald G. Sutherland and Michael J. C. Walker, "A Late Devensian Ice-free Area and Possible Interglacial Site on the Isle of Lewis, Scotland," *Nature* 309 (June 21, 1984): 701–3.

27. R. D. Guthrie, "Mammals of the Mammoth Steppe as Paleo-environmental Indicators," in David M. Hopkins, *Paleoecology of Beringia,* 425–44 (Amsterdam: Academic Press, 1982).

28. Flem-Ath and Flem-Ath, *When the Sky Fell: In Search of Atlantis.*

29. Hapgood, *The Path of the Pole.*

30. Frank C. Hibben, *The Lost Americans* (New York: T. Y. Crowell Co., 1968).

31. F. Rainey, "Archaeological Investigations in Central Alaska," *American Antiquity* 4 (1940): 299–308.

32. Hapgood, *The Path of the Pole.*

33. Ibid.

34. Ibid.

35. Flem-Ath and Flem-Ath, *When the Sky Fell,* 83–88.

36. Merritt Ruhlen, "Voices from the Past," *Natural History,* March 1987.

37. Flem-Ath and Flem-Ath, *When the Sky Fell,* 61.

38. Ibid., 167 and 168.

39. Plato, "Critias," in *Timaeus and Critias,* trans. Demond Lee (London: Penguin, 1965), book 7.

40. Ibid.

41. Bal Gangadhar Tilak, *The Arctic Home in the Vedas* (Poona City, India: Tilak Bros., 1903).

42. William F. Warren, *Paradise Found: The Cradle of Human Race at the North Pole* (Boston: Houghton Mifflin, 1885).

43. Tilak, *The Arctic Home in the Vedas.*

44. Ibid.

45. Ibid.

46. James Darmesteter, trans., "Vendidad: Fargard I," in *Sacred Books of the East* (Oxford: Clarendon Press, 1890).

47. James Darmesteter, trans., "Vendidad: Fargard II," in *Sacred Books of the East.*

48. Harold Osborne, *South American Mythology* (London: Paul Hamlyn, 1968).

49. Ignatius Donnelly, *Atlantis: The Antediluvians World* (New York: Harper & Brothers, 1882); Robin Palmer, *Dictionary of Mythical Places* (New York: H. Z. Walck, 1975).

50. Bancroft, *The Native Races of the Pacific States of North America.*

51. Warren, *Paradise Found.* (Compare with traditions on the foundations of Cuzco and Jerusalem, chapter 11.)

52. Ibid.

53. Flem-Ath and Flem-Ath, *Atlantis Beneath the Ice,* 95–97.

54. *Mahābhārata: Shanti Parva,* trans. Kisari Mohan Ganguli (www.sacred-texts.com/hin/m12/), book 12, section 347.

55. Plato, "Critias," book 4.

56. Tertullian in *De came et anima,* as quoted in Sergio Frau, *Le Colonne d'Ercole: Un'inchiesta* (Rome: Nur Neon Ltd., 2002).

57. Diodorus Siculus, *Library of History,* trans. C. H. Oldfather (Cambridge, Mass.: Loeb Classical Library, 1933), book 5; Philipp Cluvier, *Siciliae Antiquae Libri Duo* (1619), I.

58. Plato, *Timaeus,* trans. Peter Kalkavage (Newburyport, Mass.: Focus, 2001), book 3.

59. Philocori, *De Rebus Athene,* fragment in Pietro Manzi, Introduction to Cataplus of Lucianus Samosatensis, catalogued as "Lipsia 1812."

60. Francesco Prontera, *L'idea di Italia* [The idea of Italy] (Florence: Leo S. Olschki, 2000).

61. Plato, *Timaeus,* book 3.

62. Among the Egyptian sources worth listing are the writings of Wilbour, the Poem of Pentaur, Merenptah's stele, Medinet Habu reliefs, the Harris papyrus, and the bas-reliefs of Luxor and Karnak.

63. Plato, "Critias," book 10.

64. Siculus, *Library of History,* book 1, 28.

65. Elaine Sanceau, *Henry the Navigator* (Hamden, Conn.: Archon Books, 1969).

66. Edward Gaylord Bourne, *Spain in America* (New York: Barnes & Noble, 1962).

67. Flem-Ath and Flem-Ath, *Atlantis Beneath the Ice,* 120.

2. GLACIAL MELTS
AND GLOBAL FLOODS

1. Cesare Emiliani, *Planet Earth* (Cambridge: Cambridge University Press, 1992).

2. Jim Allen, archaeologist at La Trobe University in Australia in *Humans at the End of the Ice Age: The Archaeology of the Pleistocene-Holocene Transition,* ed. Lawrence Guy Straus, Berit Valentin Eriksen, Jon M. Erlandson, and David R. Yesner (New York: Plenum Press, 1996), note 4.

3. Peter Kersher, researcher of the Department of Geography and Environmental Science at Monash University in Melbourne.

4. Straus, Eriksen, Erlandson, and Yesner, *Humans at the End of the Ice Age,* 175.

5. Ibid.

6. Ibid.

7. Richard Rudgley, *Lost Civilization of the Stone Age* (New York: Touchstone, 1999).

8. N. C. Fleming, "Archeological Evidence for Vertical Movement of the Continental Shelf during the Paleolithic, Neolithic and Bronze Age Periods," in *Coastal Tectonics,* eds. I. S. Stewart and C. Vita-Finzi (London: Geological Society, 1998).

9. Thomas J. Crowley and Gerald R. North, *Palaeoclimatology* (Oxford: Oxford University Press, 1991).

10. R. C. L. Wilson, S. A. Drury, and J. L. Chapman, *The Great Ice Age* (New York: Routledge and the Open University, 2000).

11. Ibid.

12. Ibid.

13. Ibid.

14. Robert M. Schoch, Ph.D., *Voices of the Rocks: A Scientist Looks at Catastrophes and Ancient Civilizations* (New York: Harmony Books, 1999).

15. Paul LaViolette, Ph.D., *Earth under Fire: Humanity's Survival of the Ice Age* (Schenectady, N.Y.: Starburst Publications, 1997; Rochester, Vt.: Bear & Company, 2005). Citations are to the Starburst edition.

16. Cesare Emiliani, "The Cause of the Ice Ages," *Earth and Planetary Science Letters* 37 (1978): 347–54.

17. Crowley and North, *Palaeoclimatology.*

18. Emiliani, *Planet Earth.*

19. Charles H. Fletcher III and Clark E. Sherman, "Submerged Shorelines on O'ahu, Hawai'i: Archive of Episodic Transgression during the Deglaciation?" *Journal of Coastal Research* special issue, no. 17.

20. Graham Hancock, *Underworld: The Mysterious Origins of Civilization* (London: Penguin, 2002).

21. Ibid.

22. Cesare Emiliani, *The Scientific Companion,* Wiley Popular Science (New York, N.Y.: Wiley and Sons, 1995): 157, 251

23. Recorded interview with John Straw, conducted by John Grigsby, assistant researcher of Graham Hancock (1999).

24. Stephen Oppenheimer, *Eden in the East: The Drowned Continent of Southeast Asia* (London: Phoenix, 1998).

25. McGuire, W. J., et al., "Correlation between Rate of Sea-level Change and Frequency of Explosive Volcanism in the Mediterranean," *Nature* 389 (October 2, 1997): 473–76.

26. Ibid.

27. Ibid.

28. Arch C. Johnston, "A Wave in the Earth," *Science* 274 (November 1, 1996).

29. Oppenheimer, *Eden in the East.*

30. Johnston, "A Wave in the Earth."

31. Ibid.

32. Ronald Arvidsson, "Fenno-Scandian Earthquakes: Whole Crustal Rupturing Related to Post-Glacial Rebound," *Science* 274 (November 1, 1996).

33. Johnston, "A Wave in the Earth."

34. Ibid.

35. *The Guardian* (London) January 18, 1995.

36. Arvidsson, "Fenno-Scandian Earthquakes."

37. Charles Ginenthal, *The Extinction of the Mammoth,* a special double issue of the journal *The Velikovskian,* vol. 3, no. 2–3 (1997).

38. John Shaw, "A Meltwater Model for Laurentide Subglacial Landscapes," in *Geomorphology Sans Frontiers* (John Wiley and Sons, 1996), 181–236.

39. John Shaw, "A Qualitative View of Sub-Ice-Sheet Landscape Evolution," *Progress in Physical Geography* 18, no. 2 (1994): 159–84.

40. Ibid.

41. John Shaw, "Drumlins, Subglacial Meltwater Floods, and Ocean Responses" *Geology* 17, no. 9 (September 1989): 853–56.

42. John Shaw, "Sedimentary Evidence Favoring the Formation of Rogen Landscapes by Outburst Floods," University of Alberta, December 11, 1998.

43. John Shaw and Donald Kville, "A Glacio-Fluvial Origin for Drumlins in the Livingston Lake Area, Saskatchewan," *Canadian Journal of Earth Science* 21 (1984): 1442–59.

44. Paul Blanchon and John Shaw, "Reef Drowning during the Last Deglaciation: Evidence for Catastrophic Sea Level Rise and Ice-Sheet Collapse," *Geology* 23, no. 1 (1995).

45. Fletcher and Sherman, "Submerged Shorelines on O'ahu, Hawai'i," 141–52.

46. Ibid.

47. R. C. L. Wilson, S. A. Drury, and J. L. Chapman, "The Great Ice Age: Climate Change and Life," *Journal of Quaternary Science* 15, no. 8 (December 2000): 843–44.

48. Blanchon and Shaw, "Reef Drowning during the Last Deglaciation."

49. Wilson, Drury, and Chapman, "The Great Ice Age."

50. Ibid.

51. Oppenheimer, *Eden in the East.*

52. Ibid.

53. LaViolette, *Earth under Fire.*

54. Ibid.

3. ANCIENT CIVILIZATIONS
OF MEXICO AND PERU

1. Marco Zagni, *L'Impero Amazzonico* [The Amazon Empire] (Florence: M. I. R. Edizioni, 2002).

2. Jose de Acosta, "The Natural and Moral History of the Indies," book 1, chapter 4, in Harold Osborne, *South American Mythology* (London: Paul Hamlyn, 1968).

3. Garcilaso de la Vega, *Royal Commentaries of the Incas and General History of Peru* (New York: Orion Press, 1961).

4. Ibid.

5. William Sullivan, *The Secret of the Incas: Myth, Astronomy, and the War against Time* (New York: Crown Publishers, 1996).

6. Osborne, *South American Mythology,* 74.

7. Ibid.

8. Juan de Betanzos, "Suma y narración de los Incas," in Osborne, *South American Mythology,* 79.

9. Ibid.

10. Ibid.

11. Ignatius Donnelly, *Atlantis: The Antediluvian World* (New York: Harper & Brothers, 1882).

12. de Betanzos, "Suma y narración de los Incas."

13. de la Vega, *Royal Commentaries of the Incas and General History of Peru.*

14. Sullivan, *The Secret of the Incas.*

15. Graham Hancock, *Fingerprints of the Gods* (New York: Three Rivers Press, 1996).

16. Ibid.

17. Diodorus Siculus, *Library of History,* trans. C. H. Oldfather (Cambridge, Mass.: Loeb Classical Library, 1933), 1–14.

18. Graham Hancock and Santha Faiia, *Heaven's Mirror: Quest for the Lost Civilization* (New York: Three Rivers Press, 1998).

19. Harold Osborne, *Indians of the Andes: Aymaras and Quechuas* (New York: Routledge and Kegan Paul, 1952); *Feats and Wisdom of the Ancients* (Alexandria, Va.: Time-Life Books, 1990).

20. de la Vega, *Royal Commentaries of the Incas and General History of Peru.*

21. Arthur Posnansky, *Tihuanacu: The Cradle of American Man,* vol. 2 (La Paz, Bolivia: Ministry of Education, 1957), 90–91.

22. Hancock and Faiia, *Heaven's Mirror.*

23. Posnansky, *Tihuanacu,* vol. 2, 183.

24. Stephanie Dalley, *Myths from Mesopotamia* (Oxford: Oxford University Press, 1990).

25. Robert K. G. Temple, "Fragments of Berossus," appendix 2 in *The Sirius Mystery* (Rochester, Vt.: Destiny Books, 1987).

26. Hancock and Faiia, *Heaven's Mirror,* chapter 17.

27. Sullivan, *The Secret of the Incas.*

28. H. S. Bellamy and P. Allan, *The Calendar of Tiahuanaco: The Measuring System of the Oldest Civilization* (London: Faber & Faber, 1956), 47.

29. Posnansky, *Tihuanacu,* vol. 3, 57, 133–34, and table 92.

30. Posnansky, *Tihuanacu,* vol. 1, 137–39; Paul S. Martin and Richard G. Klein, eds., "Quaternary Extinctions: A Prehistoric Revolution." (University of Arizona Press, 1984), 85.

31. Posnansky, *Tihuanacu,* vol. 2, 56, and vol. 3, 196.

32. David L. Browman, "New Light on Andean Tiahuanaco," *American Scientist* 69 (1981).

33. Colin Renfrew and Paul Bahn, *Archaeology: Theory, Methods and Practice,* 5th ed. (London: Thames & Hudson, 2008).

34. Bernard Diaz de Castillo, quoted in Dale M. Brown, ed., *Aztecs: Reign of Blood and Splendour* (New York: Time-Life Books, 1999).

35. Juan de Torquemada, *Monarquía indiana,* vol. 1 in Constance Irwin, *Fair Gods and Stone Faces* (London: W. H. Allen, 1964), 37–38.

36. Peter Tompkins, *Mysteries of the Mexican Pyramids* (London: Thames & Hudson, 1987).

37. James Bailey, *The God-Kings and the Titans* (London: Hodder & Stoughton, 1972).

38. Felix Guirand, ed., *Larousse Encyclopedia of Mythology* (Amherst, N.Y.: Prometheus Press, 1959).

39. Diego de Duran, *Historia Antiqua de la Nueva España* (1585).

40. Charles Hapgood, *Maps of the Ancient Sea Kings: Evidence of Advanced Civilization in the Ice Age* (Kempton, Ill.: Adventures Unlimited Press, 1966).

41. Byron St. Cummings, "Cuicuilco and the Archaic Culture of Mexico," in the *University of Arizona Bulletin* 5 (November 15, 1933): 8.

42. Irwin, *Fair Gods and Stone Faces.*

43. Quotation from Jennifer Westwood, ed., *The Atlas of Mysterious Places: The World's Unexplained Sacred Sites, Symbolic Landscapes, Ancient Cities, and Lost Lands* (New York: Grove Press, 1987).

4. THE KINGDOMS OF THE MEDITERRANEAN AFTER THE FIRST FLOOD

1. Robert Graves, *The Greek Myths* (London: Penguin, 1963).

2. Diodorus Siculus, *Library of History,* trans. C. H. Oldfather (Cambridge, Mass.: Loeb Classical Library, 1933), 61 and 89.

3. Graves, *The Greek Myths.*

4. Siculus, *Library of History,* 51.

5. Plato, *Timaeus,* trans. Peter Kalkavage (Newburyport, Mass.: Focus, 2001), book 3.

6. Graves, *The Greek Myths.*

7. Ibid.

8. Plato, *Timaeus,* book 3.

9. Giorgio de Santillana and Hertha von Dechend, *Hamlet's Mill: An Essay Investigating the Origins of Human Knowledge and Its Transmission through Myth* (Boston: Gambit, 1969).

10. See Solange de Mailly Nesle, *Astrology: History, Symbols, and Signs* (Rochester, Vt.: Inner Traditions, 1985).

5. MEGALITHS AND GODS AMONG MEN IN THE TIME OF OSIRIS

1. E. A. E. Reymond, *The Mythical Origin of the Egyptian Temple* (Manchester, U.K.: Manchester University Press, 1969).

2. Herodotus, *The Histories,* trans. Robin Waterfield (Oxford: Oxford University Press, 1988), book 3, 28:3.

3. Robert Graves, *The Greek Myths* (London: Penguin, 1963).

4. Diodorus Siculus, *Library of History,* trans. C. H. Oldfather (Cambridge, Mass.: Loeb Classical Library, 1933), book 1, 24.

5. Ibid., book 1, 3.

6. Ibid., book 3, 74.

7. Herodotus, *The Histories,* book 3, 43.

8. Ibid., book 4, 1137.

9. Graves, "Character and Deeds of Dionysus" in *The Greek Myths.*

10. Graves, *The Greek Myths.*

11. Ibid.

12. R. Graves, "Theban Co-Kings Ruled Upper Egypt during the Hyksos Occupation of Delta" in *The Greek Myths.*

13. Robert Bauval and Adrian Gilbert, *The Orion Mystery: Unlocking the Secrets of the Pyramids* (New York: Crown Publishing Group, 1995).

14. Peter Lemesurier, *Gods of the Dawn: The Message of the Pyramids* (New York: Thorsons, 1999).

15. Ibid.

16. Bauval and Gilbert, *The Orion Mystery.*

17. Ibid.

18. Mario Pincherle, *La Grande Piramide e lo Zed* (Diegaro di Cesena, Italy: Macro Edizioni, 2000), chapter 8.

19. Bauval and Gilbert, *The Orion Mystery.*

20. R. O. Faulkner, trans., *The Ancient Egyptian Pyramid Texts* (Oxford: Clarendon Press, 1969), line 2061.

21. Peter Lemesurier, *Gods of the Dawn.*

22. Bauval and Gilbert, *The Orion Mystery.*

23. Pliny (Gaius Plinius Secundus, Pliny the Elder), *Historiae Mundi* (Venice: Giuseppe Antonelli Edition, 1844), book 8, chapter 56.

24. Mario Pincherle, *Enoch* (Diegaro di Cesena, Italy: Macro Edizioni, 2000), chapter 1.

25. Andrew Collins, "Homeland of the Primeval Ones," in *Beneath the Pyramids: Egypt's Greatest Secret Uncovered* (Virginia Beach, Va.: A.R.E. Press, 2009).

26. Piero Magaletti, *Custodi dell'Immortalità* (Foggia, Italy: Bastogi Editrice, 2011).

27. Quoted in Mario Pincherle, *La Grande Piramide e lo Zed.*

28. Selim Hassan, *Excavations at Giza* (Oxford: Oxford University Press, 1932).

29. Papyrus 3292 at the Louvre Museum

30. Ibid. Also see Hassan, *Excavations at Giza.*

31. Hassan, *Excavations at Giza.*

32. R. O. Faulkner, trans., *The Ancient Egyptian Coffin Texts* (Warminster, U.K.: Aris & Phillips, 2004), formula 1065.

33. Ibid., formula 477.

34. Ibid., lines 1256–61, 1716–17.

35. Ibid., lines 1278, 1657, 2180–81, 2882–83.

36. Robert Bauval and Graham Hancock, *Keeper of Genesis: A Quest for the Hidden Legacy of Mankind* (London: Heinemann, 1996).

37. Edouard Naville, "Le nom du Sphinx dans le livre des morts," *Sphinx, Revue critique embrassant le domaine entier de l'égyptologie* 5 (1992).

38. Faulkner, *The Ancient Egyptian Coffin Texts,* formula 1035.

39. Jane B. Sellers, *The Death of Gods in Ancient Egypt* (London: Penguin, 1992).

40. See Graham Hancock, *Fingerprints of the Gods: The Evidence of Earth's Lost Civilization,* and Jane B. Sellers, *The Death of Gods in Ancient Egypt.*

41. Faulkner, *The Ancient Egyptian Coffin Texts,* formula 1080.

42. Bauval and Hancock, *Keeper of Genesis.*

43. *Mystery of the Sphinx,* documentary, directed by Bill Cote (1993; New York: NBC).

44. Ibid.

45. Ibid.

46. The most complete study is reported in Peter Hodges, *How the Pyramids Were Built* (Washington: Lilian Barber Press, 1990).

47. Ibid.

48. Ibid.

49. Ibid.

50. Jean Kerisel, in Bauval and Hancock, *Keeper of Genesis.*

51. *Mystery of the Sphinx*, directed by Bill Cote.

52. Robert Schoch in Graham Hancock and Robert Bauval, *The Message of the Sphinx: A Quest for the Hidden Legacy of Mankind* (New York: Three Rivers Press, 1996).

53. James Henry Breasted, *Ancient Records of Egypt,* vol. 1 (Champaign, Ill.: University of Illinois Press, 1988).

54. John Anthony West, *The Traveler's Key to Ancient Egypt* (London: Harrap Columbus, 1989).

55. Professor Henri Édouard, Naville of Egypt Exploration Fund, in *London Times,* March 17, 1914.

56. John Anthony West, *Serpent in the Sky* (Wheaton, Ill.: Quest Books, 1993).

57. E. A. E. Reymond, *The Mythical Origin of the Egyptian Temple.*

58. Siculus, *Library of History,* book 3, 3–4.

59. Siculus, *Library of History,* book 1, 16.

60. Quoted in Mario Pincherle, *La Grande Piramide e lo Zed.*

61. Siculus, *Library of History,* book 1, 17.

62. Arrian of Nicomedia, *Anabasis Alexandri* (1893), trans. E. J. Chinnock (http://websfor.org/alexander/arrian/intro.asp), book 5, chapter 2; Trogus Pompeius, "Historiae Philippicae" [Philippic Histories] in *Justin: Epitome of the Philippic History of Pompeius Trogus,* vol. 1, trans. J. C. Yardley and Waldemar Heckel (Atlanta: Scholars Press, 1997), book 7.

63. Arrian of Nicomedia, *Anabasis Alexandri,* book 9.

64. Siculus, *Library of History,* book 2.

65. M. Wilford, *Chronologie des rois de Magadha* and *Mem. Sur le Mont Cancase*; Wil Johnes, *Mem. de Calcutta,* vol. 1; Voltaire wrote that one could identify the War of Moifasor and the Rebel Angels, contained in the

Indian books, with that of the Giants against Jupiter; Jean-Sylvain Bailly, *Lettres sur l'Atlantide* 1779.

66. Hesiod, "West Merkelbach, fragment 150," lines 21–24

67. Pausanias, *Description of Greece,* trans. W. H. S. Jones and H. A. Omerod (Cambridge, Mass.: Harvard University Press, 1918), book 1 (*Attica*), chapter 19.

68. Angelo Mazzoldi, *Delle Origini Italiche* [Of Italic Origins] (Whitefish, Mont.: Kessinger Publishing, 2010).

69. See Bailly, *Lettres sur l'Atlantide,* letter 23.

70. Pausanias, *Description of Greece,* book 1, chapter 5, section 8.

71. Pausanias, *Description of Greece,* book 1, chapter 31–32.

72. Pausanias, *Description of Greece,* book 10, chapter 5, section 9.

73. Mazzoldi, *Delle Origini Italiche,* chapter 15.

74. Apollodorus, *The Library of Greek Mythology,* vol. 2, trans. Robin Hard (Oxford: Oxford University Press, 2008), chapters 5–15.

75. Herodotus, *The Histories,* book 4, 13.

76. Ibid.

77. Ibid., book 4, chapter 7, 687–92.

78. "Fragment 3 Bolton," surviving fragment of the poem of Aristeas of Proconnesus.

79. "Fragments 4 and 5 Bolton," surviving fragment of the poem of Aristeas of Proconnesus.

80. Robert Bauval, "The Mysterious Origins of the Egyptians: The People of the Stars," *Hera,* January, 2009.

81. Mazzoldi, *Delle Origini Italiche,* chapter 21.

6. PELASGIAN MIGRATION TO THE INDUS VALLEY

1. Mark Kennoyer, *Ancient Cities of the Indus Valley Civilization* (Madison, Wisc.: American Institute of Pakistan Studies, Oxford University Press, 1998).

2. Ibid.

3. S. P. Gupta, *The Indus-Sarasvati Civilization* (Delhi: Pratiba Prakashan, 1996).

4. Kennoyer, *Ancient Cities of the Indus Valley Civilization.*

5. Gregory Possehl, *Indus Age: The Beginnings* (Philadelphia: University of Pennsylvania Press, 1999).

6. Gupta, *The Indus-Sarasvati Civilization.*

7. Ibid.

8. George Feuerstein, Subhash Kak, and David Frawley, *In Search of the Cradle of Civilization* (Wheaton, Ill.: Quest Books, 1995).

9. Possehl, *Indus Age.*

10. Ralph T. H. Griffith, *Hymns of the Rigveda,* vol. 1 (Whitefish, Mont.: Kessinger Publishing, 2006).

11. Ibid.

12. *Bhagvata Purana*, quoted in James G. Frazer, *Folklore in the Old Testament: Studies in Comparative Religion, Legend, and Law*, vol. 1 (London: Random House Value Publishing, 1988).

13. Ibid.

14. *Matsya Purana*, trans. A. Taluqar Oudh (New Delhi: Sri Satguru Publications, 2009), part 1.

15. Samuel Noah Kramer, *History Begins at Sumer* (Philadelphia: University of Pennsylvania Press, 1991).

16. *Satpatha Brahmana* (1882), trans. Julius Eggeling, Sacred Books of the East, vol. 12 (www.sacred-texts.com/hin/sbr/sbe12/index.htm), part 1.

17. John E. Mitchiner, *Traditions of the Seven Rishis,* vols. 17–19 (Delhi: Motilal Banarsidass, 1982).

18. Graham Hancock and Santha Faiia, *Heaven's Mirror: Quest for the Lost Civilization* (New York: Three Rivers Press, 1998).

19. Mitchiner, *Traditions of the Seven Rishis.*

20. Hancock and Faiia, *Heaven's Mirror.*

21. Possehl, *Indus Age.*

22. Graham Hancock, *Underworld: The Mysterious Origins of Civilization* (New York: Three Rivers Press, 2002).

23. Griffith, *Hymns of the Rigveda,* vol. 1.

24. Ramaswamy, Bakliwal, and Verma, quoted in Possehl, *Indus Age.*

25. Bimal Ghose, Amal Kar, and Zahid Husain "The Lost Courses of the Sarasvati River in the Great Indian Desert: New Evidence from Landsat Imagery," in Gupta, *The Indus-Sarasvati Civilization.*

26. Professor Jacobi, *Indian Antiquary*, quoted in Dr. David Frawley, *Gods, Sages and Kings* (Detroit: Lotus Press, 1991).

27. Lokamanya Ganghadar Bal Tilak, *The Orion or Researches into Antiquity of the Vedas* (Poona City, India: Tilak Bros., 1886).

28. Ibid.

29. Frawley, *Gods, Sages and Kings*.

30. Mitchiner, *Traditions of the Seven Rishis*.

31. Ibid.

32. Pliny, *Natural History*, trans. H. Rackham (Cambridge, Mass.: Loeb Classical Library, 1938), Solinus, Compendium.

33. Mitchiner, *Traditions of the Seven Rishis*.

34. Hancock, *Underworld*, chapter 7.

35. *Rig-Veda*, book 1, 32:1–12.

36. Tilak, *The Orion or Researches into Antiquity of the Vedas*.

37. *Rig-Veda*, book 4, 17:1–3, quoted in Hancock, *Underworld*.

38. Elise van Campo, "Monsoon Fluctuations in Two 20,000-Yr B. P. Oxygen-isotope/Pollen Records off Southwest India," *Quaternary Research* 26, no. 3 (1986): 376–88.

39. Lawrence Guy Straus, Berit Valentin Eriksen, Jon M. Erlandson, and David R. Yesner, eds., *Humans at the End of the Ice Age* (New York: Plenum Press, 1996).

40. Ibid.

41. Quoted in Hancock, *Underworld*.

42. Shikaripura Ranganatha Rao, *The Lost City of Dvaraka* (New Delhi: Aditya Prakashan, 1999).

43. *Journal of Marine Archaeology* 5–6 (1995–1996): 64.

44. Ananda K. Coomaraswamy and Sister Nivedita, *Myths of the Hindus and Buddhists* (Mineola, N.Y.: Dover Publications, 1967).

45. H. H. Wilson, trans., *Vishnu Purana*, vol. 2 (Delhi: Nag Publishers, 1989), 785.

46. M. W. Carr, *Descriptive and Historical Papers Relating to the Seven Pagodas of the Coromandel Coast* (New Delhi: Asia Educational Services, 1984).

47. Ibid.

48. Ibid.

49. S. R. Rao et al. "Underwater Explorations off the Coast of Poompuhur Conducted in 1993," *Journal of Marine Archaeology*, 7.

50. Hancock, *Underworld*.

51. Ibid.

52. David Shulman in Alan Dundes, *The Flood Myth* (Berkeley: University of California Press, 1988).

53. Visvanatha Kanakasabhai, *The Tamils Eighteen Hundred Years Ago* (Madras: Saiva Siddantha, 1966).

54. Ibid.

55. Schulman in Dundes, *The Flood Myth*.

56. Ibid.

57. Hancock, *Underworld*.

58. Skandananda, *Arunachela Holy Hill* (Tiruvannamalai, India: Sri Ramanasraman, 1995).

59. Ramachandra Dikshitar, *Studies in Tamil Literature and History* (Tirunelveli, India: The South India Sauiva Siddhanta Works Publishing Society, 1983).

60. N. Mahalingam, *Kumari Kandam—The Lost Continent*, Proceedings of the Fifth International Conference/Seminar of Tamil Studies (January 1981).

61. T. N. P. Haran (American College, Madurai), quoted in Hancock, *Underworld*.

62. Dikshitar, *Studies in Tamil Literature and History*.

63. Ibid.

64. Ibid.

65. Ibid.

66. Ibid.

67. Hancock, *Underworld*.

68. Mahalingam, *Kumari Kandam*.

69. N. K. Mangalamurugesan, *Sangam Age* (Madras: Thendral Pathipakam, 1982).

70. R. Spence Hardy, *The Legends and Theories of the Buddhists* (New Delhi: Sri Satguru Publications, 1990).

71. Hancock, *Underworld*.

72. Thor Heyerdahl, *The Maldives Mystery* (Crows Nest, New South Wales: Unwin Paperbacks, 1988).

73. Hancock, *Underworld*

74. Arne Skjølsvold, *Archaeological Test-Excavations on the Maldive Islands*, Occasional Papers, vol. 2 (Oslo: Kon-Tiki Museum, 1991), 66.

75. Alec Maclellan, *The Lost World of Agharti: The Mystery of Vril Power* (London: Souvenir Press, 1996).

76. José Henrique de Souza, "¿Existe Shangri-la?" quoted in Maclellan, *The Lost World of Agharti*.

77. Originally reported McClellan, *The Lost World of Agharti*, and confirmed by the Koran.

78. Robert Anthony Vitale, ed., *Edition and Study of the "Letter of Prester John to the Emperor Manuel of Constantinople": The Anglo-Norman Rhymed Version*, (College Park, Md.: 1975).

79. Tiziana Ripepi, trans., *Le leggi di Manu* [*The Laws of Manu*] (Milan: Adelphi, 1996).

80. Antonella Verdolino, "Gli Uomini bianchi del Mare di Gobi," *Hera* 101 (June 2008). See also Maclellan, *The Lost World of Agharti*.

81. Ibid.

82. Maclellan, *The Lost World of Agharti*.

83. Ibid.

84. Helena Petrovna Blavatsky, *The Secret Doctrine: The Synthesis of Science, Religion, and Philosophy* (Pasadena, Calif.: Theosophical University Press, December 1, 1999).

85. Ibid.

86. Ibid.

87. Joseph Alexandre Saint-Yves d'Alveydre, *Mission de l'Inde en Europe, mission de l'Europe en Asie: La question de mahatma et sa solution* (University of Michigan Library, January 1, 1910).

88. Ibid.

89. Michele Rossi, *Interviste con il Mistero* (Lazio: Eremon Edizioni, 2011).

90. Frawley, *Gods, Sages and Kings*.

91. Ibid.

92. Gupta, *The Indus-Sarasvati Civilization*.

93. Hancock, *Underworld*.

7. THE CONNECTION BETWEEN EGYPTIAN AND CAMBODIAN MONUMENTS

1. Giorgio de Santillana and Hertha von Dechend, *Hamlet's Mill: An Essay Investigating the Origins of Human Knowledge and Its Transmission through Myth* (Boston: Gambid, 1969).

2. George Coedès, *Angkor: An Introduction* (Oxford: Oxford University Press, 1966).

3. Ibid.

4. Ibid.

5. Robert Stencel, Fred Gifford, and Eleanor Moron, "Astronomy and Cosmology at Angkor Wat," *Science* 153 (July 23, 1976).

6. Bernard P. Groslier, *Angkor et le Cambodge au XVIe siècle d'après les sources portugaises et espagnoles* [Angkor and Cambodia in the Sixteenth Century] (Paris: PUF, Annales du musée Guimet, Bibliothèque d'Étude 1958), 63, .

7. Henri Parmentier, *Henri Parmentier's Guide to Angkor* (Phnom Penh: E.K.L.I.P. Publisher, 1954).

8. Albert le Bonheur, *Of Gods, Kings and Men: Bas-Reliefs of Angkor Wat and Bayon* (Chicago: Serindia Publications, 1995).

9. Stencel, Gifford, and Moron, "Astronomy and Cosmology at Angkor Wat."

10. A further detailed study of astronomical and cosmological symbolism of Angkor Wat is provided by Eleanor Moron, "Configurations of Time and Space at Angkor Wat," in *Studies in Indo-Asian Art and Culture* 5 (December 1977): 217–61.

11. Binod Chandra Sinha, *Serpent Worship in Ancient India* (Delhi: Books Today, 1978).

12. Alain Daniélou, *The Myths and Gods of India* (Rochester, Vt.: Inner Traditions, 1991); Felix Guirand, ed., *Larousse Encyclopedia of Mythology* (Amherst, N.Y.: Prometheus Press, 1959).

13. *Encyclopedia Britanica, Micropædia,* vol. 7.

14. Philip Rawson, *Sacred Tibet* (London: Thames & Hudson, 1933); Henry Clarke Warren, *Buddhism in Translation* (New York: Cosimo Classics, 2005).

15. Stencel, Gifford, and Moron, "Astronomy and Cosmology at Angkor Wat," 281.

16. Dawn Rooney, *Angkor: An Introduction to the Temples* (Hong Kong: Asian Books, 1994).

17. Graham Hancock and Santha Faiia, *Heaven's Mirror: Quest for the Lost Civilization* (New York: Three Rivers Press, 1998).

18. Henri Parmentier, "Dimensions," in *Henri Parmentier's Guide to Angkor*.

19. Coedès, *Angkor: An Introduction*.

20. Ibid.

21. Coedès, *Angkor: An Introduction*; Groslier, *Angkor et le Cambodge*.

22. Jean Boisselier in Marc Riboud, *Angkor: The Serenity of Buddhism* (London: Thames & Hudson, 1993), 137.

23. Hancock and Faiia, *Heaven's Mirror*.

24. Robert Bauval and Graham Hancock, *Keeper of Genesis: A Quest for the Hidden Legacy of Mankind* (London: Heinemann, 1996).

25. Graham Hancock, *Quest for the Lost Civilization*, documentary, 1998.

8. A JOURNEY INTO LANGUAGE

1. William White Howells, *Mankind in the Making* (Garden City, N.Y.: Doubleday, 1967); Beril J. Lundman, *The Races and Peoples of Europe*, IAAEE monograph no. 4, trans. Donald A. Swan (New York, 1977); Jean Hiernaux, *The People of Africa* (New York: Charles Scribner and Sons, 1975).

2. Joaquim Pedro Oliveira Martins, *A History of Iberian Civilization* (Oxford: Oxford University Press, 1930).

3. Carleton Coon, *Living Races of Man* (London: Random House, 1965).

4. Diodorus Siculus, *Library of History*, trans. C. H. Oldfather (Cambridge, Mass.: Loeb Classical Library, 1933), book 3, 53:1–3.

5. Siculus, *Library of History*, book 3, 54:4–5.

6. Louis Charpentier, *Le Mystère Basque*, [The Basque Mystery] (Paris: Robert Laffont, 1975).

7. Robert Lawrence Trask, *The History of Basque* (London: Routledge, 1997).

8. Strabo, *Geography*, trans. Horace Leonard Jones (Cambridge, Mass.: Loeb Classical Library, 1917), book 4, 1.1.

9. Joaquín Gorrochategui, *La onomástica aquitana y su relación con la ibérica*, in Jürgen Untermann and Francisco Villar, *Lengua y Cultura en la Hispania Prerromana* (Salamanca: Ediciones Universidad, 1993).

10. Dennis Stanford and Bruce Badley from the Smithsonian Museum of Natural History, interview for *Nova* episode "Secrets of Stonehenge."

11. Mark Kurlansky, *The Basque History of the World* (New York: Random House, 2001).

12. Pausanias, *Description of Greece,* trans. W, H. S. Jones and H. A. Omerod (Cambridge, Mass.: Harvard University Press, 1918), book 1 (*Attic*), chapter 19.

13. Mario Guarnacci, *Delle Origini Italiche*, vol. 2 (Venice, 1773), book 11.

14. *Universal History, from the Earliest Accounts to the Present Time* vol. 18 (London, 1781), appendix 2 "History of the Etruscans," chapter 1, section 3.

9. MISSING

1. Homer, *Iliad*, trans. Robert Fagles (London: Penguin, 1991), book 16.

2. Hesiod, *Theogony,* trans. Evelyn Whiten (www.ellopos.net/elpenor/greek-texts/ancient-greece/hesiod/theogony.asp).

3. Strabo, *Geography*, trans. Horace Leonard Jones (Cambridge, Mass.: Loeb Classical Library, 1917), book 7.

4. Diego Marin, *Il Segreto Degli Illuminati: Dalle origini ai giorni nostri, storia dell'occhio che tutto vede* [The Illuminati Secret: From the Origins to the Present Day, History of the All-Seeing Eye] (Milan: Mondadori, 2013).

5. Marin, *Il Segreto Degli Illuminati.*

6. Angelo Mazzoldi, *Delle Origini Italiche* [Of Italic Origins] (Whitefish, Mont.: Kessinger Publishing, 2010), chapter 20.

7. Trogus Pompeius, "Historiae Philippicae" [Philippic Histories], in *Justin: Epitome of the Philippic History of Pompeius Trogus,* vol. 1, trans. J. C. Yardley and Waldemar Heckel (Atlanta: Scholars Press, 1997), book 7.

8. Virgil, *Aeneid*, trans. Robert Fagles (London: Penguin, 2010), book 7.

9. Virgil, *Aeneid*, book 3.

10. Strabo, *Geography*, book 8.

11. Pausanias, *Description of Greece,* trans. W. H. S. Jones and H. A. Omerod (Cambridge, Mass.: Harvard University Press, 1918), book 1, chapter 4.

12. Diodorus Siculus, *Library of History,* trans. C. H. Oldfather (Cambridge, Mass.: Loeb Classical Library, 1933), book 3, 53–55.

13. Siculus, *Library of History,* book 3, 56, 57, and 60.

14. Sallust, *Bellum Iugurthinum* (New York: Harper Collins, 1975), 17–18.

15. Dominic Raso and Holy Ravenda, "Pelasgians in Libya—Archeo," *Hera* 28 (October 2008).

16. Theodore Monod, *Memoirs of the Society of Natural Sciences and Natural Science Museum in Milan,* vol. 26 (1993), fasc. 2.

17. Dominic Raso and Santo Ravenda, "The Pelasgian Origins of the Pharaohs" *Hera* 25 (December 2007).

18. Dionysius, *Roman Antiquities,* trans. Edward Spelman (New York: Astor Library, 1758), book 1, 19.

19. *La Civiltà Cattolica,* series 18, vol. 11 (July 18th, 1903), fasc. 1274.

20. Livy, *Histories,* trans. D. Spillan and Cyrus Edmonds (Digireads, 2009), book 1, 56:3.

21. Reported by Servius Mario Onorato in *Commentarii in Vergilii Aeneidos libros.*

22. Mario Pincherle, *Il porto Invisibile di Orbetello,* introduction (Pisa: Pacini Editore, 1989).

23. Andrea Carandini, *Roma—Il Primo Giorno* (Rome: Edizioni Laterza, 2007).

24. Judges, chapter 21.

25. Mario Pincherle, *I Mandei* (Diegaro di Cesena, Italy: Macro Edizioni, 2003).

26. Ibid.

27. Drower, *The Mandaeans of Iraq and Iran: Their Cults, Customs, Magic, Legends and Folklore* (Piscataway, N.J.: Gorgias Press LLC, 2002).

28. Ibid.

29. Quoted in Pincherle, *I Mandei.*

30. Achille Sansi, *Storia del Comune di Spoleto dal secolo XII al XVII: Seguita da alcune memorie dei tempi posteriori* [History of the Municipality of Spoleto from the Twelfth to the Seventeenth Century: Followed by Some Memories of Previous Ages] (Berkeley: University of California Libraries, 1879).

31. Alessandro Marcon, "La civiltà Ipogea" *Mystero* 15 (August 2001).

32. Sergio Frau, *Le colonne d'Ercole. Un'inchiesta* (Rome: Nur Neon Ltd., 2002), 487.

33. Quoted in Frau, *Le colonne d'Ercole.* .

34. Frau, *Le colonne d'Ercole*, chapter 42, 610.

35. Siculus, *Library of History*, book 3, 55.

36. See the entry "Sherdànu" in W. von Soden, *Akkadisches Handwörterbuch* (an essential tool for serious study, in 3 volumes), Harrassowitz, ed., 1965, 1972, 1981; (Wiesbaden: Verlag), 1216.

37. E. Lartet, "Nuvelles Recherches sur la coexistence de l'Homme et des Grands Mammifères Fossiles réputés caractéristiques de la Dernière Période Géologique," *Annales des Sciences Naturelles* 15, no. 3 (1861), quoted in Blavatsky, *Secret Doctrine*, (Cambridge: Cambridge University Press, 2011).

38. First of six lectures held by Professor A. H. Sayce, Oxford, in 1887, quoted in Blavatsky, *Secret Doctrine*.

39. See Leonardo Melis, *Shardana—Jenesi degli Urim,* and *Shardana—I Calcolatori del Tempo.* Also read Genesis 14.

40. Leonardo Melis, *Shardana—I popoli del Mare* (Sardinia: PTM Editrice, 2009).

41. Pincherle, *I Mandei.*

42. Drower, *The Mandaeans of Iraq and Iran: Their Cults, Customs, Magic, Legends and Folklore.*

43. Ibid.

44. Ibid.

45. Quoted in Christopher Knight and Robert Lomas, *The Hiram Key: Pharoahs, Freemasons and the Discovery of the Secret Scrolls of Jesus* (Gloucester, Mass.: Fair Winds Press, 2001), chapter 5.

46. Ibid.

47. See Marin, *Il Segreto Degli Illuminati,* "I popoli cugini" [The Cousin People] and "Il voto di Nazireato" [The Vow of Nazariteship].

48. Genesis 21:33 and 2 Kings 23:7.

49. Leonardo Melis, *Shardana—I Principi di Dan* (Sardinia: PTM, 2008).

50. Mario Liverani, *Oltre la Bibbia—Storia antica di Israele* (Rome: Edizioni Laterza, 2003), chapter 6.

51. Ibid.

52. Exodus 30:35 and 23:38.

53. Exodus 35.

54. Melis, *Shardana—I popoli del Mare.*

55. Judges, from 4:1 to 5:31

10. PELASGIAN RELIGION AND CULTS

1. Herodotus, *The Histories*, translated by George Rawlinson (Digireads Publishing), 76.

2. Angelo Mazzoldi, *Delle origini Italiche* [Of Italic Origins] (Whitefish, Mont.: Kessinger Publishing, 2010).

3. Lucius Annaeus Seneca, *Naurales Questiones* (Cambridge, Mass.: Loeb Classical Library, 1989), book 2, "41. Thunder and Lightning."

4. Mazzoldi, *Delle Origini Italiche*, chapter 25.

5. *Mahābhārata: Shanti Parva,* trans. Kisari Mohan Ganguli (www.sacred-texts.com/hin/m12/), section 337.

6. Acts of the Apostles, chapter 17.

7. Mazzoldi, *Delle origini Italiche*, chapters 18 and 25.

8. See two articles by Julia Morgenstern: "The Book of the Covenant," *Hebrew Union College Annual* 5 (1928); and "The Ark, the Ephod and the Tent of Meeting" *Hebrew Union College Annual* 17 (1942–1943).

9. *The Book of the Secrets of Enoch*, trans. W. R. Morfill, ed. R. H. Charles (Oxford: Clarendon Press, 1896), chapter 71 (sometime listed as chapter 3 of the appendix).

10. Genesis 25 and 29–34.

11. Genesis 27 and 29.

12. Genesis 27, 34, and 36.

13. Genesis 27, 37, and 39–40.

14. Edo Nyland, *Odysseus and the Sea Peoples: A Bronze Age History of Scotland* (Bloomington, Ind.: Trafford Publishing, 2006); Nancy Sandars, *The Sea Peoples* (London: Thames & Hudson, 1985); Leonardo Melis, *Shardana—I Principi di Dan* (Sardinia: PTM, 2008).

15. Numbers 10:25.

16. Melis, *Shardana—I popoli del Mare* (Sardinia: PTM Editrice, 2009)

17. Joshua 19:47.

18. Exodus 13:17–18.

19. Exodus 28:1–31:11.

20. Judges 18.

21. Sergio Frau, *Le Colonne d'Ercole. Un'inchiesta* [The Pillars of Hercules: An Inquiry (Rome: Nur Neon Ltd., 2002)].

22. Mario Pincherle, *Enoch—Il Primo Libro del Mond*, vol. 1 (Forlì-Cesena, Italy: Macro Edizioni, 2013), chapter 8, 1–8.

23. Ibid., chapter 14, 4.

24. Ibid., chapter 19, 2.

25. Mazzoldi, *Delle Origini Italiche*, chapter 25.

26. Ibid., chapter 25.

27. Aeschylus, *The Persians*.

28. Trogus Pompeius, Historiae Philippicae [Philippic Histories] in *Justin: Epitome of the Philippic History of Pompeius Trogus,* vol. 1, trans. J. C. Yardley and Waldemar Heckel (Atlanta: Scholars Press, 1997), book 42.

29. Bhimarao Ramji Ambedkar, *Riddle in Hinduism* (CreateSpace Independent Publishing Platform, July 14, 2008), part 3, "Riddle No. 24. The Riddle of the Kali Yuga."

30. Richard H. Allen, *Star Names: Their Love and Meaning* (Mineola, N.Y.: Dover Publications, 1963).

31. Robert Bauval, *Secret Chamber: The Quest for the Hall of Records* (London: Random House, 2000).

32. See *Historia Regum Britanniae*, written by the Welsh priest Geoffrey of Monmouth in 1135 (Milan: Imago Mundi, 2006).

33. Quoted in Pincherle, *I Mandei*.

34. Ibid.

35. Per-Em-Ra, *Book of the Dead*, trans. E. A. Wallis Budge (www.sacred-texts .com/egy/ebod/), chapter 64.

36. Micah 5:1.

37. Quoted in Christopher Knight and Robert Lomas, *The Hiram Key: Pharoahs, Freemasons and the Discovery of the Secret Scrolls of Jesus* (Gloucester, Mass.: Fair Winds Press, 2001); Pincherle, *I Mandei*.

38. Epistle of St. Clement to his disciple Theodore in relation to the sect of Carpocratians, quoted in Graham Hancock, *The Sign and the Seal:*

The Quest for the Lost Ark of the Covenant (New York: Crown Publishers, 1992).

39. Mark 14:51–52

40. *Troy*, directed by Wolfgang Petersen, DVD (Burbank, Calif.: Warner Brothers Pictures, 2004).

41. Paul Fraure, *Alexandre* (Paris: Fayard, 1985).

42. Mario Bettalli, *Storia Greca* (Rome: Carocci, 2006).

43. Pincherle, *I Mandei*.

44. George Coedès, *Angkor: An Introduction* (Oxford: Oxford University Press, 1966).

45. Ibid.

46. Bernard P. Groslier, *Angkor et le Cambodge au XVIe siècle d'après les sources portugaises et espagnoles* [Angkor and Cambodia in the Sixteenth Century] (Paris: PUF, Annales du musée Guimet, Bibliothèque d'Étude, 1958), 63.

47. Ibid.

48. Coedès, *Angkor: An Introduction*.

CONCLUSION:
THE END OF THE DIALOGUE

1. See Flavio Barbiero, *Una Civiltà sotto Ghiaccio* [A Civilisation under the Ice] (Milan: Editore Nord, 2000).

2. 2 Peter 3:1–7.

3. See Pierre Sabak, *Murder of Reality* (Castleford, West Yorkshire: Serpentigena Publications, 2010).

4. See Jan Van Helsing, *Secret Societies and Their Power in the 20th Century* (Lathen, Germany: Ewertverlag, 1995); William Bramley, *The Gods of Eden* (New York: Avon Books, 1993).

APPENDIX A:
THE SUMERIAN HOAX

1. Mario Pincherle, *La civiltà Minoica in Italia* (Pisa: Pacini Editore, 1990).

2. Quoted in Mario Pincherle, *I Mandei* (Diegaro di Cesena, Italy: Macro Edizioni, 2003).

3. Ibid.

4. Ibid.

5. Leonard Wiking, LHD, FSA, *A History of Babylonia & Assyria,* vol. 1, and *A History of Sumer & Akkad* (London: Chatto & Windus, 1923).

APPENDIX B:
CHAPTER-BY-CHAPTER COMPARISON
TO THE FINDINGS OF EDGAR CAYCE

1. See Mario Liverani, *Oltre la Bibbia—Storia antica di Israele* [Beyond the Bible—History of Ancient Israel] (Rome: Edizioni Laterza 2003), chapter 14.

2. See Andrew Collins, "The Sleeping Prophet," in *Beneath the Pyramids: Egypt's Greatest Secret Uncovered* (Virginia Beach, Va.: ARE Press, 2009).

3. Quoted in Charles Berlitz, *The Bermuda Triangle* (New York: Doubleday & Company, 1974).

4. Ibid.

Glossary and
Time Lines

Aegean Sea: A very narrow body of water located in the northeast section of the Mediterranean, between the southern Balkan and Anatolian peninsulas, with a distance between parts of Greece and Turkey of around 150 kilometers. The Aegean, with numerous gulfs, reefs, and capes along its coastlines, is connected to the Black Sea in the north by the Dardanelles through the strait of İstanbul. The more than three thousand Aegean islands include Crete and Rhodes.

Aeschylus: Greek playwright (524–456 BCE) whose play *Prometheus Bound* tells of the Titan Prometheus, who is bound to a rock as punishment from Zeus for providing fire to humans.

Agharta: known as "the Land of Immortality" or the "Subterranean World" in Buddhist teaching. In Tibetan legends it appears as a system of tunnels and cavities big enough to contain cities. Built before the flood, it went all around the world, branching from Shamballah, the capital of subterranean world, which was said to be located beneath the Himalayan chain.

Akapana Pyramid: Sacred stepped mountain south of the Underground Temple at Tiahuanaco in Bolivia that looks more like a large natural hill than a pyramid. It contains refined internal passages and at least two rooms.

Akhenaten: Of Hyksos blood by his mother, Akhenaten became pharaoh in Egypt in 1359 BCE and reintroduced the ancient religion of the one God, which he made the state cult for the god Aton.

Akkadian empire: Centered in the city of Akkad on the Persian Gulf, it extended over almost all the ancient Middle and Near East. The population spoke a Semitic language, while its priests used an artificial language called Sumerian for liturgical purposes.

Amazons: Matriarchal population that came before the Berbers in northern Africa. The Amazons entrusted magistracies, public affairs, and the army to women, while men were devoted to home life. They had a settlement on the Black Sea, in Themiskyra, now on the bottom of the Lake Simenit, fifty kilometers east of the city of Samsun in northern Anatolia.

Angkor Wat: Largest temple complex in the world, built by the Khmer king Suryavarman II in present-day Cambodia in the early twelfth century. *Angkor* is probably derived from *nagara*, the Sanskrit word for "city," but curiously assumes a specific meaning in the Egyptian language of "god Horus lives."

Angra Mainyu: In Zoroastrian teachings, "the Evil" who turned Airyana Vaejo into "an uninhabitable desolated land, with ten months of winter and only two of summer."

ankh: Represents the idea of eternal life; also the Egyptian hieroglyphic character that means "life."

Apollonius Rhodius: Greek poet and scholar, also known as Apollonius of Rhodes (third century BCE), author of the *Argonautica*, an epic poem that tells the story of Jason and the Argonauts.

Argive: The name for the Achaeans or Greeks in general, especially people from the Achaean city of Argos or the surrounding area of Argolis.

Aristotle: Greek philosopher (384–322 BCE), student of Plato and teacher of Alexander the Great, first to use a thorough system of philosophy whose writings covered many subjects including government, politics, linguistics, physics, metaphysics, biology, logic, ethics, poetry, theater, music, logic, rhetoric, biology, and zoology, and founder of Western philosophy with Plato and Socrates.

ashlar: A squared stone cut with a heavy instrument.

Avesta: A collection of sacred texts belonging to the Zoroastrian religion of pre-Islamic Persia, where Airyana Vaejo (the "Aryan homeland" and birthplace of Zoroaster) is described as a fertile land with mild climate where "the stars, the moon and the sun are only once a year seen to rise and set, and a year seems only as a day."

Aztec: Tribe that dominated northern Mexico at the time of Spanish conquest whose empire was second in size in the Americas only to the Inca in Peru.

Benben: An upright stone topped by a capstone of meteoritic iron found in the temple of Heliopolis, first venerated as a statue of Osiris, but later passed to Amon. According to Egyptian creation myth when the world arose out of lifeless waters a pyramid-shaped mound, the Benben, was the first thing to emerge.

Berbers: A white-skinned people indigenous to North Africa west of the Nile Valley. They result as a mix of four populations: Getuli, Moors, Tuareg, and Libu, the last belonging to the Sea Peoples. Their traits combine those of the Cro-Magnon and the matriarchal traditions inherited from Amazons, including the position of the woman culturally and militarily.

Callimachus: Lived in the Greek colony of Cyrene, Libya (310–240 BCE), and was a noted poet and scholar in the patronage of Egyptian-Greek pharaohs Ptolemy II and Ptolemy III. Responsible for producing a bibliographic survey, his 120-volume work, *Pinakes,* which was the foundation for the history of Greek literature.

Carthage: The site of a Semitic civilization located on the Gulf of Tunis in North Africa and a major trading area with influence over most of the western Mediterranean. In a constant state of struggle with the Greeks on Sicily and the Roman Republic, Carthage was involved in the conflicts known as the Punic Wars. Descendants of the

Phoenicians, Carthaginians spoke Punic, an extinct Semitic Canaanite language.

cartouche: An oval or oblong carving that contains a sovereign's name.

ceque lines: Found in the Andes Mountains, these alignments have an orientation based on the rising and setting of certain stars and constellations.

Chichén Itzá: With its name meaning "at the mouth of the well of the Itza," this is one of the largest Mayan cities, located in the municipality of Tinum, in the Mexican state of Yucatán.

Cholula: Central Mexican site of the Great Pyramid of Cholula, largest man-made monument in the world and oldest continuously occupied building in North America; the Spanish-built church at the top of the original pyramid is still in use.

Claudius Ptolemy: Astronomer, geographer, astrologer, and mathematician (90–168 CE, Alexandria, Egypt) who authored many scientific treatises important in Islamic and European science. His Earth-centered model of the universe is known as the Ptolemaic system.

craton: A stable, and relatively immobile, interior section of the Earth's crust that forms a continent.

Cretan hieroglyphs: Found on early Bronze Age Cretan artifacts from the Minoan era with some abstract characters but predominantly more naturally styled characters resembling human body parts, plants, animals, ships, weapons, and tools. The heiroglyphic system predated Linear A by about one hundred years but was used in parallel for most of the Minoan civilization.

Crete: The largest Greek island and fifth largest island in the Mediterranean Sea.

Cro-Magnon: Although Cro-Magnons (referred to as "early modern humans" in current scientific literature) belong to the *Homo sapiens* species, they are distinguished by a different facial type: round cranium, high cheekbones, wide and square orbits. On average they were taller than other *H. sapiens,* but without other physical or mental difference. Some physical characteristics (beard, long and thin nose, light skin and eyes, blond or red hair) were transmitted to other *H. sapiens* (like Combe-Capelle, whose burial site in southern France is considered the earliest evidence of modern *H. sapiens* in Europe), generating the Indo-European kind. Cro-Magnon people suddenly appeared in Europe in 13,000 BCE where Combe-Capelle had been more than twenty thousand years earlier. The absence of an evolutionary path traceable in any of the explored continents makes it necessary to seek Cro-Magnon origins in the unexplored Antarctica. In prehistoric times, in comparison with other men, they were real giants, a factor that can have generated the need to use the term "Giants" to indicate the Pelasgians.

cromlech: A circle of monolithic stones.

Cumae: Ancient name of the first Greek colony on mainland Italy, located on the coast of the Tyrrhenian Sea, whose ruins in Campania, Italy, are near the modern town of Cuma. The name Cuma is derived from the homonymous area of Campania (southern Italy) and its inhabitants, the Cimmerians. Another Cumae (today Aliağa) exists on the Turkish Aegean coast and its ancient inhabitants were called Cimmerians too, indicating, presumably, that it was founded by settlers who came from the west.

cuneiform writing: A mode of writing using a wedge-shaped stylus to make impressions in clay, stone, metal, and wax that originated in ancient southern Mesopotamia and was most likely invented by the Akkadians. The earliest cuneiform texts are about 5,000 years old.

Cuzco: Historical capital of the Inca empire located in southeastern Peru near the Urubamba Valley in the Andes mountain range.

Damastes of Sigeo: Greek historian and disciple of Hellanicus of Lesbos.

Danaus: King of Argos and father of the fifty daughters known as the Danaides. He is also called **Inachus, Thespius, Aegeus,** or **Titanus** and can be identified with the Egyptian god Seth.

Dashour (Dahshur): South of Giza on the west bank of the Nile, site of the "Red Pyramid" and the "Bent Pyramid," built by Snofru, father of Cheops.

diadem: A royal headband or adornment worn on the head like a crown.

Diodorus Siculus: Greek historian born in Sicily and author of forty works of history who lived in the time of Julius Caesar and Augustus and is known for the enormous universal history *Bibliotheca Historica,* covering the age of mythology to 60 BCE, the only surviving continuous historical resource due to the loss of writings of earlier authors he had used as sources.

Dionysius of Halicarnassus: Greek historian and teacher of rhetoric (ca. 60 BCE–after 7 BCE) whose 20-volume history *Roman Antiquities,* the most valuable source for early Roman history, follows Rome from its origins to the First Punic War.

Dionysius Periegetes: Greek scholar and poet, known as Dionysius the Voyager, who wrote a widely read, influential description of the then-known world. He is believed to have been from Alexandria and to have lived around the time of Hadrian (117–138 CE).

dolmen: Prehistoric monument consisting of two or more upright stones that support a horizontal stone slab.

drumlin: A long or oval hill formed by non-stratified soil and rock fragments deposited under a glacier in motion.

Duat: Region of the sky where the god Osiris reigned after ascending to heaven and the region of the southern sky containing Orion, Sirius, and the Milky Way. Egyptian burial chambers were said to provide contact between the physical world and the Duat, with spirits using tombs to travel back and forth.

Easter Island: Polynesian island in the southeastern Pacific Ocean famous for its *moai,* 887 ancient monumental statues found there.

ecliptic: Representation of the sun's apparent path among the stars in a single year, whose northernmost point on the Earth (Tropic of

Cancer) and southernmost point (Tropic of Capricorn) cross the celestial equator at the vernal and autumnal equinoxes.

Ephorus: Greek historian (ca. 400–330 BCE) of Cumae (Cyme) in Asia Minor and the first to author a universal history; his twenty-nine books were preserved by Diodorus Siculus.

Eratosthenes: Greek mathematician, geographer, poet, athlete, astronomer, and music theorist (ca. 276–195 BCE) of Cyrene, a Greek settlement in Libya, who was the first person to use the word "geography" and was creator of the discipline of geography as it is known today.

Eridanus: Mysterious river that appears in both Greek and Roman mythology and geography. It first represented the homonymous constellation southwest of Orion. Then it indicated the Po River in northern Italy or the Rhone in southeastern France.

Etruscan civilization: In an area covering current Tuscany, western Umbria, and the northern Latiums; called the Tusci or Etrusci by Romans. The old Etruscans had a close relationship with the Shardana who arrived in Sardinia and Italy from the Akkadian empire.

Fillipo Cluverio: Better known as Philipp Clüver (1580–1622), born in Danzig (Gdańsk), in Royal Prussia, a province of the Kingdom of Poland. Historian and geographer, who was the founder of historical geography.

First Time: Also called Tep Zepi, the period in Egypt when gods fraternized with humans. During this government of gods a system of cosmic order was established in the country to be maintained even after power was transferred to the mortal pharaohs.

Followers of Horus: Brought astronomy and esoteric knowledge to the people of Mesopotamia and Egypt 5,000 years ago.

forebulge: A bulge or uplift at the edge of a glacier caused by a seesaw effect, in which the Earth's crust is pushed in at the center and raised in the periphery.

Gate of the Sun: A ten-ton, solid stone arch at Tiahuanaco near Lake Titicaca engraved with calendar inscriptions and an image of Viracocha.

Glacial period: An interval of time within an ice age that lasts thousands of years and is marked by colder temperatures and the advancing of glaciers. "Interglacial" denotes periods of time with warmer climate between glacial periods (the last glacial period ended about 15,000 years ago). The Holocene epoch is the current interglacial.

Great Pyramid of Giza: The oldest and largest of the three pyramids at Giza, also known as the Pyramid of Khufu or the Pyramid of Cheops.

Gutei: The common Scythians, a nomadic people subjected by the Hyksos.

Habiru: Indebted citizens who fled Canaan to escape bondage. Groups of these Semitic people entered Egypt during the Hyksos/Shasu invasion, eventually becoming slaves, like the Hyksos, when the Egyptians regained control of their homeland. The children of the Habiru were forced to work for the armies of Ramesses II and also fought for the pharaoh's cousin, General Tot-Moses, with whom they eventually fled to Palestine.

Hecataeus of Abdera: Greek historian and philosopher (fourth century BCE) who wrote about Hyperborea.

Heliopolis: "City of the Sun" or "City of Helios," one of the oldest cities of ancient Egypt, northeast of present-day Cairo. It was the seat of the Benben.

Hellanicus of Lesbos: Greek historian (ca. 490–405 BCE) who was first to critically examine sources, selecting details from authentic materials and synthesizing that information into a narrative that could stand up to critical examination. Hellanicus was also first to mention Aeneas's founding of Rome and wrote of the Etruscans' origins as being connected to the Pelasgians.

Heracles: A divine hero in Greek mythology, son of Zeus and Alcmene, ancestor of royal clans known as Heracleidae, and known as Hercules in Rome.

Hermocrates: An Athenian general during the Peloponnesian War (431–404 BCE) and one of the characters in Plato's *Timaeus and Critias* dialogues.

Herodotus: Greek historian in the fifth century BCE known as the "Father of History" who was the first historian to systematically test the accuracy of collected materials, assembling them in a structured and engaging narrative.

Hesperides: Daughters of Ocean and guardians of the pieces torn from Tyrrenhid (the isle of Espera) during the cataclysms of 9600 BCE; each one of these nymphs protects an island or a muddy shoal, as well as the golden apple trees in the Sardinian garden of Espera.

Hittite: People of Hattusa from north-central Anatolia whose empire reached its height during the mid-fourteenth century BCE in an area that included most of Asia Minor, parts of the eastern Mediterranean, and Upper Mesopotamia.

Homer: Author of the *Iliad* and the *Odyssey* and considered the greatest Greek epic poet, with a tremendous influence on the history of literature. Homer's works offered models in writing and persuasive speaking that were copied throughout the ancient Greek culture.

Hyksos: "Heads of foreign countries" or the "elites" were the names given to them by the Egyptians; these members of the military aristocracy were the leaders of the Scythians and of those Canaanite citizens who fled Palestine to prevent debt-bondage. The Hyksos were also the leaders of the Jewish tribe who four years later were led by Moses in their escape from Egypt.

Hyperborea: A region of the empire of Osiris in what is currently the Po Valley and northern Tuscany.

hypogea: The subterranean portion of an ancient building or underground burial chamber.

ice age: A glacial age with a long-lasting reduction in the temperature of the surface of the Earth and in the atmosphere that results in the formation or expansion of continental ice sheets, polar ice sheets, and alpine glaciers. The term "ice age" can be used to indicate the presence of large ice sheets in a given area of Earth, meaning that Greenland and Antarctica are currently in their "ice age."

ice dome: Major component of an ice sheet or ice cap that has a convex surface and a symmetrical parabolic shape; can be as thick as 3,000 meters.

ice sheet: Glacial ice that covers an area greater than 19,000 square miles; also known as a continental glacier.

Ichnusa: Sardinia's ancient name, meaning "footprint."

Illyria: The Illyrians inhabited areas in the western Balkans (which eventually became Yugoslavia and Albania) and the southeastern coasts of the Italian peninsula.

Inca: The Incan culture was located in the highlands of the Andes in present-day Peru and lasted less than 200 years.

Indus Valley civilization: In the northwest region of the Indian subcontinent in the Indus River basin (currently Pakistan, India, Afghanistan, and Iran), covering over 1,260,000 square kilometers; the largest known ancient civilization and one of the world's earliest urban civilizations with a population of over five million people. New techniques in metalwork (copper, bronze, lead, and tin) were developed here and it was noted for its cities built of brick, roads with drainage systems, and houses with more than one story. The first of its cities to be discovered was at Harappa (currently in Pakistan).

Inventory Stele: Relic that contains information indicating the Sphinx, and at least one of the pyramids at Giza, had already existed in the time of Cheops/Khufu.

isostasy: Geological term for gravitational equilibrium in the Earth's surface, which can bend and distort when subjected to significant pressures (like a rubber ball when pressure is exerted on one point has an indentation in that area). Isostasy has had an important role during ice ages and for thousands of years after the melting of the ice.

Kalasasaya: A sophisticated Incan astronomical observatory in the Andes of Bolivia, oriented to the cardinal points, where equinoxes and solstices were observed and the seasons were predicted with mathematical precision.

labrys: Double ax. Instrument of the god of lightning in various civilizations. It is connected to lightning because, just like lightning, it can break the trees.

Land of Sokar: Refers to the area of Giza and the three great pyramids.

Laurentia (North American Craton): A large continental craton that forms the ancient geological core of North America, Greenland, and the northwestern part of Scotland.

La Venta: Classified a center of Olmec worship, but with many uncertainties since nothing is known about Olmec traditions. Even the enigmatic giant heads depicting men with typically African traits—broad, flat nose, full lips, and square denture—are not their work but that of a previous population.

Libu: A population originated by the diaspora of the Hyksos from Mesopotamia and Egypt, first at the time of King Utukhegal, then of Pharaoh Ahmose. They were situated between Lixus (a hill overlooking the Atlantic Ocean near the river Loukkos, in Morocco) and Dougga (near Teboursouk in Tunisia).

Linear A: The first syllabic writing of the Minoan people of the island of Crete, consisting of rectilinear abstract symbols and used in palace and religious writings; this system of writing (like Cretan hieroglyphic) has still not been deciphered. It seems the universal form of writing, Iberian (mentioned at the beginning of chapter 3), would have arrived in Crete and with minimal modifications become Cretan Linear A.

lintel: Horizontal beam found above windows or doorways.

lithosphere: The rigid, outermost shell of the Earth that is comprised of the crust and some of the upper mantle.

Lothal: One of India's most important archaeological sites of the Indus Valley civilization; its excavated dockyard held up to thirty ships of sixty tons each.

Machu Picchu: Inca site located 7,970 feet above sea level in the Cuzco region of Peru, believed to have been built for the Inca emperor Pachacuti (1438–1472). Also known as the Lost City of the Incas.

Mahābhārata: One of the two major Sanskrit epics of ancient India;the Ramayana is the other.

mandala: A symbolic diagram used both in the performance of sacred rites and as a tool for meditation.

Manu: The first, and greatest, patriarch and lawmaker of the Vedic people, described as the preserver and father of humanity and of all living creatures; also identified with the Egyptian god Osiris.

Maya: The Mayan people inhabited the Yucatán peninsula for more than a thousand years, with a common culture, religion, and unique form of hieroglyphic writing.

Medes: People who lived in the south of the Caucasus along with the Persians.

megalith: A very large stone used for monuments or building.

Mehrgarh: Neolithic site believed to be a precursor to the Indus Valley civilization, with houses built of mud bricks and agricultural practices that included the growing of wheat and barley and raising of sheep, goats, and cattle.

Memphite necropolis: Burial ground for the city of Memphis; includes the sites of Giza, Saqqara, and Dahshour.

menhir: An upright, rough stone, found singly or in groupings of similar stones. Size can vary but they are usually uneven, squared, and tapered toward the top. Widely found in Europe, Africa, and Asia, but mostly in Ireland, Great Britain, and Brittany.

Mesopotamia: The Tigris-Euphrates river region where Iraq, northeastern Syria, southeastern Turkey, and small areas of southwestern Iran are today. Bronze Age Mesopotamia included the Akkadian, Babylonian, and Assyrian empires and was considered to be the cradle of Western civilization.

Minoans: During the Victorian era archaeologist Arthur Evans did the first excavations of Cretan ruins, discovered the palace of Knossos, and baptized its inhabitants "Minoans" in honor of their personal king, Minos. The first literate culture of Europe, the Minoans had two writing systems: Linear A and Cretan hieroglyphs.

Minor Antarctica: The tip that juts out toward South America.

Minos: Also called Menes or Manes. In Greek mythology a king of Crete, son of Zeus and Europa, who became a judge of the dead in the underworld after his death. He can be equated to the Egyptian god Osiris.

Mnajdra: Megalithic temple complex on the southern coast of the Mediterranean island of Malta, among the most ancient religious sites on Earth and said to be a "unique architectural masterpiece."

monolith: A large stone in the shape of an obelisk or a column; also a term used for massive structures.

Montezuma: Aztec emperor who met the Spanish conqueror, Hernán Cortés, at the Temple of the Sun in Palenque, Mexico.

moraine: Accumulated earth and stones carried, and eventually deposited, by a glacier.

Mount Albàn: Site overlooking Oaxaca, Mexico, with an expansive area bounded by pyramids and other buildings arranged in very precise geometric forms. Next to the pyramids an observatory in an arrow-shaped building is inclined at an angle of forty-five degrees to the main axis, with several tunnels and steep stairways inside that open up to view different sections of the sky.

Nahuatl: Closely related languages that include that of the Aztec, spoken in central and southern Mexico and Central America.

navels of the world (omphalos): Reference sites on the Earth's surface whose geographical position was known from the dawn of time, marked by the presence of a carved meteorite: the omphalo.

necropolis: A large and elaborate ancient cemetery.

nuraghe: Most common type of building found in Sardinia, developed mainly between 1900 and 730 BCE, the so-called Nuragic Age, which has become the symbol of Sardinia and the Shardana civilization. The construction of the nuraghe always took place on a hill. A central tower was surrounded by a series of concentric walls and secondary structures, such as warehouses, offices, shelters, meeting rooms, armories, and workshops.

Ollantaytambo: An Incan archaeological site, this huge temple with a terraced amphitheater covers the side of a concave hill northwest of Sacsayhuaman near Lake Titicaca.

Olmec: Known as the "Mother Culture" of Central America and inventors of a calendar with annotation points and bars, with a start date of August 13, 3114 BCE, and a "catastrophic" end after 2012 CE.

omphalos: Meteoric stones that served as geodetic indicators that indicate the points of known coordinates, known as "navels of the world."

Onogoro-jima: "Island of the frozen drop," from the Japanese Shinto story of creation that tells of brine dripping from the point of a spear coagulating and forming an island.

orichalcum: An alloy (probably of gold and copper) mentioned in ancient writings including Plato's Critias dialogue. Although he only knew it by name, Critias said orichalcum was found in Atlantis and was second only to gold in value.

Osiris: A kind and gentle Egyptian ruler, beloved by his people, who taught agriculture and animal husbandry, codes of law to live by, and proper ways to worship the gods. When Egypt was finished being civilized, the population started to worship Osiris himself as a god, while the ruler brought his teachings to other lands (where he takes the names **Janus, Minos, Menes,** and **Manu**).

Palenque: Mayan temple in the state of Chiapas, Mexico, next to which is the palace, a huge complex on a triangular base with a four-story tower thought to have been used as an observatory by Mayan priests.

Pausanias: Greek traveler and geographer of the second century CE whose *Description of Greece* (firsthand observations of ancient Greece) has become an important resource for modern archaeology.

Pedra Pintada: The "Painted Rock Cave" in northern Brazil contains hundreds of characters of Iberian writing, in addition to the earliest known cave paintings in the Americas dating back 11,000 years.

Pelasgian: Exiles who escaped on ships from a catastrophe in their homeland of Antarctica to which many names are attributed, including: **Pelasgians, Danaes, Oceanides, Cainites, Vampires, Titans, Giants, Tyrrhenians, Cyclops, Sicilians, Atlanteans, Italanteans, Arii,** and **Viracochas.** We call them Cro-Magnon, as they were light-skinned with light-colored eyes and blond or red hair. Pelasgians worshipped a single deity, considered the snake a sacred animal, and assigned this epithet to their greatest men. They were masters in navigation, geography, astronomy, and architecture, mapped the whole planet, and built huge monuments throughout. We can still come across their maps today, replicated by medieval copyists and exhibited in beautiful Renaissance villas and museum windows. Their temples, constructed along riverbanks and ocean coastlines, were built with polished boulders weighing up to a thousand tons brought from quarries that were hundreds of miles away, raised and aligned with systems that we fail to understand today.

Peloponnesus: A large peninsula that makes up the southern portion of Greece.

Peoples of the Sea: Descendants of the Pelasgians; the Hyksos, Shardana, Libu, Sabines, Achaenans, and Teucrians who eventually came to be collectively known as the Sea Peoples and were the founders of an architectural rebirth throughout the Mediterranean, creating monuments like those built in Egypt.

Pillars of Hercules: Limit of the known world according to the ancient Greeks, varyingly identified by small islands and headlands. Initially they were somewhere in the Strait of Sicily, but in the third century BCE Eratosthenes of Cyrene moved them to Gibraltar to balance the boundaries of the Greek world that on the opposite side (to the east) had widened with the conquests of Alexander the Great.

Pindar: Greek lyric poet (522–443 BCE) from Thebes, author of seventeen books. Of the nine canonical ancient Greek lyric poets his work is the best preserved.

Plato: Mathematician, philosopher, and teacher, Plato (427–347 BCE) established Western philosophy and science with Socrates (his mentor) and Aristotle (his student). The Socratic dialogues (thirty-six dialogues and thirteen letters) were used to teach logic, ethics, philosophy, rhetoric, and mathematics. Speakers of the dialogue are Socrates, Timaeus of Locri, Hermocrates, and Critias.

Pleistocene: The geological epoch lasting from about 2,588,000 to 11,700 years ago and spanning the Earth's recent period of recurring glaciations.

Pliny the Elder: 23–79 CE. Roman author, philosopher, naturalist, naval and army commander in the early Roman empire; investigator of natural and geographic phenomena. Also known as Gaius Plinius Secundus and C. Plinio. Wrote *Naturalis Historia*, an encyclopedic work and model for all other encyclopedias that followed.

polis: A Greek city-state (plural: poleis).

Polybius: Greek historian (206–124 BCE) noted for *The Histories,* which covers 264–146 BCE in detail and gives an account of the rise of the Roman republic and its eventual control over Greece.

Poseidon: One of the twelve Olympian gods in Greek mythology. Poseidon's domain was the ocean. He is also called "God of the Sea."

Precession of the Equinoxes: The westward movement (opposite to the sun's) of the equinoxes along the ecliptic in relation to the stars, a gradual and continual change brought about by gravity's influence on Earth's rotational axis, like wobbling tops tracing out a pair of cones. Cycles last approximately 26,000 years.

Pumapunku: "Gate of the Puma," southwest of Kalasasaya; contains two dredged basins where hundreds of large ships could simultaneously load and unload their goods.

Quetzalcòatl (Kukulkan): The most important of the ancient Mexican gods, the "Sovereign Plumed Serpent" was prophesied to return after his death at some point in the future.

Ragnarök: According to myth, the time of the final battle between the gods of "light and order" and the Giants of "darkness and chaos." In Greek mythology the same episode is described as the battle between the gods of Olympus and the Titans. There are also strong similarities between the Ragnarök and the mythic battle between Pāndava and Kaurava in the Hindu Mahābhārata, although Ragnarök takes place in the future and the Hindu battle in the past.

Rig Veda: The oldest elements of the oral tradition of India are contained in the Vedas of which the *Rig Veda* is the oldest and most revered containing 450,000 words in 1,028 hymns formed by 10,589 verses in a very archaic form of Sanskrit.

Rostau: Ancient name of a Giza necropolis. According to Egyptian creation myth it is the first land that emerged from the chaos.

saba': "Star" in ancient Egyptian and Aramaic.

sabé: "Circumcision" in Coptic and proto-Semitic.

Sabines: Population (probably Semitic) ruled by Hyksos and with Mesopotamian origins. Many ancient writers agree they were direct ancestors of most Italic peoples, although on the lists of the Sea Peoples they do not appear as a united nation. In the fifth century a Gnostic community of Christians fled Egypt, persecuted by the Catholic archbishops of Alexandria, and took refuge in Harran,

Turkey, on the border of Syria, where they took up the same name of Sabines. They are also sometimes referred to as Sabians.

Sacsayhuaman: An ancient fortress north of Cuzco in the Andes of Peru where there are more than a thousand stone blocks, many weighing two hundred tons and even one estimated to be 361 tons, each a different size and shape. These rocks appear to have been cut and machined with ease, perfectly overlapping and interlocking.

Samothrace: A Greek island in the northern Aegean Sea facing the Straits of the Dardanelles.

sarcophagus: A stone coffin.

Sardinia: Called Ichnusa, Sardinia, and Sardo by the ancient Greeks and the Romans; the second largest island in the Mediterranean Sea and an autonomous region of Italy.

scarab: A stone or earthenware ornamental beetle.

Scythians: "The circumcised sons of Hercules" were a confederation of Semitic tribes of different social status at the top of which was an elite tribe who spoke an Indo-Iranian language.

Seth: "Evil" brother of Osiris.

Seven Sages: The wise men said to have planted the seeds of the Indo-European civilization in the Indus Valley 5,000 years ago.

Shardana: The "Princes of Dan" (from the derivation of the Akkadian *sher* = prince) left Mesopotamia in 2400 BCE and arrived in Corsica and Sardinia, having learned the route from the Akkadians who with Sargon had conquered Anatolia and its ways to the west. Once there, the Shardana had a flourishing trade with Greece, Asia Minor, and Egypt. They later led the invasions of the Sea Peoples in the east beginning in 1400 BCE.

Shasus: Indigenous Semitic nomads of the West Bank plateau, known as Suti by the Akkadians, who eventually participate in the creation of ancient Israel.

Socrates: Greek teacher and one of the founders of Western philosophy, Socrates is also known through the writings of his students Plato and Xenophon.

Sokar (Seker): Falcon god of the necropolis at Memphis. The meaning of his name is uncertain, although the Egyptian Pyramid Texts associate his name with *sy-k-ri* ("hurry to me"), Osiris's cry to Isis in the underworld.

solstice: The two points on the ecliptic at which the distance from the celestial equator is greatest and which the sun reaches each year on or around June 21 and December 21. They correspond to the longest day and the shortest day of the year.

steatite: Also known as soapstone, largely composed of talc, used for carving for thousands of years.

stele (stela): Usually carved or inscribed, a stone slab or pillar used for commemorative purposes.

Stele of Shabaka: An important religious text from the Twenty-Fifth Dynasty of Egypt found by Pharaoh Shabaka at the temple of Ptah in Memphis. Also known as the Shabaka Stone.

steppes: Vast, level, and treeless, these arid tracts are found in regions of extreme temperature in southeastern Europe and Asia.

Strabo: Greek geographer, philosopher, and historian (63 BCE–24 CE) most famous for his seventeen-volume work *Geographica,* describing the history of people and places from the known world of his time.

subglacial: Of, or relating, to the underlying portion of a glacier.

Sumerian: An artificial language invented by Akkadian priests and used for liturgical purposes. The word Sumer (from Akkadian Šumeru, "land of the civilized kings") originates in southern Mesopotamia (current Iraq), where the capital of the empire, Akkad or Agadé, was.

Tanith (Tanit): Punic goddess and chief deity of Carthage whose symbol of a trapezoid closed at the top by a horizontal line with a circle in the middle is found on ancient stone carvings and is thought to be a woman raising her hands.

Telchines: Amphibious creatures, half marine and half terrestrial, believed by the Teucrians to have great intelligence, from the first Arzawa civilization back to the Pelasgian era when the Telchines emerged from the water off the islands of Keos and Rhodes.

Temple of the Sun: Temple dedicated to Viracocha at Cuzco, also known as the Coricancha.

tephra: Solids that are thrown into the air during volcanic eruptions.

thalassocracy: Maritime supremacy.

tholoi: Stone tombs with domed roofs.

Tiahuanaco: An archaeological site in western Bolivia recognized by scholars as the most important precursor to the Inca empire.

Tifinagh: Alphabet used by the Berbers and derived from the evolution of Iberian writing, like Cretan Linear A, with which it shows strong affinities.

Timaeus: One of Plato's dialogues, written around 360 BCE, which speculates about the nature of human beings and the physical world. Timaeus was a philosopher of ancient Greece and a friend of Plato who appears in two of his dialogues.

Titans: Another name for Pelasgians; in Greek mythology they are powerful gods who belong to the generation preceding the one of Zeus, Poseidon, Hera, etc. (the Olympic gods).

torrid zone: Area in the central latitude between the Tropic of Cancer and the Tropic of Capricorn.

Tres Zapotes: One of the last Olmec centers, located in Veracruz, Mexico, which flourished between 500 BCE and 100 CE.

tuff: Porous rock.

Tuscany: Located in central Italy; area where the Etruscans created the first major civilization of the region, establishing agriculture, mining, and transport.

Tyrrenhid: Land mass that split into the islands of Sardinia and Corsica after sea level rose following the second flood in 9600 BCE.

Tyrrhenian coast: The Italian coast in the western Mediterranean (from Liguria to Calabria and Sicily), settled by part of the Atlantean diaspora.

Tyrrhenian sea: The area in the Mediterranean off the western coast of Italy associated with the Etruscans and named for the Tyrrhenian people.

Viracocha: A god revered by all the civilizations of Peru before the Incas integrated him into their religion and dedicated one of the most beautiful temples in Cuzco to him.

Virgil: 70 BCE–19 BCE; born in the Po River region and best known for the *Aeneid*, considered a national epic, chronicling Rome from the time it was founded and following the Trojan hero Aeneas as he fulfills his destiny of founding Rome.

Yucatán Peninsula: In southeastern Mexico, separates the Caribbean from the Gulf of Mexico and Central America from the rest of North America.

Zoroaster: Persian prophet and founder of Zoroastrianism, also known as **Zarathustra**.

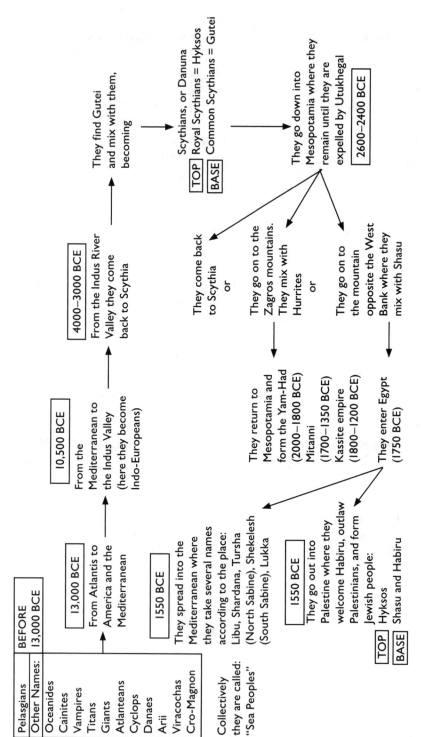

Time line 1. The journey of the Pelasgians in the Mediterranean and Indus River Valley.

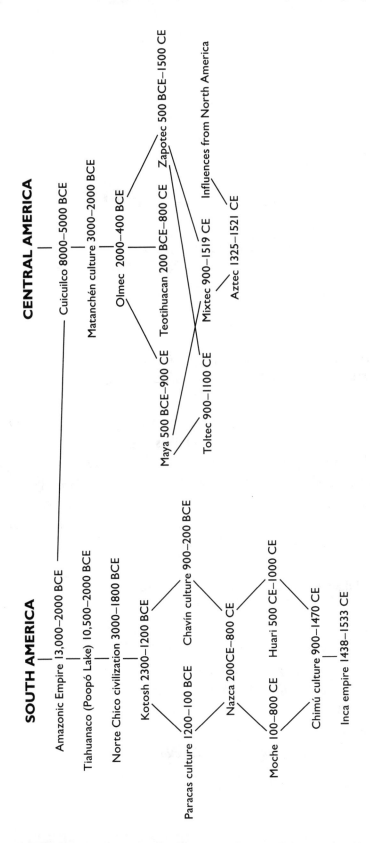

Time line 2. The journey of the Pelasgians in South and Central America.

SELECTED
BIBLIOGRAPHY

Barbiero, Flavio. *Una civiltà sotto ghiaccio*. Milan: Editrice Nord, 2000.

Bauval, Robert. *Secret Chamber: The Quest for the Hall of Records*. London: Random House, 2000.

Bauval, Robert, and Adrian Gilbert. *Orion Mystery: Unlocking the Secrets of the Pyramids*. New York: Crown Publishing, 1995.

Bauval, Robert, and Graham Hancock, *The Message of the Sphinx: A Quest for the Hidden Legacy of Mankind*. New York: Three Rivers Press, 1997.

Blavatsky, Helena Petrovna. *The Secret Doctrine: The Synthesis of Science, Religion, and Philosophy*. Cambridge Library Collection—Spiritualism and Esoteric Knowledge 1, 2 and 3. Cambridge: Cambridge University Press, 2011.

Cayce, Edgar Evans. *Edgar Cayce on Atlantis*. New York: Warner Books, 1968.

Cayce, Edgar Evans, Gail Cayce Schwartzer, and Douglas G. Richards. *Mysteries of Atlantis Revisited*. Edgar Cayce Wisdom for the New Age Series. New York: St. Martin's, 1997.

Charpentier, Louis. *Il Mistero Basco. Alle Origini della Civiltà Occidentale* [The Basque Mystery: The Origins of Western Civilization]. Paris: Robert Laffront, 1975.

Coedès, Georges. *Angkor: An Introduction*. Oxford: Oxford University Press, 1966.

Collins, Andrew. *Beneath the Pyramids: Egypt's Greatest Secret Uncovered.* Virginia Beach, Va.: ARE Press, 2009.

de Candolle, Alphonse. *Origin of Cultivated Plants.* New York: Hafner Publishing, 1959.

de Santillana, Giorgio, and Hertha von Dechend. *Hamlet's Mill: An Essay Investigating the Origins of Human Knowledge and Its Transmission through Myth.* Boston: Gambit, 1969.

Flem-Ath, Rand, and Rose Flem-Ath. *Atlantis Beneath the Ice: The Fate of the Lost Continent.* Rochester, Vt.: Bear & Co, 2012.

———. *When the Sky Fell: In Search of Atlantis.* Toronto: Stoddart, 1995.

Frau, Sergio. *Le Colonne d'Ercole. Un'inchiesta* [The Pillars of Hercules: An Inquiry]. Rome: Nur Neon Ltd., 2002.

Giacobbo, Roberto. *2012. La fine del mondo?* [2012: The end of the world?]. Milan: Arnoldo Mondadori Editore, 2009.

Gilbert, Adrian, and Maurice Cotterel. *The Mayan Prophecies: Unlocking the Secrets of a Lost Civilization.* Rockport, Mass.: Element Books, 1996.

Graves, Robert. *The Greek Myths,* vols. 1 and 2. New York: Penguin Books, 1990.

Hancock, Graham. *Fingerprints of the Gods.* New York: Three Rivers Press, 1995.

———. *The Sign and the Seal: The Quest for the Lost Ark of the Covenant.* New York: Touchstone, 1992.

———. *Underworld: The Mysterious Origins of Civilization.* New York: Three Rivers Press, 2002.

Hancock, Graham, and Santha Faiia. *Heaven's Mirror: Quest for the Lost Civilization.* New York: Three Rivers Press, 1998.

Hapgood, Charles. *The Path of Pole.* Kempton, Ill.: Adventures Unlimited Press, 1999.

King, Leonard William. *A History of Egypt, Chaldea, Syria, Babylonia, and Assyria in the Light of Recent Discovory.* Vol. 1. of *A History of Sumer & Akkad.* London: Chatto & Windus, 1923.

Knight, Christopher, and Robert Lomas. *The Hiram Key: Pharaohs, Freemasonry, and the Discovery of the Secret Scrolls of Jesus.* Gloucester, Mass.: Fair Winds Press, 2001.

Liverani, Mario. *Oltre la Bibbia—Storia antica di Israele* [Beyond the Bible—History of Ancient Israel]. Rome: Edizioni Laterza, 2003.

Maclellan, Alec. *The Lost World of Agharti: The Mystery of Vril Power.* London: Souvenir Press, 1996.

Magaletti, Piero. *Custodi dell'Immortalità.* Foggia, Italy: Bastogi Editrice, 2011.

Marin, Diego. *Il Segreto Degli Illuminati: Dalle origini ai giorni nostri storia dell'Occhio che Tutto Vede* [The Illuminati Secret: From the Origins to the Present Day, a History of the All-Seeing Eye]. Milan: Mondadori, 2013.

Mazzoldi, Angelo. *Delle Origini Italiche* [Of Italic Origins]. Whitefish, Mont.: Kessinger Publishing, 2010.

Melis, Leonardo. *Shardana—I popoli del mare* [Shardana—The People of the Sea]. Sardinia: PTM Editrice, 2009.

———. *Shardana—I principi di Dan* [Shardana—The Princes of Dan]. Sardinia: PTM Editrice, 2008.

———. *Shardana—Jenesi degli Urim* [Shardana—The Genesis of Urim]. Sardinia: PTM Editrice, 2010.

Pincherle, Mario. *Enoch. Il primo libro del mondo* [Enoch: The First Book in the World]. Vol. 1 and 2. Forlì-Cesena, Italy: Macro Edizioni, 2007.

———. *La Grande Piramide e Lo Zed* [The Great Pyramid and the Zed]. Forlì-Cesena, Italy: Macro Edizioni, 2008.

———. *I Mandei* [The Mandaeans]. Forlì-Cesena, Italy: Macro Edizioni, 2003.

Posnansky, Arthur. *Tiahuanacu: The Crandle of American Man.* La Paz, Bolivia: Ministry of Education, 1957.

Zagni, Marco. *L'Impero Amazzonico* [The Amazonian Empire]. Florence: M.I.R. Edizioni, 2002.

In addition to the above-mentioned texts, we have consulted:

- Classical works of Greek and Latin chroniclers
- Sacred texts and sagas from Christianity, Judaism, Hinduism, and Mazdaism
- The Icelandic sagas
- Spanish and Portuguese traditions
- Myths from all over the world

INDEX